Dissertations from the Department of History, Göteborg University, 34

Göteborg 2003

The Swedish-American Press and the Vietnam War

EDWARD BURTON

GÖTEBORG 2003

Cover design: Janne Saaristo
Cover picture: courtesy of *Svenska-Amerikanaren Tribunen*

Distribution: Edward Burton (hiseb@history.gu.se)
and Department of History, Göteborg University
Box 200, 405 30 Göteborg, Sweden

© Edward Burton 2003
Typeset by Janne Saaristo
Printed by Elanders Graphic Systems, Göteborg 2003
ISBN 91-88614-45X
ISSN 1100-6781

Table of Contents

iv

List of Tables

Abbreviations

ABC American Broadcasting Company (American television network).

AP Associated Press (leading American wire service).

ASNE The American-Swedish News Exchange.

CBS Columbia Broadcasting System (American television network).

DN *Dagens Nyheter* (liberal Stockholm daily newspaper).

FLT Förenade Landsortstidningar ("The United Provincial Newspaper Service").

FNL *Front National de Libération du Viet-nam du Sud* (the Vietcong political wing, NLF).

GP *Göteborgs-Posten* (liberal Göteborg daily newspaper).

NBC National Broadcasting Company (American television network).

NLF National Liberation Front, the Vietcong political organization.

NT *Nordiske Tidende* (Norwegian-American newspaper).

PLAF People's Liberation Armed Forces (the NLF military wing).

SAT *Svenska-Amerikanaren Tribunen.*

SIP Svenska-Internationella Pressbyrån ("The Swedish-International Press Bureau").

SIS The Swedish Information Service.

ST *Stockholms-Tidningen* (Social Democratic Stockholm newspaper).

SvD *Svenska Dagbladet* (conservative Stockholm daily newspaper).

SvP *Svenska Posten.*

TT Tidningarnas Telegrambyrå (leading Swedish wire service).

UD Utrikesdepartementet (The Swedish Foreign Ministry).

UPI United Press International (American wire service).

VK *Vestkusten.*

Acknowledgements

This is the place to explain my biases. As an American growing up in the Seventies, I was aware the country was not in a good mood. I could not explain it, but there was a bitter, cynical atmosphere in the air. I did not know that we had just lost a war. I had vaguely heard of Vietnam, but I had wrongly assumed it was yet another nineteenth-century conflict. It surprised me when I discovered I was wrong. The Seventies and Eighties were periods of willful amnesia in America.

I did not know much more about Vietnam by my teenage years. By then the word *Vietnam* was almost an obscenity, a metaphor to describe any endless, nightmarish trauma. Yet nobody ever talked about war openly. For example, my Uncle Barry got his draft orders in 1967 and went to Saigon. I did not even know this when I began writing this thesis. Perhaps my family did not hide it, but Vietnam was never a subject people willingly discussed. This willful amnesia has affected how most people in my generation think about the war. Few can explain what we did there, how it began, or even which side the U.S. supported. Most only have a vague idea about when the war started or ended.

These are the biases I bring with me to this thesis. I am an American. I will always see Vietnam as a foreign war, where we sent our troops to a different country. Vietnamese describe it as a war where foreign troops came to their country. The same event can look different depending on the perspective. As an American, I always wish success for my country. Losing wars is not a pleasant thing, and losing this one was especially so because it lasted so long. Still, I belong to the generation that wondered how our parents could have believed the Domino Theory. I am in the generation that grew up with the phrase "mistakes were made." Most post offices I have ever seen have a black Vietnam-era MIA-KIA flag. I grew up in the shadow of Vietnam, and people my age have never thought this was a war worth fighting. An American post-Vietnam bias occasionally appears in this thesis: a strong distrust of government.

America's myths of the Sixties have passed into history. Sweden still lives with its myths, never having them so rudely discredited. Too much Swedish writing on Vietnam, and the conflict with the United States, still echoes with Sixties' slogans. The two recent works on the U.S.-Swedish conflict, Yngve Möller's *Sverige och Vietnamkriget* and Leif Leifland's *Frostens år*, are by former UD officials. Older works include books by Foreign Minister Torsten Nilsson and Ambassador to North Vietnam Jean-Christophe Öberg. The Ambassador to China, Lennart Petri, has written an article on the U.S.-Swedish conflict. Most of these are pure apologies for the Swedish position. They assign responsibility for the broken relations mostly to the United States. They are certainly useful works. They are every bit as valuable as Lyndon Johnson's book *The Vantage Point*.

My thesis has an American outlook, and has an outsider's view of recent Swedish history. I am critical of both U.S. and Swedish foreign policy; these were not good years for either of us. Even the FNL movement, which the Swedish left has sanctified as a romantic social movement, looks different from the outside. Criticism of it may not be welcome, especially from foreigners. All these differences are in here. Yet this is why universities invite foreign students. It is to get different views on life, and avoid group-thinking and cultural self-congratulation.

I would like to thank some of the people who have helped me over the last five years. Professor Bernt Schiller was my supervisor for the first three years and helped get me started. Professor Lennart K. Persson has been my adviser for the final phases of this thesis, and I could not have completed it without him. Professors Christer Winberg and Ulf Jonas Björk have read this manuscript and given me valuable advice. It is stronger, shorter, and more readable now than it was before they saw it.

I have also made several important contacts over the years. Anders Neumueller at The Swedish Press allowed me to look through the newspaper's archives, stored in a damp basement of a nursing home. (In return for letting me see these, Neumueller wanted me to stress that *The Swedish Press* needs help. Many Swedish-American newspapers are still on the verge of bankruptcy. They would value any aid they could get from Sweden – such as stipends for journalism-students to help work on their papers.) Anders Neumueller also gave me the unlisted telephone number to Sture Wermee, *The Swedish Press's* editor in the Seventies. I have had several transatlantic telephone calls with him, and Sture Wermee has helped me immensely. He is only of the few remaining Swedish-American editors from the Sixties. I have also spoken with Jane Hendricks of *Svenska-Amerikanaren Tribunen* and Ulf Mårtensson of *Nordstjernan*. I have exchanged e-mails with Erik Hermans of *Norden* and some of Ambassador Jerome Holland's children. All I can say is thank you to all of them.

Professor Eva Queckfeldt has been kind enough to give me both encouragement and book reviews of her thesis. From the University of Wisconsin, Carl-Gustav Scott has shared documents from his research with me. Scott's thesis, *The Swedish-American Conflict Over Vietnam*, will be the first full-length academic treatment of the U.S.-Swedish diplomatic crisis. My thesis only addresses how the emigrant press reported the conflict. From the University of Victoria, Eva St. Jean has shared ideas, papers, and criticism. From our university, Karin Fogelberg has advised me on researching the Swedish media. Archivist Berndt Fredriksson has helped me find material in the Foreign Ministry's archive. From the University of Washington, archivist Gary Lundell was kind enough to give me additional help in finding and copying archive material. All he asked for in return was to listen to a tape of his second cousin, a famous musician here in Sweden.

Chapter One

Introduction

In 1965, the United States began a long and controversial war in Vietnam. The U.S. sent troops to subdue the insurgency in the Vietnamese countryside and support the government in Saigon. The South Vietnamese government had been unstable for nearly two years. Its leadership had changed seven times in the previous fourteen months in a series of military coups. Washington felt the rural uprising only worsened this instability. The U.S. hoped pacifying the insurgency would stabilize the Saigon government. If so, the U.S. might eventually reform South Vietnam into a capitalistic liberal democracy. At the moment, however, the Saigon government was hardly liberal or democratic. The military officers leading it since the overthrow of President Ngo Dinh Diem were ambitious and thoroughly corrupt. They showed little interest in democracy. Even worse, they responded to nearly any political dissent with repression. The repression only nourished more discontent, weakening the government further. This only made yet another coup more likely. The arrival of American troops also offended the patriotism of many Vietnamese. They felt that any government kept in place only by the guns of foreign soldiers was not worthy of their support. Many civilians instead backed the opposition guerrillas who promised land and social reform instead. The guerrilla movement grew, and the American troops had little success suppressing it. The U.S. public soon questioned the value of spending American blood and treasure to support the oppressive Saigon government.

An antiwar movement immediately grew in the U.S. and around the world. Before long, street demonstrations against the U.S. war became a common sight in Sweden. By September 1966, only 14%

of Swedes backed the U.S. Vietnam policy; by October 1969, only 8% of Swedes supported the American war effort.[1] The Swedish government listened to and sympathized with the mood of war opponents. Sweden's government was often out in front, leading public opinion. In particular, the ruling Social Democratic party courted voters strongly against the Vietnam War. Its foreign policy sympathized with the North Vietnamese cause.

The U.S. government ignored Sweden's criticism as much as possible. It believed drawing attention to Sweden's criticism would have lent credibility to its arguments. There were times, however, when Sweden became hard to ignore. Its antiwar movement agitated and raised money for the FNL, the guerrillas' political organization.[2] (See the following section on terminology.) Sweden also granted asylum to eight hundred American deserters. The Swedish FNL groups often celebrated the deserters as pacifist celebrities, which irritated the U.S. government. In 1969, Sweden granted North Vietnam diplomatic recognition. Sweden then offered foreign aid to North Vietnam, angering Washington still further. There were several incidents of Swedish protesters throwing eggs at U.S. diplomats. In a few cases, Swedish protesters even used racial epithets against American minority diplomats. In December 1972, Sweden's Prime Minister compared recent U.S. bombing to Nazi war crimes. In some of these cases, the United States suspended diplomatic relations with Sweden. Sweden was the only country to have its relations with the U.S. cut over the Vietnam War. In comparison, China and the Soviet Union – the countries the U.S. had hoped to contain – saw relations with America improve during the war.

The U.S. press reported Sweden's Vietnam-policy decisions, and often without much sympathy. When Sweden recognized the Hanoi government in 1969, *The Worcester Gazette* ran the headline:

---

[1] The 1969 opinion from memo "Current political opinions in Sweden," file "S-So," box 8, USIA, NA. The 1966 opinion from SIFO, which SIFO faxed to me on 18 January 1999. The 14% support reflects those who believed: "America should continue fighting with the forces currently deployed" and "America should increase its efforts."

[2] For a recent history of the Swedish FNL groups, see: Kim Salomon, *Rebeller i takt med tiden*, Stockholm, 1996.

"Americans of Swedish descent may wonder what has got into the old country: Sweden is not the country it used to be."[3] Worcester was a city with many Swedish immigrants. Other cities such as Chicago, New York, or Seattle had even more. Like other immigrants, Swedish immigrants were often among the most patriotic of Americans. They revered and supported their adopted country, and reflexively supported its foreign policy. Like other immigrants, they wanted to define their identity as loyal, true Americans. Yet that had never stopped them from expressing ethnic pride in being Swedish.

Vietnam presented a problem. Swedish-Americans now had to answer uncomfortable questions about what their Swedish cousins were doing. They had not experienced anything like this since the anti-immigrant outburst during the First World War.[4] They never had to choose sides since then. Unlike the German or Japanese-Americans, Swedish immigrants never faced pressure to disown their cousins back home. In World War Two, buying war bonds and supporting the U.S. troops harmonized with their concerns for Swedish security. Their love for Sweden never conflicted with their loyalty to the U.S. before. Now it was emotionally alarming that the homeland-Swedes could support America's current enemy. The Swedish-Americans wanted to be Swedes but still good Americans. They felt Sweden's position on Vietnam was undermining that sense of identity.

The Problem

Fifteen newspapers in North America targeted Swedish immigrants during the Vietnam War. These were the last papers remaining from the hundreds that sprang up during the nineteenth-century.[5] The remaining emigrant papers were all weeklies, and usually eight pages

---

[3] *Worcester Gazette*, 16 January 1969, quoted in memorandum "Erkännandet av Nordvietnam i början av 1969," file "Papers and Clippings – Sweden's Views on Vietnam," box "ASNE – Papers, Clippings, Swedes in America," ASNE New York, SSIRC.

[4] Carl Chrislock, "The Impact of World War I Nativism on Scandinavian Ethnicity in the Upper Midwest," *Scandinavians in America*, Decorah, Ill., 1985; and Carl Chrislock, *Ethnicity Challenged*, Northfield, Minn., 1981.

or less. Most of them still printed in Swedish. There were twelve newspapers geographically spread across the United States. For example, *Svenska Posten* served the Pacific Northwest, *Svenska-Amerikanaren Tribunen* printed in the Midwest, and *Nordstjernan* attended to the Mid-Atlantic and New England regions. Three more Swedish-language papers printed over the border in Canada. All these papers voiced Swedish immigrant values and concerns, and defended their interests. Each week they reached thousands of readers interested in Swedish affairs. *Svea* and *Svenska-Amerikanaren* alone claimed to have 26,398 and 20,304 paying subscribers respectively.[6] Also, each paying subscriber may represent an entire family of readers. As American newspapers, the Swedish-American papers watched with concern as the U.S. slipped into war, struggled without success, and eventually had to leave Vietnam. As Swedish newspapers, they also listened to Sweden's open criticism of Washington's Vietnam policy. Anyone who wanted to know Swedish-American opinion could find it here. Anyone who wanted to influence Swedish-American opinion would also have started here.

My broad questions are: *How did the Swedish-American press comment on the American military engagement in Vietnam? How did it react to Sweden's criticism of the American war?* If a paper backed the war, how did it reconcile its love of Sweden with opposing Sweden's Vietnam policy? If a paper opposed the war, how did it reconcile supporting Sweden's Vietnam policy with its patriotism for America? As I began studying these problems, it soon became clear the emigrant newspapers were in close contact with the Swedish Foreign Ministry. This raised other important questions. *Did the Swedish government influence Swedish-American coverage of Vietnam or Swedish Vietnam policy? If so, how did the Swedish government do it and did it work?*

---

[5] Alfred Söderström claims there were 1,158 different Swedish-American periodicals in the U.S. before 1910, but modern research puts the number closer to 650. (Alfred Söderström, *Blixtar på tidnings-horizonten*, Warroad, Minn., 1910: 16–53; Ulf A. Beijbom, "The Swedish Press," *The Ethnic Press in the United States*, London, 1987: 384.)

[6] Memorandum, "Swedish Publications in the United States," file 18 "Lists," box 3, Fabbe, UW.

My thesis begins by surveying the Swedish-American press in the year 1960. This was perhaps the last peaceful year in Vietnam. In 1961, the U.S. increased the number of U.S. advisers there and expanded their role in counter-guerrilla operations. My thesis formally uses 1975 as its terminal date. The war ended with South Vietnam's surrender on 30 April 1975. Yet, the Swedish-American press stopped discussing the war long before then. In practice, this thesis does not follow the Swedish-American press much past 1972. The U.S. pulled its forces from Vietnam in February 1973, ending the direct American role there.

A Note on Terminology

Perhaps more than other subjects, it is hard to find neutral language to discuss the Vietnam problem. Most words describing the combatants often take an implied position on their cause. Even the name of the country where most fighting occurred is debatable. "South Vietnam" was strictly a creation of the Cold War, which most nations recognized as a state. Many Vietnamese, however, saw it as their country's southern half that the West had illegally detached. Many other Vietnamese supported the new southern nation. The legal merit of "South Vietnam" defined many of the problems surrounding the conflict. If South Vietnam was independent, then "North Vietnam" was a separate country attacking it. The local insurgents were therefore rebels. South Vietnam's right to invite American soldiers would also be legal. If South Vietnam was not a legitimate nation, then the U.S. had illegally invaded Vietnam. The local insurgents would therefore be patriots driving out invaders and unifying their nation. Depending on how one defines the situation, U.S. involvement in Vietnam was either a moral imperative or completely immoral.

The words "South Vietnam" and "North Vietnam" may be false terms, but these are the terms commonly used to separate the combatants. My thesis will use these terms. A more difficult problem arises in what to call the southern insurgents. The Saigon government labeled them *Viet nam cong san* in the late Fifties. This phrase – meaning "Vietnamese communist" – soon got shortened to "Vietcong." This term suggested communism was the insurgents' only war aim: an assertion they rejected. "Vietcong" first had a disparaging tone, but battlefield success eventually gave the word more luster. The Swedish press rarely used the word, but called them "FNL-soldiers" instead. The FNL – *Front National de Libération du Viet-nam du Sud* – appeared in late December 1960. The FNL was a political action group struggling to overthrow the Saigon government and unify Vietnam under communist leadership. The American media rarely referred to this acronym, rejecting that communism could be liberation. When the U.S. media did use the term, they rearranged the letters as NLF: the National Liberation Front.[7] Most Americans knew of the insurgents only as the Vietcong. The guerrillas called themselves "liberation soldiers" and their organization the People's Liberation Armed Forces (PLAF).

Many of these terms appear in my thesis, and they often have implied positions on the war. Since the end of the war, people have argued over the correct terms to use. Sadly, there are few neutral terms available. Perhaps this is because the war was so contradictory, with few clear lines separating right and wrong, and had no easy answers. Political reality was just a matter of definition and perspective.

Previous Research

Most works on the Swedish-American press end around the Second World War. Most works focus either on the Swedish-American press's early days or its high-water mark from 1900 to 1924. The period of contraction, poverty, and struggle for survival has not attracted researchers. There are no books on the Swedish-American press in the Sixties and Seventies. My thesis is the only longer work on the Swedish-language press during this period so far.

There are only a few short articles on the Vietnam-era Swedish-American press. There is a 1975 obituary for *Svenska Posten's* editor, a 1973 article on *Nordstjernan's* editor, an article on *Svenska-Amerikanaren's* "Folkets Röst" page, and a chapter on *Texas Posten* in

---

[7] For a discussion of terminology in the American media, see Edwin Diamond, "Who is the 'Enemy,'?" *Columbia Journalism Review*, Winter 1970–1971: 38–39.

Larry Scott's book *The Texas Swedes*.[8] These four articles are the entire research on the Vietnam-era Swedish-American press. Apart from adding a few minor footnotes, they have had little relevance for my thesis.

My dissertation builds on three different streams of research. The first stream is the research on the Swedish-American press. This describes the earlier history of the emigrant newspapers: their creation, rise, and culture. The second research stream here includes studies on the news coverage of Vietnam. Most of these works focus on the American media, but there are a few on Sweden. These may not often appear in the footnotes, but they have helped direct the path of my thesis. The third research stream is the theoretical perspective. This helps explain why governments became increasingly involved in the flow of mass information.

The most important book from the first stream may be Herbert Finis Capps' 1966 book *From Isolation to Involvement*. Capps argues the Swedish-American press shifted from supporting neutrality in 1914 to backing an activist foreign policy by 1945. Capps' book is a survey of the emigrant papers' editorial positions. His arrangement is narrative, and in chronological order. He focuses on the debates among various editors on U.S. foreign policy problems. He describes the differences among the papers as minor. This is largely because he excludes the socialist papers. This allows him to treat the emigrant papers as a single actor, speaking with a single voice: a conservative, Lutheran voice. He often says the Swedish-Americans' agrarian and Lutheran backgrounds made them conservative. He does not explain how or why this happened. The Swedish-Americans' conservatism has roots in post-Civil War social world which Capps largely overlooks. Capps' book is eventually just a summary of the editors' editorials.[9] He uses no theory or archival material, nor has he interviewed any editors. There is no analysis of the structures that support or provide news to the Swedish-

---

[8] Marshall Wilson, "Fabbe," *Swedish Pioneer Historical Quarterly*, vol. 26, 1975: 185–192; T. Edward Karlsson, "Gerhard Rooth," *American Swedish '73*, Philadelphia, 1973: 21–27; Barbro Klein, "Folkets Röst," *Nord-Nytt*, vol. 52: 85–97; Larry E. Scott, "The Swedish-Language Press in Texas," *The Swedish Texans*, San Antonio, 1990.

American press. There is little discussion on how Sweden – or Swedish-American ethnicity – influenced the editors. Instead of analyzing the emigrant papers, Capps uses them mostly as a way to discuss world politics.

Apart from my thesis, Capps' book is the only longer work to examine the Swedish-American press's views on politics and world conflicts. There are, however, a few shorter articles. O. Fritiof Ander wrote several pieces on Swedish-American press reactions to key U.S. elections. George M. Stephenson has written on how the Swedish-American papers responded to the First World War. Herbert Capps has also published an article on U.S.-Japanese relations between 1914 and 1945. Eva St. Jean has written on how the Swedish-Canadian papers reacted to the two World Wars.[10]

The remaining works on the emigrant press focus on Swedish-American society and ethnicity before the Second World War. In some way, all revolve around the newspapers' role in assimilation. Albert Schersten's book *The Relation of the Swedish-American Newspaper to the Assimilation of Swedish Immigrants* was the first major work on the subject. Schersten shows that immigrants who read Swedish-language newspapers were less assimilated than those who did not. Sture Lindmark's thesis *Swedish-America 1914–1932* rejects this finding. He argues most Swedish-American newspaper readers were recent immigrants. They soon became Americanized

---

[9] C. A. Clausen, "Book Review: *From Isolation to Involvement*," *The Journal of American History*, vol. 54, no. 2, September 1967: 434–435; and Timothy L. Smith, "Review of Books: *From Isolation To Involvement*," *The American Historical Review*, vol. 73, no. 2, December 1967: 617; R.P., "Book Report: The Political Views of the Editors," *Vasastjärnan*, June 1967: 3.

[10] O. Fritiof Ander, "The Swedish-American Press in the Election of 1892," *Mississippi Valley Historical Review*, vol. 23: 533–554; O. Fritiof Ander, "The Swedish-American Press in the Election of 1912," *The Swedish Pioneer Historical Quarterly*, vol. 14, no 3, 1963: 103–126; George M. Stephenson, "The Attitude of the Swedish-Americans Toward the World War," *Mississippi Valley Historical Association Proceedings*, vol. 10, 1918–1921: 70–94; Finis Herbert Capps, "The Views of the Swedish-American Press Toward United States-Japanese Relations, 1914–1945," *Swedish Pioneer Historical Quarterly*, vol. 20, no. 3, 1969: 133–146; and Eva St. Jean, "From Defiance to Defence: Swedish-Canadian Ethnic Awareness During the Two World Wars," *American Journal of Scandinavian Studies*, (forthcoming).

and progressed onto mainstream newspapers. Many then canceled their subscriptions to the ethnic papers.[11] It is thus unsurprising the immigrant newspapers' readers were not as assimilated as non-readers. What then was the Swedish-American press's role in the Americanization process?

Two notable works take up this question. They include Ulf Jonas Björk's thesis *The Swedish-American Press* and Marion Marzolf's *The Danish Language Press in America*.[12] Marzolf asks whether immigrant newspapers acted to brake or speed up their readers' assimilation. She decides they mostly hastened it. Her content analysis shows that newspapers had different functions whether they served urban or rural communities. (This observation is the basis of the community-press theory, which Chapter Two will discuss further.) Marzolf notes the newspapers' social role also changed as Danish-Americans assimilated. They did not need American society explained to them as if they were new immigrants; most now got their American news from English-language newspapers. As they grew older, they became more reflective and wanted to know more about Danish society. The editors gave their communities what they wanted. They gave less space to U.S. news and fiction, but increased the volume of Danish and Danish-American news. These changes might arguably be true for the Swedes and Norwegians as well.

Ulf Jonas Björk's thesis *The Swedish-American Press* examines whether these changes applied to the Swedes or not. Between 1908–1910 and 1921–1923, he notes the Swedish-American papers changed their social role over time. Where Marzolf analyzes subject matter, Björk also examines the quality and tone of the news. Marzolf said emigrant papers had different roles if they served urban or rural communities. Björk wants to know whether the papers' news quality and tone had any relation to the communities they

[11] Albert Ferdinand Schersten, *The Relation of the Swedish-American Newspaper to the Assimilation of Swedish Immigrants*, Rock Island, Ill., 1935; and Sture Lindmark, *Swedish America 1914–1932*, Uppsala, 1971. Another essential work on immigrant assimilation versus language maintenance has been Joshua Fishman (ed.), *Language Loyalty in the United States*, The Hague, 1966.

[12] Ulf Jonas Björk, *The Swedish-American Press*, Ann Arbor, Mich., 1987; and Marion Tuttle Marzolf, *The Danish-Language Press in America*, New York, 1979.

served. He looks at three Swedish-American newspapers: *Svenska-Amerikanaren, Lindsborgs-Posten*, and *Puget Sound Posten*. They were very different papers. *Svenska-Amerikanaren* was a large newspaper, had several editors, aspired for a national audience, and was owned by a company dominated by one man. *Lindsborgs-Posten* was a small paper with one editor, and served a local rural community. It served a mainly Swedish-speaking region and assumed its readers read no other newspaper. *Puget Sound Posten*, finally, was a small newspaper edited and published by one man. It served an urban Swedish minority and ran news on the Swedish minority community. It assumed its readers also read English-language newspapers.

Björk's thesis confirms that the emigrant press's role changed over the years. *Lindsborgs-Posten* evolved into an organization sheet that focused on the local Swedish Lutheran churches. *Puget Sound Posten* began running more non-immigrant items and severely cut back its Swedish-American department. *Svenska-Amerikanaren* – the predecessor of *Svenska-Amerikanaren Tribunen*, included in my study – focused more on Sweden and cut back its American news. Sweden made up 56% of *Svenska-Amerikanaren*'s news by 1921–1923. This was a jump from 42% thirteen years earlier. Much of the news was unflattering, both for Sweden and Swedish-America. Björk estimates only around 11–12% of the Swedish news were positive news stories. In the 1908–1919 period, 49% of the Swedish news was on either accidents, crimes, or suicides. Björk notes this was part of a general bias toward the negative. Three-quarters of the Chicago news also focused on negative or threatening events.[13]

Inga Wilhelmsen Allwood's analysis of *Nordiske Tidende* shows this was also true for the Norwegian-American press. (The Norwegian and Danish emigrant papers were similar to the Swedish-American ones.) Allwood examined *Nordiske Tidende*'s 1947 output. This included 846 pages. At eight columns a page, she estimates *NT* ran around 6,768 columns of text.[14] She concludes *NT* no longer focused on American politics by 1947. It came to focus

---

[13] Björk, *The Swedish-American Press*, 113–114, 193.
[14] Inga Wilhelmsen Allwood, Knud K. Mogensen, Carl Nosjar, and Martin S. Allwood, *The Norwegian-American Press and Nordiske Tidende*, Mullsjö, 1950: 7.

on Nordic culture, religion, and politics from back home. Allwood notes that much of it had a negative tone. "At first sight it might seem that *Nordiske Tidende* specializes in Norwegian crime." Accidents and crime accounted for 8% of the paper's Norwegian news. The 1947 Quisling trial arguably inflated this sense. *NT* also watched the growth of Norway's welfare state with interest. It did not, however, always welcome the growth of socialism in Norway.[15] These are engaging conclusions. They run counter to the idea the emigrant papers might want to produce fond memories of the Old Country. These findings would have disappointed Sweden's Foreign Ministry, which wanted positive images of Sweden abroad.

My thesis also uses research on Swedish news coverage of the Vietnam War. Eva Block's thesis *Amerikabilden i svensk press 1948–1968* analyzes several Swedish papers' views of U.S. foreign policy. This includes the American war in Vietnam, among other things. Eva Queckfeldt's thesis *Vietnam: tre svenska tidningars syn på Vietnamfrågan* develops Block's research further, and focuses solely on the Vietnam War.[16] The most valuable aspect of these works is the content analysis they did on the Swedish press. My thesis will return to these theses and discuss their content analysis method in more detail in Chapter Six.

Queckfeldt's thesis is the most important work on Swedish news coverage of Vietnam. There are only a few others. Yngve Möller's *Sverige och Vietnamkriget* uses some press material, but not in a systematic way. Kari-Andén Papadopoulos' thesis *Kameran i krig* is more systematic but only addresses photojournalism. Stig Thorén has compiled large amounts of data on what news telegrams the Swedish media got, which they printed, and which they filtered out. Jörgen Westerståhl's *Vietnam i Sveriges Radio* is a content analysis of Swedish Radio's coverage of the Tet Offensive. (Its analysis method is similar to the one Peter Braestrup used on the U.S. media in *Big*

---

[15] Allwood, *The Norwegian-American Press and Nordiske Tidende*, 17–19. For a similar conclusion about the Swedish-American *Vestkusten*, see: Anders-Petter Sjödin, "Etnicitet eller assimilation i 'liberala' *Vestkusten*," Unpublished C-paper, History department, Uppsala University, 6 October 1980: 22.

[16] Eva Block, *Amerikabilden i svensk press 1948–1968*, Malmö, 1976; and Eva Queckfeldt, "*Vietnam*": tre svenska tidningars syn på Vietnamfrågan 1963–1968, Malmö, 1981.

Story, so the two works are worth comparing.)[17] These works show how the Swedish news media covered the Vietnam War. One must know how the Swedish and American media covered the war if one wants to understand fully the Swedish-American press's attitude toward the conflict.

I therefore also use several works on American news coverage of Vietnam. Most react to the myth the press undermined public support for the war with negative or violent reports. Research by George Bailey, Oscar Patterson, and Lawrence Lichty show there was negligible violence in U.S. news coverage of Vietnam. Only an average of 2.4% of TV film clips showed dead or wounded in Vietnam.[18] Daniel Hallin's *The Uncensored War* argues journalism procedures served the White House view.[19] Journalistic routines meant to uphold objectivity led the media to accept the White House version of events. This began to change with the 1968 Tet Offensive. After Tet, reporting increasingly underlined the human cost of war, often relating it in detached terms rather than as a national cause. The "guts and glory" reporting style disappeared, replaced with an image of Vietnam as a quagmire. Reporters also stopped calling Vietnam "our war" fought by "our troops," but instead termed it "the war in Vietnam."

Researchers who stress the media's supposed antiwar tone thus turn to the early Seventies to prove their point. Ernest Lefever's *TV and National Defense* analyzes CBS-TV's Vietnam coverage from 1972. His content analysis uses the White House's official position as the reference frame. Lefever decides that 69.9% of the opinions

---

[17] Yngve Möller, *Sverige och Vietnamkriget*, Stockholm, 1992; Kari-Andén Papadopoulos, *Kameran i krig*, Stockholm, 2000; Stig Thorén, "Vietnamkonflikten i telegramens belysning," *Studier i förmedlingen av utrikestelegram*, Stockholm, 1966: 64–103; Jörgen Westerståhl, *Vietnam i Sveriges Radio*, Statsvetenskapliga institutionen, Göteborg University, August 1968; Peter Braestrup, *Big Story*, vol. 2, Boulder, Colo., 1978: 302–311, 315–321.

[18] Oscar Patterson III, "An Analysis of Television Coverage of the Vietnam War," *Journal of Broadcasting*, vol. 28:4, Fall 1984: 402–404; see also: George Bailey, "Television War: Trends in Network Coverage of Vietnam 1965–1970," *Journal of Broadcasting*, vol. 20: 2, Spring 1976: 147–158.

[19] Daniel C. Hallin, *The Uncensored War*, New York, 1986.

aired on CBS urged de-escalating the war. These outnumbered statements backing the White House position by a 48-to-1 ratio.[20] Martin Herz's *The Christmas Bombing and the Prestige Press* shows the same alleged antiwar bias in the print media. *The New York Times*, Herz argues, gave more than twice as much space to Hanoi's civilian damage than its military damage. Such distortions led people to oppose the 1972 Christmas Bombings. The *Times* devoted 640 lines of text to bombing critics. It gave policy supporters only thirty-five lines.[21] These works on Vietnam reporting may not appear often in the footnotes. Still, they have influenced my approach to Swedish-American news coverage. In many ways, the Swedish emigrant papers were American periodicals commenting on the Vietnam War. They only happened to publish in Swedish. Their editors were U.S. citizens who read American newspapers and watched American television news.[22] Their knowledge of Vietnam came from the American news media.

There has been some research into the Swedish Foreign Ministry's role in news management. (The Swedish Foreign Ministry – *Utrikesdepartementet* – is commonly known as UD.) Svenbjörn Kilander's *Censur och propaganda* examines UD's news management in the First World War.[23] Before the war, UD decided it had to uphold trust in Swedish credit worthiness abroad. It took over the Swedish News Agency – Sweden's only wire service – for this purpose. Over the next few years, the Swedish News Agency spread positive news on Swedish industry's production potential. In the war, the state used the Swedish News Agency to spread news to preserve foreign faith in Swedish neutrality. It censored any incoming news telegrams that might undermine Swedish foreign policy. Kilander analyzes a period long before the Vietnam War. Still, he shows UD had a proprietary interest in news coverage of

---

[20] Ernest W. Lefever, *TV and National Defense*, Boston, Virginia, 1974: 88, 114.

[21] Martin F. Herz, *The Prestige Press and the Christmas Bombing, 1972*, Washington, D.C., 1980: tables 2 and 5, pages 29 and 40.

[22] *Vestkusten's* Karin Person was the only Swedish-American editor to keep her Swedish citizenship.

[23] Svenbjörn Kilander, *Censur och propaganda*, Uppsala, 1981.

Swedish foreign policy. UD did not hesitate to use direct methods if it felt Swedish national interests were at stake.

Johnny Wijk's *Svarta börsen* analyzes the Swedish government's role in information management in World War Two. Sweden's wartime rationing created a black market in restricted goods, such as food coupons and ration cards. The government tried suppressing this trade with propaganda that appealed to citizens' loyalty. Jörgen Weibull's article "Censur och opinionsutveckling" shows the government also censored the press during the war. It wanted to rein in the press, and ensure nothing appeared in print to anger the Germans. Again, the purpose was to maintain foreign confidence in Swedish neutrality.[24] Like Kilander, Wijk and Weibull show a state that used news and propaganda to advance foreign policy goals.

Source Material: The Swedish-American Newspapers

There were fifteen major Swedish-American newspapers still printing by the Nineteen-Sixties. These were:

Newspaper	Editor	Location	When it Closed
California Veckoblad	Mary Hendricks	Los Angeles, Calif.	Still in print
Canada-Svensken	Thorwald Wiik	Toronto, Ontario	31 Dec. 1978
Canada-Tidningen	Helge V. Pearson	Winnipeg, Man.	1 August 1970
Covenant Companion	Carl P. Anderson	Chicago, Illinois	Still in print
The Messenger	Rev. B.W. Selin	Chicago, Illinois	December 1969
Missions-Vännen	Joel Fridfelt	Chicago, Illinois	January 1961
Norden	Erik R. Hermans	Brooklyn, NY	Still in print
Nordstjernan	Gerry Rooth	New York, NY	Still in print
Svea	Anton H. Trulson	Worcester, Mass.	February 1966
Svenska-Amerikanaren	Arthur Hendricks	Chicago, Illinois	Still in print
Svenska Posten	Harry F. Fabbe	Seattle, Wash.	6 October 1976
Swedish Press	Sture Wermee	Vancouver, B.C.	Still in print
Texas Posten	Gerald B. Knape	Austin, Texas	14 January 1982
Vestkusten	Karin Person	San Francisco, CA	Still in print
Western News	Glenn Peterson	Denver, Colorado	23 April 1979

[24] Johnny Wijk, *Svarta börsen*, Stockholm, 1992: 50–64; and Jörgen Weibull, "Censur och opinionsutveckling," *Norden under 2. verdenskrig*, Copenhagen, 1979: 136–172.

The Swedish-American editors in 1975. Sitting from left to right: California Veckoblad's Mary Hendricks, The Swedish Press's representative Maj Brundin, Vestkusten's Karin Person, and Svenska Posten's Anita Myrfors. Standing from left to right: Nordstjernan's Gerry Rooth, Texas Posten's Gerald Knape, SAT's Arthur Hendricks, Western News's Glenn Peterson, Canada-Svensken's Thorwald Wiik, and Nordstjernan and Norden representative Gunnar Björkman. Photo courtesy of Vestkusten.

There were nominally fifteen papers left, but this number is rather flexible. What is a Swedish-American newspaper, really? The list above includes three Swedish-Canadian newspapers. These are Swedish emigrant newspapers printing in North America, but not in the United States. The list also includes one Finn-Swedish newspaper: *Norden*. It is a U.S.-based ethnic newspaper that targets immigrants and prints in Swedish. It writes mostly for readers from the Swedish-speaking sections of Finland: Österbotten, Åboland, Nyland, and Åland. It also reaches some Swedish-Americans.[25] I have defined "the Swedish-American press" broadly, including Swedish-language papers printing anywhere in North America. The list also includes papers that have converted to English but still targeted Swedish ethnic communities. This includes *California Veckoblad* and *Western News* (known as *Westerns Nyheter* until 1941).

---

[25] E-mail from *Norden* editor Erik Hermans to Edward Burton, 9 February 2003.

While they wrote in English, they defined themselves as Swedish newspapers.

I have included the Canadian and Finn-Swedish newspapers, but other publications presented problems. Several Swedish-American fraternal societies printed Swedish-language newsletters, for example. Are they newspapers? Also, the Salvation Army printed a Swedish-American edition of *War Cry* until 28 August 1965. These publications all had roots in the nineteenth-century, but they were never really newspapers. Some appeared in Swedish, but most had already converted to English. The publications left out of this project are:[26]

The American-Swedish Monthly	Swedish Chamber of Commerce of the USA
The Bethpage Messenger	Bethpage Mission
The California Covenanter	California Evangelical Covenant Church
The Evangelical Beacon	Evangelical Free Church of America
The Herald of Faith	Full Gospel Faith and Fellowship
The Leading Star (Ledstjärnan)	Fraternal Order of Runeberg
The Monitor	Scandinavian Fraternity of America
Musiktidningen	The American Union of Swedish Singers
The Standard	Baptist General Conference
Stridsropet	Salvation Army, Scandinavian Branch
The Svitiod Journal	Independent Order of Svitiod
Vasastjärnan	The Vasa Order of America
Vikingen	Grand Lodge of Independent Order of Vikings

These publications were Swedish-American, but most were newsletters or publicity sheets. *The Monitor, Svitiod Journal, Vikingen*, and *Vasastjärnan* were newsletters for Swedish-American fraternal lodges. *The Leading Star* was a newsletter for a Finn-Swedish fraternal order. *Musiktidningen* was a newsletter for Swedish-American choral singers. These were not news-bearing journals, except news on a narrow community. Apart from fraternal news, they did not carry "hard news" for a wider audience. *Vasastjärnan* and *The Leading Star* sometimes ran cultural features on Sweden, but nothing about Vietnam. I exclude these newsletters

---

[26] For a list of all Swedish publications printing in January 1964, see "Swedish Publications in the United States," File 18 "Lists," box 3, Fabbe, UW.

largely because they had nothing to say on Swedish Vietnam policy or the war in Asia.

California Covenanter ran topical editorials, and one could argue for its inclusion here. The national *Covenant Companion*, however, ran many of *California Covenanter*'s editorials. My thesis includes the *Companion*; many of the *Covenanter*'s views appear there. The other religious publications – *The Standard, Stridsropet, Bethpage Messenger*, and *Herald of Faith* – did not run topical editorials. These periodicals often felt like church newsletters more than religious newspapers. (The difference between the two formats is a matter of degree, and often a subjective definition.)

The remaining fifteen newspapers were often stylistically similar. Most of the news was on the front page. There was usually more, with news articles scattered throughout the paper. Sometimes there was not. Most emigrant papers had come to focus their news coverage on Sweden since the First World War.[27] Local Swedish-American clubs, like the Vasa Order, often ran columns in the Swedish-American papers. Sometimes, local Swedish-American church groups also had their own articles. The second or third pages of nearly every paper contained the "Province Notices." These had one or two terse items from each of Sweden's twenty-four provinces. Even by Swedish standards, these were of strictly local interest. These items arguably served a mostly nostalgic role. A 1971 Swedish report on the emigrant press declared the "mentioning of geographical names [in these stories] that are familiar to the readers seems to be more important than the news itself."[28]

All the Swedish-American newspapers contain serialized short stories. They were usually traditional in nature, often with a romantic portrayal of Swedish history. Frans G. Bengtsson's *Röde Orm* (*The Long Ships*) was a Swedish-American favorite. "My Lord," *Canada-Tidningen*'s editor exclaimed, "that guy can write. And back

---

[27] Björk, *The Swedish-American Press*, 193; Anna Williams, "Providing an Ethnic Identity," *Swedes in America*, Växjö, 1993; for the Danish-American press's similar focus on Denmark after the war, see Marzolf, *The Danish-Language Press in America*, 16.

[28] Svensk-Amerikanska pressutredningen, *Utvandrarnas tidningar*, Stockholm, 1971: 76.

in Canada, we thought that the art had ended with Selma Lagerlöf."[29] Selma Lagerlöf was likely the author most widely serialized in the Swedish-Americans press. Swedish officials suspected the emigrants knew little about Swedish literature "after Selma Lagerlöf and her contemporaries."[30] It may have been true. These older stories usually cost the papers little or nothing to print. The works of authors like Selma Lagerlöf were usually in the public domain, no longer under copyright. Modern writers such as Vilhelm Moberg waived their rights to royalties because of the papers' economic situation. Moberg gave *Nordstjernan* the rights to *De knutna händerna* in 1952 "as a purely personal gift" to the editor.[31]

Many papers printed at least one editorial, and occasional letters to the editor. These editorials, and most letters, were usually conservative. Finis Capps defines their social conservatism as "skepticism of idealism and insistence on the practical, pessimism of the ability of humanity to prevent war, fear of Catholicism, mistrust of the banker and the manufacturer, [and] dislike of diplomats and the military."[32] Their distrust of the military and bankers is an unusual form of conservatism. It may partly derive from the nineteenth-century Swedish Rural Party conservatism (*Lantmannapartism*). Capps also studied the Swedish-Americans of the Twenties and Thirties, when the First World War experience largely defined American conservatism. Still, even forty years later many Swedish-American papers remained suspicious of the political and economic power elite. A Lutheran air also hung over several newspapers, and some printed religious columns. *Missions-Vännen* and *The Covenant Companion* were Covenant Church newspapers, and *The Messenger* was a Methodist paper. Even secular papers like *California Veckoblad* ran religious columns.

---

[29] Arthur Andersson, quoted in M.L., "New York: Glöm inte Kanada, bön från Winnipeg," *Dagens Nyheter*, 17 January 1954: 15.

[30] Letter from Klas Böök to Olof Rydbeck, 12 February 1954, file "1954 – 1959," box I:461, PR4S, RA.

[31] Letter from Vilhelm Moberg to *Nordstjernan*, 31 March 1953, file "1950 Okt – 1953," box I:461, PR4S, RA.

[32] Finis Herbert Capps, *From Isolation to Involvement*, Chicago, 1966: 225.

The fifteen Swedish-American newspapers had much in common, but also notable differences. Some were strictly local papers, while others reached for national audiences. Some had religious affiliations, but most were secular. Some actively discussed politics while other papers remained silent.

My thesis builds on the columns, editorials, letters, and articles in the Swedish-American press. I have used the newspaper collections held at Sweden's Royal Library, Augustana College's Swenson Swedish Immigration Research Center, and Göteborg University. Other good collections exist at The Emigrants' House, Harvard University, the National Library of Canada, and the Library of Congress. *Nordstjernan* and *The Swedish Press* have sets of their own back issues. All paper collections everywhere have gaps, and even some microfilm collections are incomplete. The microfilm-makers learned that nearly all Swedish-American papers have some issues lost to history. Even with multiple collections, no major paper has been preserved in its entirety.[33] The microfilm-makers assembled near-complete runs of many papers, but their film is not always reliable. For example, they filmed the entire 1971 roll of *Svenska-Amerikanaren Tribunen* out of focus. Fortunately for me, Göteborg University has a nearly complete collection of 1971 on paper copies.[34] In short, anyone researching these papers must visit several libraries to find a newspaper's complete output.

Source Material: Newspaper Archives

Two Swedish-American papers have extisting archives from the Vietnam era. The internal letters, papers, and memoranda in these archives reveal how their editors worked and put their papers together. *Svenska Posten*'s archives are part of the University of Washington's Harry Fabbe collection. These files also have many short notes from *Vestkusten*'s Karin Person to *Svenska Posten* editor Harry Fabbe. The University of Washington also holds columnist Reinhold Ahleen's diaries. Göteborg University has some of Ahleen's

---

[33] Lilly Setterdahl, *Swedish-American Newspapers*, Rock Island, 1981: 3.

[34] Unfortunately, many libraries are destroying their paper collections to save space after buying microfilm. For a discussion of this, see Nicholson Baker, *Double Fold*, New York, 2001.

letters, and an anthology of Swedish and Swedish-American poetry that he edited. This archive is of strictly literary value and does not appear in this thesis.

The Swedish Press is the only newspaper that keeps its own archive.[35] Its papers sit in the damp basement of a Canadian nursing home. Its archives include minute details on *The Swedish Press's* existence, such as water bills from 1959, or electric bills from 1971. *The Swedish Press's* owner – the Central Press (1953) Ltd. – has its records stored at the University of British Columbia. These include details on the finances of a "typical" emigrant newspaper.[36] *The Swedish Press's* editor in the Seventies, Sture Wermee, has answered questions on the newspaper.[37] (Its current editor Anders Neumueller has also offered help.) *Norden's* Erik Hermans began editing his paper in 1962 and is still on the job today. Hermans also worked for *Nordstjernan* three days a week in the Seventies and Eighties. He has answered questions on *Norden* and *Nordstjernan's* audiences and editorial positions by e-mail. The only other remaining Vietnam-era editor, Karin Person of *Vestkusten*, is in frail health. I have not interviewed her. A short manuscript by Karin Person – "Short History of *Vestkusten*" – appears here courtesy of Ulf Jonas Björk.

Most newspapers have not saved their letters and paperwork. *Nordstjernan's* editor stressed this was largely because of a lack of space. "Look around you," editor Alvalene Karlsson said to me, referring to the small office near Times Square. "Where would we keep such an archive?" There was no room for one. When asked

---

[35] *Svea's* archives are at Pomona College in California, but these hold only bound back issues of the paper. (Telephone conversation with Ruby Trulson, 14 October 2000.)

[36] The University also has publisher Matthew Lindfors' private papers, but these have little on *The Swedish Press*. A collection of private letters between Lindfors and his wife has recently turned up. *The Swedish Press* donated these to an archive in Karlshamn. (Telephone conversation with Anders Neumueller, editor of *The Swedish Press*, 10 November 2000.)

[37] I spoke with him twice over the telephone. I did not tape either of these conversations, but noted exact quotations. Monica Lewinsky was then facing wiretapping charges for taping telephone-calls with President Clinton at the time.

about old mailing lists, *Nordstjernan* checked with the woman who wrote the mailing labels in the Sixties. This turned up nothing.[38]

Source Material: Government Archives

The Swedish government documents in this thesis have not appeared in any historical research until now. The most important sources were the Swedish Foreign Ministry's Press Bureau files. UD Press Bureau oversees and promotes news coverage of Sweden around the world. Its function is similar to the United States Information Agency in the State Department. In covering Sweden, many Swedish-American newspapers were in constant contact with this agency. Its files through 1968 are at the Swedish National Archives, but files since 1969 remain classified. These files are in UD's own archive. UD allowed me to examine these files since they likely contain no state secrets.

These files reveal a huge hidden structure behind the emigrant press that other researchers have missed. They show a network of people and institutions finding, clipping, editing, rewriting, and sending news and photos to the Swedish-American press. This network was always changing as new financial or political situations arose. UD Press Bureau directed this network and coordinated the news flow to the emigrant papers.

The UD Press Bureau files and related archives reveal close contact between UD and the Swedish-American editors. The editors occasionally wrote to UD Press Bureau, and UD always wrote back. The files also have cables between UD and its consulates discussing the editors' problems. These files are a rare source of information on how the Swedish-American press functioned in the Sixties. They give details about how the editors produced their papers. They relate what production methods they used, what machines they had, and what their drawbacks were.

A key player in this news-network was the American-Swedish News Exchange, ASNE. This was a semi-independent organ of UD. The Swedish National Archives also has the American-Swedish

---

[38] E-mail from Ulf Mårtensson, publisher of *Nordstjernan*, 1997; brief conversation with Alvalene Karlsson in the *Nordstjernan* office, 1996.

News Exchange's files. These documents reveal what kinds of news were chosen, who rewrote them, how they rewrote them, when they sent them, and how much they got for doing it. The American-Swedish New Exchange's New York office often had different views on these procedures. (Its records are at Augustana College in Illinois.) The American-Swedish News Exchange files, with the UD Press Bureau files, show how the emigrant press really worked. They show who put the newspapers together, and what went into producing them.

UD Press Bureau has published an important report called *Utvandrarnas tidningar*. In 1970, the Swedish Riksdag set up a commission to study the Swedish-American press. The Swedish-American Press Commission toured North America for three weeks in 1971. Its purpose was to find ways to help the emigrant press survive for future generations. The investigators interviewed the editors, and examined their papers' printing technology. The editors spoke frankly with them about their papers' finances and outlook for the future. Its 1971 report gives valuable data on how these newspapers functioned but has no content analysis. As "stage two" of UD's inquiry unfolded, the editors realized the plan was to reorganize the entire Swedish-American press under UD control. For whatever reason, UD believed it was worth reining in these papers. The entire project broke down with little accomplished. All that remains from this episode is one methodical report. It is an especially valuable source of information because so few emigrant newspapers have saved their files.

Disposition of the Thesis

The following chapter covers the "Historical Background of the Swedish-American Press." It introduces the three major newspapers in my thesis, which I will examine from a community-press perspective. The three major papers had different audiences which arguably influenced their editorial positions. My thesis follows them from 1960 until the early Seventies. This chapter also explains the coming generational shift in the Nineteen-Sixties. This generational shift will increasingly present an obstacle for the newspapers.

Chapter Three analyzes the source material in the Swedish-American press and the politics that may have been involved in it. The Swedish-American editors assembled their papers with news from several different sources. This chapter examines these news sources. Who wrote and edited the news articles the emigrant editors received? How much news from each source did the newspapers print? Which sources did the Swedish-American newspapers prefer to report Vietnam-related events? How much did the editors cut, add onto, or rewrite the articles they received? This chapter examines potential biases in the news the emigrant papers ran on their front pages. This news could arguably influence the editorial-page opinions.

Chapters Four through Six survey Swedish-American press opinion on Vietnam and Sweden. The title of Chapter Four is "The Swedish-American Press on Vietnam." This chapter explores emigrant editorial, columnist, and letter-to-the-editor opinions on the war in Vietnam. The chapter is in six broad sections. They include surveys of emigrant press comment on the early "military adviser" period, the 1964–1965 escalation, and America's final years in Vietnam. This chapter pays special attention to how the religious newspapers commented on the war, and how the Vietnam debate caused internal conflicts in *Svenska Posten*.

Chapter Five covers "The Swedish-American Press on Sweden." This chapter looks at six broad events (or themes) in the press commentary of Swedish Vietnam policy. These include Sweden's diplomatic recognition of North Vietnam and its sheltering of U.S. deserters. This chapter also studies how the emigrant press portrayed the main diplomatic actors of Prime Minister Olof Palme and U.S. Ambassador Jerome Holland. It also examines emigrant views on whether Sweden got distorted information on U.S. policy in Vietnam.

Chapter Six includes the content analysis method in my thesis. It introduces the method Eva Queckfeldt used in her thesis *Vietnam: tre svenska tidningars syn på Vietnamfrågan*. Using a proven and established method allows me to compare the Swedish newspapers to the Swedish-American ones. This chapter examines reporting changes in three major emigrant papers. It explains the differences in reporting and the changes over time from a community-press perspective.

Chapter Seven presents my conclusions. This gathers the chapter conclusions and offers some final analysis on how the Swedish-American press commented on the American war in Vietnam and Sweden's criticism of it.

Chapter Two

Historical Background of the Swedish-American Press

This chapter examines the state of Swedish-America and its three leading newspapers as the Nineteen-Sixties opened. The chapter comes in three main parts. The first section presents the changing face of Swedish-America, which the Sixties would partly alter. These changes would affect how they – and their newspapers – would view nearly everything, not least Vietnam. Swedish-America was shifting from the immigrant generation to a younger generation born in America. This meant the Swedish newspapers had to redirect their target audience, change their content, and even change the language they printed in. They were even reconsidering what it meant to be Swedish-American in the modern world. Many of these changes would influence their relationship with Sweden. The emigrant papers' view of Swedish foreign policy was largely the result of these sea-changes in format.

The chapter's second part presents the three main newspapers in this study. Many Swedish-American papers focused only on their local communities, but these three actively debated politics and current affairs. They would soon lead the Swedish-American debate on Vietnam. They were also different papers, writing for different communities. I will also present a theoretical framework for analyzing these newspapers.

The chapter's third section gives a snapshot of the Swedish-American papers' views of Sweden as the Sixties opened. It will show the emigrants had a divided image of Sweden: a mix of positive and negative images. I believe the Swedish-American press's criticism of Sweden's Vietnam policy was not an isolated incident. It was instead part of a long tradition of mixed feelings toward the homeland. Vietnam was a new element in emigrant criticism of Sweden, and the basis of the Swedish-Americans' mixed feelings was also changing.

Who Were the Swedish-Americans?

Where did the Swedish-Americans live? *Svenska-Amerikanaren Tribunen* printed 672 reader letters in its "Folkets Röst" section in 1960. One hundred and ten came from readers in Illinois, seventy-seven from Minnesota, seventy-five had Californian postmarks, and fifty-nine came from Sweden. This is hardly a scientific way to divine where *Svenska-Amerikanaren*'s readers lived. Still, this regional breakdown nearly matches what the U.S. Census Bureau found in 1960.

TABLE 1. *Location of Swedish-Americans by state, 1960.*

State	Immigrant Generation	First, Second, and Third Generations	Immigrant Percentage
Illinois	34,043	142,615	23.9%
California	27,041	31,067	87.0%
New York	24,532	74,125	33.1%
Minnesota	23,484	156,788	15.0%
Massachusetts	14,018	51,101	27.4%

Source: U.S. Census Bureau, cited in "Svenskar i Amerika," *Svea*, 6 September 1962: 4.

This table shows there were older and newer groups of Swedish-Americans. California was attracting new Swedish expatriates, but also many older immigrants moving there for retirement.[1] It had a high ratio of immigrants to the state's entire Swedish-American

---

[1] Theodore White, *The Making of a President, 1960*, New York, 1963: 216–217; Henrik Tallgren, *Svensk-amerikaner i Kalifornien*, Göteborg, 2000: 51, 194 note 132.

population. Older settlements like Minnesota and Illinois – states that attracted Swedes in the late nineteenth century – still had the most Swedish-Americans. Most of these, however, were in the second and third generations. These groups of Swedish-Americans were less likely to read a Swedish-language newspaper than their parents. The Swedish-American press had always relied on immigrants as its main subscription base. By 1960, Minnesota had a large Swedish-American population, but only 15% of them were immigrants. Minnesota had a distinct Swedish profile, but not enough immigrants to support a Swedish newspaper. Illinois and the Chicago region had enough immigrants to support only one emigrant paper. *Chicago-Bladet* had to close in 1952, *Covenant Weekly* reorganized in 1958, and *Missions-Vännen* closed at the end of 1960. This left only *Svenska-Amerikanaren* in Chicago.

The remaining Swedish-American newspapers still targeted the older immigrants. Most papers printed in large cities that still lured new immigrants, chiefly on the East and West coasts.[2] Their original role had been to socialize and assimilate newcomers to American society. They initially had several basic roles. One was to provide general news and information the immigrants would need in the new society. Second, these papers served as a forum for discussing political and cultural ideas. Third, they explained the laws, rules, values, and norms of American society.[3] Fourth, several newspapers sold dictionaries, almanacs, cookbooks, and study-guides for passing the American citizenship exams. Fifth, the newspapers advertised local immigrant-owned businesses that stocked hard-to-find Swedish products.[4] Sixth, these papers defended the rights and welfare of the immigrants. Lastly, they increasingly came to promote group pride and self-esteem.

These were all services for immigrants or non-English speakers. By the Sixties, younger Swedish-Americans had grown up and lived

---

[2] Beijbom, "The Swedish Press," 383; J. Oscar Backlund, *A Century of the Swedish-American Press*, Chicago, 1952: 57–59.

[3] Marion Tuttle Marzolf, "The Danish Immigrant Newspaper," *From Scandinavia to America*, Odense, 1987: 303–304.

[4] William Parker Jones, *Thor's Hammers: The Swedish and Finnish "Granitklippan" Community of West Concord, New Hampshire*, Durham, N.H., 2000: 159–160.

their entire lives in America. They did not need U.S. society explained to them. The Swedish-American newspapers had too many older readers, and not enough young ones. There were not enough younger immigrants coming to America. Mass immigration from Sweden into the U.S. had ended over forty years earlier. Two world wars sharply reduced the flow of immigrants into the United States, and Congress largely shut the doors in 1924. In Canada, immigration continued through the Twenties. Immigration into Canada may have increased after the U.S. restricted immigration. The Depression of the Thirties, however, did far more to end mass immigration to North America. The Depression also led to a greater return-flow of Swedes back to Sweden. Apart from an immigration spike to Canada after World War Two, North America's immigrant population was falling. There were too few new immigrants and too many newspapers for them to support.

TABLE 2. *U.S. and Canadian inhabitants born in Sweden, 1920–1970.*

Year	U.S.A.	U.S. decline	Canada	Canadian decline
1920	625,585		27,700	
1930	595,250	− 30,335	34,415	+ 6,715
1940	445,070	− 150,180	27,160	− 7,255
1950	325,118	− 119,952	22,635	− 4,525
1960	214,491	− 110,627	32,632	+ 9,997
1970	127,070	− 87,421	21,680	− 10,952

Source: U.S. Census and Census of Canada, 1920–1970, taken from *The Statistical History of the United States*, New York, 1972: 117; Fishman, *Language Loyalty in the United States*, 36; and Lars Ljungmark, *Svenskarna i Winnipeg*, Växjö, 1994: 13.

Note: Canadian figures are for 1921, 1931, 1941, 1951, 1961, and 1971.

Granted, even in the non-ethnic press experienced a wave of newspaper closings during these fifty years. Large papers pushed out small ones, and the small ones got ever less money from advertising. Yet, the Swedish-language press's slow erosion of its primary target audience boded ill for the emigrant papers. Nearly three-quarters of *Svenska Posten*'s readers in 1970 were immigrants, and only 21%

were born in America. (See Table 4.) Most Swedish immigrants had come to America nearly fifty years earlier. Even the Canadian immigrants that read papers like *The Swedish Press* mostly left in the mid-Twenties.[5] In the Sixties, this immigrant generation would quickly begin to die off. The Swedish-American Press Investigation expected this audience to disappear by 1975.[6] The Worcester newspaper *Svea* wrote in an editorial called "Weaker Pulse – End Near" that Swedish-America was a dying society. It was dying, and the doctors "stand at a discrete distance away so the patient can spend its last few hours in peace."[7]

These immigrants were the people who read Swedish-American newspapers. The circulation figures for the Swedish-American papers show a steady decline in readership. As the table below shows, many papers had only half the readers they had thirty years before. Some had survived only by absorbing other papers. Many newspapers closed in the First World War, and the survivors stayed alive by absorbing others. Still more papers closed during the Depression. Note the earliest figures may be imprecise: publishers often inflated their figures. Directories like *Ayer's* tried to be accurate, however. It served the publishers that paid for space in these newspapers.[8] Still, Table 3 does show the broad changes in the Swedish-American press.

---

[5] Telephone conversation with Lars Arnö, 4 February 2000; conversation with Sture Wermee, 13 February 2000; Nilsson, *De sista svenska rösterna*, 222; e-mail from University of Victoria researcher Eva St. Jean to Edward Burton, 18 February 2003.

[6] *Utvandrarnas tidningar*, 48.

[7] "Svagare puls – Slutet nära," *Svea*, 16 April 1959. See also Arnold H. Barton, "Svensk-Amerika om femtio år," *Sverigekontakt*, March 1998: 17.

[8] Björk, *The Swedish-American Press*, 36, 65 note 8.

TABLE 3. *Circulations of Svenska-Amerikanaren Tribunen, Svea, Vestkusten, Nordstjernan, and Texas Posten, 1906–1970.*

Year	SAT	Svea	Vestkusten	Nordstjernan	Texas Posten
1906	38,500	9,217	4,000	12,600	3,525
1910	34,646	11,165	4,600	14,500	3,675
1915	75,847	18,987	4,000	12,500	4,500
1920	65,282	35,432	4,500	11,475	4,000
1926	66,343	36,438	—	—	4,579
1930	69,294	35,189	4,750	—	4,860
1935	44,365	32,085	4,250	—	4,800
1940	52,373	35,008	4,800	—	3,000
1945	53,302	34,161	—	—	2,010
1950	53,831	33,105	4,500	—	1,276
1955	40,270	30,110	2,129	12,000	1,206
1960	27,103	30,263	2,289	8,050	1,215
1964	20,304	26,398	2,315	7,150	1,005
1970	20,149	—	1,250	6,500	1,500

Source: Björk, *The Swedish-American Press*, 62–63; 1964 figures from memorandum "Swedish Publications in the United States," Fabbe, UW; 1970 figures from *Utvandrarnas tidningar*, 22–32; all figures from *Ayer's*.

Table 3 shows that immigrant readers were disappearing. Papers from areas that attracted Swedes in the nineteenth century – *Svenska-Amerikanaren* and *Texas Posten* – had steep losses in the Thirties and early Forties. *Nordstjernan* and *Vestkusten* printed in areas that attracted Swedes into the early twentieth century. These papers had avoided their subscription crisis until the Fifties. Both groups faced a continued (or second) subscription dip in the Sixties. This crisis could have even been worse than the figures above suggest. Circulation figures were often self-reported, and newspapers often inflated them; high numbers implied importance. The slow decline in readership the table suggests could have been simply disastrous.

If the emigrant papers wanted to survive, they had to begin targeting the second and third-generation Swedish-Americans. In 1960, there were 832,451 Americans with at least one parent born in Sweden.[9] This second-generation represented a large untapped market for the ethnic press. If the Swedish-American press wanted these readers, they would have to print something different. Rather than explaining U.S. laws and customs to immigrants, they would have to write for people with an advanced knowledge of America. The third generation might have known America, but it knew much less about Sweden. The editors would have to change the content of their papers.

Generational change and the dynamic quality of ethnicity have long interested researchers. An early and influential theory was Marcus Lee Hansen's "third generation hypothesis." Hansen believed the immigrant generation always felt associated – by themselves and others – with their homeland. The second generation, insecure in American society, felt embarrassed by being seen as immigrants. They tried to be as American as possible, shedding the "ethnic label." The third generation was self-confident about their American identity, and may re-embrace their ethnicity. Over the years, many have challenged Hansen's third-generation theory of ethnicity. It is not a law; one should be flexible in interpreting it. Hansen's most lasting contribution to the debate on ethnicity is about its flexibility. Hansen argues that ethnicity can change, assume different purposes, and become elective over time.[10]

The face of Swedish-America was changing during the Sixties, and the ethnic identity with it. *Svenska-Amerikanaren* editor Arthur Hendricks found that Hansen's Law largely applied to Swedish-America. His second-generation readers resisted identifying themselves as ethnic Swedes.[11] If they found Swedish ethnicity vaguely embarrassing, *SAT* would have to change if it wanted to get young readers. As a major player in defining Swedish ethnicity, *Svenska-Amerikanaren* could change that definition to suit its needs.

---

[9] "Native population of foreign or mixed parentage, Sweden," *The Statistical History of the United States*, 116.

[10] Marcus Lee Hansen, *The Problem of the Third Generation Emigrant*, Rock Island, Ill., 1938; for recent interpretations of Hansen, see: H. Arnold Barton, "Emigrants' Images of Sweden," *Migrants and the Homeland*, Uppsala, 2000: 103; Dag Blanck, *Becoming Swedish-American*, Uppsala, 1997: 24–25.

[11] "What Others Say About Your *SAT*: *Hallands Nyheter*, Annonser och ungdomens intresse ger svensk USA-press ny chans," *Svenska-Amerikanaren Tribunen*, 21 February 1968: 8. See also Beijbom, "The Swedish Press," 389.

For years, the Swedish-language newspapers defined "Swedish-Americans" as immigrants who spoke Swedish. Many papers also defined the Swedish-American identity around Lutheranism and political conservatism. This was the group image the Swedish-American "ethnic leaders" had formed for the outside world.[12] Some Swedish-Americans might indeed reject the image. Rejecting it, however, meant rejecting the only ethnic identity Swedes in America ever built for themselves.[13]

As in the nineteenth-century, building ethnicity was a collective project. Dag Blanck writes in *Becoming Swedish-American* that the ethnic leaders – writers, intellectuals, and editors – created the "great traditions" of ethnic culture. This includes sensibilities on higher art, literature, history, and perhaps even politics. These traditions are "consciously created from above" by cultural ethnic leaders.[14] (There are also "little traditions" coming spontaneously from below.) Swedish editors could create new "great traditions" for the second and third generation Swedish-Americans. They could create new views on society and politics, and even redefine Swedish ethnicity for the third generation. How they redefined their ethnic ideology would affect how they viewed Sweden, America, Vietnam, and the world.

Ethnicity has a certain ideological content. Like all other groups, ethnic groups join around a set of core values.[15] Swedish-American values in the Sixties included capitalism, Christianity, "Western values," property, free trade, the Republican Party, obedience to civil authority, skepticism of idealism, and a duty to defend the nation.[16] By the Sixties, young Americans were often questioning their parents' values. In an era of change and freedom, orthodox

---

[12] Blanck, *Becoming Swedish-American*, 27; Capps, *From Isolation to Involvement*, 17; see also Victor Greene, "Becoming American: The Role of Ethnic Leaders," *The Ethnic Frontier*, Grand Rapids, Mich., 1977: 143–175.

[13] A paraphrase of Kathleen Conzen's view of German-Americans, taken from Blanck, *Becoming Swedish-American*, 28.

[14] Cultural theories from Nils Hasselmo and Raymond Breten, quoted in Blanck, *Becoming Swedish-American*, 28–29.

[15] Tallgren, *Svensk-amerikaner i Kalifornien*, 18.

[16] For a discussion of Swedish-American values from 1914 to 1945, see Capps, *From Isolation to Involvement*, 225–227.

Lutheranism and Republican politics seemed unfashionable. Getting younger generation readers would require the editors changing the content of their papers. Since they – as ethnic leaders – created the "great traditions," this would largely redefine what it meant to be Swedish-American.

Theoretical definitions of generational ethnicity can become abstract. For the Swedish-American papers, these sociological problems were not abstract at all. The first generation wanted to look back, celebrate Swedish-American culture, and take moral values from it. Younger readers wanted more sports, politics, and Swedish economic news in the paper. There was no way to satisfy both groups; switching the target audience was difficult.[17]

The Swedish-American Press Investigation urged the papers to target expatriates and the second generation. That was the conventional wisdom, but some editors questioned such advice. *Svenska Posten* resisted the "quick fix" of using sports and politics to reach new readers. Recent expatriate immigrants may initially appreciate such fare, but the effect would wear off. *Svenska Posten* editor Harry Fabbe believed this was "because they are also subject to an inevitable process: for every month, every year they live here, these interest areas will thin out. They grow into the conditions of the new land. For better or worse, they become Swedish-Americans."[18]

The largest problem facing the emigrant press was that most young Swedish-Americans spoke only English. *Canada-Tidningen* regretted that more Swedish-Canadians had not taught their children Swedish while young.[19] The children had grown up, and the Swedish-American editors faced a problem. The emigrant generation wanted their newspaper in Swedish and the second generation wanted English. Using English to reach younger readers was a sensitive issue. The language was more than a fetish, but a

---

[17] Harry Fabbe, "Hört och Hänt: Svårt att tillfredsställa alla," *Svenska Posten*, 6 March 1968: 1.

[18] Harry Fabbe, "Hört och Hänt: Svårt att tillfredsställa alla," *Svenska Posten*, 6 March 1968: 1.

[19] Arthur Andersson, quoted in M.L., "New York: Glöm inte Kanada, bön från Winnipeg," *Dagens Nyheter*, 17 January 1954: 15.

statement of basic identity. What would be the meaning of a Swedish paper if it were in English? "How can one work for Swedish culture in English?" asked *Svenska-Amerikanaren*'s Arthur Hendricks. Hendricks, and a few other editors, refused to go over to English.[20] *Svenska Posten* even began to drop the few English articles that it still printed. "We have seen too many of the mixed-language papers go under," explained editor Harry Fabbe. "We are also deeply dismayed when we see bad English printed in what ought to be a Swedish newspaper."[21] Besides, many "hard core" older readers subscribed to their papers because they were in Swedish. The editors feared that their subscriptions would plummet if they abandoned the language. There was also the feeling that younger people were not part of their natural constituency. "Young people would not subscribe anyway," insisted Arthur Hendricks.[22]

There was another problem compounding this one. The Swedish-American papers got news from Sweden written in modern Swedish. The Swedish-American readers were former immigrants. Most of them spoke a Nineteen-Twenties version of Swedish. Someone from Sweden might identify this dialect as something from a Thirties matinee film. Researchers armed with tape recorders even turned up nineteenth-century dialects still alive in America.[23]

Many readers were likely unaware the language had changed since they left. *Svenska-Amerikanaren*'s "Folkets Röst" page often carried complaints about the paper's sloppy, informal Swedish. That is, they disliked standard modern Swedish. According to the Swedish-American Press Investigation, articles in modern Swedish can "evoke a negative reader reaction. The reader simply may not even understand what they say; there are too many unknown terms, written in unknown expressions."[24]

When challenged about that assertion, *The Swedish Press*'s Sture Wermee said "it can indeed happen sometimes." According to

---

[20] Arthur Hendricks, cited in *Utvandrarnas tidningar*, 26.
[21] Harry Fabbe, cited in *Utvandrarnas tidningar*, 29.
[22] Arthur Hendricks, cited in *Utvandrarnas tidningar*, 26.
[23] Folke Hedblom, "Dialect Hunters," *American Swedish '73*, Philadelphia, 1973: 63–67.
[24] *Utvandrarnas tidningar*, 50.

Wermee, his readers had left Norrland when that dialect was quite distinct. Not only had the Swedish language changed, but its regional dialects had faded away. The problem was real.[25] The American-Swedish News Exchange's Naboth Hedin had the same opinion. (Chapter three will discuss ASNE in more detail.) Hedin believed ASNE's Swedish had "too many ultra-long words, which mean nothing to the people who have lived here for the greater part of their lives."[26] It may overstate the problem to say the Swedish-Americans could not understand modern Swedish. They could figure it out. It is likely they saw such writing as careless, or a debased version of proper Swedish.

Despite their belief that they spoke a purer language, an emigrant Swedish dialect had emerged over the years. Occasionally this dialect used words such as *streetet* and *sidewålken*, borrowed from English. (Those are expressions for *gatan* and *trottoaren* respectively.)[27] Purists derided this as "a mongrel language," and many Swedish-American editors were purists. It was easy to slip into using these words, without being aware of it. Speaking these words with a nineteenth century Värmland accent could mask, to a degree, the changes that had occurred.[28]

It sometimes amused UD that the Swedish-American papers insisted on keeping "the language of honor and heroes clean," but printed Swenglish when they wanted.[29] Their English was also immigrant-English: Swedish written with English words.[30] In short, there was no easy way to change the language to attract younger

---

[25] Telephone conversation with Sture Wermee, 13 February 2000.

[26] Letter from Naboth Hedin to Allan Kastrup, 15 June 1968, file "Correspondence – Naboth Hedin," box "Correspondences," ASNE New York, SSIRC.

[27] Arthur Landfors, "Det svenskamerikanska språket," *Svenska Posten*, 17 January 1968: 1, 3. See also: Eric Olson, "Reflektioner av Eric Olson," *Svenska Posten*, 5 July 1967: 4.

[28] Hedblom, "Dialect Hunters," 65–66.

[29] Letter from Kjell Öberg to Sven Backlund, 7 October 1959, file "1954–1959," box I:461, PR4S, RA. (Öberg attached an ad Anton Trulson had specially translated from English into Swedish: "Den finaste syrprisen i motoristens livstid . . . denne new-size Ford Falcon," *Svea*, 24 September 1959.)

[30] *Utvandrarnas tidningar*, 50.

readers. English would alienate older readers and modern Swedish might confuse them. The third generation, however, usually spoke only English. If they had learned Swedish in school, it was usually modern Swedish.

The Sixties saw more than a generational change in Swedish-America. It also saw a change in how most Swedish-Americans defined themselves. The definitions had become more fluid, and membership more voluntary. It is hard to generalize about people's ethnicity; they are all individuals. Each person has their own family history and upbringing. Collectively, however, there is a shift from one definition of Swedish-American ethnicity to another.

Earlier Definition	Later Definition
Immigrant, born abroad	Born in America
Transplantation experience	Abstract belief in common origin
First language: Swedish	First language: English
Reads older dialect of Swedish	May read some modern Swedish
Affiliation decided by society	Elective affiliation
Often politically conservative	Not bound by definition
Lutheran	Not bound by definition

It is possible the Swedish-Americans no longer formed a distinct ethnic group. Their language, appearance, citizenship status, and cultural practices associated them with mainstream America. All that they retained was a belief in a common origin overseas. In an era of desegregation and mass assimilation, this was a weak basis for keeping Swedes in the immigrant working class. If they wanted to, most Swedish-Americans could simply consider themselves American Protestant whites.

Their Swedish ethnicity was only one of several personal identities. They could consider themselves "ethnic" only occasionally, or even not at all. James McKay and Frank Lewins describe this process as moving from "ethnic consciousness" to "ethnic awareness." Swedish ethnicity changes from being the immigrant group's central identity – with an *Us* versus *Them* attitude – to being just one of many identities. Then Swedish ethnicity, and taking part in ethnic organizations, no longer excludes an American identity.[31]

Henrik Tallgren defines this process as moving from "high-active" to "low-active" ethnicity. Tallgren describes the low-active Swedish-American identity:

> Some conclusions, mainly of psychological character, can be made: Swedish-Americans have an emotional connection to an intangible reality that their forebears experienced (or, rather, what they are supposed to have experienced); a longing for an extraordinary identity, away from the everyday ones; and a symbolic connection to Vikings, who are regarded as a kind of distant relatives. Also important is family, which can be extended to the church and the Swedish-American group as a whole. Sometimes, an individual's identity can be concretized openly by, for example, making a "pilgrimage" to Sweden. But also in other ways, such as decorating (especially parts of) their home with Swedish artifacts and other memorabilia, and by "becoming" a Swede during festivals or at the ethnic club for a day or over the weekend.[32]

In McKay and Lewins' words, this low-active ethnicity is when "individuals know they possess certain ethnic traits which are no more meaningful than their other cultural, physical, social, or territorial characteristics." Low-active, ethnically aware groups will think of their ethnicity "largely in cultural terms and in terms of individuals' identities."[33] So, high-active ethnicity usually defines the individual. Individuals can largely define their own low-active ethnicity's content.

Ethnicity has an ideological content. Ideology is the ethnic group's relations of signification. That is, it is how the group uses a system of signs – or even uses culture – for its benefit.[34] High-active ethnic Swedish-Americans may not have been a class, but they were a distinct social group. As a social group, they had often clashed with other social groups in the past. (These groups included the Irish, Catholics, Norwegians sometimes, and even homeland-Swedes.)

---

[31] James McKay and Frank Lewins, "Ethnicity and the Ethnic Group," *Ethnic and Racial Studies*, vol. 1, no. 4, October 1978: 415–417. See also Eva St. Jean, "From Defiance to Defence."

[32] Tallgren, *Svensk-amerikaner i Kalifornien*, 193.

[33] McKay and Lewins, "Ethnicity and the Ethnic Group," 415–416.

[34] Definition and discussion of ideology from O'Sullivan, et al., *Key Concepts in Communication and Cultural Studies*, Second ed. London, 1994: 139–143, 209–210, 286–287.

Their group knowledge included informal symbols, codes, and myths. In moving from high to low-active ethnicity, these symbols and codes become more important. As the Swedish-Americans lost their "strange accents" and "foreign customs," they increasingly used these symbols to define their group identity. The more one could master these symbols, the more "Swedish-American" one was.

As Tallgren suggests, these symbols included Swedish clothes, Swedish artifacts, or other memorabilia. The more *lutfisk* one had at Christmas, or the more Swedish furniture in one's house, the more "Swedish-American" one was. Skills such as speaking Swedish, or knowing Swedish handicrafts, were also part of this group signification. One could say they were strategies of group cohesion. These were strategies to uphold ethnic group interests.

Many people argue the media help shape a nation's political and social ideology. The press has great agenda-setting power, deciding which issues are important or not. It largely decides what people discuss among their friends. We "know" more about world events, largely because we have read about them in the paper.[35] Few Swedish-Americans saw their Swedish newspaper as their main news-source by 1960. *The Covenant Weekly*'s 1958 survey showed that most read mainstream English-language papers.[36] By 1960, the Swedish papers were largely cultural, instead of news-bearing, media. The news they contained was mostly on Swedish events. For people living in America, Swedish news events formed an abstract reality. The events in these dispatches had little bearing on their daily lives. These stories had social and cultural meaning, but the politics in them felt distant and foreign and likely had little direct influence on the Swedish-American readers. The emigrant press's political influence came through creating a certain social and cultural atmosphere among its readers.

These Swedish-American papers were ethnic leaders. They spread the group's informal symbols, codes, and myths. For those "longing for an extraordinary identity," the Swedish-American press

---

[35] Tony Bilton, et al., *Introductory Sociology*, London, 1981: 542.

[36] Sixty-one percent of these readers subscribed to a secular English-language periodical. (Ben Bankson, "Questionnaire Study Shows Subscribers are Readers," *The Covenant Weekly*, 14 November 1958: 3.)

provided one. These papers ran ads for Swedish books, cultural artifacts, and airline tickets to Sweden. They printed recipes for Swedish foods, and many papers reported local church functions or fraternal lodge activities. Above everything else, they printed in Swedish. It was arguably more than just a language, but a linguistic ideology promoting group cohesion.

The Three Leading Newspapers: Theoretical Perspectives

Ulf Jonas Björk suggested I look at the leading emigrant papers as examples of community newspapers. Community-press theory usually deals with the rural local press, but some have used it to analyze urban neighborhood papers. Wilbur Schramm and Merritt Ludwig describe the local newspaper as "a great wide window through which readers look out into the community and into the lives of their acquaintances."[37] Unlike a major metropolitan daily, a local paper reported on the community and its members' personal events. It did not comment as much on national news, which it assumed readers got elsewhere. Björk's thesis, *The Swedish-American Press*, argues "mature" foreign-language papers adopted traits of small, rural American weeklies. A casual look at the Swedish-American papers supports this view. The Swedish emigrant press had much more news on church picnics than international politics.[38] (This may have changed when Vietnam intruded on the emigrants' tranquil world, however.) In 1972, Marion Marzolf doubted that much still separated the Danish emigrant papers from the small American weeklies. She considered the Danish-American papers to be small, American weeklies printed in a foreign language.[39]

Like the rural weeklies, the foreign-language papers were also in a struggle to survive. During much of the twentieth century, the rural weeklies were in slow decline. They were finding it hard to

---

[37] Wilbur Schramm and Merritt Ludwig, "The Weekly Newspaper and Its Readers," *Journalism Quarterly*, vol. 28, no. 2, 1951: 314.

[38] Björk, *The Swedish-American Press*, 18–19.

[39] Marzolf, *The Danish-Language Press in America*, 212–213; Wittke also considers the German papers to be "American newspapers, although still in a foreign language." Carl Wittke, *The German-Language Press in America*, Frankfort, Ken., 1957: 197.

compete with the large corporate daily papers.[40] In the new, interconnected capitalist world, people wanted more news from beyond the local area. This may have hastened the decline of the small papers that reported local community events. Their ethnic counterparts, the foreign-language newspapers, faced similar declines. Third-generation Swedish-Americans saw the tightly-knit Swedish-American community as an anachronism in the modern world. The old immigrant neighborhoods – such as Chicago's Swede-Town – exuded a brand of ethnicity from an earlier era.

The rural American weekly's specific purpose – arguably the same for foreign-language papers – was to knit its readers together. Morris Janowitz' *The Community Press in an Urban Setting* examines how this worked among Chicago's neighborhood newspapers. His conclusion was "the community press acts as a mechanism which seeks to maintain local consensus through emphasizing common values rather than solving conflicting values." These neighborhood papers stress local traditions and identities, and group cohesion. The contents of these papers all serve that purpose. They stress coverage of civic organizations, and personal and social news.[41] Ulf Jonas Björk argues this tie between purpose and content also appears in the Swedish-American press.[42] These ethnic papers also built community awareness and identification in their reporting. They covered voluntary ethnic organizations and social and personal news about immigrants. This helps explain the emphasis on church picnics and social lodges, for example. This was positive reporting on the community. The papers played down conflict in the group, stressed cooperation, and exposed outside threats to the community. An outside threat may even strengthen local solidarity against a common enemy.[43]

---

[40] Björk, *The Swedish-American Press*, 19.

[41] Morris Janowitz, *The Community Press in an Urban Setting*, London, 1967: 11, 60–61, 72, 78–79, 81.

[42] Björk, *The Swedish-American Press*, 19–20, and endnotes 14–15 on Janowitz.

[43] Douglas Blanks Hindman, "Community Newspapers, Community Structural Pluralism, and Local Conflict with Nonlocal Groups," *Journalism and Mass Communication Quarterly*, vol. 73, no. 3, Autumn 1996: 709.

Sweden was the symbol the emigrant papers used to unify their readers. It represented a common past and shared values. The Swedish-American press ran news on Sweden to give its readers a sense of a community built on ethnic social relations rather than territory.[44] Sweden was also, however, the target of the emigrants' mixed feelings about emigration. Their common past was that they all left Sweden, hoped for better lives in America, and had spent years reflecting on that decision to emigrate. Thus, Swedish-American press coverage of Sweden had traditionally been negative. The papers had often focused on crime, frauds, accidents, and suicides.[45]

Sweden and the Swedish news were their symbols of a common ethnic past. Vietnam presented a huge problem for the Swedish-American editors and their readers. Sweden was siding with America's current enemy. As Swedish leaders criticized the United States in harsh terms, the emigrants felt uncomfortable with their Swedish identities. They did not like what they read in the paper. They saw Sweden's recognition of Hanoi and sheltering American deserters as negative news. It was negative in a much different way from the usual "suicides and frauds" news they were used to seeing. That had just been gossip in the extended family. It was usually the emigrants criticizing the homeland-Swedes, not the other way around. Besides, that type of gossip had not concerned anybody but themselves. This was different. Now the mainstream press had picked up on Sweden's antiwar stance. They felt as if other Americans wondered about how much they listened to Stockholm. The emigrants may have felt the homeland-Swedes were redefining Swedishness into something different: antiwar, pro-Hanoi, and something less than fully American. Perhaps only Sweden's ruling Social Democrats took those positions, but they defined the face of Sweden in America. So, what should the emigrants do with Sweden? Like the German-Americans in the First World War, Swedish

---

[44] Björk, *The Swedish-American Press*, 25.

[45] Björk, *The Swedish-American Press*, 92–93, and Michael Sjöström, "Sverigebilden i de två svensk-amerikanska tidningar *Arbetaren* och *Nordstjernan* år 1914," B-paper, History Department, Göteborgs Universitet, HT 1995: pages 7, 9.

emigrants felt compelled to defend or condemn the old country. If they condemned it, what did that say about their Swedish ethnicity? Were they still Swedish-American? Were there other ways to harmonize their Swedish ethnicity with what the old country was doing?

My thesis examines how the Swedish-language press commented on the conflict between Sweden and the U.S. during the Vietnam War. Community-press theory suggests the emigrant press would highlight common values. How each paper does this, and how they define what the common value is, will depend on their particular communities. Some newspaper communities are territorial (limited only to Omaha, Nebraska, for example). Others are relational (limited to academics, gays, feminists, or political activists, for example).[46]

In the Sixties, three papers actively debated national and world politics: *Svenska Posten*, *Nordstjernan*, and *Svenska-Amerikanaren*. Many Swedish-American papers voiced political views now and then. These three did it often, as will soon be plain in the following chapters. Apart from their emphasis on politics, they had distinct press profiles. They were all relational papers as far as they targeted ethnic communities. The boundaries of their territorial communities were different. As their domains expanded, their hold on their readers became more precarious. No matter whether they had local or national audiences, the editors tailored their news to appeal to their communities.

Svenska Posten	*Nordstjernan*	*Svenska-Amerikanaren Tribunen*
Local audience	Regional audience	National audience
West coast base	East coast base	Midwest base
Cultural focus	Political focus	Ethnic culture focus
Corporately owned	Privately owned	Privately owned
Columnists	Editorials	Reader letters
(and editorials)	(and columnists)	(and editorials)

---

[46] Björk, *The Swedish-American Press*, 21–23.

Svenska Posten's opinion pieces came largely from political columns, but there were formal editorials too. *Nordstjernan's* opinion items came mainly from its formal editorials, but there were also regular political columns. Most of *Svenska-Amerikanaren's* opinions were from reader letters, but it also ran some editorials. There may be a direct link between the form the newspaper takes and the community it serves.

1. Svenska Posten (SvP): A Local Paper

In 1915, a sixteen-year-old Harry F. Fabbe left Sweden for Alaska. Fabbe held various jobs in Alaska, including a mining engineer at the Kennicott mines. Fabbe gathered seeds of formerly uncataloged plants for botanists at Lund and Göteborg University. (The dandelion species *Taraxacum Fabbianum* gets its name from him.)[47] He also wrote for Swedish-American newspapers such as *Svenska Socialisten*, *Verdandi*, and *Svenska Journalen*. After a few years, he migrated south to Seattle, where *Svenska Journalen* printed. In 1927, he began editing the newspaper. In 1936, *Oregon Posten*, *Svenska Journalen*, *Svenska Pressen* (Spokane), *Nya Svenska Pressen* (Vancouver), and *Puget Sound-Posten* merged into *Svenska Posten*.[48] Harry Fabbe became the managing editor of *Svenska Posten*, which then monopolized the region. Fabbe edited the paper for the next forty-six years. He was also the paper's only typesetter and advertising director. Only his name appears on the masthead.[49]

Considering this, and Fabbe's age, it is surprising that *Svenska Posten* was as good as it was. It was short, never going over six pages, but the editing and content were always professional. The Consolidated Press Company owned *Svenska Posten*. This was the corporate name of Svenska Klubben, a local group of Swedish-Americans that published the paper.

---

[47] Wilson, "Fabbe," 186; and "Harry Fabbe in Memoriam," *Nordstjernan-Svea*, 27 December 1973: 3.

[48] Backlund, *A Century of the Swedish-American Press*, 54–55; Letter from Olof Seaholm, co-signed by Sture Wermee and Einar Olson to Informationsbyrån UD, 21 January and 1 February 1972 (two copies), file "1972 febr. – december," PR4S, UD.

[49] Information from the biography in Fabbe, UW.

Svenska Posten's Harry Fabbe.

Svenska Posten was a local Seattle newspaper. It was a local sheet that reported local events. Its local news shows just how far it was – geographically and culturally – from the White House, foreign embassies, or news bureaus. On 19 October 1966, for example, the "Ancordes, Wash." section reported: Sharon Olson had married Larry Johnson, Berta Nelson and Alma Anderson were getting out of the hospital, Sylvia Nyman had returned from visiting Sweden, and that hunting season had opened for deer.[50] Svenska Posten was a local paper for serving the greater Seattle area. Few readers lived far beyond Seattle.[51]

Svenska Posten had a circulation of twenty-seven hundred copies during the Sixties. It ran serialized stories towards the back of the newspaper. The front page contained the most news and the second page contained the "Province Notices." *SvP* used UD-mediated news, but most of its commentary came from its stable of regular columnists. These included Stephen Forslund's "Pränt om Ditt och Datt," "George Lindberg synar väven," Ernest Hawkinson's "Spår Efter en Rullande Sten," Anders Mårtensson's "Och Det Begav Sig

---

[50] "Anacordes, Wash." *Svenska Posten*, 19 October 1996: 3.

[51] *Svenska Posten*'s 1941–1942 subscription list is the only complete list preserved. Nearly all subscribers outside Washington state were other emigrant papers, and ethnic and advertising organizations. There were also 49 subscribers in Sweden. ("Item 46: Subscribers, *Svenska Posten*, 1 June 1941," file 18 "Lists," Fabbe, UW.)

Rim och Reson av Reinhold Ahleen

Reflektioner av Eric Olson

Att..." and "Martin G. Johanson Berättar." Many are either cultural, religious, or nostalgic pieces. "Tankar från Palmlunden" by Kalle Palm is a clearly socialist column. (Kalle Palm was the son of radical Social Democratic agitator August Palm.) Poet Arthur Landfors also ran a column in *Svenska Posten*, and he was a socialist too.[52]

Svenska Posten was one of many Swedish-American papers to carry Adele Heilborn's "Stockholmsbrev." Heilborn was a Swedish-American living in Sweden, writing on American issues there. Her subject matter was mostly nonpolitical. She still lived in a politicized environment, and her articles occasionally related to Vietnam. Her column ran in other emigrant newspapers, but appeared most regularly in *Svenska Posten*. *The Swedish Press*, *Canada-Svensken* and *Canada-Tidningen* ran special editions of her column for Swedish-Canadians.

"Reflektioner" by Eric Olson was consistently political, and usually with a liberal viewpoint. "Rim och Reson" by Reinhold Ahleen, an emigrant from Uppland, was a more conservative political column. Ahleen and Olson debated between themselves in their columns. Lastly, *Svenska Posten*'s main editorial space was "Hört och Hänt." In "Hört och Hänt," Fabbe compiled brief stories, and mixed in his own commentaries on them. *Svenska Posten* ran 163 comment pieces on Vietnam between 1964 and 1973.

---

[52] For Landfors' biography and his views on socialism, see Alan Swanson, "A Swedish-American Poet," *Literature and the Immigrant Community*, Carbondale, Ill., 1990.

Svenska Posten was the least conservative of the Swedish-American newspapers. It may be too much to say it was liberal paper, but Harry Fabbe printed voices from the American political left.

Community-press theory argues that newspapers shape their audiences. They do, but readers also shape their local papers. It is worth noting that the Pacific Northwest Swedes had arrived later than other Swedish-American communities. The nearby *Swedish Press* printed mostly for lumberjacks, trappers, and gold prospectors from Norrland.[53] Vancouver had a significant middle-class minority. Most of these Swedes arrived between 1900 and 1930, with peak years in 1922 and 1928.[54] Postwar emigrants to Canada might have even used the porous border to take up residence in the U.S. These immigrants had experienced Swedish socialism in a way early emigrant groups had not. The Swedes on the U.S. side of the border were likely similar. *Svenska Posten* likely served a less conservative audience than most Swedish-American papers.

Community-press theory also argues that a local paper like *Svenska Posten* would have different content than a national paper like *SAT*. They are notably different papers. *Svenska-Amerikanaren* was a mainstream conservative paper, but *SvP* mixed New Deal liberalism with socialism. Even if *SvP*'s local community had readers on the political left, these were not universally popular ideas. Editor Harry Fabbe felt he could print these items in relative safety. As a local paper with local news, it had a strong claim on Seattle's Swedish-American community. No other paper provided local Swedish-American news. The political items came from columnists like Olson, Ahleen, Jacobson, and Palm. Readers may have disagreed with them, but *SvP* framed its columnists as virtual friends in the local press community. *Svenska Posten* underscored the personal quality of their politics by printing their photos above their

---

[53] Telephone conversation with Lars Arnö, 4 February 2000; conversation with Sture Wermee, 13 February 2000; and Gunnar Nilsson, *De sista svenska rösterna*, Stockholm, 1995: 222. See also Eva St. Jean, "The Myth of the Big Swede Logger: An *Arbetskarl* in the Vancouver Island Forests 1920–1948," unpublished M.A. thesis, University of Victoria, 1999: 90–93.

[54] E-mail from University of Victoria researcher Eva St. Jean to Edward Burton, 18 February 2003.

columns. Harry Fabbe had less reason to fear a flood of canceled subscriptions if he ran socialist columns. So he did. Large national papers did not have the same lock on a local community and had to be more cautious.

Until 1970, *Svenska Posten* printed the names of its subscribers that had a birthday that week. These weekly notices contained milestone birthdays, but most consisted of regular birthdays. Printing its readers' birthdays may have *SvP*'s way of reinforcing their ties to their local ethnic community. Around half of *Svenska Posten*'s subscribers agreed to have their names printed. *SvP* printed 1,196 names in 1965; it had 3,119 paying subscribers in 1964. It ran 1,622 names in 1970; it had 2,700 subscribers that year.[55] These birthday announcements exclude those who did not want their names printed. It also excludes the subscribers' family members who likely also read the paper. Back in the Sixties, many subscriptions may have been registered in the husband's name. This might undercount women readers. Still, these notices may give a reasonably representative cross-section of *Svenska Posten*'s readership. In comparison, *The Swedish Press* also used the same device. Its weekly notices had fewer names, and sometimes did not appear when space was tight. Its total birthday notices was far below the number of paid subscribers, and thus less representative.

Only a few of *Svenska Posten*'s birthday announcements listed the year the subscriber had been born. This makes reconstructing the average of *SvP*'s readers impossible. The few ages or birth years that *SvP* printed were not encouraging. If these birth years were remotely representative, *Svenska Posten*'s readers were old. These announcements report where subscribers were born, allowing one to identify immigrants. An analysis of where *Svenska Posten* readers had been born suggests why the paper had trouble surviving.

---

[55] Memo "Swedish Publications in the United States," Fabbe, UW; and *Utvandrarnas tidningar*, 27.

TABLE 4. *Svenska Posten's birthday announcements, by year.*

Year	Total	Men	Women	Immigrants	U.S. born
1960	1,649	813 *(49%)*	777 *(47%)*	1,221 *(74%)*	352 *(21%)*
1965	1,196	588 *(49%)*	579 *(48%)*	898 *(75%)*	249 *(21%)*
1970	1,622	794 *(49%)*	794 *(49%)*	1,172 *(72%)*	351 *(22%)*

Source: "Födelser under veckan," *Svenska Posten*, 1960, 1965, 1970.

Note: In 1960, *Svenska Posten* printed the names of 59 people whose sex was unclear, and 76 people whose national origin was unclear. In 1965, there was 1 Swede, 29 people whose sex was unclear, and 48 people whose national origin was unclear. In 1970, there were 7 Swedes, 34 people whose sex was unclear, and 92 people whose national origin was unclear. *Svenska Posten* stopped printing birthday announcements on 9 December 1970. This table uses three newspapers from 1969 – 10 December, 17 December, and 24–31 December – to make the 1970 figures cover a full calendar year.

Table 4 shows that immigrants still read *Svenska Posten* as late as 1970. *Svenska Posten* never managed to capture a younger generation of readers, born in America. Editor Harry Fabbe tried to keep English out of the paper. Most younger readers, however, simply could not read Swedish. As the older generation vanished, subscription rates would have to fall. This would mean the end of *Svenska Posten*.

The birthday announcements also give the town where each reader lived. Most of them lived in the Seattle area. *Svenska Posten* mostly served Seattle's Swedish-speaking population. There might have been enough Swedish speakers across the U.S. to support *Svenska Posten*, but the paper was unable to expand beyond its local profile. Breaking its local profile and becoming national while simultaneously reaching out to younger readers with English was too much. *Svenska Posten* could not do it, not within its limited budget. It converted to English late, and by then the paper was too weak to complete the transition to a national base.

The first sign of an economic problem was *Svenska Posten's* switch to a tabloid format on 20 January 1971. (*Nordstjernan* also shrank five months later.) *SvP* underwent general editorial chaos when Harry Fabbe retired in 1972. When Fabbe died on 7

December 1973, poor finances and poor editing ruined *Svenska Posten*'s chance to expand its audience. *Svenska Posten* offered the editing job to *The Swedish Press*'s Sture Wermee, but he did not take it. ("One of many mistakes," Wermee adds.)[56] Quality remained satisfactory under the new editor, Ben Ekbäck, but slipped dramatically in late 1974. The *Posten* appeared on the brink of closing in October 1974. *Svenska Posten* reappeared 23 October 1974 with another new editor, Anita Myrfors. The paper then resembled a typewritten newsletter more than a newspaper. *Svenska Posten* closed in 1976. *Svenska Posten* had a circulation of 3,119 copies per edition in the mid-Sixties.[57]

2. Nordstjernan: A Regional Paper

The leading Swedish-language newspaper in America is now New York's *Nordstjernan*. It is the oldest Swedish-American newspaper still in print, having begun on 21 September 1872.[58] Financially, the Sixties were bad times for the paper. Perhaps little known, but it nearly closed in 1964. In 1966, *Nordstjernan* merged with its Worcester, Massachusetts rival to become *Nordstjernan-Svea*. Despite this supposed merger, the *Nordstjernan* remained essentially the same. All that changed was the name *Svea* appeared on the masthead for a few years. (I will continue to call the paper *Nordstjernan* throughout this period.) *Svea*'s subscribers gave extra income, and helped *Nordstjernan* expand its base into New England. Absorbing a rival paper, and taking over its territory, was one way to expand in a shrinking market. (The other way was to open the target audience to include Danes, Norwegians, or English-speakers.) Expanding into *Svea*'s territory helped *Nordstjernan* break out of its mold as a regional New York paper. This takeover may have helped assure *Nordstjernan*'s long-term survival.

---

[56] Telephone conversation with Sture Wermee, 13 February 2000.

[57] Memo by the American Council for Nationalities Service, "Swedish Publications in the United States," January 1964, file 18 "Lists," box 3, Fabbe, UW.

[58] Bernard Lundstedt, *Svenska tidningar och tidskrifter utgifna inom Nord-Amerikas Förenade Stater*, Stockholm, 1886: 4.

NORDSTJERNAN

The Swedish North Star
Oldest Swedish Newspaper in America

Like other emigrant papers, its printing technology was obsolete and in poor condition. *Nordstjernan* owned two Linotype machines, both built around the First World War. One was in particular was in terrible shape. Like most Swedish-American papers, *Nordstjernan* had its own typesetting facilities in its office. An external printer usually did the printing and stereotyping.[59]

Nordstjernan's editor during the Vietnam War was Gerhard Rooth, considered "Mister Sweden in New York."[60] "Gerry" Rooth was born in Surahammar in October 1896. His main passion was sports, and Rooth even carried the Swedish flag in the 1912 Stockholm Olympics. He came to New York on 18 April 1923, and went to Yankee Stadium that afternoon with his girlfriend. (This game was the 1923 season opener, and the first game played in the Stadium. Babe Ruth hit a three-run shot off Boston's Howard Ehmke, leading the Yankees to a 4–1 victory over the Red Sox.)[61] Rooth began working as a sports reporter for *Idrottsbladet* in 1923. "I had been in New York a short time," Rooth recalled. "Naturally I read *Nordstjernan*, but there was seldom anything about sports, so one day I stormed into its office and started to berate Charlie K. [Johansen] for his lousy sports coverage. He looked me over and told me to write a sports column myself – if I could do better." Rooth became *Nordstjernan*'s Assistant Editor in 1936 and Managing Editor in 1953. For thirty-thousand dollars, he also became its owner in 1953.[62] Through all this, Rooth always took sportswriting seriously in *Nordstjernan*.

---

[59] *Utvandrarnas tidningar*, 77; and letter from Allan Kastrup to Sten Sundfeldt, 27 September 1966, file "1963 - mars 1967," box I:462, PR4S, RA.

[60] Telephone conversation with Lars Arnö, 4 February 2000.

[61] "Gerry Rooth," *The Swedish-Americans of the Year*, Karlstad, 1982: 125–148; Bill James, *The New Bill James Historical Baseball Abstract*, London, 2001: 127; www.retrosheet.org.

[62] Karlsson, "Gerhard Rooth," 23, 26.

NORDSTJERNAN-SVEA

In the Sixties, *Nordstjernan* printed mainly in Swedish, with almost 80% printed in that language. This high proportion fell gradually after 1970. According to a former ASNE editor:

> I once asked the editor of the old *Svenska-Amerikanaren* in Chicago if he would use a weekly news column in English. He replied very pompously: "We never allow foreign languages in the newspaper." That was the origin of the present first page column in English in *Nordstjernan*. Gerry Rooth laughed when I told him what I had heard in Chicago, and he applied the idea himself."[63]

Nordstjernan ran its English news on the front page, in a page-length column called "News in Brief." Most items were short bulletins taken from *Sverige-Nytt*. The rest of the front page had more "hard news" on Sweden than most papers. *Nordstjernan* thoroughly covered the diplomatic split between the United States and Sweden. This subject emerged on the newspaper's editorial page, usually on page four. Editor Gerry Rooth wrote most of these editorials, but *Nordstjernan* came to rely increasingly on *Sverige-Nytt* editorials. Also on page four, Associate Editor Eric Sylvan wrote a column called "Det Tycks." (Sylvan had written for *Nordstjernan* since 1925, composed several plays, and even played a judge in the Swedish movie *Domen*.)[64] *Nordstjernan* also ran short editorials from the Swedish dailies in a "press debate" column. Most of its "press debate" editorials came from *Sverige-Nytt*. Sometimes *Nordstjernan* reprinted other papers' editorials in its own editorial space. Occasionally *Nordstjernan* ran letters to the editor in a space called "Ordet är Fritt." *Nordstjernan* ran 288 comment pieces on Vietnam

---

[63] Letter from Naboth Hedin to Allan Kastrup, 25 June 1968, file "ASNE: Correspondence – Naboth Hedin," box "ASNE: Allan Kastrup, Correspondences," ASNE New York, SSIRC.

[64] Ernst Skarstedt, *Pennfäktare*, Stockholm, 1930: 187.

Nordstjernan's Gerry Rooth.

between 1964 and 1974: almost one-third of Swedish-American commentary.

Nordstjernan's news coverage of Swedish politics was also heavy. This was the paper with the most coverage of Sweden's Vietnam policy, and arguably the most "newsy" overall. Some Swedish-American papers resembled rural newspapers. *Texas Posten* and *Western News*, for example, were local sheets about church picnics and town events. *Nordstjernan*, on the other hand, was an urban Swedish-American newspaper. During the Sixties it served the northeast and eastern seaboard regions. Printing in New York City, it was the paper that most resembled a Swedish-American *New York Times*. It was large, had lots of news, used Swedish news sources, and even ran some Swedish editorials as its own. It focused on politics, and had a gravitas lacking in other papers. *Nordstjernan's* focus on political news came from New York. Perhaps it was due to New York's cultural atmosphere. Perhaps it was due to its physical proximity to the United Nations. *Nordstjernan* was the only paper to send a reporter to cover Swedish press conferences at the U.N.[65] It was also near the Rockefeller Plaza media district, and the Swedish General Consulate. Whatever the cause, *Nordstjernan* was the Swedish-language paper closest to having the tone of a metropolitan daily.

---

[65] Telephone conversation with Lars Arnö, 4 February 2000.

Dismal pay was common among the Swedish-American editors. Gerry Rooth told the Swedish-American Press Investigation that he continued the paper mostly to reach *Nordstjernan's* centennial year in 1972. If it had not been for this milestone, he said he would have closed the paper years ago.[66] Considering this, *Nordstjernan's* decline from 1969 to 1974 was foreseeable. The paper shrank in size, content, and standards. In 1967, it led the field in political news. Little remained of its extensive news coverage by 1974.

Nordstjernan is still in print. It is much stronger now than thirty years ago. In 1997, it had around twenty-three thousand readers – more than three times what it had in the Sixties.[67]

3. Svenska-Amerikanaren Tribunen (SAT): A National Paper

During the Vietnam period, *Svenska-Amerikanaren Tribunen* was among the highest quality emigrant papers still publishing. *Svenska-Amerikanaren* had survived by taking over other papers, such as the 1936 merger with *Svenska Tribunen-Nyheter*. (I will often use its everyday name of *Svenska-Amerikanaren*, dispensing with the *Tribunen* suffix.) *SAT* was also the largest of the Swedish papers, and aspired for a national subscription base. Its reported circulation reached up to twenty thousand copies, but others placed it closer to fifteen thousand.[68]

Svenska-Amerikanaren's owner was Arthur B. Hendricks. Hendricks began printing and typesetting *California Veckoblad* in 1955. Two years later, he bought the paper rather than watch it close. According to his daughter, Hendricks did not want Swedish culture and language to disappear in California.[69] In 1962, Hendricks also bought *Svenska-Amerikanaren Tribunen* and the two papers began sharing the same technical facilities. This cut typesetting and printing costs for both papers. These two papers are

---

[66] *Utvandrarnas tidningar*, 22.

[67] Karin Henriksson, "Flaggskepp firar 125-årsjubileum," *Svenska Dagbladet*, 28 September 1997: 25. See also Bengt Hansson, "Världens gång: Drakar för svensk-amerikaner," *Göteborgs-Posten*, 3 November 1996: 31.

[68] *Utvandrarnas tidningar*, 25.

[69] Telephone conversation with Jane Hendricks, editor *California Veckoblad* and *Svenska-Amerikanaren Tribunen*, 13 November 2000.

still typeset in California, although *Svenska-Amerikanaren* gets printed and mailed from Chicago. Hendricks was an entrepreneur and bought his papers as business investments. This made him an outsider among the Swedish-American editors that considered themselves cultural missionaries. UD, however, thought it was refreshing to have an economic realist among "these blue-eyed idealistic editors."[70]

Arthur Hendricks was an idealist about the Swedish language, however. *Svenska-Amerikanaren* did not compromise in using Swedish; it did not print anything in English. This is especially unusual considering that Hendricks could not read the language himself.[71] He also had a German ethnic background. This only accented his rivals' suspicion he bought the paper for purely financial motives.

Arthur Hendricks was independent and outspoken. He refused some of UD's news because he felt it might compromise his papers' independence. He did not write often on political events, according to his daughter Jane Hendricks. He took on political subjects when he felt that he was right. His papers were separate entities, but *California Veckoblad* editorials usually come from *Svenska-Amerikanaren*. Not every edition carried a formal editorial page. They became rare after 1972.

California Veckoblad and *Svenska-Amerikanaren* had two assistants from Sweden during the Sixties. According to Jane Hendricks, they initially supported the Swedish government position on Vietnam. Over time they changed their views and adopted a more conservative outlook.[72]

---

[70] Letter from Hubert de Besche to Leif Leifland, 14 January 1965, with attached memo by Sven Persson, file "1963 – mars 1967," box I:462, PR4S, RA.

[71] *Utvandrarnas tidningar*, 25–26.

[72] Telephone conversation with Jane Hendricks, editor *California Veckoblad*, 13 November 2000.

Hendricks sold his printing shop in the mid-Sixties. He made sure the terms of sale provided for *California Veckoblad* and *Svenska-Amerikanaren*. They would get their printing done at cost while the papers remained in the Hendricks family. These newspapers have dramatically lower production costs than other emigrant papers. Jane Hendricks has occasionally checked other printers, but nothing has ever proved better than this deal. One Swedish-American editor – speaking confidentially – says the printer regrets having signed this contract.

Svenska-Amerikanaren always ran a full page of letters to the editor. This section, titled "Folkets Röst," mostly contained letters about emigrants' memories of coming to America. (In the past, some papers banned these autobiographical and often repetitive letters.)[73] Some letters also focused on politics and current events. In her academic article "Folkets Röst," Barbro Klein notes: "At the end of the Sixties, the Vietnam War caught the attention of many. Occasionally extended debates broke out, and it was not uncommon for the debaters to become argumentative and bitter."[74] During 1967 and 1968, there was an extended debate on spiritualism and the essence of God's nature. By 20 March 1968, the stream of letters on religion and Vietnam became so heavy *Svenska-Amerikanaren* forbade all such letters. Some subscribers had seen the letters on religion as close to blasphemy and canceled their subscriptions.[75] Many participants considered this censorship. Others felt relieved the polemics would soon disappear. By mid-1969, however, a few letters about the war began to make their way back into Folkets

---

[73] Ulf Jonas Björk, "'Folkets Röst,' The Pulse of the Public," *Swedish-American Historical Quarterly*, vol. 50, no. 2, April 1999: 11. (This examines the letters in *Svenska Amerikanska Posten*, a Minneapolis paper with no relation to Chicago's *Svenska-Amerikanaren*.)

[74] Klein, "Folkets Röst," 87.

[75] Urlakaren, "Folkets Röst," *Svenska-Amerikanaren Tribunen*, 20 March 1968: 5. See also Klein, "Folkets Röst," 87–88.

Röst. Vietnam was fuel for arguments, but it did not have the same capacity to get subscriptions canceled. Most letters have a conservative outlook, but Vietnam had a way of crossing party lines.

The leading research on *Svenska-Amerikanaren* has been Ulf Jonas Björk's *The Swedish-American Press*. (Björk focuses on the paper before it absorbed *Svenska-Tribunen Nyheter*, however.) Björk's thesis examines three emigrant papers, each serving a different community. Björk uses *Svenska-Amerikanaren* as an example of a newspaper reaching for a national audience. Despite this goal, *Svenska-Amerikanaren's* base was solidly in Chicago and the Midwest. Its national ambitions led *SAT* to use the Swedish language, forums such as Folkets Röst, the idea of "Swedishness," and news from Sweden to create an abstract Swedish-American community. *Svenska-Amerikanaren* had a wide territorial base, but it tried reaching beyond the physically-defined plane. It also wanted a relational community that existed only within *SAT's* pages. Rather than geography, *Svenska-Amerikanaren* would base its national community on shared values and problems, and common interests and concerns.

Svenska-Amerikanaren had originally published for Chicago's Swede-Town. That was a territorially defined ethnic community similar to areas like New York's Little Italy or Chinatown. Swede-Town had largely broken up, scattering *SAT's* readers across the Midwest. Morris Janowitz argues this dispersal of the ethnic community affects the paper's content. He expects the ethnic paper to switch its focus from local news and gossip to national ethnic politics.[76] As expected, *SAT* ran national Swedish-American news and mixed in only a little ethnic Chicago news. Swedish news eclipsed the Swedish-American Chicago news by the Sixties.

Svenska-Amerikanaren courted a coast-to-coast audience, which meant uniting isolated clusters of diverse communities artificially. It was difficult to create community feelings and loyalties where no community existed. *Svenska-Amerikanaren* stressed its "Folkets Röst" page, where regular contributors formed a virtual community. This is where "grass-roots" group feelings, traditions, and consensus-

---

[76] Janowitz, *The Community Press in an Urban Setting*, 22–23.

building emerged most clearly. These letters were a symbolic way to knit together an audience that had no common local interests. It often underlined ethnic and cultural values through these letters. They were always in Swedish: *SAT* used the Swedish language as its unifying bond.

It courted a national audience, but *Svenska-Amerikanaren Tribunen* had a base in Chicago. Chicago is a large city, but with a feel for the rural Midwest: isolated and a little suspicious of the East and West coasts. Chicago is a major railway, airline, and trade center, but not a political center. Community-press theory might argue that *SAT* might emphasize trade over politics, and ethnic culture over current events.

As paper reaching for a national readership, *Svenska-Amerikanaren* was editorially conservative. The national audience *SAT* coveted likely influenced how it commented on politics. The paper's editorials often had a consensus-feel to them, even if they were a bit populist. Few, if any, editorials would have caused anyone to cancel their subscription. Harder views appeared in "Folkets Röst," the page promoting grass-roots public opinion. There were precious few political columns with personal views like in *Svenska Posten*. *SAT* was not aspiring to be a friendly neighborhood paper with familiar and politically eccentric personalities. It traded on its standing as a Swedish-American institution. *Svenska-Amerikanaren* ran 135 comment pieces on Vietnam between 1964 and 1975. Both *SAT* and its sister paper *California Veckoblad* are still in print and owned by the Hendricks family.

The Others

Svenska Posten, *Nordstjernan*, and *Svenska-Amerikanaren* dominated Swedish-American political debate in the Sixties. Other papers occasionally commented on world events, but it was hardly their regular fare. Smaller papers like *Western News* or *Vestkusten* focused more on cultural rather than political issues. Many of these smaller papers had severe financial problems, especially *Vestkusten*. The smaller local newspapers likely avoided polarizing political issues in fear of alienating readers. Even if the three political papers dominated political debate, my thesis will allow all the emigrant papers to voice their views on the Vietnam issue.

The Swedish-Canadian newspapers were small, addressed local audiences, and all had severe economic problems. Like the small papers in the U.S., the Swedish-Canadian papers ran little on Vietnam. New York's Finn-Swedish *Norden* printed in Swedish, and it kept subscription rates low to attract Swedes.[77] There had never been any dominantly Finn-Swedish settlements anywhere in America. They had always lived integrated with other Swedish-Americans, and their views were usually similar.[78] Despite being Finn-Swedish, *Norden*'s view of Vietnam was not much different from the other newspapers. Its view of Swedish Vietnam policy had a distinctly Finnish tone.

The religious newspapers actively debated the Vietnam War. Unlike the secular papers, these newspapers subsisted on difficult moral and spiritual issues. The risk of angry readers ending their subscriptions over antiwar articles was less for these "moral-based" newspapers. Both *The Messenger*, a Swedish Methodist paper, and the Covenant Church's paper, *The Covenant Companion*, debated the Vietnam War. Both papers ran editorials, but the *Companion* also ran an active letters-to-the-editor page. Clearly political views on Vietnam often appeared on these pages.

The *Companion*'s predecessor paper, *The Covenant Weekly*, did a voluntary survey of its readers in 1958. The results suggest *The Covenant Weekly*'s readers were religious, middle-class, middle-aged, and active in the Covenant Church. A large minority – 10% – were clergy. Half of *The Covenant Weekly*'s readers subscribed to other religious newspapers, perhaps *Missions-Vännen*. It is still startling that 39% of those surveyed claimed *The Covenant Weekly* was their only newspaper.

[77] Söderström, *Blixtar på tidnings-horisonten*, 69; and Backlund, *A Century of the Swedish-American Press*, 48.

[78] Söderström, *Blixtar på tidnings-horisonten*, 69.

TABLE 5. *Survey of 2,600 The Covenant Weekly readers, 1958.*

Older than 65 years	17%	Businessmen	12%
Under 24 years old	6%	White-collar workers	10%
High school graduates	29%	Skilled laborers	9%
Some college education	31%	Ministers or missionaries	10%
Professional training	11%	Subscribed since 1954	29%
Advanced degrees	3%	Subscribed since 1949	49%
Professional men	26%	Receive no other religious periodicals	49%
Housewives	16%	Receive no other secular periodicals	39%

Source: Ben Bankson, "Questionnaire Study Shows Subscribers are Readers," *The Covenant Weekly,* 14 November 1958: 3.

This survey is unique in the Swedish-American press. These figures likely do not apply to other newspapers. There is even some question whether they even apply to *The Covenant Weekly.* Twenty-six hundred readers makes a large sample, but the survey needed them to fill in the forms and mail them back. Some older readers may have been unable, or less likely, to do this. It may be unlikely only 17% of The *Covenant Weekly's* readers were pensioners, or only 22% had subscribed for more than nine years.

When asked about *Vestkusten's* readers in the Sixties, Bridget Stromberg-Brink, *Vestkusten's* current (2003) editor, wrote:

> The average subscriber [in the Sixties] was probably much like today's. Our recent survey points to a middle age, above 40, group of Swedes and Swedish Americans, more women than men. The big difference perhaps that at the time, *Vestkusten* was a local San Francisco Bay Area paper, while today we have spread along the U.S. West Coast. If anything, Ms. Karin Person's subscribers may have been older, and more Swedish-Americans than Swedish, as I know that she covered locally those organizations that catered to that segment.[79]

Vestkusten and *The Covenant Companion* were different. In the Sixties, *Vestkusten* was a local secular paper, while the *Companion* was a national religious paper. The only common thread is that their readers were middle-aged or above. No newspaper has any complete subscription list preserved from the Sixties. Only *Svenska Posten's*

---

[79] E-mail from Bridget Stromberg-Brink, editor of *Vestkusten,* 15 March 1997.

birthday announcements suggest what type of people read the emigrant papers and where they lived.

Some papers have incomplete subscription lists from the Sixties. When asked about its subscription list, *Vestkusten's* editor wrote:

> The subscription "list" we received [in 1991] was a card file – very inaccurate at that. I'm pretty sure that . . . Karin Person, who is well over 80 and in frail health, had no other lists. Since she sent the paper by bulk mail, she was not required to keep names on lists like we do under the second class mail permit.[80]

The Swedish Press still has several boxes of metal-plates that once stamped addresses on the newspapers before mailing. These boxes are undated, but likely come from the late Sixties or early Seventies. Judging from the plates scattered across *The Swedish Press's* archive floor, the stamping plates likely do not reflect an accurate subscription list.

Swedish-American Politics Around 1960

As a group, the Swedish-Americans were conservative. The Swedish-American ethnic leaders tied the group to the Republican Party in the nineteenth century, and it remained that way since then. Movements like the agrarian revolt, progressivism, and the New Deal threatened the Swedish-Americans' solidarity with the Republican Party, but the bond was always restored.[81] As a group, the Swedish-Americans were solidly conservative in the Nineteen-Fifties. When the Riksdagman – and future Swedish Liberal Party leader – Gunnar Helén visited the U.S. in 1955 he wanted to meet Swedish-Americans. Helén found the Swedish-Americans of 1955 maddeningly right-wing by Swedish standards. "I met among them some of the most ultra-conservative, narrow-minded, and chauvinistic groups in the modern American society." He even

---

[80] E-mail from Bridget Stromberg-Brink, editor of *Vestkusten*, 15 March 1997.

[81] See Ander, "The Swedish-American Press and the Election of 1892," 533–554; O. Fritiof Ander, "The Swedish-American Press in the Election of 1912," *The Swedish Pioneer Historical Quarterly*, vol. 14, no. 3, 1963: 103–126; and Capps, "Cracks and Strains in Republican Orthodoxy," *From Isolation to Involvement*, 105–132.

detected hints of fascism in their use of the Swedish flag and symbols.[82] In 1960, the Swedish-Americans' conservatism was arguably their most distinctive trait.[83]

Conservatism is a cultural concept that changes from country to country, and age to age. For example, Swedish conservatives are often royalists, but in the U.S. they are The Republicans. American conservatives are often libertarian. They see government as an unavoidable evil, but one that citizens can restrict from intruding into their lives. They believe in limited government, especially on the powers of the federal government. They hold a strict interpretation of the Constitution's "reserved powers" clause. This clause says that all powers not expressly given to the federal government belong to the states. The Republican Party also strictly interprets the Constitution's Bill of Rights. It allows citizens to own firearms, and this means exactly what it says. The Bill of Rights does not, however, specifically mention a "right to privacy." Republicans believe this so-called right comes from a mistaken reading of the Constitution.

In 1960, Republican foreign policy revolved around opposition to communism. They wanted a strong defense. This meant more military bases, new bombers and submarines, second-strike nuclear capacity, and flexible forces for brushfire wars. The Nixon campaign also wanted to reorganize the federal government, expand medical care for the elderly, and embraced the Civil Rights movement. Republicans opposed segregation, but many also resisted passing more federal laws to end it. They believed the Fourteenth Amendment was enough of a legal basis for ending segregation.[84]

The Swedish-Americans were politically conservative in the early Sixties. In the 1960 election, Scandinavian political action

---

[82] Gunnar Helén, *Alltför många jag*, Stockholm, 1991: 309.

[83] *Norden*'s editor writes, "I would say that the majority of our readers were and still are Republicans." *Vestkusten*'s editor writes, "For what it's worth, my personal experiences of those people [Swedish-Americans] is that they are warm-hearted and loveable in many respects but very conservative." (E-mails from Erik R. Hermans, editor of *Norden*, 12 February 2003; and Bridget Stromberg-Brink, editor of *Vestkusten*, 15 March 1997.)

[84] White, *Making of the President 1960*, 198, 388–390; and Barry Goldwater, "Civil Rights," *Konservatismens ansvar*, Malmö, 1964: 24–28.

Which Democratic Platform?

Which do you prefer: the socialistic, anti-Texas platform of Kennedy — or the Nixon Platform that more nearly conforms with Texas principles and ideals as expressed in the State Democratic platform?

The Kennedy platform is against nearly everything Texans are for—it is for nearly everything Texans are against.

What will be your choice? It is between a party label and the best interest of Texas and the Nation.

Allan Shivers says:

"I'LL TAKE TEXAS. I accept the Texas Democratic platform and will work for it. I repudiate the other—the Kennedy platform. I will join with my fellow Democrats to work and vote for men of maturity, experience, responsibility, and a fearless dedication to this country's best interests.

"I will vote for Richard M. Nixon and Henry Cabot Lodge."

TEXAS DEMOCRATS FOR NIXON - LODGE
ALLAN SHIVERS, Chairman

308 West 15th Street   Austin, Texas

Texas Posten ran this ad supporting Richard Nixon. Like in most of the South, The Republican Party barely existed in Texas in 1960.

committees advertised in the Swedish-American press. "Scandinavian Friends for Good Government" ran a full-page ad for Nixon in *Svenska Posten*. "Scandinavian Alliance" ran an ad for local Republicans in *SAT*. "Scandinavian Ticket" ran an ad listing candidates it felt would represent Scandinavian interests. It was a straight Republican ticket. "Scandinavian Committee" had the motto "Vote Republican from the White House to the Court House."[85] *Norden* printed its own ad for Richard Nixon – the campaign had not paid for it. It read "You bet we're Republicans!" and listed the alleged sins of the Democratic Party. It charged the Democrats had divided Korea and given control of North Korea to the communists. It also accused them of blundering into the Korean War, "but lacking the courage to win it or the ability to end it."[86] (Nixon would later try to carry the Vietnam War to victory, but without *Norden*'s support.)

---

[85] "Scandinavian Friends for Good Government," *Svenska Posten*, 26 October 1960; "Scandinavian Alliance," *Svenska-Amerikanaren Tribunen*, 2 November 1960; "Scandinavian Ticket," *Svenska Posten*, 2 November 1960; and "Scandinavian Committee," *Svenska-Amerikanaren Tribunen*, 2 November 1960.

[86] "You bet we're Republicans!" *Norden*, 6 October 1960: 7.

Some Swedish-American papers opposed John Kennedy's candidacy because he was Catholic. *Missions-Vännen* wrote weekly articles against Kennedy and Catholicism. One column asserted the Catholic Church – and the Free Churches – were sources of communism. *Missions-Vännen* said the Republicans' nomination of Richard Nixon and Henry Cabot Lodge was "a divine miracle" arranged by God. Voting for Kennedy, however, would be "a clear betrayal of Christian freedom. Vote for Nixon and Lodge, for I am convinced that **God wills it**."[87]

The Swede-Finnish *Norden* also opposed Kennedy on religious grounds. *Norden* urged its readers to vote Protestant:

> Have you examined your conscience so that you are sure you are voting for the right person? Or do you intend – like Queen Kristina of Sweden – to nonchalantly throw away everything that your forefathers gave their lives for – your religion, your fathers' faith? Do you intend to use your vote as a way to support the Papal Church's supremacy and world domination? Your fathers, who sleep under the ground back home, they call to you. Do not let them down! Do not sit uselessly at home on Election Day! Rise up to defend your fathers' faith! . . . There is nothing in this world that can compensate for freedom. The Papal Church enslaves its followers. You cannot, and should not collaborate in its spread across the free America. Do not listen to the fair promises which the Pope's representatives whisper in your ears! If history teaches anything to those with open minds, it is that the Pope's representatives can promise everything and deliver nothing.[88]

Others in the Swedish-American press rejected this. *Norden* columnist Anders Myhrman tried to distance himself from his own paper's anti-Catholicism. *Svenska Posten's* Otto Jacobson saw this anti-Catholicism as "quite simply childish!"[89] *Svenska-Amerikanaren* agreed, and reminded its readers the Constitution forbade "religious tests" for public office. (This did not stop *SAT* from running an anti-Catholic editorial called "Like Barbarians" before the

---

[87] "Communism in religion," 1 March 1960: 5; "Antikrist och kommunismen," 6 December 1960: 4; "Republikanska konventet," 2 August 1960: 8; and "Registrera och rösta," *Missions-Vännen*, 11 October 1960: 4.

[88] Elsie Mannberg, "Den stora dagen," *Norden*, 3 November 1960: 5.

[89] Anders Myhrman, "Från min kateder," *Norden*, 30 June 1960: 10; and Otto B. Jacobson, "Ett och Annat av Otto B. Jacobson," *Svenska Posten*, 2 November 1960: 6.

election.)[90] There were many in the Swedish emigrant press that opposed anti-Catholicism. A pair of *Svenska Posten* columnists even entertained thoughts of voting for Kennedy.[91]

Swedish-American anti-Catholicism had deep roots. It was one of the original reasons why the Swedish-Americans joined the Republican Party. The nineteenth-century Swedish emigrants were agrarian, Lutheran, and conservative. They came to America during an era when party loyalties often had more to do with ethnicity and religion than politics. The nineteenth-century Republican Party was the party of Protestants, temperance, and anti-slavery free-labor. The Democratic Party was a largely Southern party and favored slavery and then later segregation. It was also the party of Catholics and immigrants – especially the Irish, Italians, Russians, and Jews.[92] Swedish-Americans felt little attraction to the Democratic Party. Twentieth-century Swedish-American conservatism may partly stem from their apolitical loyalty to the Republican Party in the nineteenth century.

The Swedish-Americans were politically conservative, even if a few Kennedy-supporters lurked in *Svenska Posten*. The next few pages will examine how these papers saw the new socialist Sweden that emerged since they emigrated. Their judgment of Sweden's *folkhem* society may color how they later interpreted the Swedes' criticism of U.S. Vietnam policy. Was it something they admired? Did they respect the Swedes' opinions? Or, did they condemn their experiment with socialism as contrary to American values?

A Swedish-American View of Sweden: Eisenhower's Criticism

In late 1957, the *Swedish-American Monthly* surveyed American executives involved in trade with Sweden. Many of the thirty-four people who returned their questionnaires were Swedish-Americans.

---

[90] "Religion and USA:s president," 18 May 1960: 4; and "Som barbarer," *Svenska-Amerikanaren Tribunen*, 28 September 1960: 4.

[91] Maria Brannström, "Tankar och Rön," *Svenska Posten*, 14 September 1960: 3; and Gerda Risberg, "Intryck, infall och inkast," *Svenska Posten*, 3 August 1960: 2.

[92] David M. Potter and Don E. Fehrenbacher, *The Impending Crisis: 1848–1861*, New York, 1976: 251.

When asked what they liked most about Sweden, they often used words like: hospitality, cleanliness, and culture. They considered Swedish executives to be reliable, but did not always understand the American market. One said that Swedish business people were too pushy and forward with their American counterparts. When asked what they liked least about Sweden, the Americans usually alluded to problems with bureaucracy, morality, and socialism.[93]

Thirty-four documents do not make a solid basis for drawing irrefutable conclusions. Many responses are also less than completely serious sometimes. (When asked what he liked most about Sweden, for example, one listed Anita Ekberg.) The questionnaire effectively shows that Americans had a dualistic view of Sweden. Sweden had both negative and positive images, and a person could evoke either one anytime. Which image a person chose depended on the circumstances, and whether they felt confrontational or conciliatory.

Swedish-Americans shared this dualistic image in the early Sixties. Their newspapers used Sweden as unifying symbol, especially in areas such as culture and athletics. In the early Sixties, the Swedish-American editors filled their papers with warm praise for Ingmar Bergman's latest films.[94] They reported Sweden as a major power in the Olympics, and boxer Ingemar Johansson was a folk hero.[95] Many emigrants, however – and even emigrant editors – had mixed feelings about Sweden. This often appeared as fervent patriotism for the U.S., and sometimes as scorn for Sweden. This contempt shocked a Swede that visited in 1960, and his letter appeared in *Svenska-Amerikanaren*:

> When I came to America five months ago, I had great hopes about coming to the great land in the West. I had particularly looked forward to meeting some Swedish-Americans, who I thought I might have something in common with. Now I look back on the months I've spent here with

---

[93] Questionnaires attached to memo "angående redaktör Folkes rundfråga," 26 November 1957, file "1954–1959," box I:461, PR4S, RA. (Swedish business people described themselves in similar terms in a 1985 study. See: Åke Daun, *Swedish Mentality*, University Park, Penn., 1989: 184–189.)

[94] See for example, "Ingmar Bergmans nya film 'grym men skön'," *Texas Posten*, 25 February 1960: 1.

[95] See for example, "Svenskarna kom, såg och segrade," *Vestkusten*, 3 March 1960: 1.

bitterness and disappointment. I am not disappointed in America. . . . What has made me so bitter and angry are the negative attitudes towards Sweden and the Swedes that most Swedish-Americans that I've met have. I have never heard so much bad-mouthing of Sweden as I have heard in these months. . . . I have yet to meet an American with the same gloomy view of Sweden and its people that most Swedish-Americans have. What kinds of psychological factors make a person want to paint his old country so black? Can it be that they want to justify to themselves their decision to leave Sweden and to choose America?[96]

The emigrants' dualistic view of Sweden helped produce a love-hate relationship with the old homeland. Parts of their view of Sweden came from their collective memories of a nineteenth-century class society. Other parts came from what they had read about the new *folkhem* society. This led to incongruities in how the Swedish-American papers looked at Sweden. At times they could acidly criticize Sweden's social structure, lack of democracy, and antiquated laws. Other times, they felt a paradoxical sense of boosterism for the home country. If others criticized Sweden, they would be the first to defend it. Without any sense of contradiction, they could passionately argue that Sweden was a progressive, egalitarian democracy. They might disparage Sweden themselves, but resented others criticizing their main ethnic symbol. They might even defend Sweden from critical ideas they may have shared.

Such criticism of Sweden was almost fraternal gossip between the emigrants and the homeland-Swedes. In this light, the Swedish-American editors wanted their papers to be gossip sheets. If such discussion sold papers, created ethnic awareness, and unified the community, then the editors supported it. Having other Americans criticize Sweden was different, however. That could only create friction in the community. At worst, it could push emigrants into distancing themselves from their Swedish ethnicity.

The Swedish-American view of the homeland was complex and contradictory. The emigrant papers freely mixed modern and obsolete images of Sweden. They sometimes saw the U.S. as a democratic model for Sweden to copy. Other times, the papers

---

[96] E-son, "Folkets Röst: Bitter – besviken," *Svenska-Amerikanaren Tribunen*, 16 November 1960: 7.

might promote the Swedish model on a certain issue. Many social debates in *Svenska-Amerikanaren*'s "Folkets Röst" page, for example, revolve around whose model was better. This mix of modern and obsolete images may be what leads to the dualistic image of Sweden. Even this dualistic image changed over the following fifteen years. These are some basic views of Sweden, before and after Vietnam:

	PRE-VIETNAM	POST-VIETNAM
POSITIVE VIEW	friendly, quiet, progressive	honest, dynamic, independent
NEGATIVE VIEW	sin, sex, socialism	unprovoked moralizing

Before Vietnam, the Swedish-American press saw Sweden as a friendly land. It was socially progressive, but its people were quiet, artistic, but perhaps a little dull. After the turmoil of the Sixties, few Swedish-Americans would accuse homeland-Swedes of being inhibited or boring. By 1975, Swedish-Americans would see Sweden as a dynamic, open society.

On the negative side, the emigrants saw Sweden as a land of sin-sex-suicide-and-socialism in 1960. After Vietnam, another image attached onto this one. One in four Americans still thought of Sweden for its different liberal sexual climate, loose morals, or pornography industry.[97] Vietnam added a new image of a self-righteous critic offering unsolicited moral opinions. This image was less benign. Instead of being a little immoral, Sweden now felt mean. The emigrants' desire to interpret Sweden's behavior in moral terms may stem from their own nineteenth-century pietistic Lutheranism. Either the homeland Swedes were morally deficient or they were excessively moral (and wrong). Either way, the emigrants diagnosed it as a moral problem. The shift from one view to the other was largely a product of the U.S.-Swedish conflict over Vietnam.

---

[97] Swedish Information Service, *Knowledge of and Attitudes Toward Sweden*, Princeton, N.J., 1973: 34; see also: Swedish Information Service, *Princeton Adults' Knowledge of and Attitudes Toward Sweden*, Princeton, N.J., March 1973.

In the early Sixties, however, debate on Sweden's "moral problem" still focused on sex and suicide. An episode in 1960 reveals how complex the Swedish-American view of Sweden could get. In March 1960, *U.S. News and World Report* ran a critical article on Sweden. It argued that socialism would lead to alcoholism, suicide, and crime. Many newspapers in 1960 analyzed the alleged relation between large government and social problems. They often used Sweden as a model for both phenomena.[98] In Stockholm, UD noted this negative publicity and decided to do its own study. UD wanted a sociologist, or a journalist good at sociology, to write a memo for them. UD considered asking Gunnar Boalt, Anna-Lisa Kälvesten, or *Industria*'s Allan Lundberg to do it. They eventually got Uppsala professor Torgny Segerstedt to write it for them.[99]

The Saturday Evening Post then ran its own article on socialism and social problems, and *Readers' Digest* reprinted it. President Eisenhower was one of many people to read it. At a luncheon speech in late July, Eisenhower related his impression of the *Readers' Digest* article.

> Only in the last few weeks, I have been reading quite an interesting article on the experiment of almost complete paternalism in a [fairly] friendly European country. This country has a tremendous record for socialistic operation, following a socialistic philosophy. The record shows that their rate of suicide has gone up almost unbelievably. I think they were almost the lowest nation in the world for that. Now they have more than twice our rate. Drunkenness has gone up. Lack of ambition is discernible on all sides. Therefore, with that kind of example, let's always remember Lincoln's admonition. Let's do in the Federal Government only those things that people themselves cannot do at all, or cannot so well do in their individual capabilities.[100]

---

[98] For examples, see Werner Wiskari, "High Suicide Rate Puzzles Sweden," *New York Times* (international edition), 28 March 1960; "Backtracking," *Reading Eagle* (Pennsylvania), 5 March 1960; and "Sweden Makes Study of Reasons For Suicide," *De Kalb Chronicle* (Illinois), 22 June 1960.

[99] Letter from Gunnar Lonnaeus to Sven Backlund, 4 March 1960, and Backlund's reply 6 April 1960, file "USA 1960, 16 feb – juli 1960," box I:318, NL1, RA.

[100] Dwight Eisenhower, "Remarks at the Republican National Committee Breakfast, Chicago, Illinois. 27 July 1960," cited in *Public Papers of the Presidents: Dwight D. Eisenhower, 1960–1961*, Washington, 1961: 605.

Eisenhower did not specifically name Sweden in his speech, but it felt clear which country he meant. The press reported that Eisenhower called Sweden a "fairly friendly European country." (The adjective *fairly* is not in the official printed text, *Public Papers of the Presidents*.) Eisenhower said the Swedish people "lacked moderation in all areas." This charge likely baffled Swedes, who see themselves as very moderate (*lagom*) in all areas. It must have dismayed UD to find Sweden portrayed as something out of an Orwell novel. One of UD's main roles was to create a positive image of Sweden abroad. Having the President of the United States offset its work must have been a shock.

After reading Eisenhower's comments, ASNE's Allan Kastrup immediately went over to *The New York Times*. Both the *Times'* editorial desk and news board wanted to hear Kastrup's reaction to Eisenhower's remarks. "Not only was [the *Times*] sympathetic," Kastrup wrote to UD, "but it was also decidedly balanced and well informed." Kastrup had a "lively discussion" with the *Times* for nearly an hour.[101] Allan Kastrup told the *Times* that Swedish statistics were different from the U.S. figures. The United States (at the time) excluded teenage suicides. Sweden did not. If one takes this into account, Kastrup argued, the U.S. had a much higher suicide rate. He also asserted that Sweden and the U.S. had different demographics. If one removed blacks, illiterates, and Catholics – Sweden had few of these in 1960 – then the American suicide rate closely resembled Sweden's.[102]

Most American newspapers were every bit as sympathetic as the *Times*.[103] Many took Sweden's side, believing that Eisenhower only used Sweden as a punching-bag for domestic Cold War politics. *The Washington Post* said the President clearly meant no harm, but his comments were "extremely imprudent and undiplomatic."[104] Many

---

[101] Letter from Allan Kastrup to Ellis Folke, 29 July 1960, file "1959–1960," box A:16, ASNE Stockholm, RA.

[102] Letter from Allan Kastrup to Ellis Folke, 29 July 1960, file "1959–1960," box A:16, ASNE Stockholm, RA.

[103] For a bibliography of press reaction to this speech, see: Frederick Hale, "Challenging the Welfare State: The Case of Dwight David Eisenhower," *Swedish-American Historical Quarterly*, vol. LIV, no. 1, January 2003.

other papers agreed, seeing it as a poor idea for Eisenhower to single out an individual country for such abuse.[105] *The New York Times* story said Kastrup "insisted that the President was obviously referring to Sweden." Kastrup assured UD he had not said such a thing. If anyone was insisting, it was the *Times* people. Kastrup also pointed out that Eisenhower had referred to "a friendly European country," and not "fairly friendly." The *Times*, however, went with "fairly friendly," and most Swedish articles came directly from the *Times*.[106]

"A fairly friendly country!" wrote *Svenska Posten*'s Otto Jacobson. "What's wrong with him? Sweden is not only fairly, but very friendly to America." A *Nordstjernan* reader felt insulted that anyone would consider "our population of Swedish origin" just "fairly friendly."[107] (His wording makes no distinction between Swedes and Swedish emigrants.) *Canada-Tidningen* reported Swedish Defense Minister Sven Andersson's comment, "It almost makes one glad that his term as President is almost over if he said that about Sweden."[108]

Also, while the U.S. had a *government*, it surprised Swedish-Americans to hear that Sweden had a *regime*. The difference between the two was clear. Free people elected democratic governments, while regimes lacked popular support. *Canada-Tidningen* wrote, "A democracy is a state where you say what you want and do what you're told." A *Nordstjernan* reader argued the Swedish government ruled with its people's consent, or it would have fallen long ago.

---

[104] "Paternalism," *Washington Post*, 28 July 1960, quoted in telegram from Nils Montan to Cabinet Stockholm, 28 July 1960, file "USA 1960, 16 feb – juli 1960," box I:318, NL1, RA.

[105] Letter from Nils Montan to "Herr Ministern för Utrikes Ärendena," 8 September 1960, file "1960–1963," box A:26, ASNE Stockholm, RA.

[106] Letter from Allan Kastrup to Ellis Folke, 29 July 1960, file "1959–1960," box A:16, ASNE Stockholm, RA.

[107] Otto B. Jacobson, "Ett och Annat," *Svenska Posten*, 24 August 1960: 3; and Karl E. Wennerberg, "Ordet Fritt," *Nordstjernan*, 4 August 1960: 10.

[108] Sven Anderson, quoted in "När en president inte tänker sig för," *Canada-Tidningen*, 18 August 1960: 3. See also news telegram from Cabinet Stockholm to Bengt Rösiö, 28 July 1960, file "USA 1960, 16 feb – juli 1960," box I:318, NL1, RA.

Canada-Tidningen used the 1960 election results to affirm that argument. The Social Democrats received 48.5% of the vote.[109]

Nobody appreciated Eisenhower's comments. *Nordstjernan* ran editorial comments from the major Norwegian, Danish, and Swedish papers, and *The Washington Post*. The Scandinavian papers saw Eisenhower's comments as foolish and uninformed. *The Washington Post* described it as "extremely unwise and undiplomatic. . . . The President's stupid commentary was a form of paternalism that this country's foreign policy could have done without."[110] In comparison, the Swedish-American press was content to point out that Eisenhower was wrong. Many newspapers simply ignored the whole issue.

When Eisenhower's remarks hit the papers, UD had Torgny Segerstedt's statistics ready to rebut him. UD sent its figures to the ASNE, and from there, they went to the Swedish-American press.[111] *Vestkusten* and *Svenska Posten* ran the UD statistics on their front pages. On its front page, *Canada-Tidningen* ran a set of American suicide rates by state. Again, the numbers all came from a memo UD gave to ASNE.[112]

Only *Svenska Posten* printed its own editorial about Eisenhower's speech. *Svenska Posten* believed the carnival-atmosphere of the Republican convention had led the President astray.[113] Two weeks later, *Canada-Tidningen* reprinted the same article. *Nordstjernan* reprinted the comments of the Swedish press. *Svenska Posten* and

---

[109] *Canada-Tidningen*, 21 April 1960: 3; Karl E. Wennerberg, "Ordet Fritt," *Nordstjernan*, 4 August 1960: 10; and *Canada-Tidningen*, 20 October 1960: 4.

[110] "Eisenhowers tal," *Nordstjernan*, 11 August 1960: 6.

[111] Telegram from Cabinet Stockholm to Svensk Washington, New York, San Francisco, Minneapolis, Houston, Chicago, Montreal, Ottawa, and the Swedish-American News Exchange, 28 July 1960, file "USA 1960, 16 feb – juli 1960," box I:318, NL1, RA.

[112] "Nej, bäste Eisenhower, amerikanen dricker lika mycket som svensken!" *Svenska Posten*, 3 August 1960: 1; "Stark svensk reaktion inför Eisenhowers Chicagouttalande," *Vestkusten*, 11 August 1960: 1; and "Alkoholism och självmord ingalunda utmärkande för Sverige," *Canada-Tidningen*, 25 August 1960: 1, 4. (Memo by Lars Widén, 28 July 1960, file "1960 aug – 1960 dec," box I:318, NL1, RA.)

[113] "Hört och Hänt: Även världens mäktige kan göra misstaget att trampa i klaveret," *Svenska Posten*, 3 August 1960: 1.

Vestkusten merely printed statistics that contradicted Eisenhower's assertions. This was an unusual show of restraint, but Eisenhower was popular among the Swedish-Americans. He was a war hero, a Republican, and a respected world figure. In the wider population, 61% of Americans approved of Eisenhower's performance as president.[114]

Also, several newspapers quietly shared Eisenhower's views. *Nordstjernan*'s columnist Eric Sylvan had argued for years that Sweden's government was paternalistic. Just three months before Eisenhower's speech, *Nordstjernan* wrote that Swedish alcoholism remained a serious problem.[115] (*Nordstjernan* remained largely silent in response to Eisenhower's criticism.) Other papers had favored temperance and were unwilling to defend Swedish alcohol use.

More critical reactions to Eisenhower's speech came in syndicated columns and letters. The columnists did not feel as bound to reflect the newspapers' readers as the editor. The letter-writers reflected only their own views. *Svenska Posten*'s Otto Jacobson believed Eisenhower did not reduce poverty as he had promised. The speech only showed Eisenhower's envy towards Sweden's success.[116] Eric Olson's letter in *Svenska-Amerikanaren* ridiculed Eisenhower's literacy and knowledge of Sweden. "Clearly one of the President's golf-playing friends gave him a book that broke with his normal diet of comic books and detective novels."[117] Karl Wennerberg's letter to *Nordstjernan* described Eisenhower's speech as a political blunder. Eisenhower should not criticize others after he handled the U-2 Incident so poorly.[118] These are the only two letters to appear in the Swedish-language press on Eisenhower's speech. Also, Karl Wennerberg was a conservative, but Otto Jacobson and Eric Olson were political liberals. The conservative

---

[114] George H. Gallup, *The Gallup Poll*, New York, 1972: 3 July 1960, page 1675.

[115] "Statistik med ljusglimt," *Nordstjernan*, 26 May 1960: 6.

[116] Otto B. Jacobson, "Ett och annat av Otto B. Jacobson," *Svenska Posten*, 24 August 1960: 3.

[117] Eric Olson, "Folkets Röst: Man bör inte kasta sten," *Svenska-Amerikanaren Tribunen*, 31 August 1960: 5.

[118] Karl E. Wennerberg, "Ordet Fritt," *Nordstjernan*, 4 August 1960: 10.

writers avoided criticizing the Republican President, especially during the Republican convention.

A few weeks after Eisenhower's speech, UD noted with satisfaction, "We, in our opinion, won the first round in our special battle with the United States' President."[119] Immediately contacting the *Times* had been an effective move. It had also been useful for UD to compile its own information and give copies to the Swedish-American papers. Several emigrant papers ran the material exactly as UD wanted. UD had won the battle. Validation came two years later when Eisenhower visited Sweden. The trip was largely an apology for his critical remarks in 1960. The Swedish-American press enjoyed reporting on Eisenhower's warm reception in Sweden.[120]

A Swedish-American View of Sweden: The Welfare State

President Eisenhower's speech added fuel to debate that had been smoldering for some time in the Swedish-American press. The emigrants watched from a distance as Sweden experimented with a form of socialism. Some emigrants saw this as innovative while others saw it as vaguely threatening. Eisenhower's speech pushed the Swedish-Americans to debate the possible link between welfare and social problems. From there, the emigrants launched into a discussion about what the new Sweden was like. Was it better than the country they had left behind? Had the Social Democratic Party helped or hurt Sweden? After *Nordstjernan* columnist Eric Sylvan criticized the Social Democrats, a reader shot back:

> I honestly cannot remember a single instance when the Swedish government ever did or said anything that met with Mr. Sylvan's approval. If Mr. Sylvan had, like the undersigned, come from a poor working-class home forty years ago . . . perhaps he would better appreciate the improved conditions under which the workers today live.[121]

---

[119] Letter from Gunnar Lonnaeus to Sven Backlund, 10 August 1960, file "USA 1960 aug – 1960 dec," box I:318, NL1, RA.

[120] For example, see "Eisenhower på besök i 'Fairly Friendly European Country," 2 August 1962; and "Ike Eisenhower varmt välkommad i Stockholm," *Svea*, 9 August 1962: 1.

[121] Gösta Ericksson, "Ordet Fritt," *Nordstjernan*, 9 June 1960: 12.

Sylvan replied that the Social Democrats were different forty years ago than they were in 1960. He claimed to have even voted for Hjalmar Branting. Sylvan conceded the Social Democrats had improved conditions for the Swedish working class. "This happy fact is the last thing I would try to deny or belittle the importance of."

> What the Social Democrats have done for Swedish workers is something I would never criticize. However, it must not serve as an excuse for what the present government is trying to do to the Swedish people. It is a long step from the liberation and improvement of the working classes' living conditions to the casting of an entire people permanently in the role of children towards a parental government.[122]

Nordstjernan reader Karl Wennerberg wrote that his visits to Sweden confirmed Eric Sylvan's observations. He believed the welfare state had created a false sense of security in the people. The Swedish people thought they could get everything handed to them, without effort or error. "This is a most unhealthy situation, certainly."[123]

In *Svenska-Amerikanaren*'s "Folkets Röst" letters page, readers agreed Swedish living standards had improved. Axel Hanson noted the large manors and high nobility were no longer as visible "as in our day," and landowners could not drive their farmhands as hard as they once did. Paul Johnson remarked that even rural Swedish homes had hot and cold water, bathrooms, televisions, and refrigerators. An anonymous writer added that Swedish living standards were nearly the same as in the United States. The schools taught the English language, there was a good road system, the shops had nearly the same goods, and "most families have cars." (Most Swedish families did not have cars in 1960, however.) Helga Stromberg wrote that a person could easily get a positive view of Sweden from a quick visit, but wondered how good it was to live in Sweden over a long-term.[124]

---

[122] Eric Sylvan, "Det Tycks," *Nordstjernan*, 9 June 1960: 6.
[123] Karl Wennerberg, "Ordet är Fritt," *Nordstjernan*, 16 June 1960: 10.

Some emigrant still doubted if the land they left because of poor living conditions could have advanced as far as the U.S. Some Swedish-Americans doubted the positive reports about life in Sweden in their newspapers. A *Swedish-American Monthly* article argued Sweden's relative lack of automobiles proved that U.S. standards were far beyond those in Sweden. (After reading this article, an UD official wrote to the *Monthly*'s editor and asked: "Can anyone with an opinion on anything get it published in the *Monthly*?")[125] Even Swedish-American journalists shared doubts about Swedish progress.

A concrete discussion of Sweden's social benefits and tax burden emerged in several Swedish-American papers. Ragn V. Vennberg, from Göteborg, sent *Canada-Tidningen* information from his 1959 tax returns and a long list of social benefits from the state.[126] *Canada-Tidningen*'s Ulf Siewert conceded that Sweden's living standards were high, but believed Canadian standards were higher. "Many Swedish apartments have vacuum cleaners, TVs, refrigerators, and many other things," wrote Siewert.

> But I also know that in the equivalent Canadian homes there are refrigerators and freezers at least twice as large, a TV, hi-fi, washing machine, and ultra-modern stoves that would make the ordinary Swedish housewife green with envy. . . . The simple fact is THAT I earn 175 kronor more per week than in Sweden. THAT I pay 93 kronor less per week in taxes than for the same pay in Sweden (acc. 1959s tax table). THAT I can rent or buy housing of the same standard that exists in Sweden without a wait of several years. THAT I can get a high pension from my union . . . .[127]

---

[124] Axel Hanson, "Folkets Röst: Kan inte klaga ..." 14 September 1960: 5; Paul Johnson, "Folkets Röst: Ett tack till alla," 27 July 1960: 7; "Folkets Röst: Semesterminnen," 13 January 1960: 7; and Helga Stromberg, "Folkets Röst: Svikna förhoppningar," *Svenska-Amerikanaren Tribunen*, 27 July 1960: 7.

[125] Per Wenander, "Sweden: the Land of the Bicycle Standard of Living," *Swedish-American Monthly*, and letter from Kjell Öberg to Mac Lindahl, 15 March 1960, file "USA 1960, 16 feb – juli 1960," box I:318, NL1, RA.

[126] Ragn V. Vennberg, "Ordet Fritt: Brev från Swedish-American Club," *Canada-Tidningen*, 21 January 1960: 5.

[127] Ulf Siewert, "Ordet Fritt: Herr Vennberg och Sverige," *Canada-Tidningen*, 4 February 1960: 5.

Missions-Vännen had an ambivalent attitude towards Swedish Social Democracy. On the one hand, *Missions-Vännen* saw Sweden's welfare state, and its aid to the poor and downtrodden, as an outgrowth of Lutheran ideals. On the other hand, *Missions-Vännen* deplored Sweden's secular society. Sweden's atheism merely created an atmosphere of immorality, leading to a form of state communism. There had been progress, but *Missions-Vännen* believed the high taxes, high prices, and excessive state control were forms of repression. The paper did not dispute that people lived well in Sweden, but believed they would live better without so much state direction and regulation.[128] Ulf Siewert also believed the high taxes were repressive. Fifteen thousand young people emigrated from Sweden annually in the Fifties; Siewert believed repressive taxes caused this yearly exodus.[129]

A *Swedish-American Monthly* article, "Sweden: the Land of the Bicycle Standard of Living," agreed the tax burden was too much. The *Monthly* argued "the heavy taxation and other creeping controls over the individual probably represents a greater menace to our free way of life than the open communistic threat of which we are all aware."[130] An UD official wrote to the editor: "Right. It's not the Soviet Union or China that is the threat to humanity. It's Sweden. At least you can count on this finding its way into the Congressional Record." He pressed the Monthly's editor not to print these kinds of conservative views in future. In his view, he did not want the *Monthly* to appeal to people who "triumphantly say they have finally learned the truth about one of the most pitiful countries on Earth."[131]

This Swedish-American debate on Swedish standards largely reflected the debate in the mainstream U.S. press. For Cold War

---

[128] "The Listening Post," 13 September 1960: 6; "Sverige på väg in i kommunismen och gudlöshet," 22 November 1960: 4; and "Antikrist och kommunismen," *Missions-Vännen*, 6 December 1960: 4.

[129] Ulf Siewert, "Ordet Fritt: Därför emigrerade de," *Canada-Tidningen*, 10 December 1959: 5.

[130] Per Wenander, "Sweden: the Land of the Bicycle Standard of Living," *Swedish-American Monthly*, February 1960.

[131] Letter from Kjell Öberg to Mac Lindahl, 15 March 1960, file "USA 1960, 16 feb – juli 1960," box I:318, NL1, RA.

Missionsvännens Joel Fridfeldt.

reasons, parts of the U.S. press would not admit a form of socialism could bring progress. Some denied there was progress or the Swedish people were truly happy. San Francisco's *Daily Commercial News*, for example, ran a large story about an American youth group going to Sweden "to rehabilitate the slums" there.[132] UD believed for several weeks the whole story was just a rumor. It eventually unearthed four young Americans who spent a month at Göteborgs Stadsmission fixing substandard housing. They repaired fourteen apartments for the elderly and a recreation center for released prisoners.[133] It was good work. It was not, however, the slum clearance the *Daily Commercial News* described.

There were some articles in the American press defending Sweden, but they were not common. UD felt delighted when *The New York Times Magazine* ran an eight-page article titled "Rejoinder to Sweden's Critics."[134] "It doesn't look like a real masterpiece to me," an UD official commented, "but it's still an excellent counterweight to all the vulgar propaganda that's been poured over us over the last two years."[135]

---

[132] Telegram from Lindholm (San Francisco via Sverigeradio) to Cabinet Stockholm, 12 August 1960, file "USA 1960 aug – 1960 dec," box I:318, NL1, RA.

[133] Telegrams from Cabinet to Landberg (Svensk San Francisco) 16 and 19 August 1960, file "USA 1960 aug – 1960 dec," box I:318, NL1, RA.

[134] "Rejoinder to Sweden's Critics," *New York Times Magazine*, 26 October 1960: 61–68.

[135] Letter from Kjell Öberg to Sven Backlund, 26 October 1960, file "USA 1960 aug – 1960 dec," box I:318, NL1, RA.

In short, the Swedish-American press had an equivocal, complex view of Sweden. Parts of its view of Sweden reflected the poor, undemocratic, class society the emigrants left long ago. Another part reflected how they looked upon the place where they were born. They saw Sweden as the happy and comfortable place where they lived in their youth. This image of Sweden included a familiar – if idealized – little red cottage, village, and church. A third part of their Sweden-image revealed mixed emotions that Sweden had changed since they last saw it. Sweden may not be poor and undemocratic, but Sweden had torn down the little red cottages and replaced them with modern concrete apartment blocks. A fourth part of the emigrant papers' Sweden-image was also growing. The younger generation had never seen Sweden, never visited the local village, but had only heard their parents' stories. For these readers, Sweden was a distant place of almost mythic heroes, high ideals, and deep cultural values.[136]

Also, the emigrants – still the main audience for Swedish-American papers – had mixed feelings about their own emigration. Emigration changes a person's identity, and emigrants have mixed feelings about those changes. Many had left Sweden in anger, disgust, or perhaps feeling there were better opportunities in America. Many could have endlessly tried to justify their decisions to leave. The Swedish-American press had a predictably multifaceted image of Sweden. This often came out in the papers as either excessive idealization or undue criticism of Sweden. The Swedish-American press did both, and did it depending on circumstances. Swedish-Americans were often critical of Sweden, but reacted angrily when anyone else criticized Sweden.

Conclusions

This chapter has three main purposes: to describe Swedish-America's changing ethnicity and demographics, to present the three main Swedish-American newspapers and their communities, and to present how the Swedish-language press looked at the world around 1960.

---

[136] Barton, "Emigrants' Images of Sweden," 104.

There was a generational shift coming in Swedish-America. One generation was dying off, and the newspapers would have to attract younger readers. The newspapers had to re-target their audience, which meant redefining what it meant to be Swedish-American. The Swedish-American ethnic leaders had always defined their ethnic ideology relative to the Republican Party and Lutheranism. Like other young Americans, young Swedish-Americans questioned their parents' values during the Sixties. In the Sixties – a period of change and freedom – conservative politics and orthodox Lutheranism may have seemed hopelessly outdated. If ethnicity is an elastic concept, the ethnic press must also be elastic. The ethnic leaders – the newspaper editors – had to change their definitions of Swedish ethnicity.

In the early Sixties, most Swedish-American newspapers were socially conservative and loyal to the Republican Party. At first glance, the Swedish-American newspapers have many similarities and often minor differences. This chapter shows that while their formats were usually the same, the emigrant papers often served different communities. For example, local newspapers serve different social roles than those printing for national audiences. My thesis focuses on three newspapers with distinctly different communities. *Svenska Posten* served the local Swedish-American community in the Seattle area. *Nordstjernan* targeted a wider audience around New York and New England. It was based in the midwest, but *Svenska-Amerikanaren* aspired to a national audience. I believe that how these papers served these distinct communities influenced their social and political views. Chapter Six will do a content analysis of these three newspapers.

Around 1960, the Swedish-American press had a complex view of Sweden. It championed Sweden and the Swedish people – at times even its government – but often criticized them all. Such contradictions filled the 1960 debate over the Swedish welfare state. Emigrants were proud of Sweden's advances, and believed the Social Democrats deserved credit for it. Many also thought taxes were too high, which held back development and even oppressed the people. As cousins to the homeland Swedes, the emigrants felt they had a right to critique Sweden. If others criticized Sweden, the emigrant papers defended it; they might even defend Sweden from critical views they shared. The Swedish-Americans could not allow outsiders to denigrate the main symbol of their ethnicity. The most high-profile U.S. criticism of Sweden came in July 1960, with President Eisenhower's remarks at a Republican luncheon. The Swedish government flooded the emigrant press with statistics, memos, and news reports to deny Eisenhower's comments. *Canada-Tidningen*, *Vestkusten*, *Svenska Posten* and others ran these items on their front pages. The editors ran opinion pieces backing the Swedish viewpoint. Even several Swedish-American readers sent in letters supporting the Swedish position. Sweden's government may have felt it effectively squelched a potential problem, at least among Swedish-Americans. It seemed to be effective. When the next crisis comes, supplying news and statistics might be a good way to handle "unjust criticism" of Sweden.

Chapter Three

The Politics of Supplying News

Perhaps the hardest part of editing a Swedish-American paper in the Sixties was finding reliable news-sources. The American papers ran essentially nothing on Sweden. Relying on receiving clippings from friends back home was not satisfactory. Getting airmail subscriptions to daily Swedish newspapers was an expensive alternative. Paying royalties for their news would have cost even more. Getting wire-service reports was impossibly expensive. In this atmosphere, UD stepped in to help. In the late Fifties and early Sixties, UD set up a system to provide the emigrant papers with Swedish news. This chapter examines UD's relationship with the Swedish-American press and the news it helped provide.

The emigrant papers rarely wrote about this association with UD. Details of this relationship therefore come from UD archival sources. Most documents are between UD Press Bureau officials, and a few are between UD and the emigrant editors. These papers discuss what sorts of news UD helped provide, how it got processed, and how it got to the Swedish-American press. Mostly the emigrant papers received reliable news, but news with a distinct Swedish perspective. Other times UD arranged for the emigrant papers to get Swedish publicity material.

This chapter begins by examining the organizations UD arranged to send news to the Swedish-American press. These sections highlight what sorts of news they specialized in, what their journalistic routines were, how the emigrant editors got their dispatches, and their relation to UD. After surveying these sources, this chapter asks how much of this source material did the emigrant papers use? What were their main sources? What sources did they use to cover Vietnam-related issues? Did the editors cut, change, or add to the original Swedish source material? The purpose here is to uncover the Swedish government's role in how the emigrant press presented its news.

The American-Swedish News Exchange

A few Swedish-American papers cited their sources in the byline. These bylines mentioned sources with obscure acronyms that never appear in mainstream newspapers. News from the familiar AP or UPI was rare. Most Swedish-American news came from four organizations. These were ASNE, SIS, FLT, or *Sverige-Nytt*. The following pages will shortly explain and discuss these four organizations in detail. They are important because they provided nearly all the Swedish news to the emigrant papers. (The editors wrote their own local Swedish-American news, or got it from regional reporters.) Some of these four organizations also gave out editorials, and the editors sometimes printed them. ASNE, SIS, FLT, and *Sverige-Nytt* wrote most of the emigrant press's news on Swedish Vietnam policy.

The American-Swedish News Exchange (ASNE) first appeared in 1921, and eventually grew into the emigrant press's major news source by the early Sixties. ASNE would be the first of several hidden structures behind the Swedish-American press. ASNE was literally a news exchange. It gathered American news for Swedish consumption, and Swedish news for Americans. By 1923, ASNE had agreements with AP, UPI, Canadian Press, and several smaller organizations.

Sweden founded ASNE to repair any damage the First World War had done to Sweden's image in America. The Americans' outburst of nativist panic had made life difficult for Swedish emigrants. It also threatened U.S.-Swedish trade. Until this point, Sweden saw Russia as its prime foreign market. The Bolshevik Revolution changed that. Sweden now saw the United States as its most promising potential market. The Swedish government hoped ASNE would spread information on Sweden, and especially Swedish industry. A 1938 government report said that ASNE should "avoid anything that smells of propaganda." It would only spread nonpolitical information. Just getting Sweden into the news was promotion enough.[1] Svenbjörn Kilander argues in *Censur och propaganda* this was mostly a pretence. ASNE's cover as a nonpolitical organ made it more attractive to American newspapers. He argues ASNE was more of a publicity bureau for Swedish industry than a news office. The patina of objectivity made it more effective.[2]

ASNE was a semiofficial organ, with most of its income coming from Stockholm. It was also private: part of the American-Scandinavian Foundation. This distance from the government was also part of the plan to give ASNE journalistic credibility.[3] A closer inspection reveals substantial contact with the Foreign Ministry. ASNE worked closely with the UD Press Bureau, Sweden's organ for coordinating news and publicity abroad. (American journalists work with the United States Information Agency in the same way.) UD Press Bureau had a largely organizational role but it still influenced ASNE.

ASNE grew in the late Forties. Its New York office received 17,640 articles between 1948 and 1950.[4] Underlying tensions in U.S.-Swedish relations were surfacing during these years. Sweden's Second World War neutrality had hurt Sweden's image in America. The Cold War augured more bad publicity abroad, especially after Sweden signed a 1946 trade pact with the Soviet Union. Some U.S. politicians condemned Sweden's developing neutrality in the Cold War. Others criticized Swedish experiments with socialism.[5] Some Swedish officials believed ASNE did not do enough to calm these

---

[1] Mac Lindahl, *Svenska-Amerikanska Nyhetsbyrån i New York och Stockholm inför 30-årsjubileet*, Stockholm, 1951: 9; and *Redogörelse för tillkomsten av press och informationorganet i utrikesdepartementet*, Stockholm, 1939: 24–25.

[2] Kilander, *Censur och propaganda*, 184–185, 201.

[3] *Redogörelse for Svensk-Amerikanska Nyhetsbyråns Verksamhet, 1948–1950*, Stockholm, 1950: 36; Allan Kastrup, *Med Sverige i Amerika*, Malmö, 1985: 32–33.

[4] *Redogörelse för Svensk-Amerikanska Nyhetsbyråns Verksamhet, 1948–1950*, 28.

[5] *Redogörelse för Svensk-Amerikanska Nyhetsbyrån: Verksamhet 1/7 1947–30/6 1948*, Stockholm, 1948: 8–9; *Redogörelse för Svensk-Amerikanska Nyhetsbyråns Verksamhet, 1948–1950*, 13; and Kastrup, *Med Sverige i Amerika*, 132–133.

tensions and spread positive news about Sweden. Finance Minister Ernst Wigforss, for example, urged ASNE to do more to spread positive news about Swedish taxes and social spending.[6] The Swedish government was unhappy with Sweden's image in the United States. It saw ASNE as the organ to correct this, and began to wonder if it was doing the job.

ASNE's office in Stockholm was its main branch. This office collected Swedish news from Sweden's daily press, and edited and rewrote them for the American audience. ASNE also got information from the Swedish Institute and the International Swedish News Office. The rest came from freelance journalists.[7] ASNE's Stockholm office cabled the important news to New York, and the rest went by airmail. This format was flexible, and often a source of tension between the New York and Stockholm offices.[8] ASNE's New York office would further edit and rewrite this material, or even write new stories with American sources. It then sent these stories to various U.S. newspapers. This included its special customer – the Swedish-American press. ASNE's New York office also collected news for the Stockholm office, which it sent to Swedish newspapers.[9] ASNE always had institutional tension between its New York and Stockholm offices. Each side wanted a larger role for itself.

ASNE was a business in transition. A 1960 UD investigation advised rationalizing the Swedish information organs abroad. It suggested giving much of ASNE's workload to the Swedish Institute and the Swedish-International Press Bureau, SIP. (SIP was an organization directly in the UD political structure.) UD would eventually shut down ASNE's Stockholm office, and by extension,

---

[6] Memo by Allan Kastrup, "Utdrag ur memorandum, p. 100-," undated, file "ASNE: Papers Relating to the Activities of the American-Swedish News Exchange," page 4, box "ASNE: Allan Kastrup, Personal Papers," ASNE New York, SSIRC.

[7] Swedish Foreign Ministry, *Samverkan mellan organen för svensk upplysningsverksamhet i utlandet*, Stockholm, 1960: 35.

[8] For examples of the Stockholm-New York tension over the division of labor, see letter from Tell Dahllöf to Allan Kastrup, 25 February 1960, and Kastrup's reply to Dahllöf, 4 March 1960, file "1959–1960," box A:16, ASNE Stockholm, RA.

[9] Kastrup, *Med Sverige i Amerika*, 35.

the New York office as well.[10] The Swedish-American press was skeptical of these changes. *Nordstjernan* regarded ASNE as a good news-source, but feared direct UD control would bring changes. *Nordstjernan* argued UD Press Bureau's influence over ASNE would make "the American-Swedish News Exchange's material even more propaganda-oriented than it already is."[11] This criticism upset some at UD. Sweden's Washington attaché wanted to discuss this editorial with editor Gerry Rooth. The attaché noted that others could have written this piece. He believed that Rooth was still at the 1960 Rome Olympics.[12] The clear suspects were coeditors Mac Lindahl and Eric Sylvan.

Instead of closing these offices, UD changed their mission. Over the next six years, ASNE became the Swedish Information Service, SIS. This reorganization began as early as June 1960. ASNE selectively began using of the term "Swedish Information Service," but kept the name ASNE for the present.[13] Nobody knew how this reorganization would influence ASNE's news-distribution activity. ASNE Director Allan Kastrup warned the emigrant papers, "there will now be a drastic reduction in [ASNE's] service to them." (This overreaction surprised others: Ellis Folke was "flabbergasted at Allan's reaction" to the reorganization.) The reorganization meant the emigrant press would get its ASNE bulletins from the Stockholm office.[14]

Until 1960, the Stockholm office wrote and edited ASNE's Swedish bulletins. They would then mail them to New York, which always arrived Thursday morning. ASNE's New York office would then re-edit and stencil these bulletins for the Swedish-American press. The re-edited bulletin went out Thursday afternoon. The Swedish-American papers received these bulletins on Saturday or

---

[10] *Samverkan mellan organen för svensk upplysningsverksamhet i utlandet*, 64–66.

[11] "Nyhetstjänst till USA," *Nordstjernan*, 8 September 1960: 6.

[12] Letter from Olov Ternström to Sven Backlund, 12 September 1960, file "USA 1960 aug – 1960 dec," box I:318, NL1, RA.

[13] Protokoll 30 June 1960, file "1958–1965," box A:2, ASNE Stockholm, RA.

[14] Letter from Ellis I. Folke to Olov Ternström, 18 September 1959, file "1959–1960," box A:26; and protokoll 23 June 1960, file "1958–1965," box A:2, ASNE Stockholm, RA.

Monday.[15] Formats sometimes changed, but each weekly mailing included news releases, a four-page weekly bulletin, photographs, the Province Notes, and perhaps some cartoons, and some feature stories from Förenade Landsorttidningar, FLT. ASNE's Stockholm office was not satisfied with this procedure. It wanted to streamline the process by doing all the editing in Sweden. If the Stockholm office bypassed the New York office, the emigrant papers would get their news two days earlier. Speaking for the New York office, Allan Kastrup disagreed. He suggested the Stockholm office sent their bulletins to New York a day or two earlier. He believed this would avoid having the bulletins in transit too close to a weekend.[16]

This became a minor issue in a power struggle between Stockholm and New York. Allan Kastrup wanted a larger role for his New York office.[17] The Stockholm office increasingly by-passed New York. When it did send dispatches to New York, Kastrup would rewrite them anyway, upsetting the Stockholm office further. Some in Stockholm doubted whether he was the right person for the job. Ellis Folke of ASNE Stockholm thought, "The simple fact is that Allan is a damn good editorial writer – and information copy writer – but he knows nothing about feature material, release items, or news items."[18]

The Stockholm office respected Kastrup as a journalist but found it hard to work with him. According to ASNE's Ellis Folke, Kastrup was typically "discounting the wishes of the Council and the Board in favor of his own whims."[19] Folke believed Kastrup showed "a lack of cooperation" with the Stockholm office. People

---

[15] Letter from Tell Dahllöf to Allan Kastrup, 25 February 1960, and Kastrup's reply to Dahllöf, 4 March 1960, file "1959–1960," box A:16, ASNE Stockholm, RA.

[16] Letter from Tell Dahllöf to Allan Kastrup, 25 February 1960, and Kastrup's reply to Dahllöf, 4 March 1960, file "1959–1960," box A:16, ASNE Stockholm, RA.

[17] Letter from Allan Kastrup to Ellis I. Folke, 12 August 1959, file "1959–1960," box A:16, ASNE Stockholm, RA.

[18] Letter from Ellis I. Folke to Lars Malmström, 25 January 1960, file "1959–1960," box A:16, ASNE Stockholm, RA.

[19] Letter from Ellis I. Folke to Allan Kastrup, 19 April 1960, file "1959–1960," box A:16, ASNE Stockholm, RA.

said he proposed projects only to denounce them later. This led his colleagues in Stockholm constantly to "argue with [him] in lengthy letters." "The greatest trouble I have found is your own negative attitude," Folke eventually wrote to Kastrup. "You are a highly undependable man dealing with all kinds of childish, under-the-table games."[20]

In an 11 January 1963 meeting, members of the UD Press Bureau discussed removing Allan Kastrup from his position. It was a board meeting for the Swedish-American Foundation, but many Press Bureau personnel were present. One reason given for removing Kastrup was that he had difficulty working with his own staff. Kastrup called this "irresponsible and senseless criticism" and fumed over the accusation.[21] Nothing came of the move to dump Kastrup. Still, he held Kjell Öberg (UD's Adviser for Information Activities Abroad) and Sten Sundfeldt (UD Press Bureau's director) responsible for trying to remove him. This further worsened relations between ASNE and UD Press Bureau, and ASNE's Stockholm and New York offices.

Despite this internal conflict, the Stockholm office took over sending the Swedish-language bulletins to the emigrant press. Over time, Kastrup was "slowly getting used to the idea of the Swedish work being done in Stockholm."[22] He disliked it, but the situation was playing itself out. During 1964 and 1965, ASNE worked on the transition to become the Swedish Information Service. The archive documents do not imply ASNE's news-distribution routines changed during these years. Most documents from this era relate to practical matter of moving, changing management, and reorganizing its structure. The Swedish government finally closed ASNE in 1966, replacing it with the Swedish Information Service.

---

[20] Letter from Ellis I. Folke to Allan Kastrup, 14 December 1959, file "1957–1959," box A:21, ASNE Stockholm, RA.

[21] Allan Kastrup, "I Stockholm: Länge upp, sedan ner, eller kanske cirkus, för nyhetsbyrån," page 6, file "Papers Relating to the Activities of the American-Swedish News Exchange," box "ASNE, Allan Kastrup, Personal papers," ASNE New York, SSIRC.

[22] Protokoll 23 February 1960, file "1958–1965," box A:2; and letter from Ellis I. Folke to Lars Malmström, 25 January 1960, file "1959–1960," box A:16, ASNE Stockholm, RA.

SIS was to be ASNE's successor organization and would have only one office – based in New York. Unlike ASNE, SIS is a promotional agency with little pretense at being a news bureau. It is under UD's direct management, located in the New York General Consulate. In the Sixties SIS sent cultural and public service dispatches to the Swedish-American papers. It appeared just as Swedish criticism of the Vietnam War – and American criticism of Sweden – rose to a crescendo.

SIS printed a weekly bulletin called *Nyheter från Sverige* ("News From Sweden") in the Sixties. It was four pages long. SIS mailed these with some FLT articles, various special releases, some cartoons and photos, and the ubiquitous Province Notes. ASNE started sending these large weekly packages in 1961, when ASNE's Harriet Albert edited them. In May 1965 Maud Andersson, a Stockholm freelance journalist, took over and began assembling these packets. Andersson mailed the cartoons and Province Notes to SIS every Friday. Andersson returned to her full-time newspaper job in November 1969, and Eva-Britta Nauckhoff took over.[23] Nauckhoff edited the Notes and clipped cartoons from *Dagens Nyheter* until May 1973. After this, a Stockholm freelance group edited the Province Notes.[24]

In summary, the Swedish-American press received the Nyheter från Sverige bulletin, FLT articles, the Province Notes, special releases, and cartoons and photographs from ASNE-SIS. At various times, SIS offered other items to go with this basic package. One such offer was a weekly copy of "Veckans Klipp" – a collection of domestic political articles from the Swedish embassy's telex.[25] The

---

[23] Letter from Allan Kastrup to Harriet Albert, 27 October 1961, file "1960–1961," box A:17, ASNE Stockholm; telegram from Håkan Berggren to Odlander (SIS New York), 25 August 1966, file "1963 – mars 1967," box I:462, PR4S, RA; and letter from Eva Heckscher to Maud Andersson, 1 December 1969, and Andersson's reply, 10 November 1969, file "1969 – 1971 febr.," PR4S, UD.

[24] Telegram from Cabinet Stockholm to Inforswed New York, 29 May 1973, and letters from Anne Henriksson to all Swedish-American newspapers, 26 September 1973; and memo by Åke Berg, "Landskapsnotiser till svensk-amerikanska pressen," 18 May 1973, file "1973 – 1974," PR4S, UD.

Swedish-American papers got this material, but most also used news from a Stockholm newspaper: *Sverige-Nytt.*

Sverige-Nytt (The Swedish Digest)

In 1959, ASNE decided to intensify their service to the Swedish-American papers. With ASNE's weekly bulletins, UD also wanted to give each paper a free Stockholm daily of their choice.[26] According to this idea, *Dagens Nyheter* and *Svenska Dagbladet* were full of current news. With such papers available, there was no need for ASNE's selection, rewriting, and distribution of news. This idea never got far. A significant problem was that the news in the Stockholm papers was under copyright. Many Swedish-American papers actively pilfered news from Swedish dailies. UD could not subsidize such copyright infringement.[27] ASNE negotiated with A-Pressen, Högerpressens Nyhetsbyrå, and FLT to get the copyrights at little or no cost. ASNE had no success.[28]

Another problem was that *DN* and *SvD* wrote news for a well-informed domestic audience. Unless someone rewrote these stories, they could create more confusion than awareness. *DN*'s and *SvD*'s articles on Swedish politics and society assumed more knowledge of Sweden than most emigrants had. They also assumed a good knowledge of Stockholm. If read out of context, their articles could give the foreign reader a false impression of Swedish society.[29] Without enough background, stories on routine social problems could suggest a crisis. Minor problems in the welfare system, for example, could look like entrenched corruption. The Swedish-American editors were all competent journalists, and all could rewrite these articles. UD thought they might not want to, or have

---

[25] Letter from Swedish Embassy (Ottawa) to *The Swedish Press*, 16 March, and Sture Wermee's reply 16 July 1979, SCR, SP.

[26] Letter from Ellis I. Folke to Olov Ternström, 18 September 1959, file "1959–1960," box A:26, ASNE Stockholm, RA.

[27] Protokoll 1 December 1959, file "1958–1965," box A:2, ASNE Stockholm, RA.

[28] Protokoll 19 October 1959, file "1958–1965," box A:2, ASNE Stockholm, RA.

[29] Letter from Kjell Öberg to Ellis I. Folke, 8 October 1959, file "1959–1960," box A:26, ASNE Stockholm, RA.

Sverige-Nytt
SWEDISH DIGEST

the time.[30] A better solution was to provide them with free copies of *Sverige-Nytt*. *Sverige-Nytt* is a small Stockholm newspaper that carries national Swedish news. The ASNE director believed its Swedish news was already designed for a foreign audience. *Sverige-Nytt*'s articles were in-depth, but without demanding much previous knowledge of Swedish politics. The ASNE Director thought the emigrant papers could rewrite and edit *Sverige-Nytt*'s news with little effort.[31]

In the Sixties, *Sverige-Nytt* was a tabloid-size newspaper printed on acid-free onion-skin paper. (Unlike the Swedish-American papers, the old issues of *Sverige-Nytt* have not yellowed.) Each issue was eight pages long, with Swedish text occupying the first five pages. Most of this was Swedish national news, and often on Swedish foreign policy. The sections "Senaste nytt i korthet" ("Latest News in Brief") and "Nytt i sammandrag" ("News in Summary") had short bulletin items. News on local disturbances, arrests, and protests often appeared in these spaces. The back page had several news items in English. Also in English, pages six and seven posed as "Trade and Industry Reviews." Instead of genuine financial and business news, these stories were more promotional than news-oriented. These articles always praised new Swedish inventions, industrial developments, and business practices. Considering its indirect relation to UD and SIP, *Sverige-Nytt*'s main purpose was arguably to promote Swedish industry. The paper's news was reliable, but was mostly a lure to get people to read the promotional items.

---

[30] Letter from Sven Backlund to Kjell Öberg, 8 October 1959, file "1959–1960," box A:26, ASNE Stockholm, RA.

[31] Letter from Allan Kastrup to Ellis I. Folke, 12 August 1959, file "1959–1960," box A:16, ASNE Stockholm, RA.

Sverige-Nytt is a privately owned newspaper. Editor Erik Hummelgren called it a private organ financed only by subscriptions and advertising.[32] It also had an unofficial relationship with the Swedish Foreign Ministry. Erik Hummelgren also headed UD's Swedish-International Press Bureau, SIP. SIP is part of the Foreign Ministry's export and tourist division. *Sverige-Nytt* may earn money through subscriptions and advertising, but most of SIP's budget came from the Swedish state. SIP also shared its office space at Brunkebergstorg 14 with *Sverige-Nytt*.[33] Much of *Sverige-Nytt's* material came from SIP. Hummelgren knew this relationship with UD looked bad, but there was a certain logic to putting all the Swedish publicity organs under one roof.[34] The cooperation benefited everyone.

Hummelgren did not want UD to send copies of *Sverige-Nytt* to the emigrant papers. He knew that most Swedish-American newspapers used his material, sometimes with only minor changes. Having UD pay for their subscriptions tacitly meant they could print whatever they liked from *Sverige-Nytt*. He believed unrestricted Swedish-American use of *Sverige-Nytt* would keep him from selling more papers in the U.S.[35] ASNE's Ellis Folke tried to persuade him. Folke argued that many Swedish-American papers were using his material anyway. He insisted the emigrant papers would give *Sverige-Nytt* credit this way. This would be good publicity. It would also be a cultural service to the Swedish-American newspapers. Folke later wrote that Hummelgren "was not as happy about it as I wished him to be."[36] Rather than a cultural service, Hummelgren doubted Folke's plan was good for the emigrant papers. Using *Sverige-Nytt* would end the diversity of the

---

[32] Letter from Erik Hummelgren to Sven Backlund, 16 October 1959, file "1959–1960," box A:26, ASNE Stockholm, RA.

[33] *Samverkan mellan organen för svensk upplysningsverksamhet i utlandet*, 13–14.

[34] Letter from Erik Hummelgren to Sven Backlund, 16 October 1959, file "1959–1960," box A:26, ASNE Stockholm, RA.

[35] Letter from Erik Hummelgren to Sven Backlund, 16 October 1959, file "1959–1960," box A:26, ASNE Stockholm, RA.

[36] Letter from Ellis I. Folke to Olov Ternström, 13 October 1959, file "1959–1960," box A:26, ASNE Stockholm, RA.

Swedish-American papers. They would become all too uniform, soon becoming a pale imitation of his newspaper.[37]

Hummelgren argued that the Swedish-American papers should set up their own Stockholm office for Swedish news.[38] ASNE insisted this was absurd. ASNE director Allan Kastrup wrote that this idea arose from "a premise that doesn't exist." The emigrant press could not afford the start-up costs of setting up a Stockholm office. They probably could not even afford part of the cost. ASNE or another organ would have to bear the entire financial burden itself. This would nullify the meaning of an independent Swedish-American office. An ASNE-financed emigrant office might develop journalistic routines and standards similar to ASNE itself. They disagreed on many issues, but ASNE's New York and Stockholm offices agreed an ASNE-backed emigrant office would compete with both of them. They thus discouraged this plan as a bad idea and a duplication of services.[39] Hummelgren's idea of a Swedish-American office was a non-starter.

ASNE believed that letting the emigrant papers use *Sverige-Nytt* was a more sensible idea. ASNE's Ellis Folke pressured Hummelgren to granting them the rights to *Sverige-Nytt*'s material. If Hummelgren did not relent, Folke wrote, he would "report that [Hummelgren] would not play ball" with UD. This would have been uncomfortable for Hummelgren, since *Sverige-Nytt* worked out of UD-owned property. The threat clearly worked. Hummelgren said, "Well, he wouldn't exactly say that he didn't want to play along, but on the other hand, etc., etc. . . . ." Folke believed, "the guy wants to get paid for a service that he is already [informally] providing free of charge." More than money, Hummelgren did not want trouble with the authorities at UD's Press Bureau.[40] Three days later, Hummelgren reluctantly gave permission for the emigrant

---

[37] Letter from Erik Hummelgren to Sven Backlund, 16 October 1959, file "1959–1960," box A:26, ASNE Stockholm, RA.

[38] Protokoll 12 September 1960, and "Lunchsammanträdande med SIP:s råd den 12 Sept 1960," file "1960–1961," box A1:4, SIP, RA.

[39] Letter from Allan Kastrup to Jan Sjöby, 30 January 1961, file "1960–1961," box A:17, ASNE Stockholm, RA.

[40] Letter from Ellis I. Folke to Olov Ternström, 13 October 1959, file "1959–1960," box A:26, ASNE Stockholm, RA.

papers to use *Sverige-Nytt*. His only condition was that they reproduce his articles whole, citing *Sverige-Nytt* as their source.[41]

As Hummelgren feared, *Sverige-Nytt* instantly became the Swedish-American newspapers' main source of news. It remained a prime source through most of this survey period. The tables that appear below suggest they received it as late as 1972. By 1973, however, no emigrant paper got *Sverige-Nytt* for free any longer. UD later bought *Svenska Posten* a subscription, but *Nordstjernan* paid for its copy.[42] Its distribution manager said *Nordstjernan* received *Sverige-Nytt* but could not clip and reprint its articles. *Vestkusten's* Karin Person said her paper had exclusive rights to use *Sverige-Nytt*.[43]

Förenade Landsortstidningar (FLT)

Förenade Landsortstidningar (FLT) is "the United Provincial Newspaper Service." It is an association of seventy-three smaller, mostly rural Swedish newspapers. It plays a minor role here because no paper ran more than one or two FLT articles each week. FLT specialized in feature articles about the Swedish countryside's history and culture. ASNE-SIS also sent the Swedish-American press photographs from FLT. These were popular items: many photos in the Swedish-American press came from FLT. (ASNE and SIS included these in their weekly mailings to the emigrant papers.) Using an FLT photo cost six dollars, which ASNE would deposit into the FLT bank giro. FLT did not charge extra if ASNE sent the picture to the Swedish-American press. The emigrant papers may have paid only a nominal fee, if anything. The only condition FLT made was ASNE could only use photos or articles by FLT

---

[41] Letter from Erik Hummelgren to Sven Backlund, 16 October 1959, file "1959–1960," box A:26, ASNE Stockholm, RA.

[42] Letter from Marie Sjölander to Anita Myrfors, 6 February 1975, file "1975," and memo by Bruno Eneberg, "Svensk-amerikanska pressutredningen," 15 November 1974; and telegram from Cabinet Stockholm to Svensk New York, 30 October 1973, file "1973 – 1974," PR4S, UD.

[43] Memo by Olle Tunberg, "Redogörelse med protokoll för möte med representanter för den svensk-amerikanska (inkl. svensk-kanadensiska) pressen i Minneapolis 1975-05-27 och 1975-05-28," 8 October 1975, file "1975," PR4S, UD.

journalists. Material FLT bought from other wire services was off limits.[44]

The Swedish-American editors periodically contacted SIS to discuss the FLT pictures. They wanted photos on topical social issues, including some on current events. They warned that such pictures, while good, often had short shelf-lives. The editors wanted the regular SIS photo dispatches to contain pictures that explained Swedish life and social conditions. Anything that showed how ordinary Swedes lived their daily lives would be helpful. They wanted pictures of Swedish customs and holidays, landscapes and provinces, and jobs, trades, and stores. The editors could also use some political material too. ASNE-SIS had to remember, however, most Swedish-Americans were unfamiliar with the Swedish parties.[45]

Most Swedish-American papers did not subscribe directly to FLT, but got it through ASNE-SIS. The possible exception could have been *Svenska-Amerikanaren*. *SAT*'s owner Arthur Hendricks claimed he bought FLT's service directly for twelve-hundred dollars a year until late 1968. It is possible he did not. FLT had no records of *SAT* receiving their material. FLT editor Ivar Petersson could not find *SAT* in his address register or billing lists. He believed Arthur Hendricks had been mistaken; Petersson thought *SAT* never got FLT.[46] Another source said *Svenska-Amerikanaren* and *California Veckoblad* had indeed once used FLT. The Swedish tax system, however, forced them to drop it. Both papers had readers in Sweden. Their copies went bulk airmail to Göteborg, and then through standard mail to their Swedish readers. Once these papers went through the mail, they became domestic Swedish newspapers. Carrying FLT meant an 11% excise tax; this extra cost forced *Svenska-Amerikanaren* to drop FLT. Whatever the story was, the

---

[44] Letter from Karin Friberg to Eva Heckscher, 22 March 1967, file "1963 – mars 1967," and telegram from Ulrika Beer to Bo Kälfors, 12 December 1968, file "1967, april – 1968, dec," box I:462, PR4S, RA.

[45] Letter from Allan Kastrup to Harriet Albert, 15 May 1962, file "1962," box A:18, ASNE Stockholm; letter from Karin Person to Anne Henriksson, 27 June 1968, file "April 1967 – Dec 1968," box I:462, PR4S, RA.

[46] Telegram from Ulrika Beer to Bo Kälfors, 12 December 1968, and letter from Eva Heckscher to Ulrika Beer, 12 December 1968, file "1967, april – 1968, dec," box I:462, PR4S, RA.

excise tax on weekly newspapers ended on 1 January 1969. FLT would become tax-free after then.[47] That ended whatever legal problems there were, and SIS arranged for both papers to receive FLT. FLT service began to *SAT* and *California Veckoblad* on 20 December 1968.

Minor Sources: TT and the Swedish Dailies

Svenska Posten was one of the two newspapers that regularly cited its sources. Most of its news articles came from the sources described above. Yet, it ran some items from minor sources. In 1965, for example, *Svenska Posten* credited articles to Swedtravel, US, The Swedish-American Line, *Göteborgs-Posten, Dagens Nyheter, Sydsvenska Dagbladet,* and the Swedish news wire service Tidningarnas telegrambyrå, TT. It also ran a legally disputed article from *Svenska Dagbladet* in 1965. The Swedish-American Line and Swedtravel probably sent their publicity items directly to *Svenska Posten*. (One cannot rule out that SIS may have sent this material in its weekly Friday mailings.) *SvP* got free Sunday editions of *Göteborgs-Posten* and paid for its Sunday edition of *Dagens Nyheter*.[48] *Svenska Posten* sometimes also used material from Swedish dailies like *Aftonbladet, Sydsvenska Dagbladet,* and *Svenska Dagbladet*. According to *SvP* columnist Reinhold Ahleen, these papers sometimes surfaced at local Seattle newsstands. Some of Harry Fabbe's editorials refer to friends in Sweden that sent him news clippings. He may have had permission to print *GP*'s and *DN*'s articles, but did not have consent from other dailies. The author of the 1965 *Svenska Dagbladet* article, for example, threatened to sue *Svenska Posten* for copyright infringement.[49] The lawsuit never

---

[47] Telegram from Ulrika Beer to Bo Kälfors, 12 December 1968; and telegram from Cabinet to Inforswed New York, 13 December 1968, file "1967, april – 1968, dec," box I:462, PR4S, RA.

[48] Letter from Bruno Eneberg to Eva Heckscher, 21 May 1973, file "1973 – 1974," PR4S, UD.

[49] Letters from Jörgen Almaas to *Svenska Posten*, 7 July and 5 August 1965, file "*Svenska Dagbladet*," box 1, *SvP*; and Reinhold Ahleen's personal diary, 16 January 1967, box 1, Ahleen, UW.

happened, but it shows *SvP* would use any articles that crossed Harry Fabbe's desk.

Apart from Swedish daily papers and publicity material, *Svenska Posten* also received TT. UD paid for the Swedish-American papers to receive these wire-service reports in the early Sixties. Neither UD nor ASNE-SIS selected which TT articles the emigrant papers would get. This made TT a rare news source that did not first flow through UD channels. SIS ended this service in October 1966. It would cost SIS 6,199 kronor to give the Swedish-American press another year of these wire reports. This was just too expensive, especially since most papers made limited use of it.[50] *Svenska Posten* used just one TT item in 1965. (It continued to use TT items after this – perhaps with dubious legality.)

This development took the TT culture editor, Staffan Rosén, by surprise. He had heard the Swedish-American papers appreciated TT, but UD insisted it was not so. Rosén was personally suspicious of why UD chose to stop the TT service just then. The TT director was then in the U.S., and would return in one week. Rosén could not negotiate a compromise solution without him. Without higher authority, he could only suggest continuing TT without the expensive photo service. UD said that it understood his disappointment, and might come back to TT someday. It did not explore the idea of keeping the text service while ending only the photo service.[51]

SIS had to reduce its costs, but worried that TT's sudden disappearance would be a psychological blow to the emigrant papers.[52] Before SIS acted, it asked several editors for their opinions. *Canada-Tidningen*'s Arthur Andersson said TT's news was too specialized for Swedish-American readers. *Nordstjernan*'s Gerry Rooth agreed with *Canada-Tidningen*. They could manage without

---

[50] Letter from Lennart Tyrhammar to Harriet Albert, 14 October 1966, and letter from Kjell Öberg to Staffan Rosén, 10 October 1966, file "1963 – Mars 1967," box I:462, PR4S, RA.

[51] Letters from Staffan Rosén to Kjell Öberg, 6 and 10 October 1966, and Öberg's reply, 10 October 1966, file "1963 – Mars 1967," box I:462, PR4S, RA.

[52] Telegram from Swedinform to Anders Pers, 19 September 1966, file "1963 – Mars 1967," box I:462, PR4S, RA.

TT, but they wanted FLT to continue.[53] This was exactly what SIS expected to hear. Having them say it softened any psychological blow TT's discontinuation might have caused.

Swedish-American Press Use of its Source Material

ASNE, SIS, FLT, and *Sverige-Nytt* provided most news to the Swedish-American press. FLT had solid journalistic standing. Apart from distributing industrial propaganda, *Sverige-Nytt*'s news was also reliable. ASNE's standing was perhaps softer, but more credible than the promotional agency SIS. TT had the strongest reputation but was inappropriate for an emigrant audience. These sources were also all Swedish; they issued news by Swedish journalists in a Swedish perspective. This national bias was not a problem in reporting news such as train wrecks.[54] The Swedish national bias was a real problem in reporting the American-Swedish diplomatic tension over Vietnam. As the Sixties progressed, UD Press Bureau expanded its role in supplying the emigrant press with this Swedish news.

The question arises: how much of this Swedish source material did the Swedish-American papers use? Many Swedish-American papers cited sources in their bylines, but only *Svenska Posten* and *Vestkusten* did it regularly. Other papers were erratic about citing sources or simply did not use bylines. Even *Vestkusten* did not use bylines before Karin Person took over the paper. Only Harry Fabbe's *Svenska Posten* consistently cited sources throughout the survey period. *SvP*'s byline citation therefore allows researchers to analyze its sources. Most *SvP* news came from four different sources: ASNE-SIS, *Sverige-Nytt*, FLT, and *Stockholms-Tidningen*. A fifth source, one might say, were the uncredited items. These were likely articles that editor Harry Fabbe had written himself from various sources. He likely compiled most of these from Swedish newspapers. Some

---

[53] Telegram from Anders Pers to Cabinet Stockholm, 22 September 1966, file "1963 – Mars 1967," box I:462, PR4S, RA.

[54] For example, *Sverige-Nytt*'s "Tågolycka i Norrköping kräver nio liv," *Vestkusten*, 12 June 1975: 1, or SIS's "Fem dödade i tågkrasch," *The Swedish Press*, 15 January 1973: 2.

could have come from American sources, most notably his editorials on the war in Asia.

The table below examines *Svenska Posten*'s source material in four different years: 1960, 1965, 1969, and 1972. I had planned to survey both *Svenska Posten* and *Vestkusten* at five-year intervals. It was natural to start with 1960 and 1965, but 1970 presented problems. Apart from the 7 January issue, neither Göteborg University library nor Augustana College has *Svenska Posten* from 1970. Neither library has any 1970 copies of *Vestkusten* either. (Perhaps this is because of the New York dock-workers' embargo on surface mail to Sweden.) Both libraries have complete collections for 1969, however. There were similar problems with 1974, so I use 1972 as the survey's terminal date. This was the last year of the U.S. war in Vietnam, both newspapers were still stable, and preserved copies of each issue are available.

The table below defines a "news article" as any report longer than five lines with a bold-faced headline. Many of these also carry Swedish or American datelines. "News articles" should aspire to objectivity. The writer should have intended them as unbiased statements of fact rather than opinion pieces. The table does not count reports from social lodges, province notes, obituaries, and sports stories as "news articles." It makes exceptions for unusual obituaries, such as ones on the front page. It considers sports items not found in the sports section as news. It also excludes the strictly local news. *Svenska Posten* naturally could not have used *Sverige-Nytt*, ASNE, or FLT as sources for local stories. These major news-organs did not compete to cover local Seattle news and could not displace each other. Anyway, *Svenska Posten* ran local items as columnist-pieces rather than news articles.

The volume of Swedish news in *Svenska Posten* increased during the Sixties. Table 6 shows that *SvP* slowly decreased its use of ASNE-SIS material from 1960 to 1972. It was a marginal source, but *SvP* gradually increased its use of FLT. The big changes, however, appear in *SvP*'s use of *Sverige-Nytt*. *Svenska Posten* used twice as many *Sverige-Nytt* articles in 1969 than it did in 1960. One could say 1960 was the first year *Sverige-Nytt* was available to *SvP* and thus not a fair base-level. Even so, *Svenska Posten*'s use of *Sverige-Nytt* grew even more sharply from 1965 to 1969. As this happened, the number of articles without bylines fell sharply. These were Harry Fabbe's own stories or items that he heavily rewrote. By 1969, fewer than one in five stories did not cite a Swedish wire service as its source. The table below shows what *Svenska Posten* used as its main sources. It excludes minor sources, so percentages may equal less than 100%.[55]

TABLE 6. *Number and percentages of news articles in Svenska Posten, by source 1960–1972.*

Year	ASNE-SIS	*Sverige-Nytt*	Uncredited Items	FLT	*Stockholms-Tidningen*	Yearly Total
1960	337 *(31%)*	268 *(22%)*	573 *(47%)*	—	—	1,221
1965	307 *(26%)*	318 *(27%)*	374 *(32%)*	66 *(6%)*	69 *(6%)*	1,160
1969	552 *(27%)*	552 *(46%)*	224 *(18%)*	103 *(9%)*	—	1,208
1972	150 *(24%)*	178 *(29%)*	285 *(46%)*	62 *(10%)*	—	615

Source: *Svenska Posten*, 1960, 1965, 1969, 1972.

Note: Table 6 excludes *Svenska Posten*'s two special editions for its seventy-fifth anniversary, making 1960's total news articles to 1,324. *Stockholms-Tidningen* closed in 1966.

Table 6 shows *Svenska Posten*'s output remained steadily from 1960 to 1969. The paper had problems in 1971 and 1972: its finances were never good. Editor Harry Fabbe's health also declined, putting him in the hospital for an extended stay. His health finally forced him into retirement by 1972. Thus 1972 may be an anomaly, atypical of a general movement toward using more Swedish material. Through the Sixties, the volume of Harry Fabbe's own stories fell sharply. The amount of ASNE-SIS material rose from just over three hundred articles a year to well over five hundred. The

---

[55] *Svenska Posten* ran two *Dagens Nyheter* items and one *Aftonbladet* article in 1960. In 1965, *SvP* ran eleven items from Swedtravel, six from US, four from *Göteborgs-Posten*, and one each from The Swedish-American Line, *Dagens Nyheter, Sydsvenska Dagbladet, Svenska Dagbladet,* and TT. It ran one story each from *Svenska Dagbladet* and TT in 1969. It ran one item each from *Dagens Nyheter* and TT in 1972.

volume of *Sverige-Nytt* news more than doubled between 1960 and 1969. *Svenska Posten*'s own articles – either Fabbe's own stories, or ones he heavily rewrote – fell from 573 items in 1960 down to 224 articles in 1969. UD tried to help the emigrant papers, but the cost was more Swedish fingerprints on their contents. *Svenska Posten*'s news had an increasingly Swedish feel, and appeared in Swedish terms.

After Karin Person bought it, *Vestkusten* also used regular byline attributions. A casual examination of *VK*'s contents in 1960 shows it used many of the same sources as *SvP*. It did not cite them, however, making a formal content analysis of 1960 futile. Karin Person added bylines to her paper's non-local articles by 1965. I therefore did a content analysis of *Vestkusten* for 1965, 1969, and 1972. I used the same definition of a "news article" as before. *Vestkusten* was a local newspaper, writing for a local community. The content analysis excludes the strictly local news under the headings "San Francisco," "Oakland," "Bay Area," and "Calif." *Vestkusten* dropped some of these headings in the late Sixties, but the news remained. At times, this made deciding what was "local news" difficult. I excluded items on Oakland and San Francisco events unless they were front-page features. The table below shows what *Vestkusten* used as its main sources. As before, the table omits minor sources. Vestkusten also ran one *Göteborgs-Posten* article and a TT story in 1965, and one *Nordstjernan* story in 1969. This means the percentages may equal less than 100%.

TABLE 7. *Number and percentages of news articles in Vestkusten, by source 1965–1972.*

Year	ASNE-SIS	*Sverige-Nytt*	Uncredited items	FLT	Yearly Total
1965	182 (14%)	343 (58%)	750 (26%)	22 (1.7%)	1,300
1969	72 (16%)	62 (14%)	301 (67%)	11 (2.5%)	447
1972	45 (12%)	64 (17%)	249 (68%)	7 (1.9%)	365

Source: *Vestkusten*, 1965, 1969, 1972.
Note: *Vestkusten* continued to refer to SIS as ASNE until 17 July 1969.

Vestkusten

Tidning för Svenskarna på Stillahavskusten

Like *Svenska Posten*, *Vestkusten* also had problems. Its crisis came in early 1968 – *Svenska Posten*'s crisis came in the early Seventies. *VK* cut its news output and printed fewer pages. From January to June 1968, Vestkusten appeared only monthly. From July 1968 onwards, *VK* appeared twice a month. This meant *VK* ran much less news by the late Sixties, as column six shows.

Both *Svenska Posten* and *Vestkusten* had economic crises: *SvP* in 1972 and *VK* in 1968. *SvP* used plenty of *Sverige-Nytt* material before the crisis. By all appearances, it was gradually using ever more of this source. *Vestkusten* also used large amounts of *Sverige-Nytt* in 1965. One can only speculate that *Vestkusten* used it in 1960, and used ever more by mid-decade. When these papers finally faced their economic shocks, they cut back their number of articles sharply. Both papers ran only about half the number of items before their crises. If one looks at percentages, the share of FLT and ASNE-SIS remained steady in both newspapers. Even if raw numbers were down, *Svenska Posten* still gave SIS 25% of its space and *Vestkusten* still gave it 15%. *Svenska Posten* and *Vestkusten* still used FLT for around 8% and 2% of its stories respectively.

The change, however, came in their uses of *Sverige-Nytt*. Both raw numbers and ratios of that source fell off. *Vestkusten*'s use of *Sverige-Nytt* declined especially sharply. In each case, abandoning *Sverige-Nytt* meant a parallel increase in the share of uncredited items. In hard times, these papers preferred their own articles over *Sverige-Nytt* reports. Neither paper paid royalties for *Sverige-Nytt*'s items. The papers' financial problems were thus likely not the cause of this shift. Harry Fabbe and Karin Person did not have to rewrite *Sverige-Nytt*'s stories in their own words to avoid paying royalties. Both papers, however, ran more ads and fewer pages to survive. That put space for news articles at a premium. *Sverige-Nytt*'s stories may have been hard to shorten, but Fabbe and Person could always summarize them. They could always write their own stories to fit a specific amount of limited space. Chances are these short summaries often stemmed from *Sverige-Nytt*. Some short items had themes clearly similar to recently published *Sverige-Nytt* stories.

Whatever the reason, both *SvP* and *VK* ran less *Sverige-Nytt* news (verbatim) after their financial crises. This affected them because *Sverige-Nytt* was their major source for political news. SIS and FLT largely provided cultural news. Vietnam was a political story and most papers relied on *Sverige-Nytt* to cover it. As the table below shows, *Nordstjernan* ran thirteen Vietnam-related stories in 1965. These 1965 "Vietnam-related stories" included antiwar protests, Swedish government comment or policy decisions, or U.S. responses to Swedish actions. (These thirteen "Vietnam-related stories" all refer to Vietnam – or a combatant there – and report events that would not have happened if the U.S. had been at peace.) Twelve of *Nordstjernan*'s thirteen Vietnam-related stories came from the previous week's edition of *Sverige-Nytt*. It depended heavily on *Sverige-Nytt* to report protests and comment on Vietnam. *Svenska Posten* and *Vestkusten* – the papers that used bylines – also depended on *Sverige-Nytt* to report Vietnam. They sometimes changed *Sverige-Nytt*'s original headlines, but the text was usually word-for-word. (See table 9 for information on how much *SvP* and *VK* added or cut from its sources.)

Table 8 below counts how often each paper used *Sverige-Nytt* as its byline. As well as the local *SvP* and *VK*, it also surveys how much *Sverige-Nytt* material *Nordstjernan* used. (The national newspaper *Svenska-Amerikanaren* showed little direct use of *Sverige-Nytt*.) *Nordstjernan* did not use bylines, but usually used *Sverige-Nytt*'s original headlines. This has allowed me to survey how often *Nordstjernan* used *Sverige-Nytt* as a source. A problem was that *Nordstjernan* also used items from *Sverige-Nytt*'s "Senaste nytt i korthet" and "Nytt i sammandrag" sections. These did not carry headlines. To identify these, I compared *Nordstjernan*'s stories to what *Sverige-Nytt* printed the week before. The subject matter and wording often made these stories identifiable as "Nytt i sammandrag" items. (Table 9, however, will show that *Nordstjernan* often added to or rewrote such source material. This adds a note of caution to Table 8.)

TABLE 8. *Three Swedish-American newspapers' apparent dependence on Sverige-Nytt for Vietnam-related news.*

	Svenska Posten		Nordstjernan-Svea		Vestkusten	
Year	Sverige-Nytt	Other Sources	Sverige-Nytt	Other Sources	Sverige-Nytt	Other Sources
1965	5	0	12	1	7	0
1966	11	0	21	3	9	1
1967	12	1	21	7	15	3
1968	16	3	42	14	7	2
1969	18	4	33	20	10	13
1970	16	2	30	13	6	2
Total	78	10	159	58	51	24

Source: *Svenska Posten, Nordstjernan-Svea*, and *Vestkusten*, 1965–1970.

The table shows that as many as 159 of *Nordstjernan*'s 217 Vietnam news stories may have had some origin in *Sverige-Nytt*. Seventy-eight of *Svenska Posten*'s eighty-eight Vietnam-related stories came from *Sverige-Nytt*. That is a larger ratio than the one shown in Table 6. (In 1965, 318 of *SvP*'s 1,160 articles came from *Sverige-Nytt*.) *Vestkusten* got fifty-one of its seventy-five Vietnam-related articles from *Sverige-Nytt*. This table clearly shows the effect of *Vestkusten*'s economic problems. *Nordstjernan*'s coverage of Swedish Vietnam policy doubled from 1967 to 1968, but *Vestkusten*'s fell by half. (*VK* went from a weekly to a monthly, finally emerging as a biweekly paper.) *Vestkusten* shied away from *Sverige-Nytt*'s material during its financial crisis. *Vestkusten* took to writing its own stories on Swedish politics. However, it also became careless about using bylines. Some of its anonymous 1969 stories are identifiable as *Sverige-Nytt* articles. When possible, I listed these as *Sverige-Nytt* articles rather than "other source" items.

Sverige-Nytt was clearly the editors' favored source for Vietnam-related events. Its news was reliable even if its financial stories were purely promotional. For an eight-page newspaper, it gave Vietnam saturation coverage. (It ran 124 Vietnam-related items in 1969, for example.) The ASNE-SIS items were the emigrant press's distant second choice for such news. *Vestkusten* ran eleven ASNE-SIS Vietnam items between 1965 and 1975. Most stories recounted Riksdag speeches or policy statements by Sweden's Prime or Foreign

Ministers. *Svenska Posten* ran nine Vietnam-related SIS articles during this period. Except one story in early 1967, all of them came after Christmas 1969. *SvP*'s SIS items covered improving U.S.-Swedish relations, fewer deserters going to Sweden, cooling Swedish relations with North Vietnam, and Sweden's efforts to help find U.S. prisoners of war. All the SIS items in *SvP* had messages that might ease diplomatic tensions with the United States.

Apart from *Sverige-Nytt* and ASNE-SIS, only a few Vietnam-related stories came from other sources. *Svenska Posten* printed one article and one political cartoon from *Aftonbladet*, and one article each from *Dagens Nyheter*, *Vestmanlands Läns Tidning*, FLT, and TT. *Nordstjernan* ran two TT Vietnam-related articles, and one from the Associated Press. *Vestkusten* ran one Vietnam-related story from *Nordstjernan*. Everything else came from *Sverige-Nytt*, SIS, or did not credit a source.

Table 8 also shows how important Vietnam was to the emigrant papers. *Vestkusten* ran twenty-three Vietnam-related stories in 1969 – a year when it ran 447 news stories. Vietnam represented only 5% of *Vestkusten*'s news coverage. Roughly every *Vestkusten* edition had a Vietnam story (there were twenty-three issues that year). All but five were on the front page. These stories were in a clear minority but received high-profile treatment. *Svenska Posten* ran nearly the same number of Vietnam-related stories in 1969, but printed more than twice as much news. Roughly every other issue of *Svenska Posten* had a Vietnam-related story. Eighteen of its twenty-two Vietnam stories were front-page news. Again, Vietnam was a high-profile but occasional story. Like the other two, *Nordstjernan* treated Vietnam as a biweekly story. The difference was that *Nordstjernan* often printed multiple stories in one issue. In 1968, for example, it ran fifty-six Vietnam-related items spread across twenty-six issues. (There were fifty-two issues that year.) Thirteen issues had more than one Vietnam story; five issues had four or more. One should remember that *Nordstjernan* printed some stories in English, and top stories often appeared in both English and Swedish. This drives up *Nordstjernan*'s total volume of stories, but it is easy to exaggerate the importance of this. If one excludes the direct translations of other stories, then *Nordstjernan* had twelve issues with multiple

Vietnam stories in 1968. *Nordstjernan* gave deeper coverage than most papers during periods of conflict, but less when tensions calmed down. In all three papers, Vietnam was news that appeared in every other issue. Each paper still gave heavy coverage to cultural and social issues. These papers were, after all, cultural organs more than news-bearing periodicals. Vietnam was an important issue in 1969, but it still competed for space in the Swedish-American press against the films *Pippi Longstocking* and *The Emigrants*.

UD's Content Analysis About Editing

Sweden diplomatically recognized North Vietnam in January 1969; it was not popular among many Swedish-American readers. In June 1969, a reader wrote to *Texas Posten*: "Due to the stand taken by Sweden in recognizing North Vietnam, I cannot go along with your advertising of airline and other travel service to that country. Let them keep their Volvos and other products. We do not need any of their products, nor their propaganda." *Texas Posten's* editor Gerald Knape did not try to defend Sweden's behavior. "I stand for the United States, first, last, and always," Knape wrote. "I do not agree with the political views of any foreign government representative."[56]

This letter and tepid response brought UD's long-simmering irritation with *Texas Posten* to a boil. Houston consul Bengt Rösiö felt disgust with the sort of people who read *Texas Posten*. "Most of the Swedish-Americans [there] are extremely conservative, often of the Goldwater-type."

> The first reaction one gets when one comes to Texas is a horrible feeling of helplessness. One is confronted with people who vote for [George] Wallace, admire Rhodesia, and insist that Negroes live in slums because they prefer filth. To get into any sort of meaningful dialogue with them about Vietnam, South Africa, civil rights, or industrial policy is clearly impossible.[57]

---

[56] C.D.C., "Letters to *Texas Posten*," and G.B. Knape, "Letters to *Texas Posten*: Remarks from Editor," *Texas Posten*, 12 June 1969: 2.

[57] Letter from Bengt Rösiö to Gunnar Lonaeus, 19 January 1970, file "1970, jan. – februari," JN1Ua, UD; and memo by Bengt Rösiö, "Texas, Sverige och Vietnam," 12 January 1970, file 6, HP1Ua, UD.

In a later letter, Rösiö added that the values and lifestyles of the Texas-Swedes were "directly repulsive to me."[58] He questioned the value of spending Swedish taxpayer money on people whose values were so contrary to their own. UD Press Bureau's director agreed. "We shouldn't be looking for praise in circles that are so strongly reactionary, racist, or have values so opposed to our own understanding. It would be almost embarrassing to get positive publicity [in *Texas Posten*]."[59]

UD Press Bureau had carefully arranged for *Texas Posten* to receive ASNE, *Sverige-Nytt*, and FLT's news. *Texas Posten* had gotten a steady flow of "reliable news" about Sweden's Vietnam policy for years. Despite this stream of correct information, Swedish-American readers and editors still had scant sympathy for Sweden's position. The Texas-Swedes may be extreme examples of Swedish-Americans, but it was worrying that they had turned on Sweden. SIS's Eva Heckscher wondered if "one of their own" felt this way, how harsh was the feeling in the rest of America? She noted that several emigrant editors opposed Sweden's policy on Vietnam. She believed it was because they still did not understand the policy or Swedish society. "This makes me rather pessimistic about the degree to which they use the material they get from us. They may sort out our material in presenting the current events in Sweden."[60] She assumed Swedish-Americans would agree with Swedish policy if only they understood its good intentions. If not directly agree, she hoped they could at least respect it. Unlike the Houston consul, she still hoped this was possible, provided the Swedish-Americans got the right news.

Heckscher wanted to know how much SIS news material the Swedish-American editors filtered out. She asked SIS's Mia Brandsjö

---

[58] Memo by Bengt Rösiö, "Informationsverksamheten i Houston/USA:s sydstater," 19 April 1971, file "1971, apr. – 10 maj 1971," JN1Ua, UD. (While these are hard words, Professor Larry Scott of Augustana College – author of *The Texas Swedes* – believes they may apply to the Texas-Swedes of the time. Conversation with Larry Scott, April 2002.)

[59] Letter from Sten Sundfeldt to Bengt Rösiö, 4 February 1970, file "1970, jan – februari," JN1Ua, UD.

[60] Letter from Eva Heckscher to Hans Johansson, 15 August and 5 September 1969, file "1969 – 1971 febr.," PR4S, UD.

to do a content analysis of the Swedish-American press. Heckscher did not need anything extensive. She only needed enough to see whether her "understanding of the Swedish-American editors' Sweden-attitude was correct."[61] Brandsjö decided to focus her study on a single month, November 1969. During that month, SIS sent out four weekly issues of *Nyheter från Sverige*. Each issue was four pages each. SIS also mailed twenty articles from FLT, and these could be up to five pages each. There were also the Province Notes; SIS sent out 106 of these during November. Lastly, the editor should also have received two "special releases." One was two pages long, and the other was nine pages. Mia Brandsjö's content analysis does not include *Sverige-Nytt*. She only surveyed the material SIS gave out – the emigrant papers got *Sverige-Nytt* directly from the publisher.

From a news-supply perspective, it was an ordinary month. From a political perspective, it was not. Olof Palme had become the new Social Democratic leader, and he was hardly a popular figure in the U.S. "It will be exciting to see the content analysis results," Heckscher wrote to Brandsjö, "particularly since the 'relatively limited time period' you name includes the period when Swedish-American press had reason to note the shift in the SAP [Social Democratic Party] leadership."[62]

Mia Brandsjö made sure that she got copies of everything SIS sent to the Swedish-American papers.[63] There was some question about whether Brandsjö got the correct Salon Gahlin cartoons, but she considered those less essential.[64] Her focus would be on the FLT articles, the weekly issues of *Nyheter från Sverige*, and the Province Notes. She would count how many articles the Swedish-American papers used, and whether the newspapers cut or altered them.

---

[61] Letter from Eva Heckscher to Hans Johansson, 5 September 1969, file "1969 – 1971 febr.," PR4S, UD.

[62] Letter from Eva Heckscher to Mia Brandsjö, 7 October 1969, file "1969 – 1971 febr.," PR4S, UD.

[63] Letter from Mia Brandsjö to Eva Heckscher, 15 October 1969, file "1969 – 1971 febr.," PR4S, UD.

[64] Letter from Eva Nauckhoff to Mia Brandsjö and Eva Heckscher, 15 October 1969, and Brandsjö's reply to Nauckhoff, 29 October 1969, file "1969 – 1971 febr.," PR4S, UD.

Brandsjö's final content analysis has four categories. One counts the articles that gave the uncut *total* text of the source material. Another lists articles given only in *part*; the editors had cut these stories. The third group counts articles where editors *extended* the source material with their own added comments. The last group includes articles the editors rewrote to the extent they were different stories, but still had a *common* subject as the source material.

TABLE 9. *Swedish-American press's use of source material distributed by SIS, content analysis November 1969.*

1. *California Veckoblad* – 5, 12, 19 November 1969

	Total	Part	Extended	Common
Province Notes	–	–	4	–
FLT feature stories	–	–	–	–
Nyheter från Sverige	–	–	–	2

2. *Canada-Tidningen* – 1, 15 November 1969

	Total	Part	Extended	Common
Province Notes	1	–	1	–
FLT feature stories	6	–	–	–
Nyheter från Sverige	–	–	–	1
Special Release	–	–	–	–

3. *Nordstjernan-Svea* – 6, 13, 20, 27 November 1969

	Total	Part	Extended	Common
Province Notes	–	–	4	–
FLT feature stories	–	–	–	1
Nyheter från Sverige	4	–	3	9

4. *Svenska-Amerikanaren Tribunen* – 5, 12, 19 November 1969

	Total	Part	Extended	Common
Province Notes	–	–	4	–
FLT feature stories	2	–	–	–
Nyheter från Sverige	9	–	–	5

5. *Svenska Posten* – 5, 12, 19 November 1969

	Total	Part	Extended	Common
Province Notes	–	5	–	–
FLT feature stories	4	–	–	–
Nyheter från Sverige	7	–	–	–

6. *Texas Posten* – 4, 6, 13, 20 November 1969

	Total	Part	Extended	Common
Province Notes	–	5	–	–
FLT feature stories	4	–	–	–
Nyheter från Sverige	7	–	–	–

7. *Vestkusten* – 13, 27 November 1969

	Total	Part	Extended	Common
Province Notes	–	–	2	–
FLT feature stories	1	–	–	–
Nyheter från Sverige	2	2	–	1

Total edited stories	46	12	18	19

Source: Memorandum "Swedish-American Newspapers; Brief content analysis Nov 1969," Swedish Information Service, December 1969, mailed as attachment to letters to Sten Sundfeldt and Gunnar Lonnaeus, 20 January 1969, file "1969 - 1971 febr.," PR4S, UD.

This content analysis shows that every newspaper used the material SIS sent out, but none hesitated to change it. Indeed, *California Veckoblad* never used the SIS material as it was. It always inserted material into the articles or rewrote them. *California Veckoblad* received the FLT dispatches but did not use them. It was the only paper, maybe except *Nordstjernan*, not to run the FLT material. This analysis shows the emigrant papers often used FLT's stories and were not likely to rewrite them. *Nyheter från Sverige* was also a popular source, and it often got rewritten. *Vestkusten* was the only newspaper that ever edited its stories down; most others added to them. Together, this shows that SIS contributed significantly to the emigrant papers' news layout.

Mia Brandsjö's study shows the Swedish-American editors did not hesitate to change material when they wanted. The Swedish-American editors edited their news. UD supplied Swedish news with a Swedish perspective on world events. It reported Sweden's Vietnam policy as *our* policy, legislated by *our* government. Swedish policy came across as reasonable and prudent. If this was a deliberate policy to influence the Swedish-Americans, the editors undercut it. *Nordstjernan* added its own material to SIS's news stories, and likely to *Sverige-Nytt*'s as well. *Svenska Posten* ran some SIS articles whole, but leaving some parts out. *Svenska-Amerikanaren* and *Nordstjernan* often rewrote the Swedish material in their own words. These additions and rewording came from other media streams to complement the original Swedish text. A reasonable inference is that many were American news streams, perhaps added for balance. The rewritten articles came from editors conditioned by the mainstream American news media.

The Swedish Press's Sture Wermee considered much of the free Swedish material he received "just propaganda."[65] This may well have been a common view. *Vestkusten*'s Karin Person had reservations about the Swedish material. She thought FLT's stories were too Swedish for her audience. She also disliked SIS's *Nyheter från Sverige* partly because it lacked an American perspective.[66]

That an emigrant editor saw the Swedish news as propaganda reveals the different standards of objectivity in the U.S. and Sweden. Objectivity is a cultural idea, defined by the neutral center of society's political debate. The political debate in Sweden was further to the political left than in America. The neutral center of political debate was also further to the political left. News that Swedes might have judged objective could have seemed value-laden and biased to Americans. The system UD helped set up encouraged using this supposedly biased news. This was not a problem with most Swedish

---

[65] Telephone conversation with Sture Wermee, 7 June 1999.

[66] Letter from Karin Person to Harriet Albert, 16 February 1967, file "1963 – mars 1967"; letter from Karin Person to Anne Henriksson, 27 June 1968, file "1967, April – 1968, Dec.," box I:462, PR4S, RA; and memo "Redogörelse med protokoll för möte med representanter för den svensk-amerikanska (inkl. svensk-kanadensiska) pressen i Minneapolis 1975-05-27 och 1975-05-28," 13 June 1975, file "1975," PR4S, UD.

social news stories. It was different with Vietnam, where a left-wing bias hinted at disloyalty and social unrest.

The American understanding of objectivity is that fact and value should be separate. Opinion and news should not mix. Much of Europe has a tradition of politically-oriented papers that do not necessarily hold this mandate. The Swedish definition of objectivity had four basic parts: truthfulness, relevance, balance, and neutral presentation that does not mislead. If papers clearly linked themselves with a political party, then a degree of partiality was acceptable. The U.S. idea of objectivity demanded independence from political actors like parties or governments.[67] Swedish-American readers would have bristled at receiving news from any paper tied to any political party. This was propaganda by definition for them.

From the other side, UD Press Bureau saw U.S. media coverage of Swedish foreign policy as distorted.[68] Correcting distortions of Swedish foreign policy is a legitimate part of UD Press Bureau's role. Its job is to educate the American public of what it considered "the facts" of Swedish policy. This included Swedish-American society. UD increasingly arranged for the emigrant press to get what it saw as reliable news. It used a Swedish definition of objectivity in deciding what was reliable news. Yet, what one culture sees as educating the public may feel like propaganda to another.

Other Factors Influencing News Presentation

As the last chapter noted, Swedish-America was undergoing a generation shift. Older readers were dying and editors had to reach out to younger Swedish-American readers. Many of them could not read Swedish, which made reaching out to them difficult. Except *Svenska-Amerikanaren*, all emigrant papers underwent financial problems. Most of them eventually asked UD for help. UD became increasingly involved in the Swedish-American press's affairs during

---

[67] Westerståhl, *Vietnam i Sveriges Radio*, 1–6; Hallin, *The Uncensored War*, 63–70; Anthony Smith, *The Shadow of the Cave*, London, 1973: 1950-153; see also Herbert J. Gans, *Deciding What's News*, New York, 1979: chapter 6.

[68] Memo, "Protokoll över upplysningskommittéens sammanträde i New York den 15–16 juni 1970: bilaga 1," file "1970, juli-augusti," JN1Ua, UD.

the Sixties. This involvement, however, was at the editors' request. The major problem was a legal one. U.S. law forbids foreign states from directly supporting American papers unless they register as "agents of a foreign government." The Swedish-American press would never accept that, so UD could not give it direct cash grants.[69]

That limited what UD could do to help the emigrant papers. In the Sixties, UD mostly tried defraying their other costs by supplying as much free news as possible. If SIS gave the emigrant papers free news bulletins, they could use their news budgets for other purposes. This generosity removed more expensive American sources as realistic alternatives. The growing volume of Swedish news was largely the result of editors asking UD to help them.

Most Swedish-language newspapers still used letter-press production in the Sixties. It produced an attractive newspaper, but typesetting them was time-consuming and expensive. It usually meant the editors had to typeset their newspapers themselves or hire a Swedish typesetter. Swedish typesetters were rare, so some Swedish-language papers resorted to hiring American typesetters. Professional typesetters could set a newspaper without understanding the words they were setting, but it took longer. They also received the same hourly pay as a Swedish typesetter. Some editors asked UD to create stipends for young Swedish typesetters to work as interns for them.[70] (UD was cool to this idea.) Most editors saw converting to offset-printing as a better long-term solution. With this method, the editors would cut out articles, arrange them onto a storyboard, photograph them, and print the photograph. It was a far faster and cheaper production method than the letter-press system. The main problem was that converting to offset would be an expensive process few newspapers could afford. UD helped *Nordstjernan* raise twenty thousand dollars for *Nordstjernan's*

---

[69] For a discussion of the Foreign Agents Registration Act, see: Utvandrarnas tidningar, 40.

[70] Karin Person, quoted in Åke, "Liten intervju med duktig kollega västerifrån," *Dagens Nyheter*, 15 March 1968: 18; memo by Karin Person, "Promemoria: angående stöd åt den svenskamerikanska pressen," 23 September 1969, attached to letter from Karin Person to Harry Fabbe, 25 September 1969, file "*Vestkusten*," box 1, SvP, UW.

change-over in 1973. (It also raised around twenty-five thousand kronor for *Nordstjernan* in 1966.)[71] It did not do the same for other papers.

Svenska Posten converted to offset in February 1968.[72] This made it easier for Harry Fabbe to cut-and-paste *Sverige-Nytt* articles for *Svenska Posten*. This could be one reason why *SvP's* use of *Sverige-Nytt* jumped from 318 articles in 1965 to 552 items four years later. Also, UD encouraged the Swedish-American papers to convert to offset. SIS planned to send its news and photos in offset form in the future.

The main value in offset printing, however, is that it was cheaper. Offset printing meant editors could lower subscription rates and thus expand circulation. This expansion would largely occur among younger readers. As noted in the last chapter, younger Swedish-Americans might subscribe to a Swedish-American paper if it was in English. It would also help if it ran more news on modern Swedish society and culture rather than nostalgic items on emigration-era Sweden. The dilemma was these changes would attract younger readers but risked angering older ones. Newspapers also had to address these audience demographic problems while they addressed their production problems. The solutions to both problems pointed to more coverage of Swedish politics, implying growing coverage of Vietnam protests.

The newspapers that have survived moved quickly to solve these problems in the late Sixties. *Vestkusten* saw the younger generation as an unexploited audience and increased the amount of English for them. *VK* also printed much more political-news than the similarly local newspaper *Svenska Posten*. *Svenska Posten* resisted converting to English until it was too late, but *Vestkusten* moved quickly. *Vestkusten's* share of political Vietnam-related news was twice the percentage *Svenska Posten* printed. In the early Seventies, *Svenska Posten* embraced nostalgia and lightweight articles rather than

---

[71] Memo, "Förslag till planläggning av svensk-amerikanska pressutredningen," 25 June 1973, file "1973 – 1974," PR4S, UD; and letter from Sten Sundfeldt to Kjell Öberg, 9 September 1966, file "1963 – Mars 1967," box I:462, PR4S, RA.

[72] Letter from Karin Person to Harry Fabbe, 1 February 1968, file "*Vestkusten,*" box 1, SvP, UW.

politics and culture. It retrenched with politically safe material rather than aggressively pursuing the younger readers. Of these two similar local Swedish-American newspapers, only *Vestkusten* remains today. As a New York paper, *Nordstjernan* had long reported Swedish politics and trade. It thus found it easier to capture these younger readers, especially since it gradually switched to English. *Svenska-Amerikanaren* also exists today thanks largely to its deep pockets thirty years ago and its national base.

Conclusions

Chapter two showed UD was dissatisfied with Sweden's image in America as the Sixties began. As in the past, the emigrant papers often irritated UD with their negative portrayals of Sweden. Eisenhower's unfortunate remarks displayed a widespread tendency to link socialism to moral decay. UD effectively contained that controversy by spreading its own statistics and analyses, and the emigrant papers ran them with enthusiasm. Its position on Vietnam soon became Sweden's next major controversy in America. This dispute threatened to do even worse damage to Sweden's image in America.

This chapter shows UD increasingly provided low-cost news to the Swedish-American papers. UD soon arranged an entire news-supply system for the Swedish-American press. Tables 6 and 7 show that *Svenska Posten* and *Vestkusten* increasingly depended on Swedish news. This Swedish news came through official Swedish government channels. Table 8 shows that *Nordstjernan*, *Svenska Posten* and *Vestkusten* used one Swedish source – *Sverige-Nytt* – heavily to report Vietnam-related news. This was all news written from a Swedish viewpoint. The different perspective painted Sweden's position with more sympathy. The *we*-perspective – reporting *our* policy, decided by *our* leaders – was naturally more understanding than having it reported as a foreign government's policy. UD may have hoped this perspective would get Swedish-Americans to identify with the Swedish position.

UD arguably tried to exploit the Swedish-American press. It provided free news. The emigrant papers were impoverished and simply could not refuse anything that was free. Yet, no document directly links this news-supply policy to UD's concern over emigrant criticism of Swedish Vietnam policy. Perhaps except for UD's content analysis, there is no "smoking gun" here. There are many documents, however, showing the emigrant editors trying to exploit UD. (For example: *Western News* wanted UD to arrange for the Swedish-American papers to win a Nobel Prize, and they would all share the prize money.)[73] Their finances were a mess and their papers were collapsing. The editors tried to get whatever they could from UD. When the Swedish-American Press Commission began its work, the editors clearly saw UD had its own plans for them. Their strategy was to take as much as possible from UD, but concede as little as possible.

In the Sixties, UD mostly offered just different forms of free or low-cost news. There were better ways to support the emigrant press, even if they had dubious legality. UD could have helped find used printing machinery, give stipends for typographers to visit the emigrant papers, or give grants to Swedish organizations to advertise in the Swedish-American press. Even if these violated the Foreign Agents Registration Act, it is debatable if the U.S. government would have enforced it. UD never considered quietly slipping the emigrant papers money under the table. UD never even asked the Department of Justice to grant a limited exemption for the Swedish-American press. UD simply had a better plan: a far cheaper one. Providing free news would help these papers at little cost to the Swedish taxpayer, and might control their negative portrayals of Sweden. With the growing conflict over Vietnam, UD had good reason to fear coming criticism from them.

UD got the U.S.-Swedish conflict over Vietnam reported mostly in a national-Swedish perspective. Yet Table 9 shows that some newspapers – notably *Nordstjernan* and *Svenska-Amerikanaren* – added onto or rewrote the Swedish material. Many other stories got into print unchanged. UD was partially able to regulate what the Swedish-Americans knew about Sweden's Vietnam policy. It is reasonable to assume the data readers get on an issue affects the opinions they hold about it. By this reasoning, UD had some sway

---

[73] Letter from Enoch Peterson to UD, 24 January 1972, file "1971 mars - jan 1972," PR4S, UD.

over opinions emigrant readers might form on Swedish Vietnam policy. Was it actually enough influence to change minds? The next three chapters will examine the Swedish-American press opinion on the Vietnam War and Sweden's Vietnam policy. The following chapter looks at how the Swedish-American press commented on the Vietnam War. Did UD's news – filled with Swedish arguments about why the war was wrong – influence any emigrant editors or readers?

Chapter Four

The Swedish-American Press on Vietnam

My grandfather made several business trips to Sweden during the Sixties and early Seventies. He came to Sweden to discuss gas meters and pipelines. Each time he came, he also had to answer difficult questions on the war in Vietnam. The questions were often sharp in 1965, but softened with each passing year. He was an American with a clearly Swedish name: Hilding. Many Swedes thus assumed he would sympathize with Sweden's view of the war, at least more than other Americans did. These questions and assumptions often made his trips to Sweden uneasy experiences. Returning home, there could be even more questions about what he thought of Sweden's position on Vietnam.

My thesis examines this tension as it appeared in the Swedish-American press. Swedish-Americans like my grandfather often felt they faced two separate problems during the war. The first was how much and on what conditions they should support the war in Vietnam. How they should handle Sweden's criticism of the war was a separate but connected problem. How they would deal with the second problem would partly depend on how they resolved the first one. How did they view the war and how far did they support it? When and under which conditions did they withdraw their support? Did UD manage to influence how they thought about these problems? This chapter will examine how the emigrant papers dealt with these problems on the Vietnam War.

Most debate on Southeast Asia alone occurred from 1965 to 1967. From 1967 onward, Sweden's policy on Vietnam attracted ever more attention. Swedish Vietnam policy quickly became the main topic of discussion by the late Sixties. At times, some emigrant journalists framed nearly all their views on Vietnam relative to Sweden.

This chapter takes up Swedish-American treatment of the Vietnam issue. As much as possible, it separates the debate on U.S. foreign policy from the parallel debate on Swedish policy. There were several broad themes or subjects of discussion in the Vietnam debate. The first motif involves what the emigrant papers knew about Vietnam during the conflict's early years. The Kennedy administration made most of the crucial commitments to supporting the Saigon government. The second theme covers the 1964 and 1965 decisions to enter the Vietnam War. Events in these years pushed Lyndon Johnson to decide whether the U.S. should go to war to uphold earlier promises to Saigon. Johnson's decision created conflict among Americans. This chapter's third subject is how this dissent over Vietnam affected *Svenska Posten*. It was a typical emigrant newspaper in many ways, but it took a very different position on Vietnam than most other papers. This third section uses the newspaper's archive to examine how this happened. The religious emigrant newspapers often had different views on American society. Their opinions on Vietnam form this chapter's fourth topic. As the war went on without a victory, people looked for scapegoats for the lack of American success. The fifth theme concerns the groups Swedish-American newspapers blamed for not helping win the war. This chapter's last topic is the dirty process of extracting the U.S. from Vietnam. In summary, this chapter takes up six major themes in Southeast Asia:

- The Kennedy Administration in Indochina
- Entering the war in Vietnam
- *Svenska Posten's* internal dissent over the war
- The religious press and the Vietnam War
- Finding someone to blame: priests and protesters
- Trying to find a way out: invasions, massacres, and bombings

The Kennedy Administration in Indochina

The years from 1960 to 1964 were crucial in setting the Unites States on the inexorable path to war. These were the years when

Washington guaranteed South Vietnamese security, with American troops if need be. The U.S. military presence in Vietnam rose from 685 to 16,732 uniformed men. It was a shadowy role, with U.S. soldiers posing as advisers but secretly doing more than giving advice. By the time Lyndon Johnson became President the U.S. was spending four hundred million dollars yearly in Vietnam.[1]

The Kennedy administration wanted to downplay the story as much as possible. It wanted the press to report the U.S. role as something less than it really was.[2] The administration managed to keep debate on Vietnam at a low rumble. Debate was largely absent from the Swedish-language press. Swedish-American commentators saw Vietnam – as much as they thought about it – as part of a communist plan to take over Asia.

The Swedish-language press had much to say about communism in Asia and something to say on Indochina. It had only a little to say about Vietnam. It believed the main Indochina problem was in Laos. Already leading the Indochina debate, *Nordstjernan* wrote, "The communists are on the offensive in Laos, supported with weapons and ammunition from the Soviet Union and Red China. The chance of a new Korea is clear. It is either that or a disgraceful retreat of the Western powers, losing their foothold in Southeast Asia." *Nordstjernan*'s Eric Sylvan thought it was only a matter of time before the Soviet Union completely devoured Laos.[3]

Nobody wanted a new Korea – still the model for the long, unpopular Asian land war. Several commentators thought the U.S. should send foreign aid to help friendly Asian governments. The religious papers pointed out that in practice the money was going to the wrong purposes. *The Covenant Companion* thought U.S. foreign aid had been counterproductive so far. It had worked against the interests of both the American and Asian people.[4] *The Messenger* believed the U.S. should give money for hospitals, schools, and

---

[1] Michael J. Hunt, *Lyndon Johnson's War*, New York, 1996: 66.
[2] Philip Knightly, *The First Casualty*, New York, 1975: 376.
[3] "Dystert nyårsperspektiv," 5 January 1961: 6; and Eric Sylvan, "Det Tycks," *Nordstjernan*, 27 April 1961: 6.
[4] "A New Concept in Foreign Aid," *Covenant Companion*, 20 September 1963: 24.

Photo courtesy of Nordstjernan.

improving farming methods. Instead, it was sending weapons that threatened the welfare of the Laotian poor. The U.S. was sending military aid to Laos to solve a social problem.[5]

Others supported more military aid. *Nordstjernan*'s Eric Sylvan saw Kennedy as "sort of wimpy" in hesitating to send military aid. "He is hesitating to send American troops before it is too late and South Vietnam, like Laos, is lost. What is he waiting for? For the communists to change their minds and give up their plans for world domination?"[6]

Kennedy increased the aid and sent military advisers to South Vietnam and Laos. *Nordstjernan* thought he should send more, better, and more suitable military aid to South Vietnam. There were many examples of waste and ineffectiveness. On its front page, *Nordstjernan* ran a photo of artillery crew in Laos. The caption said "These howitzers: they shoot at random into the jungle 'wherever there is movement.'" It added that cars, trucks, weapons had gone to waste in Indochina. Many of them had simply rusted away

---

[5] Rev B.W. Selin, "The Observation Tower," *The Messenger* (*Sändebudet*), 15 May 1961: 2.

[6] Eric Sylvan, "Det Tycks," *Nordstjernan*, 9 November 1961: 6.

Svenska Posten ran this drawing of President Kennedy on 4 September 1963.

without ever having seen use.[7] In May 1964, *Nordstjernan*'s Eric Sylvan ran part of a letter by Air Force Captain Jerry Shank, recently killed in action. Shank's letter underlined the failure, waste, deceit, and poor planning of the U.S. policy in Vietnam.[8] Publishing such photos and letters told readers the U.S. should correct its Vietnam policy or not do it at all.

Nordstjernan's Eric Sylvan thought this waste and mismanagement suggested a deeper problem. The South Vietnamese people were apathetic in supporting the anti-communist cause. Americans could not defend people who were unwilling to defend themselves. If they were unwilling to risk their own lives, Sylvan argued, Washington should not risk American lives to help them. If U.S. prestige was at stake in Asia, Washington should find some other place to display it.[9] A *Nordstjernan* reader agreed: "Our involvement in South Vietnam seems utterly senseless." Samuel Youngquist also considered it ill-advised to risk

---

[7] "Laos – brandfaran i Asien," *Nordstjernan*, 6 April 1961: 1.

[8] Eric Sylvan, "Det tycks," *Nordstjernan*, 28 May 1964: 5. Captain Jerry Shank's letter from *U.S. News and World Report*, 4 May 1964. Shanks' letters have been reprinted in *Reporting Vietnam: American Journalism 1959–1975*, vol. 1, New York, 1998: 124–133.

[9] Eric Sylvan, "Det Tycks," *Nordstjernan*, 17 January 1963: 6.

American lives on people unwilling to fight communism themselves. Going into South Vietnam would thus be "a hopeless venture that may lead us into another Korea."[10]

There was not much debate on Vietnam during the Kennedy years. The consensus was the U.S. should resist communist expansion in Indochina, but avoid "a new Korea." This probably meant sending some form of foreign aid – it was unclear what form of aid would be preferable. The Swedish-American papers wanted President Kennedy to take a firm and decisive stand, but not go to war. *Nordstjernan* already led the debate on Vietnam, largely through Eric Sylvan's columns. The religious papers also discussed the Vietnam issue. Their stand was more humanistic than *Nordstjernan's*, which often saw the problem from a military and political perspective.

Entering the War in Vietnam

In the Johnson administration's early years, the caution of avoiding "a new Korea" faded. In 1963, *Nordstjernan's* Eric Sylvan called Vietnam "a hopeless situation." By 1964, rather than pulling out, Sylvan wanted to stay and fight. He now thought the insurgents received support and direction from China and the Soviet Union.[11] *Svenska Posten's* Otto B. Jacobson agreed that China and the U.S.S.R. wanted to turn Indochina into a "communist empire."[12] Few now doubted that international communist aggression threatened South Vietnam. It was an election year. The Republican Party was not running against Kennedy's decision to get involved in Vietnam. It was now running against Lyndon Johnson's reluctance to do more.

On 2 August 1964, North Vietnamese patrol boats attacked the U.S. destroyer Maddox while it mapped Northern military bases. Two days later, another American ship reported a second attack. (Rather than an attack, tropical weather conditions may have

---

[10] Samuel Youngquist, "Ordet är Fritt," *Nordstjernan*, 24 January 1963: 5.

[11] Eric Sylvan, "Det Tycks," 17 January 1963: 6; and Eric Sylvan, "Det Tycks," *Nordstjernan*, 9 January and 28 May 1964: 4.

[12] Otto B. Jacobson, "Från läsekretsen: Till vännen Sigfrid R. Johnson," *Svenska Posten*, 26 August 1964: 4.

created false radar contacts.) President Johnson responded to the reports of a second attack with air-strikes against North Vietnam. The Swedish-American press supported the White House position, and these air-strikes drew especially positive reactions. *Svenska Posten*'s Otto Jacobson thought Johnson showed firm leadership, and commended him for going on the offensive.[13] *Nordstjernan* also praised LBJ's decisive response to events in the Tonkin Gulf. It said the U.S. could not afford to have the communist world see the U.S. as a mere paper tiger. "The 'Paper Tiger' has shown its teeth."[14] The Swedish-American papers were solidly in the mainstream opinion. Eighty-five percent of the American public supported the bombing raids. Johnson's raids also found wide approval in the mainstream U.S. press.[15] Still, Otto Jacobson warned the crisis could lead to "another Korea where hordes of bloodthirsty soldiers under the monster Mao [Tse] Tung's command pour southward to defend the northern half."[16] Three of the ten Swedish-American Vietnam editorials contained warning references to "a new Korea."

America went to war in 1965. U.S. troop strength in Vietnam jumped from 23,300 to 184,300 soldiers between January and December.[17] Despite this, Swedish-American press commentary was scarce. Only *Nordstjernan* and *Svenska Posten* approached the war as a serious political issue. Most of *Nordstjernan*'s commentary came from the steadily hawkish Eric Sylvan. He argued the U.S. ought to help South Vietnam in the same way it should have helped Western Europe in the Nineteen-Thirties. The pacifists that urged negotiations in Vietnam were heirs of Neville Chamberlain's supporters in 1938. (Public opinion favor negotiating with the FNL by 1966, and even Sylvan came to this view.)[18] Sylvan spent much of 1965 condemning what he saw as the pacifists' short-sighted view of Vietnam.

---

[13] Otto B. Jacobson, "Från läsekretsen: Till vännen Sigfrid R. Johnson," *Svenska Posten*, 26 August 1964: 4.

[14] "'Papperstigern' visar tänderna," *Nordstjernan*, 13 August 1964: 4.

[15] Clarence R. Wyatt, *Paper Soldiers*, New York, 1993: 131.

[16] Otto B. Jacobson, "Från läsekretsen: Till vännen Sigfrid R. Johnson," *Svenska Posten*, 26 August 1964: 4.

[17] James S. Olson and Randy Roberts, *Where The Domino Fell*, New York, 1991: 300–301.

SVENSKA POSTEN
The Swedish Post
_{Lösnummer 10 cents.}

SPOKESMAN FOR THE SWEDISH-AMERICAN POPULATION OF THE PACIFIC NORTHWEST

Svenska Posten's Otto Jacobson used an older metaphor for Vietnam. He believed America needed another leader like Abraham Lincoln. Lincoln held his principles when defeatists urged him to seek a disastrous negotiated peace. The pacifists against the Vietnam War were moral heirs to the Copperhead Democrats during the Civil War. These appeasers were also condemning the Vietnamese to lives of slavery – bondage under communism.[19]

Svenska Posten's Reinhold Ahleen also saw the Soviets and Chinese as backing the North Vietnamese. China was trying to expand communism in Asia, but Vietnam was the scene of a civil war. If the United States got involved there, Ahleen predicted it would be unpopular and hard to leave. However, he believed American power would eventually wear down North Vietnamese resistance.[20] He also believed this was not a necessary war. Unlike the World Wars, the Civil War, or the wars with Britain, America could have stayed out of this war. It was Lyndon Johnson's voluntary decision, and thus without equivalent in U.S. history. He hoped the U.S. could get out of Vietnam through some peacefully negotiated settlement.[21] Ahleen's personal diaries show that he watched the developing situation Vietnam with unease that spring:

> 6 February – The Vietnam War is as bad as ever. Several American soldiers killed.

---

[18] Eric Sylvan, "Det Tycks," *Nordstjernan*, 23 April 1965 and 14 April 1966: 6. (In early 1966, however, 80% of Americans favored negotiations with the FNL, and 70% favored free elections even if the FNL won. William M. Hammond, *The Military and the Media, 1962–1968*, Washington, 1988: 227–228.)

[19] Otto B. Jacobson, "Ett och annat av Otto B. Jacobson," *Svenska Posten*, 5 May 1965: 3.

[20] Reinhold Ahleen, "Rim och Reson av Reinhold Ahleen," *Svenska Posten*, 7 April, 12 May 1965.

[21] Reinhold Ahleen, "Rim och Reson av Reinhold Ahleen," *Svenska Posten*, 23 June 1965: 4.

9 February – 1,000 students threw stones smashing the windows in the American Embassy in Moscow because the U.S. defended itself in the Vietnam War. Heavy Fighting in Vietnam. Looks bad. 34 soldiers killed in South Vietnam.

10 February – Wounded soldiers from Vietnam are flown to U.S. hospitals.

19 February – The Vietnam situation is still serious. China wants U.S. to withdraw the troops.

21 February – There's a struggle for power in Vietnam.

22 February – The Vietnam [situation] still looks serious. The general of the Vietnam army has resigned.

24 February – China, Russia, and France want U.S. to get out of Vietnam before peace negotiations can start.

28 February – It looks bad at present in Vietnam. No peace in sight. Russia condemns U.S. for being in Vietnam.

3 March – The war in Vietnam continues. More bombing of guerrillas by American planes.

8 March – The Buddhists in North Vietnam want the U.S. troops to withdraw from South Vietnam. Then the Reds can take over . . . The war is growing fiercer in Vietnam.

None of Ahleen's notes are profound. They do, however, effectively capture the sense of anxiety of 1965. There was a sense that America might be slowly slipping into something it was unable to handle. Ahleen's diary reveals some surprise the U.S. did not win a quick victory that summer. By 1 September 1965, Ahleen noted, "The war in Vietnam continues, and it looks to be a drawn-out affair." This subdued Ahleen's enthusiasm for the war.[22]

Svenska Posten's Internal Dissent over the War

Dissent soon began appearing in the Swedish-American press. No other paper came out against the war more than *Svenska Posten*. *SvP*'s editor, Harry Fabbe, was a liberal Democrat and once wrote for *Svenska Socialisten*. The Democratic Party saw Fabbe as a rare friend in the Swedish-American press.[23] He was one of the few editors receptive to Swedish Social Democratic views and criticism. His paper was among the few places where Swedish-Americans on

---

[22] Reinhold Ahleen's personal diary, 1965, box 1, Ahleen, UW.

[23] Letter from DNC Chairman Robert F. Wagner to Harry Fabbe, 22 December 1964, subfile "Democratic National Committee," file "Incoming Letters," box 1, SvP, UW.

the political left could still get in print. Columnist Eric Olson, for example, marked his opposition to the war quite early. In a June 1965 column, he asked, "What will it cost us to make up for and rebuild all the bridges we have bombed, all the villages we have burned with our napalm bombs – plus a starving and maimed nation that may require our help for an indefinite future?"[24] *Svenska Posten* ran such controversial views in 1965 when Vietnam was still a popular cause.

Editor Harry Fabbe turned against Johnson's Vietnam policy in 1966. Most Swedish-American papers identified with the Republican Party, and fighting communism was an article of party faith. Fabbe's opposition to the war brought him into conflict with some of his pro-war columnists. *Svenska Posten*'s loudest voice for war was columnist Otto B. Jacobson. He believed North Vietnam was forcing communism on South Vietnam, and provoked the U.S. into action. If the U.S. let North Vietnam take the South, then "the overlords of communism" would swallow the entire area.[25] Jacobson could not understand those – including his editor – that argued for leaving Vietnam. Relations between Jacobson and Fabbe were poor during 1965. As a result, Jacobson vanished from *Svenska Posten* for several months. He returned in early 1966, but public unity masked deep bitterness between the two men. "Maybe you don't agree with me," Jacobson wrote in a personal letter to Fabbe. "Maybe you believe as the majority of Swedes do that we ought to pull out of Vietnam . . . but personally I believe that regarding Vietnam you're all **Blind!!**"[26]

Fabbe edited his columns, enraging Jacobson. The cuts sometimes implied things Jacobson never meant. "My last article in particular was shorter than all the rest," Jacobson wrote to Fabbe, "yet you deliberately cut it to a severe minimum. My friend – if you want me to disappear from your pages – just keep cutting a little

[24] Eric Olson, "Från Läsekretsen," *Svenska Posten*, 23 June 1965: 4.

[25] Otto B. Jacobson, "Answers Murray, Mullen on Viet Nam," *Skagit Valley Herald*, early 1966. (Attached to letter from Otto B. Jacobson to Harry Fabbe, 28 February 1965, file "Incoming Letters," box 1, SvP, UW.)

[26] Letter from Otto B. Jacobson to Harry Fabbe, 28 February 1965, file "Incoming Letters," box 1, SvP, UW.

Ett och
Annat
Av Otto B.
Jacobson

Svenska-Posten's Otto B. Jacobson.

while longer and I'll be glad to do just that."[27] The end came for
Jacobson in July 1966. Harry Fabbe printed a caustic editorial based
on information from a "daily newspaper." Fabbe wrote:

> Civilization is celebrating a military triumph in Vietnam against some of the
> world's poorest peasants. Giant planes dump bombs, helicopters and other
> planes fire at people with automatic weapons. So-called war correspondents
> count bodies. Peace and goodwill are spread with cluster bombs, bombs that
> explode over a large area and send shrapnel or even small droplets of napalm.
> . . .[28]

It was Fabbe's most outspoken condemnation thus far. Otto
Jacobson was furious:

> Dear friend, I have long suspected your personal views as to our effort against
> our common enemy, communism in Vietnam. Now after reading your last
> editorial where you wholeheartedly seem to sanction the view of that "daily
> press" (American or Swedish?) what it may be, I personally feel it useless for
> me to support your paper anymore but I think it best that we now part
> forever as editor and writer . . . It's best to quit now instead of trying to
> convince a blind nation, a blind people that our boys (of which one is mine)
> are fighting and dying in Vietnam in order to preserve not only your and my
> future freedom only, but the future freedom of Sweden as well.[29]

---

[27] Letter from Otto B. Jacobson to Harry Fabbe, 18 March 1965, file "Incoming
Letters," box 1, SvP, UW.

[28] "Hört och Hänt: 'Civilisationen' vinner terräng," *Svenska Posten*, 6 July
1966: 1, 4.

[29] Letter from Otto B. Jacobson to Harry Fabbe, "7-8-66," file "Incoming
Letters," box 1, SvP, UW.

Jacobson believed Fabbe based his editorial on Swedish material. "Your 'daily press' forgets to mention the real reasons our boys are dying out there," Jacobson wrote.[30] He thought the Swedish press did not put the conflict in the proper context. Europe's media questioned U.S. official policy, and the Cold War ideology had less influence over them.[31] Harry Fabbe thus used Swedish material in his editorials for just this reason. (This developed into a debate in itself, discussed in the following chapter.)

Early in the war, Jacobson wrote about U.S. experiments with non-lethal gases in Vietnam. This included battlefield use of tear gas, and gases that caused diarrhea and nausea. "I could hardly contain myself when I thought about it," wrote Jacobson. "Just think if one – or many – of the enemy had their guns trained on a South Vietnamese or American adviser. Right then they would have to throw their guns down and run behind the nearest bushes."[32] Most of Europe's media saw this as far less humorous. The European press widely criticized the use of gas, which suggested a new and sinister policy in Asia. The debate showed just how isolated the United States had become on the Vietnam issue.[33]

Sverige-Nytt ran an article on the gas episode, and *Nordstjernan* picked up the story.[34] It gave a European view of the event. Only the last line of *Sverige-Nytt*'s article reveals the gas was not lethal. It instead mentioned "chemical and biological weapons and even nuclear weapons."[35] *Sverige-Nytt*'s version ran this phrase in boldface type – which *Nordstjernan* omitted. The article excluded the U.S. Army's view that tear gas could help immobilize guerrillas without

---

[30] Letter from Otto B. Jacobson to Harry Fabbe, "7-8-66," file "Incoming Letters," box 1, SvP, UW.

[31] Louis Herren, deputy editor of *The Times* (London), "The Media and Vietnam: Comment and Appraisal," *Columbia Journalism Review*, Winter 1970–1971: 26.

[32] Otto B. Jacobson, "Ett och Annat av Otto B. Jacobson," *Svenska Posten*, 7 April 1965.

[33] Hammond, *The Military and the Media 1962–1968*, 155–157.

[34] "Regeringen beklagar tårgasinsats i Vietnam," *Sverige-Nytt*, 18 May 1965: 3; and "Regeringen beklagar tårgasinsats i Vietnam," *Nordstjernan*, 27 May 1965: 1.

[35] "Regeringen beklagar tårgasinsats i Vietnam," *Sverige-Nytt*, 18 May 1965: 2.

killing them.[36] It delivers the opinions of Swedish officials without comment or reply. It treats them as sensible, trustworthy sources. By doing so, the article adopts an implied editorial content.

A church newspaper, *The Messenger*, listened to the Swedish message. The Swedish press opposed the use of tear gas, and foreign opinion alone should be a reason not to do it again. "We certainly do not believe we are justified in using any type of gas," *The Messenger* wrote, "for its use will be misconstrued by peoples of the entire world."[37]

The Religious Press and the Vietnam War

In the Sixties, there were three active denominational newspapers left in Swedish-America. (A fourth, the Covenant Church's *Missions-Vännen* closed in 1960.) The Salvation Army's Swedish-American edition of *The War Cry – Stridsropet* – published in Chicago. It closed in 1965 without ever discussing Vietnam. *The Covenant Companion,* also from Chicago, was the voice of the Covenant Church. It served church members further to the political left of *Missions-Vännen*'s readers. Also from Chicago, *The Messenger* was a newspaper for Methodist Swedish-Americans. *The Messenger* and *The Covenant Companion* could not support war on religious grounds.[38] Their discussion of U.S. foreign policy often revolved around ethical problems more than politics. Secular papers often shied from controversy, afraid of losing subscriptions. *The Messenger,* and especially *The Covenant Companion,* willingly discussed Vietnam as a moral problem. The *Companion* was a national periodical. Like *SAT,* it knit its audience together with an active letters-to-the-editor page. Its debate on the war's morality often appeared on this page.

---

[36] Hammond, *The Military and the Media 1962–1968,* 154, 154 note 17, 203.

[37] Rev. B.W. Selin, "The Observation Tower," *The Messenger (Sändebudet),* April 1965: 2.

[38] For an analysis of Swedish-American religious pacifism in the Twenties and Thirties, see: Roger Wesley Pettenger, *The Peace Movement of the Augustana Lutheran Church as a Catalyst in the Americanization Process,* Ann Arbor, Mich., 1987.

The Covenant Companion believed the U.S. must help the Vietnamese. It hesitated to endorse war as the way to help them.[39] Negotiations and nonviolent methods were the preferable ways for Christians to help Vietnam. Even the *Companion's* columnists backing the war doubted that war alone could bring a lasting peace. Peace would only come to Vietnam through economic, political, social, and educational reforms.[40] The *Companion's* commentary emphasized peace, reform, and humanitarian issues over military and political ones. It leaned towards an antiwar position, but never openly said this in an editorial. Both hawkish and antiwar positions appeared in the *Companion's* "Our Readers Write" section. In 1966 and 1967, *The Covenant Companion* printed eight pro-war letters and five with an antiwar view. (This excludes three brief letters on missionary activities in Vietnam.)

The Covenant Companion's letters from missionaries and surgeons make up the Swedish-American press's few "in-country" reports. (It also ran several items on missionary activities, such as a 1968 guerrilla murder of six missionaries.)[41] In 1967, the *Companion* ran a letter from Thomas C. Kolstad, a missionary in Vietnam who ministered to refugees. He felt his work was valuable, but felt isolated doing it.[42] In 1967, *The Messenger* ran an article by a Methodist missionary from Qui Nhon. She saw Vietnam as overburdened by problems, both natural and manmade. She could not stop the war, but she was helping one hundred and fifty families build houses in Tin Lanh. She concluded by writing, "it is not some religious act which makes Christians what they are, but participation in the suffering of God in the life of the world." She urged *Messenger* readers to accept Christian duty to help for their neighbors, especially those in Vietnam.[43]

---

[39] "What about Vietnam?" *The Covenant Companion*, 25 February 1966: 32.

[40] Ben Hartley, "Vietnam: My View," *The Covenant Companion*, 25 February 1966: 12.

[41] "War Claims Six Missionaries," *The Covenant Companion*, 8 March 1968: 24.

[42] Thomas C. Kolstad, "Our Readers Write: A Soldier's Thanks," *The Covenant Companion*, 21 April 1967: 28.

[43] Tharon McConnell, "Vietnam: A Different Perspective," *The Messenger* (*Sändebudet*), October 1967: 1, 4.

A 1967 article by Wendell E. Danielson recounted some experiences as an Army chaplain. He wrote that one of his soldiers – Private Barker – always questioned him with concrete spiritual issues. "Could Jesus be a point man (first man in the patrol)?" Private Barker would ask. "Is genocide ever justified? . . . Would Jesus fight for us if he were here?" Reverend Danielson considered these fair questions. He was unable to answer these questions relating the Bible to the war, leaving him frustrated. He closed his article by appealing to the Lord to help end the suffering around him. "Why doesn't God do something? Soon . . . like today?"[44]

Chaplain Lt. Col. Thomas A. Harris believed answering such hard questions was the Army chaplain's duty. The Army needed soldiers that dared to weigh difficult moral problems. Drugs and disorder were becoming issues in Vietnam, and the Army needed mentally and morally healthy soldiers.[45] Reverend Richard H. Larson disagreed. He had spent nine months in Vietnam, also as a U.S. Army chaplain. He also left Vietnam disillusioned and morally compromised. He sensed that he had been an accomplice to killing. "First of all," Larson wrote,

> the Army has one function . . . waging war and killing the enemy as we are doing in Vietnam. Basically everyone's job in the Army is either to kill or make the process more efficient. . . . Likewise, the Army view of the chaplain's function is to assist in preparing the men emotionally and spiritually to wage war, not to prepare them for a productive life after the Army is done with them. . . . The cost in lives and damage to body and mind is too much of a price to pay.[46]

Even medical staff faced moral issues in Vietnam. Beverly Greene Hinkel wrote that her husband had been a Quaker medic there for two years. Many doctors in the field hospitals felt they had to pull out when the North Vietnamese invaded the South in 1975. The doctors left for their own safety, but left many wounded behind.

[44] Wendell E. Danielson, "Incidents Real," *The Covenant Companion*, 19 May 1967: 7.

[45] Thomas A. Harris, "Today's Soldier – No Sad Sack!" *The Covenant Companion*, 22 September 1967: 12–13, 28.

[46] Richard H. Larson, "Our Readers Write: Too Much For Me," *The Covenant Companion*, 20 October 1967: 2.

"The decision to stay or leave is a hard one and can only be answered by each of us, after which we must live with our answer."[47]

The Covenant Companion opposed war as a rule, but avoided criticizing the government's Vietnam policy. The *Companion* discussed Vietnam as a social issue, not as a political one. However, the Methodist newspaper *The Messenger* questioned U.S. politics in Vietnam. It was the only paper to cite foreign opinion as a reason to withdraw from Indochina.[48] *The Messenger* doubted the North directly controlled the insurgency in the South. Even if the U.S. might have a role in South Vietnam, *The Messenger* thought it had no right to attack North Vietnam. The bombing campaign in the North was "akin to a big bully attacking some helpless person of lesser size." The paper urged Washington to stop this bombing, but contain its activities to defeating the insurgents in the South. Before it closed, *The Messenger* had described Vietnam as "a terrific quagmire of impossibility."[49]

The Covenant Companion became the last denominational paper when *The Messenger* closed in 1969. The *Companion* also became aggressively antiwar as the Seventies began. It could no longer comfort the distressed while remaining neutral on the source of their distress. Columnist Dr. Karl Olson urged Christian readers to be more active in opposing the Vietnam War.[50] In a reply letter, Rev. Douglas Cedarleaf wrote that he withheld 40% of his income tax – the amount given to the military – to protest the war. Another reader wrote in to support Cedarleaf's controversial action.[51] Nobody wrote in opposing this plan; if they did, the *Companion* did not print it.

---

[47] Beverly Green Henkel, "Our Readers Write: Bloodbath?" *The Covenant Companion*, 15 August 1975: 2. See also article on the Hoa Khanh Children's Hospital, *The Covenant Companion*, 1 May 1975.

[48] Rev. B.W. Selen, "The Observation Tower," *The Messenger (Sändebudet)*, April 1965: 2.

[49] Rev. B.W. Selen, "The Observation Tower," *The Messenger (Sändebudet)*, March 1965, November 1966, May 1967, and July 1967: 2.

[50] Dr. Karl A. Olson, "Trust," *The Covenant Companion*, 15 April 1971.

[51] Rev. Douglas G. Cedarleaf, "Our Readers Write: On War and Taxes," The *Covenant Companion*, 1 June 1971: 2; and David H. Johnson, "Our Readers Write: Admires Stand," *The Covenant Companion*, 15 September 1971: 2.

The Covenant Companion reacted to the My Lai Massacre with apocalyptic horror. It considered My Lai to be a national sin, evidence of how far Americans had moved from God. The *Companion* quoted Isaiah 1:4-6 to describe America as a morally corrupt nation. It warned of the Lord's coming judgment: "Americans today are sowing the wind and reaping the whirlwind. Our ears twitch to hear almost anything but the strong, abiding word of God."[52] *The Companion's* sister paper, *California Covenanter*, wrote this was a sign of spiritual malnutrition. If America continued its obsession with violence, sex, and impurity, it would kill the nation.[53] The war had become a source of shame; the *Companion* described Vietnam as America's national sin.

The sin of war even tainted events that should have been joyous, such as the 1973 release of the American POWs. The U.S. prisoners brought back stories of torture in the Vietnamese camps. The *Companion* wrote that Father Philip Berrigan – a Catholic priest who tried negotiating their release – felt shocked, betrayed, and lied to. The paper noted one POW said he did not blame the North Vietnamese for torturing them. "We would have probably done the same thing," he said. America had become a corrupt society, and Vietnam had poisoned even these moments of joy.[54]

Such opinions had become standard among the *Companion's* emigrant readers, but not always welcome from Swedish readers. The *Companion* ran a letter from Falköping that accused the U.S. of aggressively pursuing a self-defeating policy. The writer said America's adventure in Vietnam gave liberal democracy a bad name. It may have even made communism appear as a palatable alternative. Worse, the U.S. had entered Vietnam as the leading Christian nation. America's distinctly un-Christian warfare there could arguably turn young people away from Christian ideals.[55]

---

[52] "In Conclusion: God Save Our Land," *The Covenant Companion*, 1 May 1971: 32.

[53] Rev. C. Calvin Herricott, "Christian Patriotism," *The California Covenanter*, 26 June 1969: 1.

[54] "In Conclusion," *The Covenant Companion*, 1 May 1973: 32.

[55] Leif Svensson, "Our Readers Write: World is Watching U.S." *The Covenant Companion*, 1 April 1972: 2.

Such views were common among Swedish-Americans readers, but unwelcome from Swedes.

A Swedish-Canadian reader wrote that the Falköping letter ignored history. The way to solve problems like Vietnam, he argued, was not to walk away from them. Only an active foreign policy, one that defuses crises before they begin, can prevent such wars.[56] Another letter-writer thought it was hypocritical for Swedes to offer moral advice to Americans. Swedes had their own problems, if different ones. He suggested, "the Swedes straighten themselves out before giving gratuitous advice to Americans."[57] (This also developed into a debate in itself, which the next chapter will take up.)

Finding Someone to Blame: Priests and Protesters

"The war is not going as it should," *Nordstjernan's* Eric Sylvan noted in 1967.[58] Swedes and Americans alike realized the war had reached a deadlock. There would be no military victory, at least not soon. The U.S. would not be able to leave Vietnam without losing prestige. *Svenska Posten* columnist Reinhold Ahleen's personal diary reveals the frustration of 1967.

> 19 January – The newspapers say that great losses in Vietnam were reported on both sides last week. The U.S.A. has lost 6,875 dead and 39,261 injured since the war began.
> 7 February – During the five-year war in Vietnam, the U.S.A. has lost 1,172 planes and 630 helicopters according to the papers. They don't talk about how many lives have been lost and the misery war brings.
> 10 February – There is a rumor there may be a cease-fire in the Vietnam War. Hope there's a kernel of truth in it.[59]

There was no lasting cease-fire. *Nordstjernan's* Eric Sylvan noted "a tone of bitterness and recrimination" entering the Vietnam

---

[56] Rev. P.A. Langvand, "Our Readers Write: Don Quixote . . . Rides Again," *The Covenant Companion*, 1 June 1972: 2.

[57] Robert E. Anderson, "Our Readers Write: Should Swedes Criticize?" *The Covenant Companion*, 15 May 1972: 2.

[58] Eric Sylvan, "Det Tycks," *Nordstjernan-Svea*, 20 July 1967: 4.

[59] Reinhold Ahleen's personal diary, 1967, box 1, Ahleen, UW.

debate.[60] Sylvan himself was a leading critic, bitterly accusing different groups of not supporting the war. Even in late 1965, Sylvan accused professors, intellectuals, and artists for undermining the war effort. He thought they ignored history, Vietnam's strategic significance, and the need to stop aggressive dictatorships.[61]

There was a recurring anticlerical theme in Sylvan's columns from 1965 and 1966. He argued that church support for the war was soft, and possibly even antiwar. When a coalition of churches urged passive resistance to the U.S. escalation, Sylvan called them hyper-sensitive "bleeding hearts." When a Cincinnati clerical group suggested withholding their 1964 taxes in protest, he said it was just an excuse to avoid taxes. When Rev. Martin Luther King condemned the war, Sylvan said it was arrogant and presumptuous of him. Sylvan considered Rev. King an appeaser, and a self-promoting tool of the communists.[62] *Svenska Posten*'s Otto Jacobson also criticized the "fat and well-meaning men" in the priesthood. He saw them as appeasers, and the moral equivalent of the Copperhead Democrats in the Civil War.[63]

As the war stalemated, this anticlerical sentiment jelled around Swedish-American anti-Catholicism. *Svenska Posten*'s Oscar Kulle wrote, "certain religions, and one in particular," had led America into Vietnam. Kulle suggested John Kennedy intervened in Vietnam to support fellow Catholic Ngo Dinh Diem. *SvP*'s Stephen Forslund agreed that this was why the U.S. had entered Southeast Asia. "It is no great secret that the one Holy Church bears the greatest guilt in this mess."[64]

By 1967, Sylvan argued that Washington politicians would not let the military win the war. Eric Sylvan thought the U.S. could win militarily. Washington elites, however, feared the political and

[60] Eric Sylvan, citing *The New York Times*' columnist James Reston, in "Det Tycks," *Nordstjernan-Svea*, 20 July 1967: 4.

[61] Eric Sylvan, "Det Tycks," *Nordstjernan*, 27 May, 15 July, 22 July, 7 October, 1965: 4.

[62] Eric Sylvan, "Det Tycks," *Nordstjernan*, 18 February, 15 July, 16 September 1965: 4.

[63] Otto B. Jacobson, "Ett och annat av Otto B. Jacobson," *Svenska Posten*, 5 May 1965: 3.

diplomatic price of a violent victory. Vietnam was an example of what can happen when weak-willed civilians try to wage war. President Johnson should give complete control of the war to General Westmoreland. If freed from political constraints, Westmoreland would win the Vietnam War.[65] This argument recurs in many unsuccessful wars, not just Vietnam. (A memorable example was the idea Abraham Lincoln had kept General George McClellan from winning the Civil War.)[66]

In the first few years, Eric Sylvan accused intellectuals and ministers for not supporting the war. *Svenska Posten*'s columnists focused on Catholic priests for undermining the Vietnam cause. The antiwar movement soon became the most convenient outlet for frustration. In 1965, Eric Sylvan described people against the war as unaware of the area's strategic significance. Some, he argued, wanted "peace at any price."[67] These were common views among policy supporters; a few even believed the communists secretly encouraged this thinking. Not many argued in the war's early stages the antiwar partisans were anything more than wrong. As the war continued without success, parts of the Swedish-American press began to paint the antiwar movement as unpatriotic, immoral, or insincere.

Even antiwar Swedish-American columnists began turning against the antiwar movement. *Svenska Posten*'s Arthur Landfors was one of Swedish-America's last socialist voices.[68] Writing to editor Harry Fabbe, Landfors described disgust over Boston antiwar rallies led by YIP leader Abbie Hoffman. Hoffman may have made positive

---

[64] Oscar J. Kulle, "Om sådant som hänt och händer ibland oss," *Svenska Posten*, 19 April 1967: 6, Stephen Forslund, "Pränt om ditt och datt," *Svenska Posten*, 10 May 1967: 5. (More sophisticated versions of this argument suggest the influence of Roman Catholic moral absolutism helped shape U.S. foreign policy in the Cold War. See: James Carroll, "The Church and Foreign Policy in the U.S.," *The Boston Globe*, 15 August 2002: A15.)

[65] Eric Sylvan, "Det Tycks," *Nordstjernan-Svea*, 19 December 1966, 9 March and 20 July 1967: 4.

[66] See: David Herbert Donald, *Lincoln*, New York, 1995.

[67] For examples, see Eric Sylvan, "Det Tycks," *Nordstjernan*, 23 April, 6 May, 27 May 1965, and 16 June 1966.

[68] Åke Leif-Lundgren and Bernt Linné, "Arthur Landfors," *Tiden snöar från trädet*, Luleå, 1993: 49–58.

comments, but he buried them in a cascade of obscenities and crude language. Hoffman urged the crowd to march on Yale University "and send it to the fucking moon." He also invited a Black Panther to address the crowd, which he urged "to take up the gun against the pigs." Landfors told Harry Fabbe that people like Abbie Hoffman and Jerry Rubin should be in jail.[69] *Nordstjernan*'s columnist "Uncle Joe" considered such talk as analogous to vandalism and rioting. He thought talk that degraded American society was equivalent to treason. He proposed deporting such people to some communist country.[70]

Such excesses helped critics reduce the antiwar movement to a caricature of "long-haired, bearded individuals who run riot in our streets and parks." *SvP*'s Reinhold Ahleen dismissed them as young mobs "who think it is fun to kick up rows, make noise, throw rocks, and burn flags."[71] The emigrant papers reported similar incidents in Sweden, completing the picture of a violent and immature movement.

California Veckoblad in particular actively promoted an unflattering image of the antiwar movement. It had been silent on Vietnam until 1967, when it began running political cartoons. Many of them appeared on its front page. Most drawings disparaged the antiwar protesters as lazy, unpatriotic, drug-taking hippies. A few pictures even had a broadly anti-youth tone. As *California Veckoblad* began running political cartoons, it also printed photos of soldiers in Vietnam. *California Veckoblad* ran seven photos in 1967, and twenty more appeared in 1968.[72] These pictures clearly

---

[69] Letter from Arthur Landfors to Harry Fabbe, undated (likely from late 1969 or early 1970), and letter from 15 April 1970, file "Landfors, Arthur," box 1 incoming letters, SvP, UW.

[70] Uncle Joe, "Uncle Joe's Corner," *Nordstjernan-Svea*, 21 April 1966: 9.

[71] Carl H. Olson, "Folkets Röst: Hälsning från Värmland," *Svenska-Amerikanaren Tribunen*, 11 March 1970: 5; and Reinhold P. Ahleen, "Ordet Fritt: Herr Redaktör!" *Nordstjernan-Svea*, 25 April 1968.

[72] *California Veckoblad*, 27 January, 28 April, 13 October (two photos), 27 October, 15 December 1967 (two photos), 9 February, 8 March (three photos), 22 March (two photos), 17 May (two photos), 26 July (two photos), 9 August, 23 August-8 September, 20 September (two photos), 27 September, 25 October, 1 November, 8 November 1968 (three photos).

California Veckoblad's drawings often contrasted the forces of order in society with the forces of disorder.

contrasted with the satirical cartoons on the antiwar movement. Three of the 1968 pictures had a religious reference, and one showed soldiers shaving and bathing. The idea behind was likely to boost support for the soldiers, and by extension their mission. Juxtaposing active soldiers against lazy hippies suggests the military – not the antiwar movement – was the better force for positive change. If the U.S. was in a quagmire, America could rely on its soldiers to finish the job. The antiwar movement, however, was defeating America at home. This shifted guilt from those who pursued the war to those who opposed it.[73]

California Veckoblad's sister paper – *Svenska-Amerikanaren* – ran frequent letters about hippies. For example, a 1968 letter called them "asocial individuals . . . mentally unbalanced dirty little people

---

[73] Keith Beattie, "Stab Wounds," *The Scar That Binds*, London, 1998: 21.

EASY DOES IT . . .
Sp5 Daniel Kolarsky leads
the way across a bamboo
bridge built over a tribu-
tary of the Saigon River.
Soldiers of the 1st Infantry
Division were on a recon-
naissance-in-force mission
near Saigon.

*California Veckoblad regularly
ran photos from Vietnam, the
only newspaper to do so.*

. . . who manifest their contempt for common moral standards and discretion through their bizarre clothing.[74]" *SAT* remained socially conservative, loyal to the Republican Party, and had not turned against the war. In 1967, however, it ran an article warning young Swedish-Americans and visiting Swedish students about their draft status. It suggested they "immediately return home before their conscription orders arrive." (*Western News* ran a similar warning in late 1966.) *SAT* ran an article on a Swedish student who returned to Halmstad after getting draft orders. The story did not condemn the action but presented it as a sensible move.[75] These articles suggest that young Swedish-Americans may find being in Vietnam highly undesirable. They may even implicitly encourage draft-dodging.

---

[74] Adolf W. Jacobson, "Folkets Röst: Funderingar vid årsskiftet," *Svenska-Amerikanaren Tribunen*, 10 January 1968: 5. See also: Hilma P., "Folkets Röst: Skrivlåda," *Svenska-Amerikanaren Tribunen*, 26 March 1969: 5.

[75] "En immigrant med visum är prospective G.I. för Vietnam," *Svenska-Amerikanaren Tribunen*, 8 March 1967: 1; "Questions and Answers: As an Alien, Am I Subject to Draft and Military Service?" *Western News*, 26 November 1966: 2; and untitled article, *Svenska-Amerikanaren Tribunen*, 7 August 1968: 1.

Almighty God, we make our earnest prayer that thou will keep the United States in thy holy protection, that thou wilt incline the hearts of the citizens to cultivate a spirit of subordination and obedience to the government; and entertain a brotherly affection and love for their fellow citizens of the United States at large...

(Washington's Prayer at Valley Forge, 1783)

California Veckoblad's drawings sometimes argued that civil disorder can undermine democracy.

SAT's article also suggests ways for Swedish nationals to volunteer for Vietnam. This feels as if *SAT* included it for balance only.[76]

The American antiwar movement and Sweden's FNL movement were natural lighting rods. They attracted attention among those looking to explain U.S. futility in Vietnam. *SAT* ran many letters hostile to draft-evaders, but there were some that sympathized with them. Emigrant veterans of World War One could particularly understand why young people wanted no part of Vietnam. In 1914, Olof Lindberg, an *SAT* reader, was a sailor in the Swedish navy. Many of his comrades thought Sweden should enter the war, which everyone assumed would be an adventure. The Swedish government knew better. In retrospect, Lindberg was glad Sweden remained

---

[76] "En immigrant med visum är prospective G.I. för Vietnam," *Svenska-Amerikanaren Tribunen*, 8 March 1967: 1.

neutral. He also wished the United States had shown the same restraint before going into Vietnam.[77]

Alf Carlsson was a young immigrant in 1917. He was living in the United States when he got his draft orders. Immigrants could have asked for draft deferments, he told *SAT*, but Swedish-Americans wanted to fight for their country. He could not respect deserters, but conceded Vietnam was cruel and destructive, "a miserable war."[78] Knut Almgren, another *SAT* reader, received his U.S. draft orders in July 1917. The army doctors had rejected him as unfit for service, but both his sons served in the Second World War. In 1969, his grandson got his draft papers and "declared healthy and fit for duty as a shooting target," Almgren wrote. "End this war."[79]

"Carl" from Chicago was also a First World War veteran. He wrote to *SAT* after his nineteen-year-old friend said good-bye before shipping off to Vietnam. His young friend was unsure about fighting in this war, and "Carl" said he felt the same way about the First World War. It reminded him of a peace-song that Swedish soldiers sang, but the army had forbidden.[80] "Carl" was the third *SAT* reader to print a version of the illicit peace ballad. Two other veterans sent in different versions of the same song in early 1969. Carl's version ended with "let us lay our weapons down and conclude eternal peace." Birger Hanson's variant ended with "peace is and shall ever be life's highest poetry."[81]

The Messenger ran a feature story on a First World War veteran's conversation with a soldier returning from Vietnam. The story

---

[77] "Skånepågen" Olof Lindberg, "Folkets Röst: Dömen icke så varden I dömda, kriget är skulden," *Svenska-Amerikanaren Tribunen*, 23 April 1969.

[78] "Boxholmaren" Alf N. Carlson, "Folkets Röst: En oförlåtlig handling," 23 February 1966; and "Folkets Röst: Mer om Vietnam," *Svenska-Amerikanaren Tribunen*, 26 July 1967.

[79] "Tegelslagarens" Knut Almgren, "Folkets Röst: Bort med krigen," *Svenska-Amerikanaren Tribunen*, 25 June 1969.

[80] "Carl," "Folkets Röst: På väg till krigsfronten," *Svenska-Amerikanaren Tribunen*, 26 April 1967: 5.

[81] Birger W. Hanson, "Folkets Röst: Freds sången," 9 April 1969: 5; and G. Johansson, "Folkets Röst: Kan någon fredssången?" *Svenska-Amerikanaren Tribunen*, 19 March 1969: 5.

contends the soldiers may be honest and reliable, but that Vietnam was a terrible war. American soldiers faced "the heat, and the wetness, and the swamp, and the mud, and the food (rice and C-rations), and the guerrilla warfare, and the booby traps, and the snipers, and actual fighting." The soldiers were good men, and worthy of a better war.[82]

Several *SAT* letters directly or implicitly related Vietnam to World War One. Very few – if any – compared Vietnam to the Second World War. World War Two was the Good War, a metaphor that legitimized U.S. foreign conflicts.[83] The American imagination still considered World War One a brutal, pointless, and avoidable conflict. As W.W. I veteran Olof Lindberg said, Vietnam was yet another war caused by politicians "who had promised not to send our brave boys into war in a foreign land. Yet after the election they broke their promise."[84]

Trying to Find a Way Out: Invasions, Massacres, and Bombings

The United States began the Seventies fumbling around for a way out of the Vietnam Quagmire. It negotiated with the North, turned the war over to the South, and invaded Cambodia. When nothing else worked, it stepped up its bombing campaign. As people hoped things might get better, everything seemed to get worse first.

The U.S. invaded Cambodia in late spring 1970. *Nordstjernan's* Eric Sylvan thought Nixon had probably made the right decision. Like other emigrant columnists, he now ascribed the Vietnam policy to the President rather than the nation. Sylvan thought Nixon had listened to reliable and experienced advisers who knew what they were doing. The President had by-passed Congress, but Sylvan still held that he made the right decision.[85] *Svenska Posten's* Reinhold

---

[82] Olin Clarke Jones, "Visiting With an American Soldier On His Way Home From Viet Nam," *The Messenger* (*Sändebudet*), February 1967: 1, 2.

[83] Daniel C. Hallin, "Images of the Vietnam and Persian Gulf Wars in U.S. Television," *Seeing Through the Media*, New Brunswick, N.J., 1994: 50; Hallin, *The Uncensored War*, 175.

[84] "Skånepågen" Olof Lindberg, "Folkets Röst: Dömen icke så varden I dömda, kriget är skulden," *Svenska-Amerikanaren Tribunen*, 23 April 1969.

[85] Eric Sylvan, "Det Tycks," *Nordstjernan-Svea*, 7 May 1970: 4.

Ahleen also believed Nixon ignored Congress in invading Cambodia. Rather than a wise decision, he wondered whether it was even legal. Ahleen considered the 1971 invasion of Laos reckless, and another step down the road to destruction. These invasions were to contain an aggressive China, but the price of containment had become too high. He could only pray they might speed an end to the war.[86]

The invasion of Cambodia provoked protests on American campuses. At Kent State, National Guard troops shot and killed four students. *Nordstjernan* saw the invasion and shooting at Kent State as signs of an apocalyptic breakdown of society. It described the violence as, "the beginning of the end." (It did not say of what.)[87] Also printing in New York, *Norden* ran the photo of the Kent State shooting. *Norden's* Erik Hermans had long opposed the war, but avoided public statements about it because of the risk of losing subscribers. Cambodia and Kent State were the events that pushed editor Hermans into speaking out. He wrote that the war had torn America apart, and nothing was more important than creating unity. "If the price of that harmony is leaving Vietnam," *Norden* wrote, "that price must be paid."[88]

A September 1971 editorial let readers know an editorial change was coming. *Norden* wrote, "we cannot hope that every reader will agree with us, but in any case, we want our opinions heard." The paper had become completely opposed to the White House's Vietnam policy by early 1972. Richard Nixon became *Norden's* symbol of the Vietnam War. It used the epithet "Tricky Dick," and ran a drawing of Nixon behind prison bars. A September 1972 drawing made Nixon look diseased.[89] It ran antiwar poems on its editorial page. No other Swedish-language paper shifted its opinion as dramatically as *Norden*. *Norden's* Erik Hermans was a young

---

[86] Reinhold Ahleen, "Rim och Reson av Reinhold Ahleen," *Svenska Posten*, 13 May, 27 May, and 10 June 1970, and 24 February and 14 April 1971: 2.

[87] "Kambodja," *Nordstjernan-Svea*, 21 May 1970: 4. (Reprinted from *Handelstidningen*, 4 May 1970.)

[88] "Nixon och de unga," *Norden*, 14 May 1970: 8; e-mail from Erik Hermans, 12 February 2003.

[89] "På tal om Nixon," *Norden*, 30 September 1971; see cartoons on 13 April 1972, 7 September 1972, and 11 January 1973.

editor, a generation younger than most of his peers in the Swedish-language press. It may not be surprising that Hermans' paper opposed a war where soldiers his age were doing the fighting and dying.

●

Svenska Posten was the other explicitly antiwar newspaper. Its Vietnam position softened in 1971 when poor health pushed editor Harry Fabbe into retirement. News of the My Lai massacre brought *SvP*'s antiwar opinion back out again. Eric Olson called the incident just one of many crimes against humanity. Lieutenant Calley was only the most visible offender in an inhuman system of warfare. Lt. Calley might have ordered the massacre, but the true guilty parties were in Washington. The commanders that sent men like Lt. Calley into villages like My Lai were the true criminals. One could even say that all Americans still backing the war deserved blame for the massacre. (An *SvP* reader thanked Olson two weeks later for his words on the American collective guilt for the Vietnam War.)[90] Olson indicted the U.S. public, the military, and a faceless bureaucracy for the massacre. He diffused the responsibility so wide that nobody was really to blame for it.

Western News called Calley a "blindly obedient military robot" – a vicious product of the military. Exposing the system that produced such men might be the only valuable lesson from Vietnam. The paper also believed Calley's commanding officers bore final responsibility. *Nordstjernan*'s Eric Sylvan identified Lieutenant Calley's superior officer as Company Officer Captain Medina. Medina denied ordering Calley to kill civilians at My Lai, but it was unclear what orders he gave. Both *Western News* and Eric Sylvan believed Calley was a political scapegoat for others. Putting Calley on trial was only a way to release pent-up frustrations over a brutal

---

[90] Eric Olson, "Reflektioner av Eric Olson," *Svenska Posten*, 7 April, 14 July, and 4 August 1971: 3; and "Från Läsekretsen," *Svenska Posten*, 21 April 1971: 6.

war.[91] Like the mainstream press, Swedish-American discussion of My Lai centered on William Calley's trial. It put the massacre into a legal perspective which made it easier to deal with the atrocity.[92]

Many Americans downplayed or disbelieved the My Lai massacre.[93] Eric Sylvan said the My Lai massacre was a trivial incident in the war. The guerrillas' style of warfare was savage. The U.S. bombing of North Vietnam had killed far more people than any number of village massacres. Sylvan warned that all wars have massacres. *Western News* agreed wars are always brutal, and innocent people die on all sides.[94] *SvP*'s Eric Olson added that World War Two was hardly a Good War. Even the Second World War had massacres of civilians and prisoners the press had never publicized. Eric Sylvan added that American bombing of Germany had killed thousands of innocent Germans. Yet, he believed it was dangerous to focus too much on incidents like My Lai. Sylvan thought Americans should not let sensationalist horror paralyze their ability to act. If such stories can influence U.S. actions, then uncivilized nations indifferent to such horror will use it to their advantage.[95]

The U.S. stepped up its bombing campaign during North Vietnam's 1972 Easter Offensive. *Nordstjernan* wondered whether there was any point to it. Without U.S. ground troops, the U.S. could not prevent Northern conquest of South Vietnam. The U.S. could only drop bombs, and that would only delay the inevitable. Continuing to fight would "only prolong a war we have already lost."[96] Brooklyn's *Norden* agreed with its cross-town rival. The U.S.

---

[91] "Swedish Newspapers Comment on Calley Case," *Western News*, 22 April 1971: 1; "More Comment in Swedish Newspapers on the Calley Case," and "Many Calley Cases in South Vietnam," *Western News*, 24 June 1971: 1; and Eric Sylvan, "Det Tycks," *Nordstjernan-Svea*, 13 April 1971: 4.

[92] Hallin, *The Uncensored War*, 180.

[93] For analysis of these denials, see: Edward M. Opton Jr., "It Never Happened, and Besides, They Deserved It," *Sanctions for Evil*, San Francisco, 1971.

[94] "Swedish Newspapers Comment on Calley Case," *Western News*, 22 April 1971: 1.

[95] Eric Sylvan, "Det Tycks," *Nordstjernan-Svea*, 13 April 1971: 4; "Swedish Newspapers Comment on Calley Case," *Western News*, 22 April 1971: 1; and Eric Olson, "Reflektioner av Eric Olson," *Svenska Posten*, 4 August 1971, 3.

[96] "Skall Nordvietnam vinna?" 20 April 1971: 4; and "Vägen ur Vietnam," *Nordstjernan-Svea*, 27 April 1972: 4.

could not send the troops back, and bombing was the only U.S. solution. A better option would be to leave and "let Saigon fight for its own skin. Saigon is not worth any more of our lives." Instead, President Nixon continued to bomb and cause more bloodshed.[97] *Svenska Posten* thought the U.S. bombing was disproportionate to South Vietnam's value. America could have used the effort put into pounding North Vietnam for better purposes. *SvP* thought the bombing revealed "an insane superpower mentality."[98]

Nordstjernan ran two letters from a Swedish critic of American foreign policy in 1972. Torgny Rumert's first letter called the Vietnamese a heroic people who inspired all of humanity. (His reference to "the Vietnamese" implied there was just one Vietnam, not two. It also implied that all Vietnamese supported one cause: the FNL cause.) Rumert's second letter – covering one full page of five columns – said the Americans were trying to wipe such people out

Svensk G. I. avled för U.S.A.

Den 2 maj jordfästes i Golden Gate National Cemetery en svensk medborgare, vilken som frivillig i amerikanska armén hade dödats i kriget i Vietnam den 4 april efter endast två månader fält som medlem av "A battery, 6-33 artillery".

Modern säger: "Vi hör så mycket om Sveriges antikrigskänslor och om U.S.A.:s desertörer där, men här hade vi en man som gav sitt liv för Förenta Staterna." — En heroisk son till en heroisk familj.

Vestkusten reported the death of a local Swedish volunteer in the U.S. Army. His mother says: "We hear so much about Sweden's antiwar feelings and the U.S. deserters there, but here we had a man who gave his life for the United States."

---

[97] "Hanoi-attack," *Norden*, 13 April 1972: 8.

[98] Harry Fabbe, "Hört och Hänt," *Svenska Posten*, 24 May 1972: 2.

with napalm. "America! Where are you going? Why are you suddenly beyond all common sense? Must you really mass-kill everyone else before you, just so you can survive?"[99] His letter continued in this manner for thirty-three more paragraphs.

Rumert's letters brought in several replies. J. Alvar Anderson described it as Swedish anti-American propaganda. Instead of promoting better U.S.-Swedish relations, such diatribes only created needless discord. G. Wallin called the letter a politically-motivated "Niagara of drivel." Rumert said he liked America, but Wallin held that he felt more hate than anything else. Brett-Larson Oliver wrote a reply-letter that also filled an entire page of text, across five columns. Oliver had been in Vietnam for two years and believed the guerrillas were far more brutal than the Americans. "They never took any of our men prisoners in the field unless he had a high rank," Oliver wrote. "Any patrol that was overrun or ambushed was killed to the last man. On retaking the area we found their tortured and sliced-up bodies – and you call that a heroic struggle for high ideals."[100] It was partisan, but Oliver's letter was a rare firsthand account in the Swedish-American press of events in Vietnam.

The Swedish-American press gave the war's end scant attention. It gave the Paris Peace Treaty only a subdued welcome. Many papers conveyed aversion to discussing an issue they felt was distasteful. *Norden* said it would have rejoiced over the peace treaty if the war had been honorable. The war instead awoke only disgust over the carnage: 3.3 million people injured and 6.8 million tons of bombs dropped. *Norden* did not believe Paris marked an honorable peace after such a disgraceful war.[101]

Two weeks after the Paris treaty, North Vietnam began releasing its American prisoners. *Svenska Posten* noted that three local Swedish-American families would not get their children back. North Vietnam's prisoner list did not include the sons of *Svenska*

---

[99] Torgny Rumert, "Så här efteråt..." 1 March 1973; and "Ordet är Fritt: Kära vänner och läsare av *Nordstjernan-Svea*," *Nordstjernan-Svea*, 30 November 1972: 10.

[100] J. Alvar Anderson, "Ordet är Fritt," and G. Wallin, "Ordet är Fritt: Re. 'Så här efteråt,'" *Nordstjernan-Svea*, 15 March 1973: 3; and Brett Larson Oliver, "Ordet är Fritt: Sweden Where Are You Going?" *Nordstjernan-Svea*, 24 May 1973: 10.

[101] "Fred – Men hur?" *Norden*, 1 February 1973: 12.

Posten subscribers in Puyallup or Oak Harbor, or the daughter of *SvP* readers in Seattle.[102] *Svenska Posten, Nordstjernan,* and *Vestkusten* had all reported Swedish and Swedish-American casualties in Vietnam.[103] There would not be any more.

Conclusions

This chapter has focused on how the Swedish-American press reported on the Vietnam War. It shows that the emigrant papers knew little about Vietnam before the 1965 intervention. Most papers backed the U.S. Vietnam policy in the Kennedy years. Those against the policy believed America did not do enough to fight communism, or that it was ineffective and wasteful.

When the U.S. entered the Vietnam War, the Swedish-American press gave the move its uneasy support. Only *Svenska Posten* openly opposed the U.S. intervention. *Svenska Posten*'s files show that editor Harry Fabbe's views on Vietnam led to conflict with one of his leading columnists. Otto Jacobson ultimately resigned his position rather than let Fabbe edit his columns. The *SvP* files also show that columnist Reinhold Ahleen was very wary about the U.S. intervention.

Svenska Posten was the only secular paper to oppose the Vietnam War. The two religious papers – the *Companion* and *Messenger* – leaned toward pacifism on principle. Until the late Sixties, the *Companion* avoided openly criticizing Washington's politics. It discussed Vietnam as a moral and spiritual problem rather than a political one. It slowly came to define America's Vietnam policy as amoral, and by the end a positive sin.

---

[102] "Hört och Hänt," *Svenska Posten*, 31 January 1973: 1–2.
[103] "Svensk befälhavare på sprängd USA-båt," 8 September 1966: 12, and Otto H. Loven, "Vietnam krigare hedrad," *Nordstjernan-Svea*, 12 January 1967: 9; "Svenskättling har stupat i Saigon," 28 February 1968: 4, and "Svensk svårt sårad i Vietnam," *Svenska Posten*, 26 June 1968: 5; "Svensk befälhavare på sprängd USA-båt," 8 September 1966: 1, "Svensk G.I. avled för USA," 9 May 1968: 1, and "Svenskättling erhåller posthumt Congressional Medal of Honor: Tilldelad Paul Foster av San Francisco, stupad i Vietnam," *Vestkusten*, 11 September 1969: 1.

As the war led to a stalemate, policy supporters looked for reasons why the U.S. was unsuccessful. They focused first on the Religious Left, the original core of the antiwar movement. *Nordstjernan*'s Eric Sylvan in particular blamed the liberal clergy for undermining the war effort. Sylvan said the clergy did not support the war enough, but others said the church supported the war too much. Some *Svenska Posten* columnists specifically blamed the Catholic Church for causing the war. This is a very different criticism than not helping win it. Still, the message was the same: the church is responsible for our national problems.

The antiwar movement became a student movement rather than clerical one by the late Sixties. The criticism of church leaders faded. Condemnation of student protesters and hippies grew accordingly. The student protest movement was often loud, noisy, and adversarial, and thus an easy target for criticism. Many reader letters in *SAT* said that such protesters undermined the war effort. Many others – especially those from First World War veterans – could still express understanding for the student antiwar movement.

Commentary on Vietnam slowly declined by the late Sixties. This was partly because Sweden's Vietnam policy became the new focus of emigrant attention. (The following chapter will discuss Swedish policy in more detail.) By the Seventies, however, Swedish-American commentary was down everywhere. Most newspapers were more preoccupied with their poor finances. Vietnam had become a nasty war and an unpleasant subject. The emigrant papers saw it as a litany of massacres, pointless bombings, and invasions of neutral countries. *The Covenant Companion* believed the sin of war had poisoned the entire country. There were few vocal policy supporters left in the emigrant press. War hawks like Eric Sylvan either retired or died, and their papers did not replace them with similar columnists. Quiet war doves like *Norden*'s Erik Hermans eventually decided they could no longer stay silent. By the Seventies, the emigrant papers did not like the subject of Vietnam. Discussing it was not the way to win new subscribers. They instead pressed consensus issues – Swedish food, music, and literature – rather than the divisive Vietnam issue.

Chapter Five

The Swedish-American Press on Sweden

The previous chapter focused on how the emigrant papers saw the crisis in Southeast Asia. It showed the Swedish-language press initially backed the war. Over the years, it became increasingly receptive to antiwar opinion. How did they receive the homeland Swedes' criticism of the war? Did they agree with it? They slowly began to oppose the war themselves, but may have resented Swedes disparaging their adopted land. Perhaps the only thing they disliked more was when Americans disparaged their homeland. This often happened in the late Sixties as the U.S. media reported Swedish Vietnam policy. Did they defend Swedish Vietnam policy as they had defended Sweden from Eisenhower's 1960 criticism?

This chapter examines these problems related to Sweden's criticism of the Vietnam War. These are large and often vague issues, however. This chapter splits emigrant press commentary into parts. It explores the press commentary of six major events in Sweden's Vietnam policy. These events (or themes) were the most frequent subjects of debate in the Swedish-American press. In their own way, each reveals a particular facet of the emigrant press mentality in dealing with Swedish criticism. These six events (or themes) are:

- Swedish news coverage of Vietnam (most discussion in 1966–1967)
- Sweden's sheltering of U.S. deserters (most discussion around 1968–1969)
- Olof Palme as a person and symbol (early 1968 and mid-1970)
- Sweden's diplomatic recognition of North Vietnam (all discussion in 1969)

- U.S. Ambassador Jerome Holland's reception in Sweden (1970)
- Olof Palme's speech following the Christmas Bombings (1973)

These may not have been the most common subjects in Sweden's debate on Vietnam, but they often arose in the emigrant papers. Most of these subjects arose in the years between 1968 and 1970, when debate on Swedish policy raged hottest. This chapter ends by examining how *Svenska Posten, Nordstjernan,* and *Svenska-Amerikanaren* reported Sweden's Vietnam policy in these three years. I feel the news on the front page is an integral part of how the emigrant press presented its readers with this issue. The way they presented stories often decided which opinions readers would draw from them. In this view, "hard news" can be a subtle editorial. News may even be more persuasive than editorials because they pose as undisputed facts.

The Swedish-American press had reported Swedish reaction to the Vietnam War as early as April 1965. *Svenska Posten, Nordstjernan,* and *Svenska-Amerikanaren* all reported a 14 April 1965 student protest on the war. (The *Sverige-Nytt* article they ran – "Stockholm Students Demonstrate For Vietnam" – referred to a single Vietnam.)[1] For the next two years, Swedish reaction to Vietnam was most on the emigrant papers' news pages. In 1965, they reported stories of Swedish concern and misgivings about the war. In 1966, they reported more stories about protests and stronger condemnation of American policy. There were some editorials about Sweden's criticism of the war. In 1967, the Swedish view of the Vietnam War moved off the news pages and into the comment pages. It soon became the main topic of debate in the Swedish-American press. By 1968, Swedish Vietnam policy was much more important than the war in Southeast Asia.

---

[1] "Stockholmsstudenter demonstrerade för Vietnam," *Nordstjernan*, 15 April 1965: 1, "Ungdom i Stockholm gilla ej US:s insats i Vietnam," *Svenska-Amerikanaren Tribunen*, 14 April 1965: 1, and "Uppropsprotest mot Vietnam-politiken," *Svenska Posten*, 14 July 1965: 4, were all based on "Stockholmsstudenter demonstrerade för Vietnam," *Sverige-Nytt*, 6 April 1965: 2.

In 1965 and 1966, the Swedish-American newspapers were still debating Johnson's escalation of the war. By this point, the mainstream U.S. newspapers began picking up stories on the growing protests in Sweden. In June 1966, *The Washington Post* ran a story – "Police Guard American Embassy in Swedish Capital" – which UD Press Bureau regarded as critical of Sweden. *The New York Times* also reported the protests and flag-burnings near the Stockholm embassy.[2] This was not the publicity the Swedish-American editors wanted to see about Sweden. Something was wrong. These stories led the emigrant papers to wonder whether Sweden got accurate information about what the U.S. was doing in Vietnam.

Swedish News Coverage of Vietnam

Like other Swedish-American columnists, *Nordstjernan*'s Eric Sylvan used Swedish news material in his columns.[3] He also considered much of it biased. Sylvan wrote, "the Swedish press must bear some responsibility for the Swedish people's distorted view of America and American policies. Certain organs publish sensational quotes without the slightest responsibility of checking the truth or accuracy of what they put into print."[4] Syndicated Swedish-American columnist Adele Heilborn thought the Swedish press ran antiwar viewpoints indiscriminately.[5] *Vestkusten* also believed that Radio Sweden "spreads left-wing propaganda" against the U.S.[6] These were the opening salvos in an intense debate about Sweden's news

---

[2] Memo by Von Knorring, "Sverige i amerikansk press 1966," attached to letter from Sven Frychius to Sten Sundfeldt, 13 January 1967, file "USA 1967 jan – 1967 mars," box I:323, NL1, RA.

[3] *Svenska Posten*'s Reinhold Ahleen's diaries suggest what a "typical" Swedish-American columnist read. He bought any Swedish newspaper his local newsstand had available. In addition to mainstream American papers, Ahleen subscribed to *American-Scandinavian, Literary Digest, Nordstjernan,* the Mormon *North Star, Svenska-Amerikanaren, Svenska Posten, Sverige-Nytt* (in 1967), *Vasabladet,* and *Vestkusten.* (Personal diaries, 16 January 1965, 12 January 1967, and passim 1965, box 1, Ahleen, UW.)

[4] Eric Sylvan, "Det Tycks," *Nordstjernan-Svea,* 16 June 1966: 4.

[5] Adele Heilborn, "Stockholmsbrev för *Svenska Posten*," Svenska Posten, 22 November 1967.

Eric Sylvan:
DET TYCKS

coverage of Vietnam. This debate appeared in all three major emigrant papers.

In a later column, Eric Sylvan criticized Sweden's media for drawing news from biased sources. "It will publish news from North Vietnam but much more seldom anything from South Vietnam." Sweden even used partisan American sources. The Swedish media related the views of Senators Fullbright and Kennedy, and editorials by *The New York Times*. Sylvan blamed the Swedish media's "one-sided reporting" for the friction between America and Sweden.[7]

Svenska Posten's Harry Fabbe preferred Swedish news on Vietnam. On Vietnam, "The Swedish press is particularly knowledgeable on the international level. . . . What is special about the Swedish press? Nothing except that it is free, does not muzzle itself, and reports conditions realistically and as it sees them." Fabbe also believed Swedish reporters covered the war from both North and South Vietnam.[8] Actually, the North Vietnamese distrusted foreign journalists and rarely allowed them into the country.[9] A few visitors got temporary visas, however. The North Vietnamese allowed left-wing Swedish author Sara Lidman to visit Hanoi briefly

---

[6] Bertil Frödin, "U.S.A.-Sverige," *Vestkusten*, 22 August 1968: 1. Editor Karin Person writes that she "agrees wholeheartedly with the above."

[7] Eric Sylvan, "Det Tycks," *Nordstjernan-Svea*, 7 September 1967: 4. For a dissenting reply to this column, see E.I. Folke, "Ordet Fritt," *Nordstjernan-Svea*, 25 April 1968. Despite Sylvan's assertion, there was really very little news from North Vietnam in the Swedish media. (Queckfeldt, "*Vietnam*," 60.)

[8] Harry Fabbe, "Hört och Hänt: Svensk press är välinformerad," *Svenska Posten*, 27 April 1966: 1; Harry Fabbe, "Hört och Hänt: Svensk press är välinformerad," *Svenska Posten*, 27 April 1966: 1. Many in the mainstream U.S. press believed this too. *The Minneapolis Star* for example wrote, "Television newscasts in Sweden use Vietcong propaganda films extensively." ("Sweden, The Phony Neutral," *Minneapolis Star*, 3 February 1969.)

in 1966. Harry Fabbe ran part of Lidman's article in *Svenska Posten*, including her interview with Ho Chi Minh.[10]

Svenska Posten's Adolf Jacobson considered the Lidman article simple Hanoi propaganda. Jacobson thought she portrayed Ho Chi Minh as "a veritable Christ figure," but "President Johnson, on the other hand, is a thug." American planes drop bombs at random, without regard for human lives, while Lidman described the Vietnamese as determined and heroic.[11] Lidman wrote that the capitalist press distorted facts about events in Vietnam. Jacobson concluded it was hard to know who was telling the truth, since "truth is a relative concept." He strongly implied that whatever truth was, there was not much of it in Lidman's article.[12]

Svenska Posten's conservative columnist Reinhold Ahleen echoed Lidman's complaint in his own terms. "Media barons control the press in the U.S. and portion out what they want the reader to know and nothing more." Ahleen thought they were doing the same thing with the Vietnam story. In reporting Vietnam, most American news magazines "only deliver the government's views and not the people's." Ahleen also believed the U.S. press had not yet told the complete story on Vietnam.[13]

---

[9] *Expressen's* Vietnam correspondent Ulf Nilson writes, "The other side did not admit anyone, and a few [reporters] that wandered in by mistake were killed. Hanoi admitted one or two dedicated supporters, but a reporter like me never got a visa despite many attempts." Sweden's chargé d'affarés to Hanoi wrote the North Vietnamese "press is totally controlled, and only things relating to the Vietnam War get published . . . this is a hard, a very hard information climate, mostly because of the close character of the communist society." (E-mail from Ulf Nilson to Göteborg B-student Jonathan Karlsson, 8 May 2001, courtesy of Nilson and Karlsson; Letter from Jean-Christophe Öberg to Eva Heckscher, 19 April 1971, file "1971–1985," JN1Xv, UD.)

[10] Harry Fabbe, "Hört och Hänt: Sara Lidman skriver om sitt besök nyligen i Nordvietnam," *Svenska Posten*, 4 May 1966: 1.

[11] As an FNL supporter, her allusion to "the Vietnamese" referred to a single country. Americans specifically had the South Vietnamese in mind when they referred to "the Vietnamese" – whom they might agree were heroic for resisting "the North Vietnamese."

[12] Adolf W. Jacobson and Sara Lidman, "Fakta och Funderingar," *Svenska Posten*, 25 May 1966: 4. Jacobson does not quote the 4 May 1966 "Hört och Hänt" editorial in *Svenska Posten*, but Lidman's original article in *Vi*.

[13] Reinhold Ahleen, "Rim och Reson," *Svenska Posten*, 9 February 1966: 4.

On 26 May 1965, *Svenska Posten* printed an editorial called "Facts are Facts." This *Stockholms-Tidningen* editorial, critical of U.S. policy, also said that much had not yet been told. The author, Sture Källberg, had visited North Vietnam in 1962. He had seen the destruction and exhaustion from the last war, and the willingness to fight again. He said that nobody had welcomed the Americans as liberators in this current war.[14] "The article is a real eye-opener," Reinhold Ahleen wrote three weeks later. "It should be translated into English and sent to the nation's leadership. If there is any truth in that Vietnam has become a field for military maneuvers, I cannot think of a greater stain on the reputation of our times."[15]

Most Swedish-American commentators were not as open to Swedish criticism. Most of them just hardened their hawkish views. *Svenska-Amerikanaren* hated Källberg's editorial. "Facts are Facts" and other *ST* editorials, were "clearly communist-inspired and without any hint of true information." *Svenska-Amerikanaren* dismissed *Stockholms-Tidningen*'s printed letters to the editor as anti-American "hate propaganda."[16] A *Svenska-Amerikanaren* reader wrote, "A large part of the Swedish press . . . has cast their lot with the Communists and Vietcong . . . Has this press been brainwashed by Russian propaganda?"[17] The view that the Swedish media were under communist control became increasingly common as the war went on. Swedish critics saw the U.S. press as a propaganda machine, but some (not all) Swedish-Americans saw the Swedish press as communistic. Both saw their news as accurate, but the other's as distorted, value-laden, and biased. Swedish and American standards of objectivity were drifting apart.[18]

---

[14] "Hört och Hänt: Facts are Facts," *Svenska Posten*, 26 May 1965: 1, 4.

[15] Reinhold Ahleen, "Rim och Reson," *Svenska Posten*, 16 June 1965.

[16] Arthur Hendricks, "Vad den som vet bättre säger om amerikansk utrikespolitik," *Svenska-Amerikanaren Tribunen*, 5 January 1966: 4.

[17] "Boxholmaren" Alf N. Carlson, "Folkets Röst: En frihetens symbol," *Svenska-Amerikanaren Tribunen*, 20 July 1966: 5. See also Carlson's letter in the 26 July 1967 edition of *SAT*. For similar letters see: Berit Gustavsson, "Sverige och Vietnam," *California Veckoblad*, 23 June 1970 and *Svenska-Amerikanaren Tribinen*, 21 June 1970; Harry C. Seaburgh, "Ordet Fritt," *Nordstjernan-Svea*, 13 February 1969; and Helga Stromberg, "Folkets Röst: Kritik från svensk press," *Svenska-Amerikanaren Tribunen*, 20 July 1966: 5.

Many mainstream American newspapers agreed that the Swedish press was drifting to the left. Many small conservative American papers ran a 1967 article by Åke Thulstrup claiming an anti-American bias in Swedish Television.[19] Many American papers ran extracts from the 1965 *Stockholms-Tidningen* debate-articles "Why We Hate the U.S.A." The American papers referred to these debate-articles as *ST* editorials. These appeared frequently during Tage Erlander's trip to America. (Many papers ran these items believing the Social Democratic *ST* was an official organ of the Swedish government.)[20] *Nordstjernan* and *Svea* ran a *Sverige-Nytt* editorial as a rebuttal. It recognized that many Swedes thought the U.S. made a serious mistake in sending troops to Vietnam. It was simply wrong to assume Swedes had come to hate ethnic Americans because of this.[21]

Sweden and the United States were also developing different standards of television reporting. American TV news often has a documentary feel, but Swedish TV news uses film with symbolic images and artistic camera angles. This difference in reporting styles emerged as a problem in January 1969. *Svenska-Amerikanaren* wrote that a Swedish TV reporter had used the U.S. flag as a doormat, wiping his feet on the Stars and Stripes. Reporter Per-Martin Hamberg visited the Marxist-Leninist Party, an anti-American group which had a doormat shaped like a U.S. flag. The television film showed Hamberg using the doormat as he entered the apartment. Some of these details did not appear in *SAT*'s report. *SAT* instead wrote that Hamberg had staged the film for its symbolism.[22] American TV networks have been known to stage

---

[18] The American definition of objectivity – Hallin, *The Uncensored War*, 68 – includes an emphasis on political neutrality not as widely accepted in Sweden. By American values, Swedish reporters may well have violated this standard.

[19] Memo by Lennart Alvin, "Sverige i Amerikansk press 1967," attached to letter from Sven Frychius to Sten Sundfeldt, 8 December 1967, file 90 "Januari – Februari 1968," box I:324, NL1, RA.

[20] Memo from Hubert de Besche to UD, "Sverige i Amerikansk press år 1965," file 83 "April – September 1966," box I:322, NL1, RA.

[21] "Hatar vi USA?" *Nordstjernan* and *Svea*, 20 January 1966.

[22] "Stjärnbaneret skymfat i svenskt TV-program av obildade reporters," *Svenska-Amerikanaren Tribunen*, 29 January 1969: 1.

footage, but the networks condemn the practice as highly unprofessional. Many *Svenska-Amerikanaren* readers found this story disturbing. It implied the Swedish media was not only unprofessional but also ideologically biased. Many "Folkets Röst" readers presumed this episode marked a new, anti-American policy in Swedish Television. Some readers argued the Swedish government encouraged such anti-Americanism. John T. Karlsson wrote to say that he was ashamed to say that he came from Sweden. Hilma Anderson thought, "That hippie reporter ought to be sent to Siberia for a few months."[23]

Swedish news coverage of American society was also becoming unflattering. *Nordstjernan* wrote that a recent Congressional report judged that Sweden's mass media focused mostly on crime, racial conflict, hippies, and Vietnam in reporting American society.[24] A *Svenska-Amerikanaren* reader was visiting Sweden during the "fall of Saigon." The coverage of the U.S. that she saw on Swedish Television astonished her. "My husband worked as a carpenter there," she wrote.

> All day long, he had his co-workers against him, because of what they had seen the night before about the bad conditions in America. All the reports and film clips came from Hanoi. He tried to explain to them that these were just propaganda films, but they wouldn't believe it. What my husband said was just propaganda. It got even worse for my husband, hearing them disparage the U.S. every day. We never dreamed how hated America had become in working circles in Sweden.[25]

Another Swedish-American visitor noticed the same phenomenon. "I watch on Swedish TV just how bad it is in America," a *Svenska-Amerikanaren* reader wrote.

---

[23] John T. Karlsson, "Folkets Röst: [sic] Skräcker USA-turisterna," 12 March 1969: 4; Hilma P., "Folkets Röst: Åsikt," *Svenska-Amerikanaren Tribunen*, 25 June 1969: 5; for other Folkets Röst comments, see: Bertil, "Åsikt," 5 March 1969; Carl Borgervall, "Amerika och Sverige," 26 November 1969; Birger W. Hanson, "Här och där," 15 April 1970; and Holger Hesselmark, "Till broder Carlson," 14 May 1969.

[24] "Svensk kritik skapar oro i Amerika," *Nordstjernan-Svea*, 21 March 1968: 4.

[25] E.S., "Folkets Röst: Vad två svensk-amerikaner upplevde i Sverige," *Svenska-Amerikanaren Tribunen*, 4 June 1975: 4.

They only show propaganda films about slums and misery. You never hear about the many good things about life and living here. On Vietnam and the war there, you never hear about the communists' ravage the land. It's always about how the U.S. bombs hospitals and kills innocent people. When you listen to the radio or watch TV, you only see and hear condemnation of the U.S.[26]

Many Swedish-Americans described this as a growing culture of anti-Americanism in Sweden. Adolf Jacobson wrote in *SAT* that many Swedish critics were "mean and hateful." For whatever reason, they wanted to paint American society as black as possible. A *Nordstjernan* reader thought the U.S. had become a Swedish scapegoat for anything they disliked. He had often visited Sweden, but said he did not want to hear "Here come the damn emigrants," and "Yankee go home" again.[27]

American media coverage of Sweden was also changing rapidly. In 1965 UD prided itself on positive U.S. coverage of Sweden, especially on technology and industry.[28] Swedish antiwar protests were rapidly displacing these positive articles in 1966. Conservative papers often used Sweden as a lurid warning example in criticizing LBJ's social programs.[29] *U.S. News and World Report*, for example, used Sweden as an example of how welfare programs lead to crime and moral decay. *Look* magazine's article "Sweden and Sex" was not completely negative, but rehashed some old, familiar charges.[30] By extension, these imply moral decay can lead to social turmoil and political protests.

---

[26] E.S., "Folkets Röst: Vad två svensk-amerikaner upplevde i Sverige," *Svenska-Amerikanaren Tribunen*, 4 June 1975: 4. See also: "TV-Guide anser svensk TV anti-USA," *Vestkusten*, 9 March 1972: 1.

[27] Adolf Jacobson, "Folkets Röst: Lite småprat," *Svenska-Amerikanaren Tribunen*, 20 November 1975: 5; and Harry C. Seaburgh, "Ordet Fritt," *Nordstjernan-Svea*, 13 February 1969: 6.

[28] Memo "Material Published in the American Press January 1 – 30 June, 1965," attached to letter from Holger Lundbergh to Sten Sundfeldt, 6 July 1965, file 81 "USA mars 1965 – aug 1965," box I:322, NL1, RA.

[29] Memo from Torsten Henriksson, mailed by L. Schönander, 9 February 1966, file 82 "USA September 1965 – Mars 1966," box I:322, NL1, RA.

[30] Alfred Zänker, *U.S. News and World Report*, 7 February 1966: 58; "Sweden and Sex," *Look*, 15 November 1966.

In brief, by 1966 the Swedish-American papers noted the antiwar protests in Sweden. Most emigrant papers still supported the war at this stage, and these protests signified a new cultural dissonance. Many papers tried to downplay these protests' significance. One way to do this was to suggest the protesters did not reflect the views of Sweden's Silent Majority. Another way – common after 1968 – was to describe the protests as driven by irrational anti-Americanism. This label stripped some legitimacy from their criticism. A third way – common before 1968 – was to deny the protesters really understood what was happening in Vietnam. *Nordstjernan*'s Eric Sylvan, for example, dismissed the Swedish protesters as "significantly lacking in knowledge or understanding of our situation in Vietnam."[31]

For people who thought the protesters did not understand the situation, it was only a short step to blaming the Swedish media. The Swedish press had a duty to explain and inform the public about Vietnam. If the Swedish people did not know or understand the U.S. situation in Vietnam, the press had failed them. There seemed to be just three possible causes for this. The Swedish press was either inept, used biased sources, or was ideologically hostile to America. Commentators who supported the war – such as Eric Sylvan – used some or all of these reasons. Antiwar commentators – such as Harry Fabbe – liked the Swedish press interpretation of Vietnam. Yet, even Fabbe assumed Sweden's media used supposedly biased North Vietnamese sources.

Few Swedish-American commentators listened to or absorbed Swedish criticism or protests. Swedish critics were people to rebut, oppose, support, undermine, or pointedly ignore. Few listened. Only *Svenska Posten* and *The Messenger* seemed to take Swedish criticism of the war seriously. *The Messenger* ran two editorials on Vietnam editorials in 1965. Both of them cite hostile public opinion "in friendly countries" as a reason for the U.S. to change policy.[32] *Svenska Posten* often agreed with the substance of Swedish criticism,

---

[31] Eric Sylvan, "Det Tycks," *Nordstjernan*, 15 July 1965: 7.

[32] Rev. B.W. Selen, "The Observation Tower," *The Messenger* (*Sändebudet*), April and March 1965: 2.

only *The Messenger* argued the existence of foreign opposition was itself a reason to leave Vietnam.

Sweden's Sheltering of U.S. Deserters

The first U.S. deserters to come to Sweden arrived in August 1967. The Erlander government decided to grant them asylum for humanitarian reasons.[33] At first, only a handful of deserters followed. By mid-1968, ever more deserters were turning up at Swedish immigration centers. (Unlike the draft evaders that went to Canada, the deserters had already joined the U.S. military.) The U.S. press widely reported Sweden's acceptance of the deserters, and few supported the policy.[34] Some papers believed – incorrectly – Sweden gave the deserters asylum for political reasons. These papers did not consider going "absent without leave" from a military base as an expression of political beliefs. They did grasp, however, how giving U.S. deserters asylum could benefit certain Swedish leaders politically. Other newspapers reacted against Sweden sheltering the deserters for humanitarian reasons. These newspapers doubted the U.S. would treat any returned deserters inhumanely.[35] As Boston's *Christian Science Monitor* wrote, "No Swedish government can say that the United States is a land of persecution."[36]

Swedish-American coverage of the deserters started in late 1967 after the first of them arrived.[37] Coverage of the deserters grew

---

[33] Documentary "Hell No, We Won't Go," Swedish Television, Channel 2: 24 April 1997.

[34] Press Intelligence Inc. found 103 news articles in the U.S. press on Sweden's deserter policy from 1 October 1969 to 1 June 1970. It judged 74 of them to have a neutral tone, 26 had a negative tone, and only 3 stories had an positive tone about Sweden's deserter policy. (Memo "Protokoll över upplysningskommitténs sammanträdande i New York den 15–16 juni 1970: bilaga 4," file "1970, juli–augusti," JN1Ua, UD.)

[35] Memorandum by Lennart Alvin, 5 February 1968, attached to letter from Sven Frychius to Sten Sundfeldt, 5 February 1968; courtesy of Carl-Gustav Scott, University of Washington.

[36] *Christian Science Monitor*, 7 February 1969, from UD Pressbyrån, *Sverige i utländsk press, 1969*, (yearly series) Stockholm: 23.

[37] "Desertören kom till Sverige," *Svenska Posten*, 30 August 1967: 1, and "En 20-årig färgad desertör," *Vestkusten*, 31 August 1967: 1.

Drawing courtesy of Nordstjernan.

dramatically over the next two years. For example, *Nordstjernan* ran fifty-six news articles about Swedish Vietnam policies in 1968. Six of these were about the deserters. By the first six months of 1969, this percentage had jumped to one story in every three.[38] *Svenska-Amerikanaren* ran seven "deserter stories" in 1969, and an eighth linked the deserters to foreign trade. Here too, news of the deserters occupied almost one-third of the news coverage.

Svenska Posten was relatively quiet on the deserter issue. *SvP*'s Adele Heilborn wrote two articles in 1968 on the U.S. defectors. One cited a *Borås Tidning* editorial critical of the deserters and the decision to accept them.[39] In a later article, she conceded Sweden did not aim its policy directly at the U.S. She noted that Sweden accepted French soldiers deserting from the Algerian War. There was a legal precedent for Sweden's policy, which she considered "a very important thing."[40]

Svenska Posten's Stephen Forslund pushed the Algerian analogy further. Sweden "has accepted both Poles, Balts, and Germans under similar circumstances, and even Frenchmen who didn't want to fight in Algeria. Why should Americans be in a different category when the circumstances are the same?"[41] The usually nonpolitical *Western News* agreed. It pointed out that even the U.S. had welcomed deserters in similar circumstances.[42] An *SAT* reader in Stockholm urged emigrant readers to forget the deserters were in uniform. To

---

[38] Of thirty-two stories between 16 January and 17 July 1969, ten were on the deserters.

[39] Adele Heilborn, "Stockholmsbrev," *Svenska Posten*, 24 July 1968.

[40] Adele Heilborn, "Stockholmsbrev," *Svenska Posten*, 22 May 1968: 3. Carl-Gustav Scott points out, "While it is true that Seden began to accept foreign deserters as early as World War II and had recieved French deserters during the Algerian War, no actual *legal* precedent existed at the time when the first American deserters arrived. It was added retrospectively." (Carl-Gustav Scott, "Swedish Sanctuary of American Deserters During the Vietnam War," *Scandinavian Journal of History*, vol. 26 no. 2, 2001: 126)

[41] Stephen Forslund, "Pränt om ditt och datt av Stephen Forslund," *Svenska Posten*, 1 May 1968. Carl-Gustav Scott adds, "Sweden did not begin to accept German deserters until the war had begun to turn against the Third Reich. Prior to the Allied victory at Alamein in November 1942, German deserters were simply repatriated to their units in Norway and Finland." (Scott, "Swedish Sanctuary of American Deserters During the Vietnam War," 126, note 12.)

her, they were simple refugees that had come to Sweden for shelter.[43] Sweden had a long-standing tradition of granting shelter to those who needed it, and was not just targeting Americans. It had sheltered Nazi persecution years earlier, *Western News* wrote, "so we can hardly complain now."[44]

Like the U.S., Sweden also accepted deserters and refugees from communist countries. *Nordstjernan* stressed that Sweden had accepted over twenty-five thousand such refugees. *Vasastjärnan* believed many Americans were unaware that other countries had accepted many more deserters than Sweden. *Western News* listed these countries as France, Switzerland, and Canada. For some reason, *Vasastjärnan* thought the U.S. media focused relentlessly and unfairly on the Swedish deserters.[45]

Stephen Forslund also asserted that many Swedes had emigrated to escape military service. His point that many Swedish "corporals took their farming-leave to slip away across the Atlantic" resonated in some readers.[46] An *SAT* reader recalled Swedish soldiers easily buying black-market emigration papers in Norway or Denmark. Another reader guessed that several hundred Swedish draftees had fled to America. A third reader wondered why the United States never returned these Swedish deserters.[47] *Canada-Svensken* thought a new wave of Swedish deserters might develop. Sweden had its own

---

[42] Enoch Peterson, "America Also Holds Deserters From Other Countries," *The Western News,* 22 January 1970: 1.

[43] Gurli Crona. "Folkets Röst: Hälsning från Stockholm," *Svenska-Amerikanaren Tribunen*, 14 May 1969: 5.

[44] "Sweden, Vietnam, and Neutrality," *The Western News*, 13 November 1969: 6.

[45] Rune Moberg, "Sänd Nixon 'USA-Sweden,'" *Nordstjernan-Svea*, 2 October 1969: 4. Reprinted from *Se*; "Interviewers From Sweden's TV Found Americans Mostly Misinformed About Sweden," *Vasastjärnan*, April 1970: 9; and George Kane, "Bad Publicity For Sweden Scored," *The Western News*, 31 October 1968: 1.

[46] Stephen Forslund, "Pränt om ditt och datt av Stephen Forslund," *Svenska Posten*, 1 May 1968. See also: Viktor Johansen, "Folkets Röst: Paleface," *Svenska-Amerikanaren Tribunen*, 2 April 1969.

[47] John E. Eriksson, "Folkets Röst: Olycksmoln," 21 January 1970: 5; Mrs. Fritz R. Stenborg, "Folkets Röst," 19 November 1969: 5; and Allen Berg, "Folkets Röst: På Krigsstigen!" *Svenska-Amerikanaren Tribunen*, 22 April 1970: 5.

laws against desertion. Such laws would be harder to enforce now that Sweden's government had condoned desertion.[48]

Nordstjernan thought these analogies were weak. This was partly because "no Americans ever glorified the Swedish deserters, turned them into folk heroes, or used them as a political tool to be used against the Swedish government and Swedish society." *Western News* added that Sweden had not been at war either.[49]

For some Swedish-Americans, their own youthful lives had not been much different from the deserters' lives. "I have always been an anti-militarist," wrote *Svenska Posten*'s Kalle Palm. "I remember how I, eighty years ago, sold recruiting ballads outside the Stockholm induction office. ... When I got older, I gave out anti-military propaganda instead. It was *Think First and Act Later* by Leo Tolstoy, *To Our Comrades in Uniform* and *Down With Arms* by Berta von Sutter." Palm speculated that hatred for the war was likely prevalent in the army. War brutalizes and dehumanizes a person, so there was likely resistance to it.[50] Palm's paper, *Svenska Posten*, was openly antiwar. It also served an emigrant community further to the political left than most papers. It may not be surprising to find these views in *Svenska Posten*, but similar views also appeared in *SAT*'s "Folkets Röst" page. Support for the deserters existed in both large and small communities, traditional and more recent emigrant centers.

In summary, the mainstream U.S. press disapproved of Sweden's sheltering of American deserters.[51] Many in the Swedish-American press also resented the Swedish policy. It may be perhaps surprising that this was far from a universal view. The Swedish-American press was not a bastion of antiwar feeling, but some commentators could support the deserter policy. When the deserter question arose in the late Sixties, there was growing opposition to the war. One could

---

[48] Thorwald Wiik, untitled editorial, *Canada-Svensken*, 16 April 1968: 2.

[49] Quote from *Nya Wermlands Tidningen*, cited in "Erlander upptäcker USA:s goda vilja i Sydvietnam," *Nordstjernan-Svea*, 12 February 1970: 4; and George Kane, "Bad Publicity For Sweden Scored," *The Western News*, 31 October 1968: 1.

[50] Kalle Palm, "Tankar från Palmlunden," *Svenska Posten*, 13 March 1968.

[51] *Sverige i utländsk press 1968*, 12; and *Sverige i utländsk press 1969*, 23–25.

interpret the support of Sweden's deserter policy as a militant expression of antiwar feeling. It certainly was a militant idea by American standards, however. One could speculate that Swedish-Americans were perhaps more willing to agree with the deserter policy simply because it was Sweden. They wanted to agree with Sweden; they wanted to respect its policies. Some Swedish-Americans even expressed sympathy with the deserters' personal plight. The readers that identified with the deserters were often older men who had been young during the First World War. Vietnam war-hawks usually described the current conflict as a continuation of World War Two. Some aging emigrants saw it as more akin to the meaningless bloodbath of World War One. This aging readership could have been more receptive to antiwar opinions than younger readers were.

Olof Palme as a Person and Symbol

Much of the Swedish-American criticism of Swedish Vietnam policy focused on the critics themselves. The emigrant press saw Foreign Ministers Torsten Nilsson and Krister Wickman as near embodiments of the Swedish policies. (The emigrant papers usually spared elder statesman Tage Erlander from criticism.) No politician, however, became more of a lighting-rod than Olof Palme.

In July 1965, cabinet adviser Olof Palme gave a widely publicized speech on Vietnam. It was a tame speech by later standards. Its main theme was that military force would likely not win social justice. Palme did not even directly mention the U.S., and referred to Vietnam only once at the end.[52] It was, however, Sweden's first statement of opposition to the war. This Gävle speech helped propel Palme into the forefront, making him the party's leading debater on social issues. He became Minister of Education in 1967, but continued to speak on Vietnam. Some Swedish-American commentators wondered why the Erlander government allowed its Education Minister to take such a large role in foreign policy.[53] As

---

[52] Möller, "Olof Palmes Gävletal," *Sverige och Vietnamkriget*, 37–52.

[53] Gösta Guston, "Ordet är Fritt: Öppet brev till Hans Excellens, Statsminister Tage Erlander," *Nordstjernan-Svea*, 28 March 1968: 7; and "Varken hjälte eller martyr," *California Veckoblad*, 3 May 1968. Reprint from *Göteborgs-Posten*.

Olof Palme continued speaking on Vietnam, his political influence in the party grew. By early 1968, most political observers predicted he would be the next Prime Minister.

On 21 February 1968, Olof Palme marched in an antiwar demonstration in Stockholm's Sergels Torg. Hanoi's ambassador to Moscow, Nguyen Tho Chan, marched by his side. Palme's speech criticized America's war, supported the FNL, and recommended negotiations. Unlike his Gävle speech, this one condemned U.S. policy in direct terms.[54] Ambassador Nguyen's address was radical – from a Western perspective. Although Palme was on the same stage as Nguyen, he did not disavow or temper Nguyen's sentiments.

The Swedish-American press did not like Palme's speech, or the march with a North Vietnamese diplomat. *Svenska-Amerikanaren* reported it with the headline: "Anti-USA Demonstration in Stockholm." *California Veckoblad* carried the headline: "Sweden's Top Officials Join Anti-USA Demonstrations in Stockholm."[55] Such headlines frame the following stories. As Lyndon Johnson once said, "The headlines were all I read, and they're all the people read."[56]

Sverige-Nytt's article played down the event and Palme's role in it. *Sverige-Nytt's* text does not even mention Palme until the final third of the story.[57] The segment on Palme appears in small type, which the paper used to mark nonessential news that emigrant editors could omit. *Sverige-Nytt* provided a relatively mild quotation about negotiations from Palme's speech.[58] *Svenska Posten* ran this tepid story as it was.[59] *Nordstjernan* ran it as "New Attacks Against

---

[54] Möller, *Sverige och Vietnamkriget*, 119–120; Palme's speech appears in Olof Palme, *USA-kriget i Vietnam*, Stockholm, 1968, and Swedish Foreign Ministry, *Sverige och Vietnamfrågan: Anföranden och uttalanden*, Stockholm, 1968: 59–64.

[55] For example, see: "Anti-USA demonstration i Stockholm," *Svenska-Amerikanaren Tribunen*, 13 March 1968: 10; and "Sweden's Top Officials Join Anti-USA Demonstrations in Stockholm," *California Veckoblad*, 15 March 1968: 1.

[56] Lyndon Johnson, cited in Kathleen J. Turner, *Lyndon Johnson's Dual War*, Chicago, 1985: 185.

[57] The story covers twenty-one centimeters of text. Palme appears on the thirteenth centimeter.

[58] See Palme's speech, *USA-kriget i Vietnam*, page 10; and compare it to "Hanois Moskvasändebud på informationbesök," *Sverige-Nytt*, 27 February 1968: 3.

America in Shameless Demonstration: Palme Disgraces Swedish People With Speech."[60]

Sverige-Nytt issued a photograph of Palme marching with Ambassador Nguyen, which *Nordstjernan* printed. Arthur Hendricks, *Svenska-Amerikanaren* and *California Veckoblad*'s editor, was in Sweden in February 1968. He found a photo of protesters holding signs such as "Military Help for FNL," "Hitler – LBJ," and "USA Murders." This photo was far more inflammatory, and Hendricks used it for his newspapers. "Read the banners," Hendricks wrote. "How can you say, honestly, that Olof Palme respects and admires America so much when he leads anti-USA demonstrations?"[61]

There was little U.S. comment on the episode largely because the Tet Offensive still dominated U.S. papers. The emigrant papers began by printing Swedish press opinion instead. *Nordstjernan* and *Svenska-Amerikanaren* ran a *Svenska Dagbladet* editorial critical of Palme for linking Sweden's government with the communist side in the war. *Göteborgs Handels- och Sjöfarts-tidning* noted that Palme marched with people protesting his own government. *Göteborgs-Posten* thought Palme drew support from "vocal revolutionaries . . . the parliament of violence and the street."[62] *Nordstjernan*'s Eric Sylvan said Palme made "common cause with the thankfully small number of America-haters and communist-sympathizers who have no better outlet for their antisocial tendencies than flag-burning, egg-throwing, and window-smashing."[63] This loose association of

---

[59] "Nordvietnams sändebud i Moskva på besök," *Svenska Posten*, 28 February 1968: 1.

[60] "Nya attacker mot Amerika i skamlös demonstration: Palme skandaliserar svenska folket med tal," *Nordstjernan-Svea*, 7 March 1968: 1.

[61] Photograph "Anti-USA demonstration i Stockholm" appears in *California Veckoblad*, 15 March 1968: 1, 6 June 1969: 1, and *Svenska-Amerikanaren Tribunen*, 13 March 1968: 6. For Arthur Hendricks' presence in Stockholm, see "We Still Say Olof Palme is Anti-USA," *California Veckoblad*, 6 June 1969: 1.

[62] "Kring Palme," *Nordstjernan-Svea*, 7 March 1968: 4; and *Svenska-Amerikanaren Tribunen*, 13 March 1968: 8.

[63] Eric Sylvan, "Det Tycks," *Nordstjernan-Svea*, 28 March 1968: 4. *Nordstjernan* also took the unusual step of printing the names and addresses of all Swedish reporters in the U.S. The clear but unstated message was that angry readers should complain to those people. (*Nordstjernan-Svea*, 7 March 1968: 5.)

Anti-USA demonstration i Stockholm

Olof Palme, antiwar protests, and social turbulence was common among the critics. *California Veckoblad* argued that Olof Palme may not have condoned any specific anti-American incidents. Yet, "his open approval of these acts adds fuel to 'the popular thing.'"[64]

Palme's speech incensed the U.S. government. Ambassador William Heath was furious, and told Prime Minister Erlander, "You are making a hero out of our enemy." The White House soon called Heath ambassador home "for consultations." President Johnson followed Sweden's criticism for years – with anger and resentment – but resisted action.[65] William Heath recommended the withdrawal this time. According to Heath, official Swedish policy had "created an environment where threatening actions and degrading forms of protest against American representatives could occur, even against the Ambassador himself." Heath said the Swedish authorities did

---

[64] Arthur B. Hendricks, "We Still Say: Olof Palme is Anti-USA," *California Veckoblad*, 6 June 1969: 1.

[65] William Heath, cited in memo from Wilhelm Wachtmeister to Sverker Åström, "Amerikanske ambassadören besöker statsministern för samtal om svensk-amerikanska förbindelserna," 7 March 1968, file 7, HP1:Xv/spe, UD; letter from Hubert de Besche to Sten Sundfeldt, 3 February 1966, file "1966–1968: Vietnam," box I:605, U6, RA.

nothing to stop egg-throwing demonstrators, "for fear of losing a handful of votes."[66]

It was short-lived, but recalling Ambassador Heath was popular in the Swedish-American press. This was more true among columnists and letter-writers than the Swedish-American editors. The editors thought they were in a difficult position, where strong positions could only anger readers.[67] Among letter-writers, *Svenska Posten* ran a letter saying, "Uncle Sam's patience ... has finally ended with Sweden."[68] *Svenska Posten*'s conservative columnist, Reinhold Ahleen, wrote that the recall filled him "with sorrow and shame." The recall was a justified action and purely Sweden's fault.[69] (This was not *Svenska Posten*'s opinion, so Ahleen's piece appeared in *Nordstjernan*.) Another letter to Nordstjernan called Palme's march "indecent and immoral. No wonder we decided to recall our ambassador 'for consultations.'"[70] *Canada-Svensken* believed Palme

Olof Palme, Anti-USA Leader, May Be Next Premier Of Sweden

---

[66] William Heath, cited in memo from Wilhelm Wachtmeister to Sverker Åström, "Amerikanske ambassadören besöker statsministern för samtal om svensk-amerikanska förbindelserna," 7 March 1968, file 7, HP1:Xv/spec, UD. Even the North Vietnamese did not appreciate this. According to Sweden's main negotiator, "The North Vietnamese government would appreciate it if we re-established friendly relations with USA." (Telegram from J.C. Öberg to Cabinet Stockholm, 13 July 1968, file 8, HP1:Xv/spe, UD.)

[67] Gerry Rooth, "Ordet är Fritt: Dear Mr. Muentzing," *Nordstjernan-Svea*, 23 October 1969: 10.

[68] Bertil, "Från Läsekreten: Uncle Sams tålamod slut ..." *Svenska Posten*, 13 March 1968: 3.

[69] Reinhold Ahleen, "Ordet Fritt: Herr Redaktor," *Nordstjernan-Svea*, 25 April 1968.

[70] Sigfrid K. Lonegren, "Ordet Fritt: Sweden-U.S.A." *Nordstjernan-Svea*, 25 April 1968.

had ruined Sweden's neutrality. It suggested that his ouster might help restore relations with the U.S.[71] The liberal *Svenska Posten* argued the President was punishing Sweden for voicing ideas widespread in America. *SvP* detected domestic politics at play.[72]

●

Olof Palme became Sweden's Prime Minister in late 1969. By this point, some Swedish-American readers saw him as "the darling of Sweden's extremist organizations."[73] When a *California Veckoblad* reader tried to defend Palme, the paper ran a caustic editorial on its front page as a rebuttal.[74] In this editorial, as elsewhere, *California Veckoblad* wrote that Palme was becoming Sweden's new *Premier*. The word had a clear Soviet ring to it. The paper called Tage Erlander the *Prime Minister*, which had a familiar British sound.

Olof Palme visited the United States in early June 1970. His stated purpose was to visit Kenyon College and accept an honorary degree. Palme hoped his visit to America might help improve U.S.-Swedish relations. He scheduled his trip just weeks after a racially-charged incident involving the new U.S. ambassador. (More about this below.) *Nordstjernan* reprinted a *New York Daily News* editorial that said, "he can keep his advice. We don't owe Palme even a polite hearing, particularly since his countrymen have gone out of their way to insult our envoy, Ambassador Jerome Holland, at every opportunity."[75]

Svenska Posten's Reinhold Ahleen reported that Palme's visit to the White House was less than a success. According to *U.S. News and World Report*, Ahleen wrote:

---

[71] Thorwald Wiik, "Neutralitet, skatter och socialreformer," *Canada-Svensken*, 16–31 March 1968.

[72] Harry Fabbe, "Hört och Hänt: Relationerna Sverige-USA," *Svenska Posten*, 27 March 1968: 3.

[73] Adolf W. Jacobson, "Lite Småprat," *California Veckoblad*, 31 October 1969: 6.

[74] Åke Sandler, "Dr. Åke Sandler Likes Mr. Olof Palme," and Arthur B. Hendricks, "We Still Say Olof Palme is Anti-USA," *California Veckoblad*, 6 June 1969: 1. (Professor Åke Sandler – the son of former Prime Minister Rikard Sandler – currently writes for *Vestkusten*.)

[75] "Prime Minister Olof Palme," *Nordstjernan-Svea*, 4 June 1970: 4.

Palme had a long talk with Secretary of State William Rogers. A photo of the meeting shows the mature and sober Rogers with deep lines in his forehead and Palme making an effort to answer correctly and diplomatically. . . . Here he couldn't get away with witticisms as he can in Paris or London. The Americans are of a different breed. After this crossfire, Palme can draw a sigh of relief to be on the plane back home.

"The magazine in question is openly Sweden-hostile," editor Harry Fabbe inserted into Ahleen's column. Fabbe added that Rogers had arranged the meeting with Palme and scheduled a follow-up meeting.[76] According to Fabbe, *Svenska Posten* received special shipments of clippings from the Swedish press sent daily from Stockholm.[77] Perhaps UD was making sure Fabbe took a correctly Swedish interpretation of Palme's trip.

Palme changed few opinions on Sweden's Vietnam policies during his trip, but may have won some respect in the U.S. The Swedish-American press still viewed him as a leftist radical. He was still the man who marched with a North Vietnamese diplomat. Yet for him to visit America seemed bold, showing a sincere desire for better relations. Some Swedish-American columnists predicted relations would soon improve. The conservative *California Veckoblad* admired Palme's courage in facing a hostile crowd.

One hundred dock workers had come [to his speech] . . . to protest the Swedish Vietnam policy. They carried signs like "Palme the Racist," "Palme – Sweden's George Wallace," "Palme – War Monger," and "Palme – Peace Saboteur." When the Prime Minister began speaking they moved forward and shouted their slogans, booed, and roared "Go home you bum" and "Go back to Hanoi," etc."

Svenska-Amerikanaren, Svenska Posten, and *California Veckoblad* all noted with satisfaction that Palme condemned the protesters that attacked Ambassador Holland. He told his American audience those protesters had tried to undermine his trip to the U.S. "It only made me more determined to come here," Palme told his audience, to

---

[76] Reinhold Ahleen, "Rim och Reson av Reinhold Ahleen," *Svenska Posten,* 24 June 1970: 4. See also: "Sweden's Hate-America Campaign – Why?" *U.S. News and World Report,* 18 March 1968.

[77] "Hört och Hänt: Smånotiser från skilda håll," *Svenska Posten,* 24 June 1970: 4.

great applause, "even if I were carried here on a stretcher."[78] Perhaps Olof Palme never erased his Sergels Torg image, but it helped add to his growing image as a dynamic leader. Gerry Rooth regretted printing the *New York Daily News* editorial in *Nordstjernan*. "Here we willingly admit that it was a hasty decision and not fully contemplated move."[79] *California Veckoblad* did not go that far, but started using the phrase "Prime Minister Palme."[80]

Olof Palme became a lightning-rod for criticism over the next few years. One can only speculate why that was so. His image in the emigrant press, however, became fixed when he marched with Nguyen Than Cho on Sergels Torg. To the aging conservative Swedish-Americans, he was a protester. Unlike many Swedish politicians, Palme was young, affluent, well-spoken, and well-educated. Even these virtues worked to link him with the college students protesting on American campuses. His appearance in the film *I Am Curious Yellow* – banned as pornography in most U.S. states – only solidified Palme's reputation among some Swedish-Americans.[81] To those that supported the war, he arguably represented everything they disliked. To those against the war, he was a well-spoken and erudite spokesperson.

Sweden's Diplomatic Recognition of North Vietnam

On 10 January 1969 – with twelve days left in the Johnson presidency – Sweden recognized the government of North Vietnam. Sweden was the first noncommunist nation to recognize Hanoi's Democratic Republic of Vietnam. Sweden had recalled its Saigon envoy in April 1967, and gradually cut all ties to South Vietnam.

---

[78] "Vietnam och neutraliteten är vad Olof Palme fick redogöra för här," *Svenska-Amerikanaren Tribunen*, 24 June 1970; *California Veckoblad*, 26 June 1970; and "Hört och Hänt: Vad Palme sade på Nationella Pressklubben i Washington," *Svenska Posten*, 17 June 1970: 1, 4.

[79] Gerry Rooth, "Vad Nytt På Stan," *Nordstjernan-Svea*, 18 June 1970: 3.

[80] The first use of the words appear in "Prime Minister Olof Palme Tells the UN of Sweden's 'Strategy for Survival'," *California Veckoblad*, 6 November 1970: 1.

[81] For comment on Palme's appearance in the film, see: E.H. "Folkets Röst: Epoken Erlander," 19 November 1969: 5; Hilma Anderson, "Folkets Röst: Bäste Urlakare och läsekrets," 26 November 1969: 5; and P.H.K., "Folkets Röst: Hippiepropaganda," *Svenska-Amerikanaren Tribunen*, 24 February 1971: 5.

The U.S. media saw the recognition of Hanoi as unfriendly, un-neutral, and unlikely to bring peace.[82] The mainstream newspapers in the nation's capital condemned the move. Papers in traditional Swedish areas like Moline or Worcester were also critical. Only a handful of mainstream American papers supported Sweden.[83]

The first reactions in the Swedish-American press were immediately and emotionally negative. A *Nordstjernan* reader called Sweden's move "an expression of hate and ill-will against our land and people."[84] (*Nordstjernan* ran this letter twice.) *Nordstjernan* ran the *New York Daily News*'s cartoon of Ho Chi Minh rising from a can of Swedish surströmming. The accompanying editorial said Sweden's goal was to strengthen the communist position in the Paris peace talks. New York's other paper, *Norden*, had the same view.[85]

Two weeks later, *Nordstjernan* ran a more measured commentary from the *Washington Post*. (Denver's *Western News* printed the article in May 1969.) The Post also believed Sweden wanted to help Hanoi's position at Paris. This need not be a problem, however. The editorial argued, "legal recognition by Sweden is less significant than

---

[82] *Sverige i utländsk press 1969*, 19–21. Press Intelligence Inc. found 125 news articles in the U.S. press between 1 October 1969 and 1 June 1970 on Sweden's Vietnam policy and aid to Vietnam. It judged 55 of these to have a neutral tone, 54 had a negative tone, and only 16 news stories reported positively on Sweden's Vietnam policy, including foreign aid to Vietnam. (Memo "Protokoll över upplysningskommitténs sammanträdande i New York den 15–16 juni 1970: bilaga 4," file "1970, juli-augusti," JN1Ua, UD.)

[83] "Sweden Recognizes Hanoi, Affects Talks – Reds' Hand Bolstered at Paris," *Washington Evening Star*, 10 January 1969; Warren Unna, "United States Hits Sweden on Bid to Hanoi," *Washington Post*, 11 January 1969; *Post* and *Star* editorials reprinted in United States Congress (House), *Congressional Record*, Ninety-First Congress, First session, Washington D.C.: 13 January 1969, page 455; Kastrup, *Med Sverige i Amerika*, 333; and memo "Erkännandet av Nordvietnam i början av 1969," file "ASNE – Papers and clippings – Sweden's views on Vietnam," box "ASNE – Papers, clippings, Swedes in America," ASNE New York, SSIRC.

[84] Harry C. Seaburgh, "Ordet Fritt," *Nordstjernan-Svea*, 13 February 1970: 6, and reprinted 13 March 1970: 4. See also Henry Bengtson's reply letter, 27 February 1970: 5.

[85] "Swedish Sideswipe," *Nordstjernan-Svea*, 16 January 1969: 4. Reprinted with a new introduction from *The New York Daily News*; and "Svensk diplomati," *Norden*, 23 January 1969: 8.

PHEW!

Redaktionell teckning i N. Y. Daily News med anledning av
Sveriges erkännande av Hanoi.

Reprinted courtesy of Nordstjernan.

the de facto and more substantial recognition the United States gives Hanoi by talking about peace at Paris." Sweden's new legal position might even make it a possible mediator, if the U.S. so wanted.[86] A *Nordstjernan* reader suggested Sweden might send peace-keeping troops if it could help bring peace to Vietnam.[87]

Svenska Posten pointed out that Sweden was the first European country – after France – to recognize the United States in 1783.[88] Sweden was also among the first to recognize the People's Republic of China, the Soviet Union, and the Algerian Republic.[89] Some Swedish-Americans saw recognizing Hanoi as part of a tradition of Swedish diplomatic independence. Columnist Adele Heilborn wrote, "When Sweden was the first in the world to recognize the new state U.S.A., what did the master of the world England think?" "Fly förbaskade," answered editor Harry Fabbe.[90]

Another argument was that recognizing a foreign government need not imply approval of its ideology. Olof Palme maintained that the U.S. had ambassadors in Greece, South Africa, Spain, and Bulgaria. *Nordstjernan* pointed out that none of these were democracies.[91] The U.S. kept its ambassadors in these countries, but withdrew its representative to Sweden. Johnson's ambassador to Sweden left his post on 24 January, and Nixon did not appoint a new one. The Swedish-American newspapers treated the ambassador question with a mixture of defiance and unease. For

---

[86] "Chagrin at Sweden," *Nordstjernan-Svea*, 30 January 1969: 4; and "The Position of Sweden Re: North Vietnam," *Western News*, 8 May 1969: 2. Reprinted from *The Washington Post*, 14 January 1969.

[87] G. Gustafson, "Ordet är Fritt: Swedish Foreign Office indicates willingness to commit Swedish troops for peacekeeping in Vietnam," *Nordstjernan-Svea*, 27 November 1969: 10. Information taken from Dick Nolan, *San Francisco Examiner*, 14 October 1969.

[88] Harry Fabbe, "Hört och Hänt," *Svenska Posten*, 15 January 1969: 4. See also Ivar Lundskog, "Ordet är Fritt: History Repeating," *Nordstjernan-Svea*, 23 January 1969: 10.

[89] Torsten Nilsson, *Åter Vietnam*, Stockholm, 1981: 146.

[90] Adele Heilborn, "Stockholmsbrev," *Svenska Posten*, 7 May 1969: 3; Harry Fabbe (citing Rune Moberg in *Se*), "Hört och Hänt," *Svenska Posten*, 15 October 1969: 4; see also Moberg's article reprinted in "Sänd Nixon 'USA-Sweden,'" *Nordstjernan-Svea*, 2 October 1969: 4.

[91] "Sändebudet som saknas," *Nordstjernan-Svea*, 4 December 1969: 4.

example, a *Nordstjernan* reader blamed Sweden for the current poor relations. After Palme's "notorious torchlight parade," Washington had no choice but to withdraw its envoy.[92] As 1969 continued, calls to resume relations increased, the U.S. having already made its point.

In the mainstream media, Swedish recognition of Hanoi resurrected the image of Olof Palme marching with the North Vietnamese diplomat. Much of the U.S. media connected that incident – which "proved" Swedish anti-Americanism – to Swedish recognition of Hanoi. UD Press Bureau wrote, "Every time they wrote about the recognition [of Hanoi], they dragged up the entire catalog of Swedish sins, preferably with new deserters or demonstrations."[93] It was much the same in the Swedish-American press. Recognizing North Vietnam was not itself a problem, but it was yet another incident in a pattern of unfriendly moves.

In late 1969, Sweden announced it would give North Vietnam forty million dollars in aid after the war.[94] It may have been humanitarian aid, but it hardly improved relations with Washington. Parts of the U.S. press saw this as a direct insult to the United States. Two years later, a reporter for WNEW-TV in New York said, "May I also add that this money from Sweden comes from you, American tourists, who buy Swedish products, who send checks to Sweden. You are helping to shoot down American planes every day, in every way, through our good neutral friend, Sweden."[95] It may have been an exaggeration, but this reflected a real sentiment in parts of the American public opinion.

Svenska Posten's Martin Johanson wrote, "Sweden will be giving America's enemies in North Vietnam 45 million dollars. What do

---

[92] Oke J. Spendrup, "Ordet är Fritt: Sweden Versus USA," *Nordstjernan-Svea*, 6 November 1969: 10.

[93] *Sverige i utländsk press 1969*, 20.

[94] "News in Brief: Swedes $44M for Hanoi," *Nordstjernan-Svea*, 20 November 1969: 1.

[95] Martin Abend of the WNEW-TV Ten O'Clock News, 11 January 1973, cited in memo by Radio TV Reports, Inc., "Discuss Sweden's Criticism of United States," file "1972, nov – jan 1973," JN1Ua, UD.

you think of that?"[96] "It made me purely discouraged," *Svenska Posten*'s columnist Arthur Landfors wrote in reply.

> We have different view on things and we have the right to express them, but we don't have the right to do it in a way that leads to false conclusions. That's the case here. Someone without any knowledge of Sweden's position in this war, doesn't know what purpose this money is for, can get a totally false impression from words like these. That the money will go to America's enemies is just not true. The greater part will be used only when the war is over. North Vietnam will hardly be an enemy any longer then.[97]

Landfors believed Sweden's aid resembled America's own Marshall Plan after World War II. This view was controversial. Harry Fabbe's decision to print this as an anonymous letter reflects this.[98]

At *Texas Posten*, a reader wrote in and explained that he was canceling his subscription in protest. Sweden was giving North Vietnam aid and moral support while American soldiers died in the field. *Texas Posten* still advertised airline service to Sweden and other Swedish goods. The reader urged editor Gerald Knape to drop their advertising and boycott their products.[99] This was a disturbing threat. Texas Posten always kept subscription rates low, trying to earn its income from advertising. A similar paper, *Canada-Svensken*, earned around 90% of its income from advertising revenue.[100] This meant *Texas Posten*'s Gerald Knape could not easily refuse any advertising income. This threat of a reader boycott came while UD debated putting large standing ads in *Texas Posten*. Gerald Knape deflected his reader's protest with a personal disavowal of Sweden's position.[101] Knape's reply dismayed UD, which considered too weak in its support of Swedish policy. This is when UD decided to do a

---

[96] Martin G. Johanson, "Martin G. Johanson berättar," *Svenska Posten*, 21 January 1970.

[97] Letter from Arthur Landfors to Harry Fabbe, February 1970, file "Landfors, Arthur," box 1 incoming letters, SvP, UW.

[98] "Hört och Hänt: Ingen rätt uttrycka en åsikt så att felaktiga slutledningar dras," *Svenska Posten*, 11 February 1970: 1.

[99] C.D.C., "Letters to Texas Posten," *Texas Posten*, 12 June 1969: 2.

[100] Letter from Thorwald Wiik to Informationsbyrån UD, 21 January 1972, file "1972, febr. – december," PR4S, UD.

Texas Posten's Gerald Knape.

content analysis of the entire Swedish-American press. (See Chapter Three for more on this content analysis; its results appear in Table 9.) Newspapers like *Texas Posten* were in a difficult position. They had to serve conservative readers, and reflect their communities. Yet, still had to appeal to UD's news network and financial resources that indirectly supported them.

U.S. Ambassador Jerome Holland's Reception in Sweden

On 12 January 1970, Washington appointed Dr. Jerome Holland as its new ambassador to Sweden. Sweden had a new Prime Minister – Olof Palme – and it was time to give a fresh start to U.S.-Swedish relations. (Sweden also showed a desire to start over by helping get information on U.S. prisoners in North Vietnam.)[102] Ambassador Jerome Holland was an academic, not a professional diplomat. He had been Hampton Institute's president since 1960, and president of Delaware State College for seven years before that. The emigrant press's response was collective relief that Sweden finally had a U.S.

---

[101] Letter from Hans Johansson to Eva Heckscher, 24 July 1969, file "1969 – 1971 febr.," PR4S, UD; and G.B. Knape, "Letters to *Texas Posten*: Remarks from Editor," *Texas Posten*, 12 June 1969: 2.

[102] The American press received Palme's recent efforts to find news on the POWs with gratitude. For example, see "Will Sweden Get Names of U.S. PWs? [sic]," *Chicago Sun-Times*, 20 October 1969, "U.S. Seeking Neutrals' Aid on POWS," 14 November 1969, and "Officers' Wives Given Hope," *Virginian-Pilot* (Richmond), 28 November 1969. For a critical view, see "Envoy to Sweden," *New York News*, 19 January 1970.

envoy. Some columnists noted Holland was a black man. In early 1970, this attracted as much attention as his resume.

Nordstjernan's conservative Eric Sylvan saw it as a good move by Nixon. The time was right, it was the right country, and it was an excellent opportunity. "His choice of Dr. Holland must be considered wise, logical, and well-suited," Sylvan concluded.[103] A different opinion came from *Svenska Posten's* conservative columnist. On 28 January 1970, astonished *SvP* readers saw this paragraph in Reinhold Ahleen's column:

> One can wonder if it is pure revenge, cheap and petty revenge that motivated President Nixon to appoint a former football-playing Negro as American ambassador to Sweden. The post has been vacant a year. We have nothing against the race, but one might think that Sweden would have been worth the courtesy of sending a white person as American envoy. . . . This Negro, no matter how educated he may be, has no external advantages: he does not have a distinguished appearance. . . . It is a humiliation for such an enlightened and prosperous land like Sweden to have a Negro as its American ambassador, for America is the white race's land.[104]

Like many Swedish-American columnists, Ahleen was getting old. Comments like these reflect prejudices from a different era, and an old man's inability to hide them. Whatever the reason, Ahleen had a history of racist articles. In 1968, Ahleen printed his solution to America's race problem: deporting blacks to Africa.[105] Editor Harry Fabbe condemned these articles, but some readers still canceled their subscriptions in protest.[106] According to columnist Arthur Landfors, Ahleen was "extremely conservative." Ahleen wrote poetry, which many Swedish-Americans liked, so he filled a

---

[103] Eric Sylvan, "Det Tycks," *Nordstjernan-Svea*, 29 January 1970, reprinted in "Hört och Hänt," *Svenska Posten*, 4 February 1970: 4.

[104] Reinhold Ahleen, "Rim och Reson av Reinhold Ahleen," *Svenska Posten*, 28 January 1970: 4.

[105] Reinhold Ahleen, "Rim och Reson av Reinhold Ahleen," *Svenska Posten*, 27 November 1968: 4.

[106] Information on the canceled subscriptions came from a conversation with Professor Larry Scott, Augustana College, August 1997. Editor Harry Fabbe distanced himself from Ahleen's article in "Hört och Hänt: De frivilliga medarbetarnas idéer och åsikter är deras egna, inte alltid Svenska Postens," *Svenska Posten*, 27 November 1968: 4.

Jerome Holland.

niche in Swedish-America's cultural world. "However," Landfors concluded, "I have lost all respect for him and no longer keep in touch with him."[107]

The reaction to Ahleen's article was quick and critical. A reader from Seattle called it "pitiful and ridiculous." One from Colorado called it "idiotic," but admitted many "so-called Swedish-Americans" had similar views. *Smålandsposten's* editor wrote to *SvP* to say Ahleen proved some emigrants "learn absolutely nothing by seeing the world."[108] Håkan Berggren, the head of SIS, wrote to *Svenska Posten*. Berggren insisted the Swedish people certainly would welcome Ambassador Holland warmly. He also pointed out the U.S. had sent black envoys to Denmark, Finland, and Norway, where they had served with distinction.[109] A *Svenska Posten* reader even reacted to Ahleen's line about Richard Nixon having "cheap

---

[107] Letter from Arthur Landfors to Harry Fabbe, undated letter, file "Landfors, Arthur," box 1 incoming letters, SvP, UW.

[108] Lisa Bryzell, "Från Läsekretsen: Är detta Rim och Reson?" *Svenska Posten*, 18 February 1970: 2; Håkan Carheden, "Från Läsekretsen: Om USA:s svarte ambassadör," *Svenska Posten*, 18 February 1970: 2; and Gustaf Lövqvist, "Från Läsekretsen: Mr Ahleen utan rim och reson," *Svenska Posten*, 8 April 1970: 4.

[109] Håkan Berggren, "Hört och Hänt: Om USA:s nye ambassadör i Stockholm, dr Jerome Holland," *Svenska Posten*, 4 February 1970: 1, 4. (However, Joseph Holland points out: "My father was only the second African-American U.S. ambassador to be appointed to a European country, which was reflected in the racial character of some of the protests [he encountered in Sweden]." E-mail from Joseph Holland to Edward Burton, 19 April 2003.)

and petty revenge." He asked, "How can a man with President Nixon's importance plan revenge against such a small country, which most people think has Copenhagen as its capital?"[110]

In a more cautious tone, columnist Eric Olson wondered if Nixon indeed sent Sweden a message by appointing Holland. "He is a clever man, this Nixon," Olson wrote, "and he knows more tricks than a circus seal."

> If the Swedes feel offended or annoyed by the Negro appointment, it would show that Sweden really is not as humanistic – with a beating and bleeding heart for the oppressed – as their self-righteous criticism of the U.S.A. has tried to maintain. Instead, it would show that they harbor racial prejudice, and that Sweden's leading men therefore deserve the ugly epithet "racists."[111]

Olson believed the appointment would either mute the Swedes' criticism of the U.S., or expose them as hypocrites. A *Svenska Posten* reader predicted it would be the latter. "Far too many Swedes are racists, almost comparable to our Southern Democrats." *SvP's* Stephen Forslund also foresaw the risk of a "white backlash" below Sweden's dignity.[112] Many of these concerns were also current in Sweden. Speaking broadly, most Swedes were willing to accept a black ambassador but some suspected the U.S. was setting them up.

Jerome Holland assumed his post in Sweden in April 1970. An anti-American attitude then prevailed in Sweden, mostly due to the recent U.S. invasion of Cambodia. Holland arrived at Arlanda Airport on 9 April 1970. Protesters had assembled to meet him, but a large police escort was also there to ensure they did not enter the airport terminal. Holland left the airport by a side route, so demonstrators never came in close contact with the Ambassador. Despite heavy security, one demonstrator – a Swedish Uppsala-student – pushed past the barricades. He was the first to call to Holland: words *Aftonbladet's* and *Expressen's* reporters heard as "Go

---

[110] Anders Raman, "Från läsekretsen: Om den nya US-ambassadören," *Svenska Posten*, 11 February 1970: 4.

[111] Eric Olson, "Reflektioner av Eric Olson," *Svenska Posten*, 11 February 1970: 4.

[112] John Sandell, "Från Läsekretsen: Många svenska är rasister," *Svenska Posten*, 11 Mars 1970: 6; and Stephen Forslund, "Pränt om ditt och datt av Stephen Forslund," *Svenska Posten*, 4 Mars 1970: 4.

home, murderer. You're not wanted here." They heard these phrases repeated several times.[113] *Svenska Dagbladet* reported the U.S. delegation also heard the demonstrator shout "We don't need you here, nigger," with such racial epithets repeated in both English and Swedish. The police arrested and questioned the demonstrator that pushed past the barricades. No further incidents happened that day.[114]

A week after his arrival, Ambassador Holland was to give the King his credentials at the Royal Palace. Holland's cortege from the Grand Hotel to the palace was in a closed horse-drawn carriage, according to tradition. Again, there was a large police escort to keep the FNL-protesters back behind the barricades in Gamla Stan. The Swedish press reported that individual demonstrators managed to break through and charge the carriage a couple of times. Exactly what these demonstrators shouted is unclear, but only *Svenska Dagbladet's* reporter gave a specific quote: "Go home, you're not wanted."[115]

Holland held a press conference after his reception with the King, and he discussed his views on the demonstrations he had faced. He had mentioned on television the previous evening that he had heard the phrase "Nigger go home" at the airport. At the press conference, he said he heard similar phrases outside the Palace that

---

[113] Lars Bjelf, "Demonstranter och 100-tals poliser mötte ambassadören," *Aftonbladet*, 9 April 1970: 8; and Barbaro Flodquist, "Han som skrek på Arlanda: 'Jag fick plötsligt en ide'," *Expressen*, 10 April 1970: 7. Yngve Möller's *Sverige och Vietnamkriget* (page 239) claims the demonstrator was an American deserter and shouted the phrase "house-nigger" – reporters do not confirm either of these assertions. The demonstrator denied he had said anything racist, and a week later charged Holland with slandering him. (Lars Svegård, "USA-ambassadören blir polisanmäld," *Expressen*, 15 April 1970: 23.)

[114] Ingmar Lindmarker, "USA-ambassadören skymfad: Polisen stod passiv vid arlanda dramatik," *Svenska Dagbladet*, 10 April 1970: 3. For more on this interpretation, see: Ruth Link, "Ambassador Holland and the Swedes," *Crisis*, vol. 78, March 1971: 43-48; and Fredrik Logevall, "The Swedish-American Conflict Over Vietnam," *Diplomatic History*, vol. 17:3, 1993: 436-437.

[115] Mats Orwin, "4 FNL-aktivister greps, smädelser mot tom vagn," *Svenska Dagbladet*, 15 April 1970: 11. *Dagens Nyheter* and *Expressen* report either the American delegation's account or give second-hand information. *Aftonbladet* did not report the event.

afternoon. He regarded these as a personal attack and not as a general anti-American expression.[116] Ambassador Holland told *Jet* magazine a few weeks later:

> They [demonstrators] are part of the political life in a free, democratic nation. However, I am a little bit concerned when I hear such remarks as "nigger," both at the airport and when I was driving to the palace. They shouted "Nigger, nigger go home." That was a personal attack on me, and I resent it. I haven't heard that for many years, and only then in the most racist areas of the United States.[117]

For his part, Prime Minister Palme denied the protesters had used any such language. Palme wrote to Jerome Holland, and urged him to stop claiming that racist incidents had occurred:

> Recollections of persons who had been in the procession, both in horse-drawn coaches and in motor-cars, were noted. A tape recording made by the Swedish Radio when you arrived at Arlanda airport was studied. In the material available to the Swedish authorities, there has been found no evidence of an abuse of a racial character.[118]

---

[116] Klas Bergman, "'Nigger åk hem' ett slag under bältet för mr. Holland," Dagens Nyheter, 15 April 1970: 14; Sture Lindmark, "Demonstrationerna slag under bältet," *Svenska Dagbladet*, 15 April 1970: 3, 11; Stig Kamph, "Mr. Holland fick åka ända till Sverige för att höra ordet 'nigger,'" *Expressen* (Reflex) 15 April 1970: 31.

[117] "U.S. Envoy In Sweden Told, 'Nigger, Go Home,'" *Jet*, 30 April 1970: 4. In a recent e-mail, Joseph Holland, the Embassador's son, writes: "There is no doubt that racial pejoratives were used against my father the day of our arrival. I remember vividly the protester who broke free from the crowd and rushed my father shouting words that were later translated for me 'Nigger go home.' A few days later, as my father traveled to present his credentials to the King, I was there once again and heard protesters use words like 'Nigger, we don't want you here.' . . . These protests continued. I remember being with my father on several occasions when the car we were riding in was blanketed by eggs thrown by protesters. . . . However, I can't say I remember hearing a Swedish person use the word 'Nigger.' I do remember being told and reading about that word being used against my father." (E-mail from Joseph Holland to Edward Burton, 16 and 19 April 2003.

[118] Letter from Olof Plame to Jerome Holland, 25 July 1970, reprinted in Bertil Östergren, "Ett brev säger så mycket," *Vem var Olof Palme?* Stockholm, 1984: 177–178.

Most mainstream U.S. papers trusted Holland; few accepted the idea nothing had happened. The American media interpreted "nigger go home" as a racist expression.[119] In Chicago, the *Sun-Times* said there was no basis for Sweden's good reputation for race relations. The Swedish press held biases against Southern Europeans, the *Sun-Times* wrote, and blacks had problems renting hotel rooms in Stockholm. *The Chicago Sun-Times'* cross-town rival, the *Chicago Daily News* also focused on the incident. The *Daily News* wrote, "There is obviously some room in Sweden for some soul-searching." Sweden, it wrote, could learn something about race relations from the United States. Four days later, the *Daily News* ran a cartoon of the Swedish King saying [*sic*] "Velkomm to Sveden Mr. U.S. Ambassador" – while placing a large sign on Holland's back: "Nigger go home."[120]

The Swedish-American papers felt the same anger, but mixed with sometime acute embarrassment. *Svenska-Amerikanaren's* editors, for example, printed in the same city as the *Daily News* and *Sun Times*. Its editors could have scarcely avoided seeing the "Velkomm to Sveden" cartoon. At *Nordstjernan*, Eric Sylvan had confidently predicted "a warm reception" because Sweden was "a land free of prejudice, and its social conventions more advanced than any other."[121] Perhaps embarrassed by the event, Sylvan did not write a follow-up to this prediction. *Nordstjernan's* Anny Säfström – the only Swedish-American columnist living in Sweden –

---

[119] Press Intelligence Inc. found 67 news articles in the U.S. press on Jerome Holland's reception in Sweden before 1 June 1970. It judged 33 of these to have a neutral tone, and 34 had a negative tone. Press Intelligence Inc. did not find any news stories to report positively on Holland's reception. (Memo "Protokoll över upplysningskommitténs sammanträdande i New York den 15–16 juni 1970: bilaga 4," file "1970, juli-augusti," JN1Ua, UD.)

[120] "Racism on the Palace Steps," *Chicago Sun-Times*, 17 April 1970; "Swedish Manners," *Chicago Daily News*, 16 April 1970; and *Chicago Daily News*, 20 April 1970. All three Chicago editorials quoted in Allan Kastrup, memo "Some editorial headings spring 1970," file "Misc Notes and Quotes," box "ASNE Misc Papers and Writings on Sweden," ASNE New York, SSIRC.

[121] Eric Sylvan, "Det Tycks," *Nordstjernan-Svea*, 29 January 1970, reprinted in "Hört och Hänt," *Svenska Posten*, 4 February 1970: 4.

condemned the demonstrators. She quickly added that the U.S. had irresponsible demonstrators too.[122]

One function of ethnic newspapers is to disclose threats to the community. Exposing outside threats will keep the community safe, but can also enhance ethnic solidarity. Such threats can even come from renegade Swedes or emigrants that could possibly disrupt the community. Parts of the emigrant press labeled these specific demonstrators as a dangerous element. *Svenska Posten* noted that UD condemned the demonstrators and described them as hooligans. *Svenska Posten* also ran an *Arbetarebladet* editorial that used this description. It described such protesters as "a deranged element" outside the FNL movement with little interest in Vietnam. Such elements could only hurt Vietnam's cause. The editorial ended by comparing these protesters to the Nazi Brownshirts of the Thirties.[123] These labels place such hostile demonstrators outside the Swedish debate on Vietnam. This device preserves the integrity of legitimate Swedish debate. The label "hooligan" signifies an outsider, and a threatening one. The emigrant press certainly preferred this label than calling the threatening element as "Swedish."

Canada-Tidningen and *Nordstjernan* also ran parts of this editorial. They also added an editorial from *Norrköpings Tidningar* they received from *Sverige-Nytt*. This editorial accepted UD's disavowal, but argued Foreign Minister Torsten Nilsson indirectly encouraged such actions. He had appealed to society's worst elements, and "stroked them with provocative speeches." The Foreign Minister could not disavow responsibility when the results of his political pandering developed.[124] These were the hardest words a *Sverige-Nytt* editorial ever used for a Swedish official. *Sverige-Nytt* also distributed an *Aftonbladet* editorial taking Olof Palme's interpretation that nothing had happened.[125] No Swedish-American

---

[122] Anny Kristina Säfström, "Sverige Brevet," *Nordstjernan-Svea*, 29 July 1970: 9.

[123] UD statement, reported in "Hört och Hänt: Om politiska busfasoner, seger som blir moraliskt och politiskt nederlag och farliga militärräd," *Svenska Posten*, 13 May 1970: 1.

[124] "Brännmarkning," *Canada-Tidningen*, 1 June 1970, and *Nordstjernan-Svea*, 14 May 1970: 4.

[125] "Tyckt i veckan," *Sverige-Nytt*, 16 June 1970: 2.

paper printed it. The emigrant press only used material with the critical interpretations of events.

Svenska Posten's Reinhold Ahleen wrote that Ambassador Holland should realize such protests were not against him personally. They were the ugliest possible expression of anger surrounding the Vietnam War.[126] Ahleen likely still smarted from the criticism on his article about Holland's appointment. He was ironically the only Swedish-American columnist to correspond directly with the new ambassador. Ambassador Holland wrote back to Ahleen twice in 1970.[127] Instead of discussing the racial incidents, Holland assured Ahleen "the [Swedish] people are quite friendly and respectful."[128]

Over the next two years, Holland impressed many in the emigrant press with such diplomacy under pressure. As *Nordstjernan's* Gerry Rooth wrote:

> He has . . . been given a collossally difficult mission. According to news in two private letters sent to *Nordstjernan-Svea*, he has invited demonstrators to his home in Stockholm. Even if he doesn't succeed in convincing any of his guests [about the U.S. position on Vietnam and Cambodia], they must come to respect him.[129]

The next two years were difficult, and by 1972 he had enough. *Svenska-Amerikanaren* then wrote, "He has been called 'nigger' and 'murderer' and been subjected to egg-throwing. We have all reason to regret that this intelligent, skillful, and friendly man – who has been so tolerant of the Swedish leftist groups and their provocations – has tired of Sweden and is moving back to the U.S."[130]

In summary, the Swedish-American press widely publicized many of Ambassador Holland's ordeals. Nothing, however, came to match the reaction following the "nigger go home" incident. This

---

[126] Reinhold Ahleen, "Rim och Reson av Reinhold Ahleen," *Svenska Posten*, 17 June 1970: 4.

[127] Reinhold Ahleen's diary, 17 May 1970 and 12 October 1970, box 2, Ahleen, UW.

[128] "Rim och Reson av Reinhold Ahleen," *Svenska Posten*, 10 June 1970: 4.

[129] Gerry Rooth, "Vad Nytt på Stan?" *Nordstjernan-Svea*, 4 June 1970.

[130] "Vill Jerome Holland Flytta?" *Svenska-Amerikanaren Tribunen*, 9 August 1972: 1. Reprinted from *Nya Wermlands Tidningen*.

was a minor episode in Sweden's Vietnam debate, but was a major part of the emigrant debate on Sweden's FNL movement. The Swedish-American press accepted that something had happened. No paper ran the *Sverige-Nytt* denial that an incident had occurred. In 1970, newspapers in America's northern states were conditioned to doubt such denials about civil rights incidents. Civil rights was a consensus issue that even non-political northern papers could support.[131] Nearly all of them reported the events around Jerome Holland as racist to some degree. They only disagreed on whether the FNL movement had a racist underside, or whether it was "a deranged element" outside the movement. Only *Svenska Posten's* Reinhold Ahleen suggested the incident had more to do with Vietnam than race.

The rest of the emigrant press asserted the incident was racist. Under this interpretation, the FNL movement – or some of its followers – were indefensibly in the wrong. The American ambassador appeared as the aggrieved party. For papers backing the war, this news story stripped some moral high ground from the FNL movement. Most papers in the antiwar camp also sympathized with civil rights issues. These newspapers were not receptive to the argument that "nigger go home" was progressive criticism. This story squeezed the FNL movement from both the political right and left.

Olof Palme's Speech Following the Christmas Bombings

On 20 and 21 November 1972, Henry Kissinger and Le Duc Tho made an important breakthrough in the Paris peace talks. They drafted an agreement allowing the U.S. to leave Vietnam while North Vietnamese troops remained in South Vietnam. The talks broke down on December 13: Saigon demanded changes, while

---

[131] Erik Hermans writes, "*Norden* and me, being liberal, took a very strong stand for the blacks, not least in connection with the Selma upheaval. I had a Swedish guy – Sjögren was his name – in Brooklyn that wrote several articles for us about the mistreated blacks. . . . I remember a visit to New Orleans in 1952, when I sat down far back in a bus, not seeing the sign 'For black patrons only.' The stares I got from the ones up front were brutal." (E-mail from Erik Hermans to Edward Burton, 12 february 2003.)

Hanoi backed away from their concessions. The White House decided to force the North Vietnamese back to the negotiating table with more bombing. The bombing lasted from 18 until 29 December 1972. The President and White House said nothing during the bombing. This intentional coldness disturbed many Swedish leaders, especially during the Christmas season. Prime Minister Olof Palme told a TV interviewer, "Things should be called by their proper name."

> What is happening today in Vietnam is a form of torture. There can be no military motives for the bombings. . . . What is happening is that people are being tormented, that a nation is being tormented in order to humiliate it, to force them to submit to the language of force. That is why the bombings are an outrage. There are many of this kind in modern history. They are often connected with names – Guernica, Oradour, Babij Jar, Katyn, Lidice, Sharpeville, Treblinka. Violence has triumphed, but the judgment of history has been hard on those who carried the responsibility. Now there is another name to add to the list – Hanoi, Christmas 1972.[132]

Richard Nixon did not like Palme comparing the bombings to Stalinist or Nazi war crimes. Palme's reference to racist atrocities also came with ill grace. Sweden's controversial reception of Jerome Holland was still a recent memory. After Palme's remarks, the White House withdrew its chargé d'affaires John Guthrie. It would neither send a new ambassador to Sweden nor accept Sweden's new ambassador to Washington.[133]

Nordstjernan devoted nearly its entire front page to Palme's remarks. It ran his television comments front and center, and in boldface type. Below this quotation, it reprinted the 1968 photograph of him marching with North Vietnam's ambassador to Moscow.

---

[132] Translation partly from Fredrik Logevall, "The Swedish-American Conflict Over Vietnam," 440–441 (this translation omits one sentence), and partly from telegram from Svensk Washington to SIS New York, 3 January 1973, file "ASNE Press Releases and Clippings," box "ASNE Papers, Clippings, Swedes in America," ASNE New York, SSIRC. See also the Reuters translation in Leif Leifland, *Frostens År*, Stockholm, 1997: 46.

[133] Logevall, "The Swedish-American Conflict Over Vietnam," 441.

UD was not happy to see this picture again. "This photo has been for many years a source of irritation in many quarters in this country," the New York General Consul wrote. "I was quite surprised when I found that *Nordstjernan* had again printed it on the front page."[134] Consul Gunnar Lonaeus called *Nordstjernan's* Gerry Rooth to complain about the Sergels Torg photograph. Rooth asserted that he received the photograph from UD with the latest batch of FLT material. Lonaeus wanted to know how this could have happened. If true, it was poor journalistic practice to distribute such photos during the current crisis. It was, after all, both inflammatory and five years out of date. He did not advocate UD censorship, but Lonaeus wanted more oversight in distributing such pictures.[135] At UD, Eva Heckscher thought there had been a misunderstanding somewhere. The woman that distributed such material, Eva Nauckhoff, confirmed that Rooth's story was indeed true. She had sent out an article on Palme on 10 November 1972, including several pictures of him. One of them was the Sergels Torg photograph. Rooth exaggerated slightly in claiming that *Nordstjernan* got the picture in "the latest batch" of FLT material.[136]

As the distributor of such pictures, Nauckhoff had no litmus-test for what was appropriate for non-Swedish readers. She usually did not distribute news stories on violence, crime, youth crime, drugs, or pornography. Such stories offset the positive image of Sweden that UD wanted to promote abroad. She also left out many stories about Riksdag issues, and tax and labor market questions. These were too heavy for foreign consumption. If someone who did not know Swedish society read them in isolation, these articles would leave an undue negative impression. In all, Nauckhoff believed she sent the Swedish-American press only about half the FLT material available.[137]

---

[134] Letter from Gunnar Lonaeus to Eva Heckscher, 19 January 1973, file "1973 – 1974," PR4S, UD.

[135] Letter from Gunnar Lonaeus to Eva Heckscher, 19 January 1973, file "1973 – 1974," PR4S, UD.

[136] Letter from Eva Nauckhoff to Gunnar Lonaeus, 29 January 1973, and Nauckhoff's note in the margin of letter from Lonaeus to Eva Heckscher, 19 January 1973, file "1973 – 1974," PR4S, UD.

It may have been impossible to manage the Swedish-American press's treatment of Palme, no matter what Nauckhoff sent. Even the mainstream U.S. newspapers carried his comments. The large domestic papers probably had much more influence than UD's dispatches. Most U.S. papers saw Palme's comments as gratuitous, unfair, and overstated. Few printed his explanations and partial retraction. *The Cincinnati Enquirer* wrote that Palme's "honest moral arguments inevitably degenerated into hair-pulling and mudslinging." *The Los Angeles Times* foreign news editor told UD that Sweden's foreign policy had an "attitude of superiority." He did not oppose Sweden's Vietnam policy, but he thought Sweden was "damned sanctimonious" about it. Editors for the *San Francisco Examiner* and the *Oregon Journal* had similar views.[138] Conservative papers used Palme's interview as a chance to review Sweden's role in the Second World War.[139] These editors voiced a feeling widespread in the mainstream press, and the emigrant papers agreed with it. Several of these critical newspapers printed in cities with Swedish-American papers. If they did not directly influence the emigrant editors, they likely changed public opinion in the cities where they worked.

Many mainstream papers agreed with Palme that the Christmas bombings were needless and brutal. Many other newspapers saw the decision not to name an ambassador as petty and vindictive. Some commentators even saw the White House's position as faintly ridiculous. Syndicated columnist Art Buchwald wrote that Nixon had found a new enemy: the Yellow-Haired Peril. Washington and Stockholm could never have normal relations, Buchwald wrote, "as long as Sweden continues to enslave its people and spread its diabolic massage parlors around the world."[140]

---

[137] Letter from Eva Nauckhoff to Gunnar Lonaeus, 29 January 1973, file "1973 – 1974," PR4S, UD.

[138] "Scandinavian Opposition Damage to U.S. Position," *The Cincinnati Enquirer*, 14 January 1973; *Sverige i utländsk press 1973*, 53–54; and memo by Håkan Berggren, "Informationsmarknaden i USA, 2: Västkusten," file "1970, maj – juli 14," JN1Ua, UD.

[139] "The Peacenik Premier of Sweden," *The New York Daily News*, 3 January 1973, cited in *Sverige i utländsk press 1973*, 54.

[140] Art Buchwald, cited in *Sverige i utländsk press 1973*, 60.

The Swedish-American press took a subdued stance toward the latest rupture in diplomatic relations. *Nordstjernan* and *Svenska Posten* ran editorials "sent out by the Swedish news service in Stockholm." Reprinting editorials from *Dagens Nyheter* and *Vestmanland Läns Tidning*, *Svenska Posten* supported Palme's description of the bombings as "an outrage."[141] *Nordstjernan* ran a *Vestmanland Läns Tidning* editorial describing the bombings as "disgusting," but it also hoped the diplomatic problems would soon pass.[142]

Nordstjernan's editor Gerry Rooth usually did not write his own editorials anymore. He instead reprinted comment from the domestic Swedish press. Eric Sylvan's often critical columns had disappeared back in 1971. Much of the paper's independent comment disappeared with him. *Nordstjernan* ran a reader letter, however, which solidly blamed Palme for the latest crisis. Oke Spendrup argued government protests should go through the proper diplomatic channels. "In order to be effective, the language of the protest is all-important. It is to be correct, perfectly cool, and detached. If this basic rule is not observed, the protest is more likely than not to be counterproductive." (A *Svenska-Amerikanaren* reader later added that effective criticism should be subtle, "so that nobody even notices it.")[143] Spendrup thought Palme had been undiplomatic, imprudent, and acted like an international amateur.[144]

Harry Clifford wrote in to *Nordstjernan* to say that Olof Palme certainly breached diplomatic bounds, but he was no amateur. Clifford wanted to focus the debate back on Vietnam. "At issue was the horrendous bombing of North Vietnam," he wrote. "It is important to remember that North Vietnam did not declare war on the United States; also that this small Asian nation is not guilty of

---

[141] "Hört och Hänt: Illa ställt med julfriden," *Svenska Posten*, 10 January 1973: 1.

[142] "USA tänker klara sig utan," *Nordstjernan-Svea*, 11 January 1973: 4.

[143] Helmer Furuholm, "Folkets Röst: Samhällskritik," *Svenska-Amerikanaren Tribunen*, 9 July 1975: 5.

[144] Oke J. Spendrup, "Ordet är Fritt: The Importance of Keeping Cool," *Nordstjernan-Svea*, 18 January 1973: 6; and Helmer Furuholm, "Folkets Röst: Samhällskritik," *Svenska-Amerikanaren Tribunen*, 9 July 1975: 5.

any acts of aggression against our country." In that perspective, it was trivial to focus on Palme's undiplomatic language.[145]

In his column "Sverige-Fronten," however, Albin Widén dismissed Palme's criticism as "communist-inspired propaganda." "There are many Swedes," Widén wrote, "maybe even most, regret the Swedish mass-media has taken such a one-sided view of the Vietnam conflict, and certainly hope that the anti-American propaganda coming out of neutral Sweden will stop once a peace treaty is signed."[146] In the next week's column, Widén feared a treaty would not stop the anti-American criticism. Still, "it is some reason for satisfaction that the transatlantic contacts in the economic and cultural planes continue unaffected by this propaganda."[147] Widén's labeling of Swedish criticism as anti-American propaganda – plus the idea that most Swedes reject it – is likely a reflexive defense mechanism. In a painful period, this removed some sting from Sweden's criticism of their adopted country.

In early 1973, the Swedish-American press paid more attention to the diplomatic crisis with Sweden than events in Asia. Few argued that withdrawing the ambassador was unreasonable after Palme's comments. Within a few months, the satisfaction of withdrawing the American ambassador began to fade. *Norden* asked for new diplomatic relations as early as May 1973.[148] By autumn, the Swedish-American papers began looking at the diplomatic problem with regret. Several papers hoped Washington would appoint a new ambassador without a long delay.[149]

By late 1973, the Swedish-American press had become eager for normal relations again. Even parts of the mainstream press thought the time had come. *Canada-Tidningen* ran a *New York Times* editorial saying the U.S. showed "a morbid over-sensitivity" toward Swedish criticism.[150] *Nordstjernan* reprinted another *Times* editorial

---

[145] Harry W. Clifford, "Ordet är Fritt," *Nordstjernan-Svea*, 8 February 1973: 7.

[146] Albin Widén, "Sverige-Fronten: Anti-amerikansk propaganda," *Nordstjernan-Svea*, 8 February 1973: 2.

[147] Albin Widén, "Sverige-Fronten," *Nordstjernan-Svea*, 13 February 1973: 2.

[148] Lawrence Backlund, "Sverige Nixons samvete?" *Norden*, 31 May 1973.

[149] For example, see: "Smått, kort och gott," *Svenska Posten*, 12 September 1973: 1; and "New York Times on Sweden," *Nordstjernan-Svea*, 13 September 1973: 4.

quoting Senator Hubert Humphrey as calling Washington's position "infantile petulance."

> Experience has repeatedly demonstrated that the withdrawal of ambassadors is an ineffectual, self-defeating method of showing disapproval of a foreign country. That is true even if the other country is a bloodstained dictatorship or a totalitarian tyranny. But when the country is the peaceful democracy of Sweden, the position of the United States is not only inconsistent but ridiculous.[151]

In the same week, *SvP* noted that if the time had come for relations with communist China, then it was also time to appoint an ambassador to Sweden. *Svenska Posten* wrote that Henry Kissinger should make a side-trip to Stockholm on his coming trip to Moscow. "Perhaps someone can remind him that those terrible Swedes, under dangerous conditions, saved thousands of his brothers in faith from Hitler's executioners."[152] In debating Palme's remarks, critics often used Sweden's Second World War history against it. (Even one Riksdags-member used Sweden's wartime record as a reason to stay out of the Vietnam debate.)[153] *Svenska Posten* reminded readers there was another side to Sweden's wartime role.

Svenska Posten's columnist Eric Olson even wrote to President Nixon. He printed an extract of it in his *SvP* column. "I sincerely urge you to offer your humble apology to the Swedish government and to its people, exchange ambassadors at the earliest date, and restore for both nations the useful trade post in the city of Gothenburg."[154] *Svenska Posten*'s backing organization, Svenska Klubben, wrote an open letter to Henry Kissinger urging renewed relations. Both *Svenska Posten* and *Nordstjernan* printed it: highly

---

[150] Anthony Lewis, "Americans Misunderstand Swedish Criticism," *Canada-Tidningen*, 1 November 1969. Reprinted from *The New York Times*.

[151] "New York Times on Sweden," *Nordstjernan-Svea*, 13 September 1973: 4. Reprint of "Why Punish Sweden?" *The New York Times*, 5 September 1973.

[152] "Hört och Hänt: Smått, kort och gott," *Svenska Posten*, 12 September 1973: 1.

[153] Nils Nilsson, "Ordet Fritt: Svensk riksdagsman om Vietnam," (see also: Sigfrid K. Lonegren, "Ordet Fritt: Sweden-U.S.A.,") *Nordstjernan-Svea*, 25 April 1968: 8.

[154] Eric Olson, "Från läsekretsen," *Svenska Posten*, 28 November 1973.

unusual for rival papers.[155] In his column, Eric Olson amplified the appeal of the open letter. Olson considered the present conflict foolish, and the quarrel behind it "both baseless and arbitrary."[156] Editor Bengt Ekbäck added, "it is more than just baseless and arbitrary."

> It also shows the kind of pettiness and puerility that so often flows out of the White House, not just at Sweden but all opposition. Never before has this building occupied such a chauvinist, so little suited to lead a democratic land like the U.S.A. From his role as a bully investigating "un-American activities" in the Fifties, to today's Watergate and fascist tactics, the present White House president has written his name into American history.[157]

These were easily among the harshest words any Swedish-American newspaper ever said about a Republican leader. They would have been almost inconceivable just a few years earlier. The Watergate scandal was rapidly undermining the Swedish-American press's faith in the Nixon White House. By extension, Watergate further eroded support for the White House policy on Vietnam. Also, Bengt Ekbäck had only been editing *Svenska Posten* for ten months. He was part of the generation-shift taking place in Swedish-America. As a young editor, fresh off the plane from Sweden, he was more critical of U.S. foreign policy than long-time editor Harry Fabbe.

The Swedish-American press welcomed President Nixon's appointment of Robert Strausz-Hupé in March with relief. *Vestkusten* spoke for many when it described a sense of "universal elation" following the exchange of ambassadors.[158] These episodes show just how far the Swedish-American press had moved since 1960. It would have been hard to imagine in the Hammarskjöld years the emigrant press could hold a Swedish Prime Minister in so little regard as Olof Palme in 1973. It would have been hard to

---

[155] "Ett 'öppet brev' från Svenska Klubben," *Svenska Posten*, 24 October 1973: 1, and "Öppet brev till Kissinger," *Nordstjernan-Svea*, 15 November 1973: 2.

[156] Eric Olson, "Från läsekretsen," *Svenska Posten*, 21 November 1973.

[157] Bengt Ekbäck, comments appended to "Från läsekretsen," *Svenska Posten*, 28 November 1973.

[158] Karin Person, "På tal om . . .: Ambassadörsutbyte Sverige-USA," *Vestkusten*, 28 March 1974: 1.

imagine *Svenska Posten* pouring such wrath over a Republican President either. Vietnam had made the country angry, cynical, and less willing to believe in political ideals.

Differences in Swedish-American News Coverage

The emigrant press's editorial pages convey opinions on Sweden's Vietnam policy to the reader. They set the agenda for debate; they offer opinions for the reader either to accept or reject. Yet, the editorial pages are only part of the papers' overall presentation of Sweden's Vietnam policy. The front-page news gives the information the emigrant debate will interpret and argue over. This "hard news" defines which facts policy-supporters or opponents will use to back their positions. The front page may even define the scope and limits of the editorial-page debate. It is worth looking at what sorts of issues got reported in the news sections. How did these papers present Sweden's Vietnam policy? Did they present Swedish policy in a way that might lead to supporting it or opposing it?

Of the Swedish emigrant papers, *Svenska Posten*, *Nordstjernan*, and *Svenska-Amerikanaren Tribunen* ran the most news about Vietnam-related issues. This thesis has reviewed their sources in an earlier chapter. In summary, they all used at least one daily Swedish newspaper, SIS's dispatches *Nyheter från Sverige*, and most used *Sverige-Nytt*. By 1969, all three papers received FLT as well.

Source	Svenska Posten	Nordstjernan-Svea	Svenska-Amerikanaren
Nyheter från Sverige	Yes	Yes	Yes
FLT	Yes	Yes	By 1969
Sverige-Nytt	Yes	Yes	No
Daily paper	*GP, DN*	*VLT*	*NWT, GP, Barometern*

Nearly all their Vietnam-related stories were about Sweden. If Southeast Asia appeared in the paper, it was usually in the editorial pages. There were exceptions, however. Some emigrant papers reported on local Swedish-Americans killed in battle. *Nordstjernan* and *Vestkusten* even reported on a Swedish officer killed in Vietnam. A few items on Vietnam or antiwar protests sometimes reached the

Leaflet distributed by the International Longshoremen's Association, New York City, 1970.

DEMONSTRATE AGAINST

OLOF PALME
Prime Minister of Sweden

PRO-COMMUNIST - ANTI-AMERICAN

YOU'RE NOT WELCOME IN AMERICA

VISIT YOUR MAOIST, NORTH VIETNAMESE AND RUSSIAN FRIENDS' THEY LIKE YOU BETTER IN COMMUNIST, TOTALITARIAN COUNTRIES, THAT'S WHERE YOU BELONG....

● Palme has permitted the American Ambassador to be humiliated by Communists in Sweden. He has been attacked, spat on and insulted.

● Palme has encouraged and participated in Anti-American demonstrations.

● Palme has carried Viet Cong flags in parades and encouraged the desecration of the American flag.

● Palme has welcomed Communist butchers to his country.

● Palme has made vicious attacks against the U.S.

● Palme has welcomed American military deserters and traitors to Sweden.

● Palme backed the Swedish declaration recognizing the Viet Cong as the sole representative of the South Vietnams people.

Boycott Volvo & Saab Cars

HOTEL WALDORF ASTORIA
JUNE 10, 1970 at 12 Noon
Lexington Ave. at 49th Street, N.Y.C.

Sponsored by Rank and File of the International Longshoremen's Assoc., AFL-CIO

I.L.A.- "I Love America"

Source: ASNE New York, SSIRC

emigrant news pages. *Nordstjernan*, for example, reported President Johnson's decision to quit the 1968 election, pause the bombing, and offer to negotiate.[159] Most of the Vietnam-related news, however, involved Swedish reaction to the war. As the Swedish role in the Vietnam debate grew, the number of articles covering it grew as well.

TABLE 10. *Number of Vietnam-related articles in three Swedish-American newspapers, 1965–1970.*

Year	Svenska Posten	Nordstjernan-Svea	Svenska-Amerikanaren
1965	5	13	3
1966	10	24	6
1967	14	28	7
1968	19	56	17
1969	22	53	26
1970	19	43	19

Source: *Svenska Posten, Nordstjernan-Svea,* and *Svenska-Amerikanaren Tribunen,* 1965–1970.

---

[159] "Svensk befälhavare på sprängd USA-båt," *Nordstjernan-Svea,* 30 August 1966: 2, and *Vestkusten,* 8 September 1966: 1; and "President Johnson drar sig ur valstridens hetta," *Nordstjernan-Svea,* 4 April 1968: 1.

No newspaper ran anything that referred to Vietnam in 1964. In 1965, when Swedish criticism of the war began, *Nordstjernan* quickly took the lead in reporting it. The disparity between *Nordstjernan*'s intense coverage and *Svenska-Amerikanaren*'s reporting until 1967 is striking. *Nordstjernan* ran almost twice as much as its nearest competitors. (This is a little misleading because *Nordstjernan* ran some stories in both Swedish and English.) Even so, *Nordstjernan* ran four times more about Sweden's Vietnam debate than its Chicago rival in 1966. *Svenska-Amerikanaren*'s sister paper, *California Veckoblad*, ran nothing on the subject in 1966. These were simply different papers, in different areas, writing for different audiences.

Apart from intensity, *Nordstjernan*'s coverage was different in other ways. *Nordstjernan* reported American-Swedish non-government relations while others focused on diplomatic relations. Many such stories involved boycotts of Swedish goods, both real and threatened. Sweden's sheltering of U.S. military deserters angered much of New York's working class. For several months, New York Harbor longshoremen discussed refusing to unload Swedish ships. This threat worried many in U.S.-Swedish trade.[160] No formal boycott ever took place, but the dock workers often balked at unloading Swedish goods. *Nordstjernan* was a New York paper and had a special interest in this story. These boycotts directly affected *Nordstjernan*. Subscribers in Sweden often got their newspapers several months late. The dock workers stopped the surface mail to Sweden until late 1971.[161] (There were many stories about the blocked mail. Most did not mention Vietnam, so they do not appear in the content analysis tables.)

Nordstjernan also featured the Swedish government's criticism of the war. In *Nordstjernan*, articles on diplomatic protests outnumbered those on FNL demonstrations eight to four. *Svenska-*

---

[160] Letter from Paul G. Sturges (Sturges Advertising) to Eric Lindström (Svenska Handelsbanken), 15 April 1968, file "1968, maj – juni 14," box I:326, NL1, RA. See also: Victor Reisel, "Aid to Deserters May Cost Sweden Millions," *Oakland Tribune*, 10 April 1968, and "Swedes Fear G.I. 'Haven' May Trigger U.S. Boycott," *Wall Street Journal*, 12 April 1968.

[161] "Postgången USA-Sverige åter normal," *Nordstjernan-Svea*, 9 December 1971: 1.

Amerikanaren had the opposite emphasis, and chose to emphasize violent street demonstrations. *SAT*'s writing had changed since the war began. In 1965, *SAT*'s first story on a Swedish demonstration had described the protesters in childlike terms. "The young people . . . were stopped by the police and fifteen placards were confiscated. The young people were taken to the police station, and later released after talking through the problem."[162] By mid-1967, *SAT* described the protesters as fanatics. One article described "demonstrators [as] vandalizing a Danish bus . . . the protesters smashed [the bus windows] and they burned [an American] flag. On the bus doors, they painted 'death to the U.S. army.' The hooligans then entertained themselves by jumping up and down on the bus roof."[163] *SAT* always described the protesters as unthinking, but exchanged innocence for insanity. Detroit, Watts in Los Angeles, and 150 other U.S. cities had felt race riots by 1968. This list includes *SAT*'s hometown of Chicago. After Chicago's 1968 Democratic Convention – ruined by riots – *SAT* ran stories urging peaceful demonstrations.[164] By the late Sixties, *Svenska-Amerikanaren* loosely linked mindless protests with Sweden's diplomatic policy.

Table 11 below shows what three major Swedish-American papers thought were the most important issues at the war's height. It separates the Swedish-American news stories into thirteen broad groupings. Most news items fall within these categories. Many of these stories reported the then-poor relations between the United States and Sweden. I divided these news articles between those on relations between governments and those between the countries. The first type reported diplomatic relations among top leaders, diplomats, and ambassadors. I labeled these diplomatic stories "official relations." The "unofficial relations" reported on U.S.-Swedish relations outside this strictly diplomatic level. Stories on "unofficial relations" might include threats of boycotts of Swedish

---

[162] "Ungdom i Stockholm gilla ej USA:s insats i Vietnam," *Svenska-Amerikanaren Tribunen*, 14 April 1965: 1.

[163] "En järnring av polismän runt amerikanska ambassaden," *Svenska-Amerikanaren Tribunen*, 9 August 1967: 1.

[164] "Vill begära av Sveriges ungdom att demonstrera ordningsfullt" and "Demonstrera fredligt föreslog Erlander i debatt i Stockholm," *Svenska-Amerikanaren Tribunen*, 29 May 1968 and 12 June 1968: 1.

goods, for example. Stories claiming that underlying relations were still good – even if the governments quarreled – also fell into this group. Naturally, problems in "unofficial relations" may be issues for diplomats to solve. They just land in this category if a civilian voiced the problem.

The emigrant press also reported the Swedish protests over the Vietnam War. I also codified these according to their source. Rallies supporting the FNL were "FNL protests," as were antiwar statements from the Swedish FNL groups. I called antiwar statements by government officials a "government protest." I labeled a protest from a non-government Swedish leader an "other protest." Antiwar criticism from Olof Palme was a "government protest," but criticism from Jan Myrdal was an "other protest."

Other issues were easier to define. *Nordstjernan* in particular ran items reviewing whether Sweden's Vietnam policy clashed with its neutrality policy. There were also several stories on Swedish efforts to negotiate a peaceful settlement of the war. In 1968, there were several reports speculating Sweden might grant diplomatic recognition to North Vietnam. I labeled these stories "Swedish recognition." Sweden granted its recognition in early 1969. News on the wisdom or progress of the Stockholm-Hanoi relations has its own category for 1969 and 1970. Stories about American deserters and Olof Palme's 1970 visit to the U.S. were easy to classify. "Miscellaneous war news" included stories about local Swedish-Americans casualties or other war news. I excluded two items from Svenska Posten that did not easily fit these broad definitions.

TABLE 11. *Three Swedish-American newspapers' news themes in Swedish Vietnam policy, 1968–1970.*

News Subject	Svenska Posten			Nordstjernan-Svea			Svenska-Amerikanaren		
	68	69	70	68	69	70	68	69	70
Official relations	4	4	2	10	9	5	2	2	3
Unofficial relations	–	3	–	13	7	4	–	6	1
FNL protests	3	–	2	4	–	9	6	1	2
Other protest	1	1	2	3	7	1	–	5	–
Government protest	2	2	3	8	1	6	1	1	1
Debate on "neutrality"	1	–	–	3	1	3	–	–	1
Swedish peace negotiations	1	1	1	4	1	2	1	2	1
Aid to North Vietnam	3	1	4	2	7	4	2	2	1
Swedish recognition?	–	x	x	2	x	x	–	x	x
North Vietnam relations	x	2	1	x	6	1	x	–	1
American deserters	–	8	–	5	11	3	3	7	5
Palme's U.S. visit	–	–	3	–	–	4	–	–	2
Miscellaneous war news	3	–	–	2	2	1	2	–	1
Total	18	22	18	56	52	43	17	26	19

Source: *Svenska Posten*, *Nordstjernan-Svea*, and *Svenska-Amerikanaren Tribunen*, 1968–1970.

The table shows *Nordstjernan* ran the most news related to Vietnam or Swedish debate on the war. It ran more than twice as many Vietnam-related news articles as its nearest competitor. It ran some articles in both English and Swedish, which arguably inflates the total. If one excludes the English articles, *Nordstjernan* ran forty-two items in 1968, forty in 1969, and thirty in 1970. Even these adjusted totals are far above its competition.

Stories on the strained relations were most important to *Nordstjernan*. It is, after all, a New York newspaper. Is it based near the Swedish General Consulate, United Nations, and other power centers. It is also a port city, one that risked dock-workers refusing to unload Swedish products. New York's blockage of surface mail to Sweden directly affected *Nordstjernan*, but few signs it touched any other paper. As a paper from a political center, *Nordstjernan* showed the most interest in U.S.-Swedish relations. By 1968 and 1969, its volume of stories on diplomatic relations fell, but there were more on the American deserters. (These issues naturally relate to one another.) Relative to total volume, *Svenska Posten* and *Svenska-Amerikanaren* showed more interest in the deserters than diplomatic relations.

Most news stories reported protests or new aspects on U.S.-Swedish relations. These articles often reveal the current standards of journalistic objectivity. Stories on diplomatic relations rely heavily on official sources, and usually Swedish ones. There is the assumption that government officials have an institutional right to make news. These stories reported their views with little or no interpretation or analysis. Of course, Swedish-American editors often added analyses to *Sverige-Nytt* text they got as "straight news." The original source favored stories built around official sources, resulting in many stories on diplomatic relations. They often had a horse-race quality. Who were ahead or behind, were they successful, and what was their strategy?[165] This "horse-race" journalism impeded any deeper reporting on the fairness or accuracy of the Swedish or American positions. Instead, these stories report the opinions of Swedish officials as though they were fact.

Coverage of the deserters jumped across the board in mid-1969. These also show technical "horse-race" reporting. Many stories relate the latest statistics on the deserters. Few stories discuss their motives for desertion.[166] The rare exceptions were when the deserters issued public statements, which got reported without comment. It was naturally easier for journalists to report weekly statistics on the deserters. This focus also avoided reader complaints the reporters had biases. All readers could agree on the objectivity of deserter statistics. Discussing their motives may have invited questions of

---

[165] Hallin, *The Uncensored War*, 70–74, 205–207; Gaye Tuchman, *Making News*, London, 1978: 92; and Daniel C. Hallin, "The American News Media: A Critical Perspective," *Critical Theory and Public Life*, London, 1985: 121–146.

[166] For example, *Nordstjernan-Svea* ran the following stories in 1969: "News in Brief: Count 167 Deserters," 30 January 1969: 1; "Ytterligare åtta amerikanska desertörer får stanna," 27 March 1969: 1; "Uppehållstillstånd för ytterligare 16 USA-desertörer," 1 May 1969: 1; "Ytterligare 13 USA-avhoppare får stanna," 17 July 1969: 1; "16 avhoppare dömd tillförvisning med uppskov," 4 December 1969: 1.

conflict of interest or perspective.[167] These stories were most common in *Nordstjernan*, which based its reports on *Sverige-Nytt*.

It was different in *Svenska-Amerikanaren*, a paper that did not use much Sverige-Nytt material. *Svenska-Amerikanaren* and *California Veckoblad* in particular depicted the deserters as part of the "unpatriotic" antiwar movement. These were conservative-populist newspapers with a record for supporting the war. For them, it was as safe to call desertion unpatriotic at it was to consider statistics objective. (What is true and thus objective reporting is ideologically relative.)[168] Their coverage of the deserters grew increasingly negative. Until early 1969, "deserter stories" focused on the Swedish government's policy of granting deserters asylum. In 1970, "deserter stories" usually focused on the individuals. They were always negative: there were no positive stories about them. Stories on their psychological problems, drug habits, and criminal records were most common in Svenska-Amerikanaren.[169] (This follows the mainstream press's lead: *The Boston Globe, Los Angeles Times, Washington Post*, and *Houston Post* all reported on the deserters' criminal records.)[170] For *Svenska-Amerikanaren*, treating the deserters like this may have been a consensus issue. Community papers need stories that unify their readers. Exposing the deserters as a threat to their way of life might even renew solidarity against a common cultural enemy.

Svenska Posten's news coverage was nowhere as intense as *Nordstjernan*'s reporting. It is still notable that eight of *SvP*'s twenty-two news stories in 1969 were on the deserters. Swedish aid to North Vietnam was another area *SvP* emphasized. *Nordstjernan*'s output was consistently twice that of *Svenska Posten*, but *SvP* matched or exceeded *Nordstjernan*'s coverage of Swedish aid to

---

[167] Hallin, *The Uncensored War*, 206.

[168] Tuchman, *Making News*, 177–179.

[169] For example, *Svenska-Amerikanaren Tribunen* ran the following stories in 1970: "Vietnamdesertörer i Sverige är avslöjade narkotikasmugglare," 8 April 1970; "USA-desertör greps vid rån i Köpenhamn," 15 April 1970; and "För brott dömda desertörer få ej stanna i Sverige," 29 April 1970: 1.

[170] *Sverige i utländsk press 1969*, 23, and *Sverige i utländsk press 1970*, 34. (See also *Boston Globe* 6 April 1968, *Los Angeles Times* 12 October 1968, Washington Post 12 October 1968 and 3 May 1970, and *Houston Post* 11 May 1970.)

North Vietnam in 1968 and 1970. *Svenska Posten* also ran three articles on the war itself – including two on Swedish-American casualties. Only *California Veckoblad* ran more news on the war: twenty-four articles or photos in 1968 alone.

Svenska Posten got most of its Vietnam-related news from *Sverige-Nytt*. *Svenska-Amerikanaren* did not get this news source. It showed. *SAT* ran one story on Senator McCormack criticizing Olof Palme. *Sverige-Nytt* distributed an article on another Senator – Claiborne Pell – defending Sweden. *Nordstjernan* printed it.[171] *Svenska Posten* ran another *Sverige-Nytt* article, on yet another Senator: "Senator Fullbright Asks a Question: Fascist Greek Junta Gets Blessing, Democratic Sweden Gets Punished." (*SAT* argued Senator Fullbright did not reflect America's silent majority on Vietnam.)[172] *Svenska Posten*'s *Sverige-Nytt* deserter-articles, far from being provocative, explain Swedish policy. Using *Sverige-Nytt* as its source, *SvP* ran stories like "Deserters Get a Priest From the U.S." and "Generous Attitude, Not Asylum For Deserters."[173] These were the positive kinds of stories UD would have wanted to see in the Swedish-American press. By supplying *Sverige-Nytt* to *Svenska Posten*, UD was giving a positive spin to potentially bad news.

The worst news, however, were the stories of the racially-loaded attacks on Ambassador Jerome Holland. Several emigrant papers ran *Sverige-Nytt* news and editorials in reporting this story. Most of *Sverige-Nytt*'s items were critical of the protesters. Not one, however, ever mentioned the racial content of these incidents. At most, they only used vague references to "abusive words" or "anti-American slogans." Most *Sverige-Nytt* articles ignored the racial slurs but focused on the rock and egg-throwing that went with it.[174] This was

---

[171] "Krav av USA-senator," *Nordstjernan-Svea*, 7 August 1969: 1,"and Ambassadör till Sverige, krav av USA-senator," *Sverige-Nytt*, 29 July 1969. See also: "Senator kräver ny ambassadör," *Nordstjernan* and *Vestkusten*, 30 October 1969: 5, also from *Sverige-Nytt*.

[172] "Senator Fullbright ställer en fråga: Fascistiska grekjuntan välsignas, demokratiska Sverige får straff," *Svenska Posten*, 19 November 1969: 1; and Arthur Hendricks, "Till USA," *California Veckoblad*, 19 June 1970 and *Svenska-Amerikanaren Tribunen*, 17 June 1970: 6.

[173] "Desertörerna får en präst från US," 26 February 1969: 1; and "Desertörerna: Generös hållning, ej asyl," *Svenska Posten*, 12 March 1969: 1.

perhaps *Sverige-Nytt's* way of protecting its image of objectivity. It avoided choosing between "racism" or "criticism" interpretations simply by not reporting either one. The essence of the story got lost, but nobody questioned *Sverige-Nytt's* objectivity either.

By 1969, the Swedish FNL movement was notable for its absence. Neither *Svenska Posten* nor *Nordstjernan* ran any stories on Swedish street demonstrations. The FNL movement surfaced in only one *Svenska-Amerikanaren* article.[175] As in the U.S., the American troop withdrawals quieted the Swedish antiwar movement.

Also new in 1969 was a shift to printing criticism of Sweden as news. *Nordstjernan* ran *Newsweek's* article "The World's Conscience Sweden is Unscrupulously Neutral." *Svenska-Amerikanaren* ran a story on Senator John McCormack with the subheadline: "We can take criticism, but Palme was needlessly provocative – We can be glad Sweden has taken in the deserters."[176] Such stories stung. Sweden's government claimed such American criticism was unfair and unjustified. The emigrant papers sometimes printed these assertions.[177] While rare, these stories stand in ironic contrast to the ones justifying Swedish criticism of the U.S.[178] It may have been possible that editors were fully aware of the irony. Instead of justifying the Swedish criticism, it gave it a complaining tone. Sweden may criticize others, but was hyper-sensitive to criticism itself.

---

[174] See: "Polisen lurade alla demonstranter utom en när USA-ambassadören kom till Arlanda," 14 April 1970: 1; "Dr. Jerome Holland," 14 April 1970: 1; "USA-ambassadören på besök i kanslihuset," 28 April 1970: 2; "Starkt fördömande i utrikesdebatten av demonstrationerna mot USA-ambassadören," 5 May 1970: 1; and "Lymlar," *Sverige-Nytt*, 5 May 1970: 1.

[175] "Amerikadagen var lyckad i Halmstad trots röda plågan," *Svenska-Amerikanaren Tribunen*, 20 August 1969: 1.

[176] "Newsweek: Världssamvetet Sverige skrupulöst neutralt," *Nordstjernan-Svea*, 18 September 1969: 1; and "Relationerna USA-Sverige har blivit mycket dåliga: Vi kan ta kritik men Palme uppträdde onödigt utmanande – Avhopparna kan vi vara glada Sverige övertagit," *Svenska-Amerikanaren Tribunen*, 18 June 1969: 1.

[177] For example, "Sverigekritiken i amerikansk press berörs i utrikesminister Torsten Nilssons 1:a majtal," *Vestkusten*, 8 May 1969: 1.

[178] For example, "Felaktigt att tolka kritik som fiendskap, anser statsminister Palme," *Vestkusten*, 11 December 1969: 1.

Svenska-Amerikanaren often presented its news in an inflammatory way. On 29 January 1969, *SAT* ran on its front page: "The Stars and Stripes Desecrated on Swedish TV by Ignorant Reporters." This story also had three follow-up reports.[179] Several stories on the American deserters were unsympathetic. "U.S. Deserters Are Treated Like Heroes in Sweden," for example, is provocative by American standards. The only positive news for Sweden came at the end of the year. *Svenska-Amerikanaren* reported in positive terms Olof Palme's effort to get news on U.S. pilots held captive in North Vietnam.[180]

There were limits to how negative the Swedish-American press was willing to get. The emigrant papers did not use every article available to them. It is hard to infer conclusions about the items they did not print, except excluded articles often focused on strictly local protests. Yet, it is notable that *SAT* – a paper almost eager to run disparaging news on deserters – abstained from a story on a traitor. In 1968, *Sverige-Nytt* reported that three students had painted a swastika on an American flag and were arrested for desecrating a national symbol. A Swedish court acquitted them on the basis that the swastika accurately depicted current U.S. foreign policy. None of the Swedish-American papers touched that story. In 1970, *Sverige-Nytt* twice reported Sweden sheltered a deserter who defected to North Vietnam and voluntarily made FNL propaganda films.[181] No Swedish-American newspapers ran those stories either. *Svenska-Amerikanaren* was willing to report on flag desecration, but not that. It was just too much, too negative for a newspaper that championed Sweden and Swedish values. There were no respected figures like

---

[179] "Stjärnbaneret skymfat i svensk TV-program av obildade reporters," 29 January 1969: 1; "De som i Sverige bar skymf mot vår USA-flagga åtalades," 12 February 1969: 1; "Frikänd för flaggskändning," 7 May 1969: 1; and short notice on after-effects, *Svenska-Amerikanaren Tribunen*, 11 June 1969: 1.

[180] "En USA-desertör i Sverige av dylik kaliber en hjälte," 9 April 1969: 1; short notice on POW pilots, 5 November 1969: 1; and "Hustrur till flygare störtade i Vietnam besökte Palme i Stockholm," *Svenska-Amerikanaren Tribunen*, 17 December 1969: 1.

[181] "Senaste nytt i korthet," 5 November 1968; and "Nytt i sammandrag," *Sverige-Nytt*, 1 September and 10 November 1970.

Jerome Holland that could bring readers together. It was just bad news with no social function.

The individual papers' characters show what kinds of news interested them most. *Svenska-Amerikanaren* was still reaching for a national audience, and was socially conservative. Its conservatism often had a populist feel, reaching for popular consensus issues. *SAT* focused on the American deserters, whom it scornfully portrayed as drug addicts and hippies. The local *Svenska Posten* reported mostly on the Swedish government Vietnam position. It did not run anything about the deserters. *Nordstjernan* reported mostly on protests, especially ones that risked damaging U.S.-Swedish relations.

Conclusions

This chapter examines how the emigrant press commented on six aspects of Sweden's reaction to the Vietnam War. These six themes were common and often recurring subjects in the emigrant press. They may not have appeared frequently in the Swedish or mainstream American press, but often arose in the emigrant papers.

Swedish protests over the war grew dramatically in 1966 and 1967. This led some Swedish-Americans to wonder if the homeland-Swedes got accurate news on the war. They likely assumed that opposition to the war derived from misunderstanding its purpose. All believed Sweden's media had different views on the war, perhaps because it used different sources. The emigrant papers widely felt, however, the Swedish media portrait of America focused on the negative. This reached the emigrant press and immediately posed problems. These community papers preferred to downplay conflict and emphasize social harmony. Having Swedes deride America threatened the unity of Swedish-America. The Swedish-American press downplayed this threat's seriousness by blaming "the media," a faceless entity. This was preferable to conceding that broad opposition to U.S. policy existed in Sweden. The Swedish media was either careless in its sources, or worse, controlled by a clique of fanatics. This eventually became an untenable position. Swedish-Americans wanted to imagine their homeland cousins as noble rather than foolish. *Svenska Posten* chose to embrace the Swedish media for what it defined as superior and independent reporting.

Sweden's sheltering of U.S. deserters and recognizing North Vietnam attracted attention in the emigrant press. These issues also drew some mainstream American newspapers' attention: most critical of Sweden. This time, the risk was that Americans might start deriding Swedes. This would also injure Swedish-American unity. Parts of the emigrant press came to support both the deserter and recognition policies. They were policies impossible to deny and hard to blame on small left-wing cliques. It was better to describe these policies as wise rather than foolish. The emigrant press often described them as part of a humanitarian tradition in Swedish foreign policy. *Svenska Posten*'s columnists in particular backed these (by U.S. standards) controversial policies. The politically conservative *Svenska-Amerikanaren* opposed Sweden's deserter policy. Much of *SAT*'s news coverage, however, avoided focusing on Sweden's policy. It instead found it easier to blame the deserters (for various offenses) rather than condemning Sweden. *SAT* had little comment on Sweden's diplomatic recognition of North Vietnam, however. This was a phenomenon it could not attribute to others. *SAT* downplayed this story as far as possible. The paper could always argue it was a story too political for a mainly cultural paper. Its choice of news – often reporting the negative results of both policies – make *SAT*'s views clear.

The emigrant newspapers often reported the U.S.-Swedish diplomatic friction in personal terms. Instead of a conflict between states, they reduced it to a personal conflict among various actors embodying their nations. Prime Minister Olof Palme almost appeared as the physical symbol of Sweden's Vietnam policy. In this study period, Palme never shed the image as a young radical who marched with North Vietnamese diplomats. The image of him protesting on Sergels Torg tightly associated him with America's current enemy. There was thus wide dislike for him among the Swedish-American newspapers. They disliked him most when they felt his arguments assumed a moralizing quality. They accepted him most when they felt he had made extra efforts to reach out to

Americans. The ethnic press wanted to stress cooperation and harmony, and they liked Palme most when he played to that goal.

Ambassador Jerome Holland often appeared as a symbol for the United States. Unlike Olof Palme, they portrayed him as patient and forbearing despite intense provocation. (Black men from the segregation-era U.S. South learned to tolerate provocation from an early age.) This made Holland an ideal symbol for the United States. He was a symbol of cooperation and harmony for a community press looking for such symbols. The emigrant press depicted him as making extra efforts to reach out to Sweden: efforts often rejected. This made him a near folk-hero in the Swedish-American press. The emigrant papers instantly identified with his difficulty of not having the homeland-Swedes accept him. They could relate to that; they also felt mistreated by their Swedish cousins. Here, the Swedish-American press used an African-American to strengthen community bonds. The emigrant papers would prefer to unify around Sweden as a symbol, but Jerome Holland embodied values the emigrants respected more.

Chapter Three showed UD gave lots of news to the emigrant press, even if table 9 shows the editors often changed it. This chapter analyzes the emigrant press's news coverage of Swedish Vietnam policy in more detail. All the newspapers got UD's news, but often used it differently. *Nordstjernan* reported most on the state of relations – diplomatic and otherwise – between the U.S. and Sweden. *Svenska-Amerikanaren* had more interest in deserter stories and FNL protests. *Svenska Posten* ran stories on diplomatic relations and Swedish aid to North Vietnam. UD might supply news to the Swedish-American press, but it did not control what they would choose. That privilege belonged to the editors. They arguably chose some stories because they cast Swedish policy in a negative light (by U.S. standards). Some stories went completely unreported, likely because they were too inflammatory. Still other stories got rewritten in ways that would have disappointed UD. Table 9 shows *SAT* rewrote or extended more than half of its SIS-distributed news. Its hostile articles on Sweden's FNL protesters and deserters clearly deviate from UD's official line. UD was certainly a gatekeeper in the flow of news to the Swedish-American press. Yet, the editors often used the critical articles (but not excessively so) that passed UD's gates. After that, they might alter them to suit their paper's editorial stands.

The facts in these dispatches were the basis for the emigrant community's debate on Sweden's Vietnam policy. The editors and columnists always knew the latest events in Sweden. They did not get this news from the mainstream American press; there was scant coverage of Swedish politics there. One can only speculate they got this news from imported Swedish newspapers or UD-mediated dispatches. Despite all this Swedish information, the emigrant community's opinions do not have a notably Swedish perspective. One gets the impression the editors, columnists, and readers interpreted UD's news according to their own understanding of the war. For example, a Swedish condemnation of the war would have had little effect if it clashed with how the emigrants believed the war was going. If the mainstream media said the U.S. was making progress, the emigrants would reject Swedish assertions the war was futile. Such criticism would only create an image of Swedish ignorance of "the facts." It might also build an image of Swedish antipathy to the United States. Sweden and the U.S. understood the war in different ways. If UD did not appeal to the American way of understanding it, it arguably could not appeal to Swedish-American doubts about it.

Chapter Six

Content Analysis of the Swedish-American Press

The last two chapters describe how the Swedish-American press commented Vietnam and Sweden. Those chapters used certain quotations from select editorials to show how the newspapers viewed issues. This chapter does a statistical breakdown on every editorial, column, and letter debating the Vietnam War. The value with such a statistical approach is that every item gets analyzed. Done correctly, this will reinforce conclusions drawn in previous chapters. It ideally shows the thesis did not select quotations selectively. It shows in an easily measurable way how the emigrant papers changed over time. The chapter will first introduce and explain a content analysis method. This method will help examine the amount and direction of comment in the three leading Swedish-language papers from 1965 to 1972. Next, the chapter will examine the content analysis results year by year. Lastly, this chapter explores possible reasons why the Swedish-American papers changed over the years.

Methodological Reflections

Content analysis is one way to judge how a newspaper presents a certain subject. It is a statistical method. The idea is to count how often a particular message appears in a book, newspaper, or broadcast. For example, George Bailey's thesis counts which names the American TV networks used to describe the "other side" in the Vietnam War. He used a rather simple form of content analysis.

Bailey watched videotape of evening news broadcasts, and whenever a key word appeared, he jotted it down. If a reporter said *Vietcong*, he wrote it down. If a reporter said the enemy was a *VC terrorist*, he wrote that down too. When he was through, he had an interesting table.

TABLE 12. *Names the U.S. television network news anchormen used to label the United States' enemy, number and percentage, all extant broadcasts 1965–1970.*

Name in story	ABC	CBS	NBC	All
None	49 *(37%)*	45 *(25%)*	59 *(39%)*	153 *(33%)*
Hanoi	1 *(1%)*	3 *(2%)*	4 *(3%)*	8 *(2%)*
Vietcong, V.C.	16 *(12%)*	22 *(12%)*	14 *(9%)*	52 *(11%)*
Communists	7 *(5%)*	18 *(10%)*	7 *(5%)*	32 *(7%)*
V.C. guerrillas	3 *(2%)*	2 *(1%)*	2 *(1%)*	7 *(2%)*
Communist North V.N.	2 *(1%)*	10 *(6%)*	4 *(3%)*	16 *(3%)*
Vietcong communists	1 *(1%)*	2 *(1%)*	2 *(1%)*	5 *(1%)*
North Vietnam	12 *(9%)*	21 *(12%)*	24 *(16%)*	57 *(12%)*
Enemy	21 *(16%)*	25 *(14%)*	20 *(13%)*	66 *(14%)*
Hanoi and N.V.N.	1 *(1%)*	4 *(2%)*	0 *(–)*	5 *(1%)*
Communist enemy	4 *(3%)*	9 *(5%)*	2 *(1%)*	15 *(3%)*
Vietcong enemy	1 *(1%)*	2 *(1%)*	4 *(3%)*	7 *(2%)*
N.V.N. enemy	5 *(4%)*	3 *(2%)*	1 *(1%)*	9 *(2%)*
All others	11 *(8%)*	12 *(7%)*	10 *(7%)*	33 *(7%)*
Totals	134 *100%*	178 *100%*	153 *100%*	465 *100%*

Source: George A. Bailey, *The Vietnam War According to Chet, David, Walter, Harry, Peter, Bob, Howard, and Frank*, Ann Arbor, Mich.: University Microfilms, 1973: 218.

Note: Only those names accounting for at least 1% of the total are listed here.

Some critics of TV news say reporters often used the value-laden and prejudicial term *communists*. They might even argue they heard it "all the time." George Bailey shows this is simply untrue. Bailey even shows that ABC and NBC specifically avoided the word. He even shows that television anchormen – supposedly neutral observers – avoided the partisan word *enemy*. Use of the catch-all term *enemy*, however, did increase over the years.[1]

Bailey has examined large volumes of videotape: everything that still exists. His survey is non-selective, unlike most qualitative methods of analysis. This kind of analysis claims to be more objective than methods that make broad conclusions from selected quotations. The empirical analysis that uses select citations, however, is also important. It adds an important interpretative level to these dry statistics. One also has to survey examples, to illustrate quality. The statistical method should complement the qualitative discussion. Content analysis can be a useful tool, but it can also be maddeningly problematic. The most difficult aspect is defining what to choose and classifying what to count.

A study from 1968 entitled *Vietnam i Sveriges Radio* shows some of content analysis's pitfalls. It set out to discover if Swedish Radio had presented the Tet Offensive in a nonpartisan and accurate way. The suspicion was that the Swedish media ran more news unfavorable to the American and Saigon forces. The study drew up a list of "positive news," favorable to the United States, and a list of unfavorable "negative news." Positive news included: civilian support, release of prisoners, willingness to negotiate, cease-fires, good morale, and military success. Negative news included: murdering civilians, executing prisoners, inability to instate order, poor chain of command, poor morale, desertion, and censorship.[2] This study wanted to see if Radio Sweden balanced this negative news against positive news.

Studies that label news as positive and negative have a long tradition in mass-communication research. The trouble is deciding exactly what is positive and what is not. Killing civilians and prisoners is certainly negative by Judeo-Christian standards. Western culture assumes peace is the normal state of affairs and that war is not. War is only acceptable if continued peace leads to continuing an intolerable situation. This forces Westerståhl to weigh

---

[1] George Arthur Bailey, *The Vietnam War According to Chet, David, Walter, Harry, Peter, Bob, Howard, and Frank*, Ann Arbor, Mich. 1973: 368.

[2] Westerståhl, *Vietnam i Sveriges Radio*, bilaga 2. See also: Per-Gunnar Ekeblad and Christer Samuelsson, "Vietnamkonfliktens behandling i Sveriges radio-TV under perioden 11/2–9/3 1968: inledning, syfte och metod," unpublished essay, University of Göteborg, September 1968: 10.

the relative value of "intolerable peace" in Vietnam. Some of his definitions suggest Westerståhl valued compromise and cease-fire over an anti-communist victory. *Nordstjernan*'s Eric Sylvan, however, disagreed with this. Sylvan wanted the U.S. to increase its force to end the war sooner. He would have labeled military escalation as something positive. This type of analysis method is inevitably relative to culture and politics.[3] This comes out clearly in the words positive and negative. These are value judgments whose logical conclusions wind up endorsing one view of the war as correct and the other as incorrect. I would like to avoid these value judgments.

Another problem with Westerståhl's approach is that war is hardly a positive experience. Little in Vietnam was going well for the United States by 1968. In the end, this is what *Vietnam i Sveriges Radio* measured. Absolutely, there was more poor morale among the U.S. troops than good morale. Reporting otherwise for the sake of balance would have been to distort reality.

Another content analysis approach came out of Lund in the late Seventies. It arose in two theses: Eva Block's *Amerikabilden i svensk press 1948–1968* and Eva Queckfeldt's *"Vietnam": tre svenska tidningars syn på Vietnamfrågan 1963–1968*. These two works avoid the problematic positive-negative labels, which are culturally and politically relative. They instead use a shift in Swedish press opinion as its basis. They also define almost every imaginable opinion as a view common before or after that shift. They call one set of opinions an Earlier View and another set a Later View. Perhaps at their core, their detailed definitions are as subjective as Westerståhl's broad subject themes. The virtue of Block and Queckfeldt's method is its transparency: everything has a clear code. They do not use undefined standards of what hypothetical politically moderate people might judge positive news. The labels Earlier and Later avoid prejudicial terms such as positive and negative. My thesis will adopt

---

[3] In 1997, I tried using Westerståhl's positive-negative content analysis method on the news the Swedish-American papers printed. I soon ran into endless interpretation problems. Other people in the inter-coder reliability tests often produced very different results from mine. I soon decided to scrap it and find another method with clearer guidelines.

their method of content analysis. It is a proven method, and its use will allow an easy comparison of the Swedish and Swedish-American press.

Eva Block's thesis *Amerikabilden i svensk press* examines how the U.S. image has changed in the Swedish press. America had a good reputation in the Swedish press after the Second World War. It was a progressive democracy that defended others from communism. The U.S. had some problems, but its leaders worked honestly and wisely to overcome them. Racism was a problem, but only in the South. Politicians were trying to end it, and had made progress. Block calls this the Earlier View of America. This well-defined image produces a more satisfying content analysis than simply counting "positive news."

Over the next twenty years, this idealized image changed. The Swedish press started forming a more antagonistic image of America. In its pure form, the U.S. was a reactionary superpower that supported right-wing dictatorships. Instead of protecting others, the U.S. was partly responsible for the East-West tension. Racism was a profound problem, even in the North, and politicians did little to change it. America's leaders now seemed like dishonest and opportunistic Cold Warriors. Block calls this a Later View of the United States. Both Earlier and Later Views are ideal types. Newspapers may have leaned toward one or the other, but none ever ran a pure version of either image.

Block wants to find out when America's image shifted from one to the other. She believes the shift from an Earlier to Later View was not uniform. Parts of the idealized Earlier View began to chip away first. This led to changing opinions in other areas later. She breaks her analysis of the United States' image into five parts. Two of them are domestic: American domestic politics and racial discrimination. Three more involve U.S. foreign policy. These are U.S.-Soviet conflict, U.S. policy in Latin America, and U.S. policy in Vietnam.

She concludes the change was not uniform. A change in one "image part" may have caused changes in other "image parts." For example, a shift in views about Latin America may have influenced the image of U.S. policy in Vietnam. The early image shift of the

U.S. as neo-imperialistic in Latin America may have been a precondition for the Later View of U.S. policy in Vietnam.

Block focuses on the Kennedy years of the Vietnam War. She discusses Vietnam as an issue in the 1968 election, but her analysis of Vietnam largely ends with the 1965 escalation. Looking at more would be beyond the scope of Block's thesis. That would be an entire dissertation in itself. Eva Queckfeldt wrote that dissertation in 1981, called *"Vietnam": tre svenska tidningars syn på Vietnamfrågan 1963–1968.*

Block's thesis divided the image of America into five parts, with Vietnam perhaps being the most serious one. Queckfeldt further subdivides that one image part into eight themes. Those themes and their most defining features appear in the table below.

TABLE 13. *Most defining features of Queckfeldt's eight Earlier and Later View themes.*

Theme	Earlier View	Later View
1. Cause of war	The war is world Communist aggression.	The war is imperialist aggression.
2. The FNL	The FNL is a communist group.	The FNL is a nationalist group or noncommunist.
3. North Vietnam	The war is Soviet or Chinese aggression.	The Soviets or Chinese are not behind Hanoi.
4. South Vietnam	South Vietnam could become a democracy.	South Vietnam will not become a democracy.
5. United States	The U.S. is stopping communist aggression.	The U.S. has attacked North Vietnam.
6. War events	The U.S. bombing is legal and effective.	The U.S. bombing is not effective, is terroristic.
7. Chance for peace	The U.S. will win, or is willing to stop.	The U.S. will lose, there is no military solution.
8. Sweden-U.S.	The demonstrators are naive or communists.	The demonstrators are socially aware.

Source: Queckfeldt, *"Vietnam,"* 131–139.

It is irrelevant whether one view is correct and another false. Neither image is, by itself, accurate nor correct. They are only ordering concepts, useful for making comparisons. Queckfeldt wants to measure and compare the editorial views of three Swedish newspapers: *Dagens Nyheter, Svenska Dagbladet,* and *Stockholms-Tidningen. DN* is tied to the liberal bourgeois People's Party and *SvD* has ties to the conservative party. *Stockholms-Tidningen* was a Social Democratic newspaper. (Queckfeldt continued her analysis with the similar Social Democratic newspaper *Aftonbladet* after *ST* closed.) She wants to know when the newspapers changed their views on Vietnam. Like Block, Queckfeldt argues that certain theme groups changed first and others later.

She concludes the themes "United States" and "Chance for Peace" dominated Swedish press opinion. *Dagens Nyheter's* editorials resembled *Stockholms-Tidningen's* views more than *Svenska Dagbladet's* opinions. These newspapers chose U.S. sources much more often than North Vietnamese sources. (She refers to this as "news imperialism.")[4] Critics of the U.S. predominated in all three newspapers. More than 90% of that criticism directly related to antiwar views current in America. More than half came from U.S. critics like William Fulbright, Robert Kennedy, Arthur Schlesinger, and Harrison Salisbury.[5] This means the Swedish antiwar views in the emigrant press have their roots in the American debate.

She has defined Earlier and Later views for each theme with a series of codes. (These codes appear in an appendix.) Her coding scheme is extensive, covering nearly every potential opinion on the Vietnam War. This is extremely helpful. Everything is transparent, coding is less subjective, and makes an inter-coder reliability test far less urgent. However, the coding scheme for theme eight is not as extensive as the others. Theme eight covers the Swedish conflict with the United States. Queckfeldt has only used twelve codes to define this theme. The Earlier View press opinions were current in the 1963, and the Later View opinions prevailed in the 1968 debate. One should note the "Earlier View" did not always support the U.S., nor was the "Later View" always consistently hostile. Queckfeldt's codes do not reflect a Postive-Negative value judgment but a shift over time. Her codes for the Swedish conflict with the U.S. are:

---

[4] Queckfeldt, *"Vietnam,"* 66. (Queckfeldt says this phrase sounds dated and would use other words today.)

[5] Queckfeldt, *"Vietnam,"* 55.

TABLE 14. *Eva Queckfeldt's theme group Eight: Sweden-Vietnam.*

Earlier View	Later View
1. Sweden risks its neutrality by criticizing the U.S.	1. Sweden does not risk its neutrality by criticizing U.S.
2. Swedish criticism is unclear, naive, left-wing.	2. Swedish criticism builds on U.S. material.
3. Support for U.S. Vietnam policy exists in Sweden.	3. Criticism of U.S. Vietnam policy exists in Sweden.
4. Sweden must restrain its criticism of the U.S.	4. Sweden must increase its criticism of the U.S.!
5. Criticism of Swedish Vietnam policy exists in Sweden.	5. Critics of Swedish policy are Cold Warriors.
6. The Swedish government condemns the U.S. Vietnam policy.	6. The Swedish government does not take a strong enough stand against the U.S. Vietnam policy
7. The Swedish Vietnam criticism is one-sided, aimed only at the U.S.	7. The Swedish government has also criticized others, such as the Soviets.
8. Swedish government has strong public support on Vietnam.	8. Certain politicians, circles exploit Vietnam to become popular.
9. Sweden can mediate war.	9. Sweden cannot mediate war.
10. Rules and interventions at demonstrations are necessary.	10. Interventions often unnecessary or provocative.
11. Demonstrators are fanatics, communists, leftist radicals.	11. Demonstrators against U.S. Vietnam policy in all quarters.
12. Demonstrators are ignorant, naive, deceived, troublemakers.	12. Demonstrators are knowledgeable, socially aware.

Source: Queckfeldt, "*Vietnam*," 139.

Twelve codes cannot adequately cover any possible opinion that might arise. They may cover most, but not all. This is unfortunate for me, because theme eight is the one that appears most often in the Swedish-American press. In applying her codes myself, I frequently found opinions that Queckfeldt has not covered. In coding these editorials, I sometimes had to stretch the codes given above to cover these opinions. I simply had to reflect on the underlying values of each Earlier and Later code. An ambiguous editorial often falls under the penumbra of other codes. Another code can often implicitly express values that may cover ambiguous editorials. Sometimes looking at Eva Block's codes on U.S. domestic politics can help clarify and solve the problem.

For example, the Swedish-American press often wrote that Sweden was damaging its relations with the U.S. Queckfeldt does not give a specific code for this opinion. I listed this statement as an Earlier View opinion. It is a view implied in the codes "Sweden risks its neutrality by criticizing the U.S." and "The Swedish Vietnam criticism is one-sided, aimed only at the U.S." One-sided, unfair criticism would tend to damage relations. By the early Seventies, this opinion faded. More commentators blamed the U.S., instead of Sweden, for the broken relations. Blaming the United States, in turn, was a Later View opinion.

Most editorials easily fall into one of these two ideal types. Queckfeldt's codes help classify editorials that do not seem to express an opinion openly. Her codes classify how editorials frame issues and reason about them. There are some inconsistencies in her codes, however. (For example, the statement "South Vietnam is an American puppet dictatorship" is Earlier View code 4stU. One could call the same thought, rephrased with the U.S. as its subject, "the United States supports a dictatorship," the Later View code 5dem.) In applying Queckfeldt's codes, some moments demand careful reflection about her codes' original intent. Sometimes, one must stretch the letter of her coding pattern to remain within its intended spirit.

Content analysis is the art of simplifying complex realities down to the level of statistics. This helps measure growing or shrinking phenomena, but sometimes things get lost. Statistics often hide intangible values such as quality and intensity. That is the case here. For example, code "Later 5kram" is the view "News from Vietnam is covered up, and facts are silenced or distorted." Queckfeldt gives all editorials with this view the same code. For example, *Aftonbladet* once wrote, "The lies in the official American propaganda are obvious to everyone who has followed the Vietnam War's development." *Svenska Dagbladet* wrote, "Over the last few years, President Johnson has gone through one test after the other, but considering his and his nation's situation, he has certainly tried to project the most optimism possible." Both editorials say

Washington has distorted the situation in Vietnam. They only say it differently, with different intensity of opinion. They may have the same view, but the two statements are unequal.[6] This is a problem with most forms of content analysis. The statistics are important, but they need support from examples and a thoughtful qualitative analysis. Statistics by themselves are not enough.

There have been three main objections to Queckfeldt's thesis. First, it only goes up to January 1969. As one critic put it, "The period under review ends just as the Vietnam debate is heating up, both in Sweden and the United States."[7] Second, she surveys only formal editorials. She does not examine the debate on the culture pages, their reader letters, or most political columnists.[8] (For some reason, she includes James Reston's *New York Times* column that *Svenska Dagbladet* printed.) She does not look at front page reporting at all. *Svenska Dagbladet* commented, "Sven Öste's pioneering reporting for *Dagens Nyheter* has not been taken up at all, although it may have done more than anything else to swing public opinion in this country."[9] Lastly, she compares a conservative paper with liberal and socialist ones. This largely predetermines her conclusions in advance. It comes as little surprise that different parties had different views on Vietnam. Some of her findings have the feel of confirming the obvious.[10]

This thesis avoids most of these objections in applying her method. First, I carry the content analysis through the end of 1972: four years more than Queckfeldt covers. Second, I include the columnists and reader letters in the content analysis. There is also a discussion of front-page news. Third, I am comparing newspapers

---

[6] Bo-Kage Carlson, "Vietnam och vi," *Svenska Dagbladet*, 8 July 1981.

[7] Joseph P. Board, "Eva Queckfeldt: "Vietnam": tre svenska tidningars syn på Vietnamfrågan 1963–1968," *Statsvetenskaplig Tidskrift*, 1982(3).

[8] For criticism on this, see: Bo Grandien, "Hur tidningarna bytte åsikt i Vietnamfrågan," *Dagens Nyheter*, 17 May 1981; and "Vietnam i debatten," in Per Rydén, "Ljus från Lund," *Sydsvenska Dagbladet*, 23 October 1981. (All reviews courtesy of Eva Queckfeldt.)

[9] Bo-Kage Carlson, "Vietnam och vi," *Svenska Dagbladet*, 8 July 1981.

[10] For example, she proves that half of the Swedish press criticism came from American critics like William Fullbright or Robert Kennedy. *Nordstjernan's* Eric Sylvan pointed this out back in his 7 September 1967 column.

that lean to the political right. By-passing the political variable may produce more interesting conclusions. Queckfeldt mixes socialist and conservative papers, but she also compares two morning dailies with the evening tabloid *Aftonbladet.* (*Aftonbladet* fills only part of her survey period, however.) Morning papers and evening tabloids fill quite different roles in the mass-communications world. My thesis removes that variable as well: the emigrant papers are all weeklies.

Despite some minor flaws, I believe Queckfeldt has a solid method for analyzing press opinion on Vietnam. The three most political papers – *Svenska Posten, Nordstjernan,* and *Svenska-Amerikanaren* – dominated debate on Vietnam. These three papers account for over 70% of the Swedish-American opinion pieces on the subject. It is perhaps natural to run Eva Queckfeldt's analysis method on these three newspapers. I uncovered 834 items comment items about Vietnam in the entire Swedish-American press. The three dominant papers ran well over five hundred of these. These "comment items" included editorials, columnist articles, and letters to the editor. I read through these items, looking for any of Queckfeldt's enumerated opinions. When I found certain opinions, I assigned the articles various codes for the views they express.

Most comment pieces received several codes. Only short or narrowly-focused pieces got fewer than two or three different codes. Some got five or six. Many expressed a mix of Earlier and Later views too. Eric Sylvan's *Nordstjernan* column from 28 August 1969, for example, took the codes: Earlier 7brned, Later 7mil, and Later 7Ntr.[11] He had the Later Views the Vietnam War had no military solution, and was open to negotiating with Hanoi with North Vietnamese troops still in the South. There were two Later View codes, and only one Earlier View opinion. That one opinion, however, outweighed the others. Some of his views may have changed, but he still insisted North Vietnam and FNL broke international cease-fires. That was the thrust of Sylvan's entire column. When there is a mix of Earlier and Later Views, content analysts must ask themselves: what is the item's primary message? What is the secondary message?

---

[11] Eric Sylvan. "Det Tycks," *Nordstjernan-Svea*, 28 August 1969: 4.

I labeled items as either Earlier or Later view pieces, depending on what the central opinion – or plurality of opinions – was. I coded everything and defined them as either Earlier or Later view items. There were exceptions, however. The major exception was *Nordstjernan*'s editorial columns – items from *Sverige-Nytt* – called "Saxat ur de svenska ledarspalterna." These columns presented editorials from several Swedish newspapers: as many as seven or eight. *Nordstjernan* tried to balance the conservative and socialist papers, but one set of codes usually dominated these columns. There were some cases when it was hard to decide what the predominating view was. Rather than making a questionable decision, I simply left these editorials out of the statistics.

A note on standards: I examined 834 opinion pieces. (It is possible there were some I did not find.) For me to consider an editorial a "Vietnam piece," it must explicitly mention the war or Sweden's Vietnam policy. Several alluded to foreign American conflicts or domestic protests. For example, a 1967 *Nordstjernan* editorial opened with the line:

> Sweden's young people, who now use every opportunity to go through the streets of Stockholm and express their hatred for the U.S. and President Lyndon Johnson, have discovered a difficult dilemma, writes *Norrköpings-Tidningar*.[12]

It may seem clear these protests are opposing the Vietnam War, but the editorial never says so. These young people could have been protesting almost anything. I decided not to assume it was Vietnam. For me to label an editorial as a Vietnam item, the word "Vietnam" had to appear somewhere in the text. I also accepted synonyms such as "Southeast Asia" or allusions to the combatants such as the FNL or Vietcong.

Sometimes just mentioning Vietnam was not enough. Some comment pieces named Vietnam but only in passing. For example, Eric Sylvan's 1 September 1966 *Nordstjernan* column mentioned the war. His subject, however, was the draft: just using the word Vietnam was not enough. There had to be at least three sentences

---

[12] "Vad nu då? Inga protester?" *Nordstjernan-Svea*, 15 June 1967: 4.

with an opinion on the war or Swedish Vietnam policy.[13] These rules may have slightly reduced the survey size, but did not create any noticeable bias in the results.

Eva Queckfeldt's method is most useful here for tracing the breakdown of the Cold War ideology. It is less helpful in tracking the emergence of a new, postwar ideology in America. The Cold War ideology collapsed in America, but nothing quite like the Swedish "Later View" really developed there. The Later View may describe parts of Swedish society by 1975, but only a minority in America. Her Later View does not altogether fit the United States.

Creating a new set of codes describing an exhausted, disillusioned, and cynical nation would be one solution. This was a tempting idea. It did, however, have some serious drawbacks. One could no longer compare the Swedish-American press to the homeland-Swedish press. This created yet another drawback. It would then be hard to measure how successful UD's press policy had been. UD had arranged for the emigrant papers to get Swedish news. Had this indeed brought the emigrants around to the Swedish way of looking at Vietnam? It would be hard to tell. I eventually decided not to create a new set of codes. It did not seem wise to create an American Later View coding system when the news in the emigrant papers was mostly of Swedish origin. This thesis, then, retains Eva Queckfeldt's Later View coding. This allows a final comparison of the Swedish-American and Swedish newspapers.

One may also object that the Swedish dailies and the emigrant papers had different subject matter. *Dagens Nyheter* and *Svenska Dagbladet* are daily news organs. The Swedish-American newspapers are mostly social and cultural organs. The Swedish dailies focused on the topical themes "United States" and "Chance for Peace." The Swedish-American press emphasized the cultural conflict of "Sweden-Vietnam." This theme was a relatively minor element in Eva Queckfeldt's study, but not so here. The emigrant papers devoted around half of their commentary to the Swedish Vietnam policy. In times of crisis, they printed even more. The emigrant

---

[13] Some reader letters in *Svenska-Amerikanaren* had run-on sentences, so I was flexible with this rule. For some letters, I looked for two or more independent clauses about Vietnam.

papers perhaps stressed "Sweden-Vietnam" to the point where it ruined a valid comparison to the Swedish dailies. Maybe so: it is a legitimate concern.

Queckfeldt's method is still a good way to measure changing press opinion of the Vietnam War. The emigrant papers often focused on Sweden, but concern over Vietnam was never far away. One often suspects that debate on Sweden was so acrimonious because the war in Asia was not going well. Vietnam was a raw nerve and Swedish critics had struck it. Chapter Five showed that the Swedish-Americans often struck back in kind, because of the raw nerve. The Swedish-Americans often focused their arguments on Sweden, not Vietnam. Still, the national nightmare in Southeast Asia was mainly why they were argumentative.

The Results

This thesis examines how all fifteen Swedish-American newspapers viewed the Vietnam War. Not all newspapers covered the Vietnam debate equally. *Svea* ran only six editorials before it closed, *Canada-Svensken* ran eleven, and *Western News* printed nineteen editorials. On the other side, *Svenska-Amerikanaren* ran 135 and *Svenska Posten* printed 202 comment pieces. *Nordstjernan* printed as many as 288 comment pieces on Vietnam and Sweden's Vietnam policy. Some pieces fell outside the content analysis time-frame of 1965–1972. Others related only indirectly to Vietnam. *Svenska Posten* has 187 items in this survey, *Nordstjernan* 218, and *Svenska-Amerikanaren* 102.

These three newspapers led the debate on Vietnam. They also represented three different Swedish-American communities. Eva Queckfeldt's analysis method may show how these different community newspapers responded to Vietnam. This thesis therefore focuses its content analysis on them. *Svenska Posten, Nordstjernan,* and *Svenska-Amerikanaren* were distinct papers. They all wrote for older Swedish-Americans, but had individual identities. Their different communities – local, regional, and semi-national – meant they had different ways of serving them. *Svenska Posten's* opinion items came from its wide stable of in-house columnists. *Nordstjernan* ran editorials. It had one columnist (Eric Sylvan) whose article read like a guest editorial. *Svenska-Amerikanaren* ran an active letters-to-the editor page and ran a few editorials.

These papers had little to say on Vietnam before the 1965 escalation. *SvP* ran three Vietnam-items in 1964, *Nordstjernan* had four, and *Svenska-Amerikanaren* mentioned Vietnam only once in a discussion of foreign policy problems.[14] All comments were brief, and all had an Earlier View of Vietnam. *Nordstjernan* and *Svenska Posten* had far more to say in 1965. *SAT*, however, ran only two Vietnam-editorials that year: both were Earlier View. For 1965, when *SAT*'s comment was still scarce, the content analysis compares *Nordstjernan* and *Svenska Posten* to the other papers. The column "All Others" includes *Svea*'s five editorials, *Norden*'s four, and *California Veckoblad*'s and *Canada-Tidningen*'s one editorial each.

TABLE 15. *Two Swedish-American newspapers' attitude toward the Vietnam War, by opinion type, 1965.*

	Svenska Posten		Nordstjernan		All Others	
Opinion Type	EARLY	LATER	EARLY	LATER	EARLY	LATER
Editorial	–	2	4	1	8	3
Columnist	10	12	12	–	–	–
Reader Letter	1	–	–	1	–	–
Total	11	14	16	12	8	3

Source: *Svenska Posten, Nordstjernan*, and *California Veckoblad, Canada-Tidningen, Svea, Norden*, and *Svenska-Amerikanaren Tribunen*, 1965.

While *SAT* ran only two items on Vietnam, *Nordstjernan* printed eighteen comment items in 1965. *Svenska Posten* ran twenty-five. Comment on Vietnam thus came mostly from the northern papers on the Atlantic and Pacific coasts. Unlike 1964, Vietnam was no longer abstract, but a palpable political crisis. It was not yet a domestic social problem, however, and the friction with Sweden had

---

[14] "Utrikespolitisk översikt," *Svenska-Amerikanaren Tribunen*, 14 October 1964; Eric Sylvan, "Det Tycks," *Nordstjernan*, 9 January, 28 May, and 3 December 1964; "Papperstigern visar tänderna," *Nordstjernan*, 13 August 1964; "Ett och Annat av Otto B. Jacobson," *Svenska Posten*, 6 August and 2 September 1964; and "Rim och Reson av Reinhold Ahleen," *Svenska Posten*, 9 December 1964.

not really begun. *SAT* may have seen Vietnam as unfit for a Swedish-American paper without a direct Swedish role.

Nordstjernan projected a solidly Earlier View of Vietnam. Columnist Eric Sylvan was the most avid debater, and was consistently hawkish on Vietnam. His early articles backing the war had a reasonable, measured tone that became sharper by the year's end. *Nordstjernan* ran four editorials on Vietnam in 1965. The one Later View editorial came from *Sverige-Nytt*.[15] Many *Sverige-Nytt* editorials were collections of press commentary from the Swedish dailies. Most Swedish dailies were less supportive of the U.S. Vietnam policy than American papers. *Sverige-Nytt* also had links to UD, so the press commentary it chose often lightly favored UD's position.

Svenska Posten also printed two Later View editorials. One of them clearly derives from a *Sverige-Nytt* editorial.[16] (*Svea* also ran an editorial based on UD material; unusually, it gave an Earlier View of Vietnam.)[17] Most of *Svenska Posten*'s opinion came from its stable of in-house columnists. Editor Harry Fabbe added antiwar columnist Eric Olson to the stable in 1965. This added to *Svenska Posten*'s rapid shift to a Later View. The paper ran eight columns supporting Johnson's Vietnam policy in 1965. Seven appeared before July. The eighth, which appeared in November, was only tepid in its support. *SvP* largely stopped promoting the White House position by early 1966. This fall in *SvP*'s support is unusual because American support for the war rose rather than fell in 1965. In November 1965, 64% of Americans backed the war; 59% supported the war in

---

[15] "Vietnam ur svensk synpunkt," *Nordstjernan* 2 September 1965 is based on "Saxat ur ledarspalten: Vietnam," *Sverige-Nytt*, 24 August 1965. "Anti-Amerikanism," *Nordstjernan* 18 November 1965 is based on "Saxat ur ledarspalten: Anti-Amerikanism," *Sverige-Nytt*, 9 November 1965.

[16] "Hört och Hänt: Svenska regeringen om Vietnam," *Svenska Posten*, 22 September 1965 is based on "Saxat ur ledarspalten: Vietnam," *Sverige-Nytt*, 24 August 1965.

[17] "Boheman om USA," *Svea*, 30 December 1965 is based on "Saxat ur ledarspaltarna: Boheman om USA," *Sverige-Nytt*, 7 December 1965.

[18] John E. Mueller, *War, Presidents, and Public Opinion*, London, 1973: 55, 143, 271, 275.

early 1966.[18] *Svenska Posten*'s commentary thus resembled the Swedish dailies more than the American ones in 1965.[19]

Svenska Posten's editor Harry Fabbe was a New Dealer and sympathized with the Swedish Social Democrats.[20] This may have made him more receptive to Swedish Social Democratic arguments on Vietnam. As a Seattle editor, Fabbe was also far from Washington or the New York media center. The West-coast culturally treats East-coast assertions with skepticism, often thinking quite independently. Eastern assertions about Vietnam's strategic value may have met more skepticism in the West. The other West Coast newspapers paid little attention to Vietnam. *Svenska Posten* only continued to oppose the war in 1966, and became more vocal about it. Table 16 below shows a huge jump in *Svenska Posten*'s commentary.

TABLE 16. *Three Swedish-American newspapers' attitude toward the Vietnam War, by opinion type, 1966.*

Opinion Type	Svenska Posten		Nordstjernan-Svea		Svenska-Amerikanaren	
	EARLY	LATER	EARLY	LATER	EARLY	LATER
Editorial	–	5	4	2	2	–
Columnist	6	29	14	1	–	–
Reader Letter	–	–	1	–	3	4
Total	6	34	19	3	5	4

Source: *Svenska Posten, Nordstjernan-Svea,* and *Svenska-Amerikanaren Tribunen,* 1966.

Svenska Posten's Vietnam commentary leaped from twenty-five comment items in 1965 to forty in 1966. Editor Harry Fabbe openly opposed the war in 1966 and stopped writing Early View editorials. This directly led to Otto Jacobson pulling his pro-war columns from *Svenska Posten*. Without Jacobson's columns, *SvP* presented an almost solidly Later View of the war.

---

[19] Block, *Amerikabilden i svensk press 1948–1968,* 84–87; Uncas Rydén, "Vietnamkriget i svensk press – en kvalitativ analys," AB-uppsats, History Department, Göteborg University, VT 1993: 6–8.

[20] Wilson, "Fabbe," 190.

Nordstjernan's opinion on the Vietnam War had not changed much since 1965. *Nordstjernan* editor Gerry Rooth was silent on Swedish Vietnam policy. It may be worth noting *Nordstjernan* had been printing with two letter-press machines, both built around the First World War. One needed minor repairs costing around two thousand dollars, and the other needed a six thousand-dollar investment. So far, Rooth's daughter had paid for repairs of these machines. By 1966, *Nordstjernan* asked UD and SIS for help in raising twenty-five thosand kronor to convert the paper to offset printing.[21] UD raised some money for *Nordstjernan*, but not enough for the offset conversion. These plans went through summer and autumn 1966, and might have chilled *Nordstjernan*'s criticism of UD foreign policy. Instead columnist Eric Sylvan led the debate on Vietnam. His columns account for most Earlier View comment in *Nordstjernan*.

Table 16 also shows the war finally came to Chicago. *Svenska-Amerikanaren* ran seven letters on Vietnam in 1966, but none the year before. *SAT* ran two Vietnam-editorials in 1964, two more in 1965, two in 1966, and as table 17 below shows, two more in 1967. The paper's attention to Vietnam was quite consistent and understated. Vietnam was beginning to engage the Swedish-American public, and *SAT*'s readers, but not its editors.

In 1967, *Nordstjernan* focused on Sweden's FNL movement and the Russell Tribunal that met in Stockholm. *Nordstjernan* approached these subjects with a mainly Earlier View of Vietnam. Its editorials were discreetly Earlier View, but Eric Sylvan's columns were bluntly so. *Svenska Posten*, however, focused on American policy in Vietnam. More than ever, *Svenska Posten* explicitly described Vietnam as a civil war. *Svenska Posten*'s commentary and Eric Sylvan's columns were easy to classify. *Nordstjernan*'s editorials were more subtle, however, and one should see those statistics more as a judgment call.

---

[21] Letter from Allan Kastrup to Sten Sundfeldt, 27 September 1966; memo from Allan Kastrup to Allen Hernelius, 26 June 1966; and letter from Sten Sundfeldt to Kjell Öberg, 9 September 1966, file "1963 – Mars 1967," box I:462, PR4S, RA.

TABLE 17. *Three Swedish-American newspapers' attitude toward the Vietnam War, by opinion type, 1967.*

Opinion Type	Svenska Posten EARLY	Svenska Posten LATER	Nordstjernan-Svea EARLY	Nordstjernan-Svea LATER	Svenska-Amerikanaren EARLY	Svenska-Amerikanaren LATER
Editorial	–	1	8	6	2	–
Columnist	2	15	11	2	–	–
Reader Letter	–	–	3	–	4	5
Total	2	16	22	8	6	5

Source: *Svenska Posten, Nordstjernan-Svea,* and *Svenska-Amerikanaren Tribunen,*
1967.

Table 17 shows that Vietnam continued to engage the Swedish-American press. Commentary fell a bit in *Svenska Posten,* down from 1966's near-saturation levels. *Nordstjernan's* Eric Sylvan continued to turn in his yearly twelve to fourteen columns on Vietnam. The volume of editorials, however, jumped since 1966 from six to fourteen. (*Nordstjernan* got many of these from the Swedish newspaper *Sverige-Nytt.*) *Svenska-Amerikanaren* still handed in its two annual Vietnam editorials, but the volume of reader letters on Vietnam continued to rise. Even *Nordstjernan* had more letters about Vietnam coming in.

These tables for 1965, 1966, and 1967 show several trends. First, the amount of commentary rose as America deployed more troops (and more soldiers died). Second, the increases were in different areas for each newspaper. Eric Sylvan turned in the same number of columns each year, but the number of *Nordstjernan* editorials was growing. Letters-to-the-editor were another growth sector. The tables may not show it, but the commentary increasingly focused on Sweden and Swedish Vietnam policy. As more American soldiers went into harm's way, Swedish criticism of "U.S. imperialism" became a more emotional subject. This emotional charge produced more letters, columns, and editorials from the Swedish-Americans. These trends continued into 1968, as the table below shows.

TABLE 18. *Three Swedish-American newspapers' attitude toward the Vietnam War, by opinion type, 1968.*

Opinion Type	Svenska Posten		Nordstjernan-Svea		Svenska-Amerikanaren	
	EARLY	LATER	EARLY	LATER	EARLY	LATER
Editorial	1	9	12	7	5	5
Columnist	3	23	11	–	1	–
Reader Letter	1	–	8	3	3	–
Total	5	32	31	10	9	5

Source: *Svenska Posten, Nordstjernan-Svea,* and *Svenska-Amerikanaren Tribunen,* 1968.

Table 18 shows the amount of commentary kept growing. Svenska Posten saw a dramatic jump in comment over 1967's levels: more than twice as much. *Nordstjernan* ran forty-one items; it ran thirty items in 1967. More editorials, and many more letters accounted for this increase. Vietnam and the emotional Swedish role were becoming popular issues among editors and readers. The flood of political reader-letters became so heavy *Svenska-Amerikanaren* banned them on 20 March 1968.[22] *Svenska-Amerikanaren* ran fewer letters on Vietnam, but the editorials jumped five-fold over earlier levels.

Nordstjernan, for example, had a largely Earlier View of the war. Most of its Early View editorials criticized Sweden's Vietnam policy. The amount of Later View comment on the U.S. role in Vietnam was rapidly growing. Two-thirds of *Nordstjernan's* remarks on the war – only the war – were Later View statements. This is notable, but it is unwise to exaggerate its importance. Many Americans felt more hostile to the antiwar movement than the war itself. This antipathy for the war critics may have indirectly created a negative support for the war. It would be specious to separate completely feelings on the war from feelings on the antiwar movement. No such neat divisions exist in life. (See Table 28 for a breakdown on how *Nordstjernan* commented on codes 1–7 as opposed to code eight.)

---

[22] Urlakaren, "Folkets Röst," *Svenska-Amerikanaren Tribunen,* 20 March 1968: 5.

HITTING BACK . . . An infantryman watches for enemy acitivity as fellow soldiers aboard an armored personnel carrier return enemy fire during action near Long Binh, Vietnam.

In 1968, Svenska-Amerikanaren's sister paper ran twenty photos of U.S. troops in Vietnam.

By 1968, Sweden's Vietnam policy was the dominant issue in *Nordstjernan* and *Svenska-Amerikanaren*. Most *Nordstjernan* opinion items were on the Swedish role in the war. The paper ran only ten comment pieces strictly on the war itself. Conservative columnist Eric Sylvan wrote eight of those ten: all were Early View opinions. *Svenska Posten* did the complete reverse. Twenty-three of its thirty-seven comment items had little to do with Sweden. *SvP*'s columnists showed far more interest in Vietnam. *SvP*'s discussion about Swedish politics arose mostly in Harry Fabbe's editorials.

This division between Swedish Vietnam-policy and war-commentary was clearest in *Svenska Posten*. *Nordstjernan* often mixed comment on the Swedish policy with discussion of Vietnam and vice-versa. There were many comment items on the war that did not mention Sweden. There were many comment pieces on Sweden's Vietnam policy, and most had clear views on the war fused into their arguments. It is difficult to separate Swedish-American views on Vietnam and emigrant views on Sweden's reaction to the war.

Svenska Posten was the paper that most often treated Vietnam in isolation. Of these three papers, *SvP* was perhaps most able to treat Vietnam on its own merits. *Nordstjernan*, however, often linked Vietnam to the symbolic subject of Sweden. Vietnam was something complicating U.S.-Swedish relations. In defending the

U.S. from (what it saw as) gratuitous criticism, *Nordstjernan* indirectly backed the war.

Nordstjernan was printing more editorials – and specifically more Later View editorials – with each passing year. In 1968, it ran seven Later View editorials; in 1969, this doubled to fourteen Later View editorials. Many of these came from Sweden, supplied by UD's press bureau. *Svenska Posten* had a Later View of Vietnam in 1968, and had the same view in 1969. Still, the twenty-three Later View columns it ran in 1968 declined to just thirteen in 1969. *Svenska-Amerikanaren*'s volume of comment rose significantly, but no other change is statistically certain.

TABLE 19. *Three Swedish-American newspapers' attitude toward the Vietnam War, by opinion type, 1969.*

Opinion Type	Svenska Posten		Nordstjernan-Svea		Svenska-Amerikanaren	
	EARLY	LATER	EARLY	LATER	EARLY	LATER
Editorial	2	6	15	10	6	–
Columnist	4	13	9	5	1	1
Reader Letter	–	–	13	4	11	10
Total	6	19	37	19	18	11

Source: *Svenska Posten, Nordstjernan-Svea,* and *Svenska-Amerikanaren Tribunen,* 1969.

Svenska Posten ran twenty-five comment pieces on Vietnam in 1969. This continued its odd yearly fluctuation from twenty-five to forty pieces. The other two papers continued increasing their coverage of Vietnam. Each year since 1964 had seen large jumps in the volume of comment. This year was no exception. *Nordstjernan* jumped from forty-one to fifty-eight pieces, and *SAT*'s commentary more than doubled. *SAT* had plainly forgotten it had banned letters on Vietnam a year ago. Nordstjernan printed more letters than ever before. This was the first time *Nordstjernan*'s volume of Vietnam-related letters had not doubled over the previous year. This time it was only a 38% increase.

The balance between Early and Later View opinion had remained fairly stable since 1966. Perhaps the most striking aspect of Table 19 is the constant steady rise in commentary. As the United States stepped up the war, Swedish-American opinion intensified with it. Much of the expanding commentary was on the growing Swedish reaction to the ever-growing war. The growth rate in the opinion pieces did not precisely mirror the troop growth-rate. The quantity of both troops and opinion pieces had been rising for years, however.

By now, many of *Nordstjernan*'s editorials on Swedish Vietnam policy came from *Sverige-Nytt*. *Nordstjernan*'s editorial on Sweden's diplomatic recognition of North Vietnam, for example, came from *Sverige-Nytt*.[23] *Nordstjernan*'s use of these editorials partly accounts for its gradual shift to a Later View of Vietnam. This suggests the paper's editors were slowly changing their minds on Vietnam. *Nordstjernan* printed what it wanted, and it increasingly wanted to run *Sverige-Nytt*'s Later View editorials.

Svenska Posten continued to run fewer and fewer Early View opinions with each passing year. *SvP*'s columnists were among the most antiwar voices in the Swedish-American press. They drew most of their news and opinions from the mainstream American press. They were largely unaffected by UD's news-supply policies, but still gave a Later View presentation of Vietnam.

TABLE 20. *Three Swedish-American newspapers' attitude toward the Vietnam War, by opinion type, 1970.*

Opinion Type	Svenska Posten EARLY	Svenska Posten LATER	Nordstjernan-Svea EARLY	Nordstjernan-Svea LATER	Svenska-Amerikanaren EARLY	Svenska-Amerikanaren LATER
Editorial	2	9	10	6	3	4
Columnist	4	11	12	4	1	–
Reader Letter	–	2	2	–	9	10
Total	6	22	24	10	13	14

Source: *Svenska Posten, Nordstjernan-Svea,* and *Svenska-Amerikanaren Tribunen,* 1970.

---

[23] "Nordvietnam," *Nordstjernan-Svea,* 23 January 1969; and "Saxat ur ledarspaltera: Nordvietnam," *Sverige-Nytt,* 14 January 1969.

The volume of Swedish-American commentary had peaked. These three newspapers – which collectively ran 112 comment items in 1969 – printed eighty-eight items in 1970. *Nordstjernan*'s Vietnam-related output fell for the first time: fifty-eight items down to thirty-three. *SAT*'s commentary did not grow, but stabilized. The Later View opinion in *SAT* finally equalled the amount of Earlier View material. Just over half *SAT*'s editorials and letters in 1970 had a Later View of the war.

For the first time, the amount of commentary on Vietnam fell. The commentary in the Swedish-American press was still acrimonious, but there was less of it. The plan to withdraw the American troops dampened the intensity of the war criticism. UD surmised in mid-1970 that Americans also might have gotten used to the Swedish criticism. Sweden had also not done anything dramatic since it gave recognition to North Vietnam either.[24] Then, in mid-1970, Jerome Holland arrived in Sweden. This produced more news and more comment items critical of the Swedish FNL movement. The share of Later View items dropped markedly in the political *Nordstjernan*, largely as fallout from the Holland-affair. This fall in Later View items came mostly from articles on Sweden; ones on U.S. policy changed little from 1969.[25]

Over the past few years, *Nordstjernan*'s Later View comments had swelled from four, to eight, to ten, and then to twenty-two pieces a year. In 1970, *Nordstjernan* reverted to an Earlier View of Vietnam. Fewer formal editorials took up the Vietnam issue. *Nordstjernan* showed most interest in protests, especially those that risked damaging U.S.-Swedish relations. *Nordstjernan* started writing more on Sweden's Vietnam policy and the increasingly ugly protests there. For a paper concerned with diplomatic and trade relations, there was much for it to criticize. Diplomatic relations had

---

[24] Memo "Protokoll över upplysningskommitténs sammanträdande i New York den 15–16 juni 1970: bilaga 1," file "1970, juli-augusti," JN1Ua, UD.

[25] Theme code "Sweden-Vietnam." 1969: Earlier View – 29 times. Later View – 21 times. 1970: Earlier View – 18 times, Later View – 7 times. Theme code "U.S.A." 1969: Both Views – 6 times each. 1970: Earlier View – 4 times, Later View – 5 times.

rarely been more tense. *Nordstjernan* itself had to deal with foreign subscriptions not arriving in Sweden because of the blocked mail.

After 1970, the emigrant press's desire to discuss Vietnam collapsed. The volume of commentary fell in all papers. This could have been because the U.S. was clearly losing an ugly war. It may have been because America was then withdrawing its ground troops, resulting in fewer protests. It could also be because of the poor economic state of the Swedish-American press. These were also its nadir years. All papers cut their journalistic standards, printing output, and paper size. Political commentary also faded. Lastly, the emigrant papers needed help. Sweden's Riksdag had just recently appointed an UD-led investigation into ways to help them.[26] The emigrant papers possibly chose not to criticize the organization they hoped might soon help them.

TABLE 21. *Three Swedish-American newspapers' attitude toward the Vietnam War, by opinion type, 1971.*

Opinion Type	Svenska Posten		Nordstjernan-Svea		Svenska-Amerikanaren	
	EARLY	LATER	EARLY	LATER	EARLY	LATER
Editorial	–	–	1	5	–	2
Columnist	1	9	3	–	1	–
Reader Letter	–	1	1	–	2	2
Total	1	10	5	5	3	4

Source: *Svenska Posten, Nordstjernan-Svea*, and *Svenska-Amerikanaren Tribunen*, 1971.

Table 21 shows far less interest in Vietnam. These three newspapers ran only 15% of what they printed two years earlier. *Nordstjernan's* Vietnam-related output was only 17% of what it printed in 1969.

---

[26] Utrikesutskottets utlåtande nr. 22, "Utlåtande i anledning av väckta motioner om stöd till den svensk-amerikanska pressen i Nordamerika," Bihang till Riksdagens protokoll 1969, femte samlingen, förste avdelningen, Andra Kammaren, protokoll 1969, 41: 156; and "Svar på frågan ang. tidpunkten för tillsättande av utredning om stöd till den svensk-amerikanska pressen i Nordamerika," 14 May 1970, Motion i Andra Kammaren, Bihang till Riksdagens protokoll 1970, Nr. 25: page 7–8.

Eric Sylvan became ill and died, reducing the number of Earlier View columns. Even so, *Nordstjernan* ran only six Vietnam-related editorials in 1971. This was a sharp fall from the twenty-six editorials in 1969. *SAT*'s output also fell by more than 75% from the 1969 level. *Svenska Posten*'s output was also down, perhaps related to Harry Fabbe' declining health. Even so, *SvP*'s output had tumbled to just under one-third of the 1970 level.

The lack of interest is the most striking feature in Table 21. Perhaps this because 1971 was a quieter year than most, and Nixon had removed most American soldiers from Vietnam. Ending the draft and replacing it with a lottery system largely calmed American universities. This took much of the steam out of the student-led protest movements. America had withdrawn two-thirds of its soldiers from Vietnam in the last two years. The bombing was still intense, however. One would expect more commentary than this considering how antiwar the U.S. public had become. The reasons for this sharp fall-off are largely speculative.

The Swedish-American press was falling into crisis and chaos. *The Swedish Press* went into liquidation, *Svenska Posten* and *Nordstjernan* shrank into tabloids, and *Vestkusten* needed a five-hundred dollar advance on advertising to survive. This sudden disintegration consumed the editors' time and energy. They sacrificed standards where they could, if it the savings would keep their newspapers alive. Fewer pages and more advertising meant less news. The content also shifted to broadly acceptable cultural items, away from trenchant political debate.

Kjell Öberg's press commission visited the Swedish-American papers in early 1971. He wrote his analysis that summer, and filed his report in December 1971.[27] The anticipation of what he might recommend may have led the editors to quiet their partisan politics. Prime Minister Palme had been a popular – if not a populist – object of wrath in 1968 and 1969. The editors must have known UD did not welcome critical editorials on Swedish leaders and policies.

---

[27] Telegrams from UD to Svensk Ottawa, Svensk Washington, Svensk San Francisco, and Inforswed New York, 1 March 1971, file "1969 – 1971 febr."; and letter from Kjell Öberg to UD, 6 December 1971, file "1971 mars – jan 1972," PR4S, UD.

Perhaps they toned down their populist opinions while UD considered supporting the emigrant press.

It is also possible the editors now began covering Vietnam in a blanket of silence. The war started as crusade, then a challenge, and had finally become as an obscene scar. Swedish-Americans were conservative, and fiercely patriotic for their adopted country. It might have been easier to pass over Vietnam in silence. It may have been difficult for them to voice Later View criticism of America. Instead of shifting from an Earlier to a Later View of Vietnam, perhaps the Swedish-American press shifted to silence. As tables 20 and 21 show, the drop-off in commentary from 1970 to 1971 fell mostly among Early View supporters.

The following table gives an idea of 1972's opinion distribution in the three leading newspapers.

TABLE 22. *Three Swedish-American newspapers' attitude toward the Vietnam War, by opinion type, 1972.*

Opinion Type	Svenska Posten		Nordstjernan-Svea		Svenska-Amerikanaren	
	EARLY	LATER	EARLY	LATER	EARLY	LATER
Editorial	–	3	1	5	1	–
Columnist	–	–	2	–	–	–
Reader Letter	–	1	–	1	2	–
Total	–	4	3	6	3	0

Source: *Svenska Posten, Nordstjernan-Svea,* and *Svenska-Amerikanaren Tribunen,* 1972.

Swedish-American press interest in Vietnam fell even further in 1972. This was the bloodiest year of the entire war, even if the Americans did not suffer it. The December bombing of Hanoi awoke controversy and protest around the world. Mainstream press coverage of the war remained intense. Debate turned even further against the war. None of this appears in table 22. The only sign of changing attitudes may be a slight drop in Earlier View opinion and an unwillingness to discuss Vietnam. From 1973 onwards, measurable opinion in these three newspapers slowed to a trickle.

What Does it Mean?

New York's *Nordstjernan* was the most political newspaper, usually seeing Vietnam in geopolitical terms. Seattle's *Svenska Posten* was also political, but balanced social politics with ethics. In the Midwest, *Svenska-Amerikanaren* mostly resented Sweden's Vietnam policy. Its sister paper, *California Veckoblad*, mostly resented the antiwar movement. *The Covenant Companion* and *The Messenger* were the midwestern papers most active in the Vietnam debate. They leaned toward antiwar positions on religious grounds, but avoided criticizing the U.S. government. If one had read *Svenska Posten, Nordstjernan,* and *Svenska-Amerikanaren* cover-to-cover from 1965 to 1972, this is what one would have seen.

TABLE 23. *Three Swedish-American newspapers' attitude toward the Vietnam War, 1965–1972.*

Year	Svenska Posten		Nordstjernan-Svea		Svenska-Amerikanaren		Total
	EARLY	LATER	EARLY	LATER	EARLY	LATER	
1965	11	14	16	2	2	–	45
1966	6	34	19	3	5	4	71
1967	2	16	22	8	6	5	59
1968	5	32	31	10	9	5	92
1969	6	19	37	19	18	11	110
1970	6	22	24	10	13	14	89
1971	1	10	5	5	3	4	28
1972	–	4	3	6	3	–	16
Total	37	151	157	63	59	43	510

Source: *Svenska Posten, Nordstjernan-Svea,* and *Svenska-Amerikanaren Tribunen,* 1965–1972.

This table combines editorials, letters, and regular columns. It gives each newspaper's overall presentation of the conflict over Vietnam. In reality, readers may trust a formal editorial more than a letter from someone they likely did not know. Those letters were often short opinion statements, while columnists usually wrote analytical pieces. This table simply shows each newspaper's overall presentation.

After having said that, Table 23 reveals several different things. First, it shows that these were three quite different newspapers. Second, comment on Vietnam rose almost across the board from 1965 until 1969 and then fell sharply after 1970. Third, the rising tide of Earlier View opinion in *Nordstjernan* and *Svenska-Amerikanaren* peaked in 1969. Later View opinion in these two newspapers peaked at around the same time. It is unclear when – or if – a transition from an Earlier to Later View happened.

Academics have too often treated the Swedish-American press as a unified conservative block. True, most were conservative and had similar journalistic formats. All of them contained the same ubiqitous Province Notes, for example. Their treatment of Vietnam and Swedish Vietnam policy was quite different, however. Nearly three-quarters of *Nordstjernan*'s commentary reflected the Earlier View of Vietnam. *Nordstjernan* has little sign of a shift from one Vietnam-view to the other. Later View items only outnumber the Earlier View pieces in just one year, 1972.

Svenska Posten, however, ran more than four times more Later View comments than Early View opinion. The Earlier View was never the dominant opinion in *SvP* after 1964. Its shift from an Earlier to Later view came extremely early. *Svenska Posten*'s support for the war fell in 1965. U.S. public support for the war actually rose, not fell, in 1965. *Svenska-Amerikanaren*, on the other hand, was far more centrist. Before 1969 – when discussion was heavy – it tilted slightly toward the Earlier View of Vietnam. From 1970 onwards – when discussion was light – it leaned toward a Later View. Compared to the other two papers, *SAT* had only half the number of comment items. *SAT* had three times more readers than *Nordstjernan*, seven times more than *Svenska Posten*, and none of their financial problems. The strongest newspaper followed public opinion rather than leading it. The smallest newspaper had the more controversial politics.

The level of comment changed dramatically over these eight years. The United States stepped up its role in Vietnam every year from 1964 until 1969. Every year saw more Swedish-American press interest in Vietnam over the year before. A slight hiccup in this upward trend came in 1967, caused mostly by *Svenska Posten*'s columnists. (This was when Swedish-American interest shifted from Asia to Sweden. Disillusionment with the war had also begun to set in.) Swedish-American comment swelled as the American military commitment to Vietnam grew. As table 24 shows, the eight-fold increase in troop strength from 1964 to 1965 created a six-fold increase in commentary. American troop commitment to Vietnam nearly doubled the following year. Swedish-American commentary also grew 63% from 1965 to 1966.

TABLE 24. *Number of Swedish-American comment items relative to U.S. troop strength in Vietnam, 1964–1972.*

Year	U.S. troops in Vietnam at year's end	Number of Swedish-American comment items
1964	23,000 soldiers	8 items
1965	184,000 soldiers	45 items
1966	385,000 soldiers	72 items
1967	485,000 soldiers	59 items
1968	536,000 soldiers	92 items
April 1969	*543,000 soldiers*	–
1969	475,000 soldiers	112 items
1970	334,000 soldiers	88 items
1971	156,000 soldiers	28 items
1972	23,400 soldiers	16 items

Source: U.S. Department of Defense statistics, cited in *Reporting Vietnam*, 784–799.

The amount of commentary climaxed in 1969. This was the same year U.S. troop strength crested at 543,000 soldiers. Commentary then fell as the U.S. began pulling troops from Vietnam. U.S. troops strength fell by nearly one-third between 1969 and 1970. Swedish-American commentary fell 22% that year. This is no direct linear relation, but intensity of debate roughly followed the national manpower and resources invested overseas.

The volume of opinion rose and fell. Table 24 shows when opinion was most intense, but not when it shifted from an Earlier to a Later View. This thesis has used Eva Queckfeldt's content analysis method to help calculate this. A benefit to using her method is that I can compare the Swedish and emigrant press side-by-side. The table below shows the percentage of Earlier View opinion printed each year in three Swedish and three emigrant papers.

A percentage of Earlier View items gives an easily understood statistic. Eva Queckfeldt's thesis used an arcane ratio that was less accessible than a zero-to-one-hundred percentage. She created a formula where she divided (Later − Earlier) by (Later + Earlier) to reach a scale from -1 to +1. A negative number would show an Earlier View, and a positive number showed a Later View. If a newspaper printed nothing but Earlier View commentary, it would have a perfect -1. If it ran nothing but Later View items, it would be +1. In 1966, for example, *Dagens Nyheter* had a score of +0.07, *Stockholms-Tidningen* had +0.32, and *Svenska Dagbladet* had a -0.27 score.[28] This is needlessly confusing and not very accessible. People relate to percentages more easily than ratios.

The table below shows what percentages of Earlier View comments were part of the total. The easiest way to turn Queckfeldt's "-1 to +1" ratio into a percentage was to add one to her score and multiply it by fifty. The table below compares the Swedish and Swedish-American press treatment of Vietnam.

TABLE 25. *Percentage of Earlier View opinion in Dagens Nyheter, Stockholms-Tidningen, and Svenska Dagbladet compared with Svenska Posten, Nordstjernan-Svea, and Svenska-Amerikanaren Tribunen, 1964–1971.*

Year	DN	ST	SvD	SvP	N-S	SAT
1964	61%	61%	67%	100%	100%	–
1965	54%	37%	68%	44%	89%	100%
1966	47%	34%	64%	15%	86%	56%
1967	46%	33%	60%	11%	73%	55%
1968	43%	38%	55%	14%	76%	64%
1969	–	–	–	24%	66%	62%
1970	–	–	–	21%	71%	48%
1971	–	–	–	9%	50%	43%

Source: Queckfeldt, *"Vietnam,"* 75; *Nordstjernan-Svea*, *Svenska-Amerikanaren Tribunen*, and *Svenska Posten*, 1964–1972.

---

[28] Queckfeldt, *"Vietnam,"* 75.

The emigrant newspapers rely on Swedish sources, but they simply do not resemble Swedish newspapers. If UD hoped that providing Swedish news – with Swedish values – would get these papers to think of Vietnam in a Swedish way, UD was wrong. The statistics suggest the free news had little effect; the free editorials in *Nordstjernan* may have had some. *Nordstjernan* used some *Sverige-Nytt* editorials as its own. Eric Sylvan's hawkish column, which appeared on the same page, offset whatever impact they had. UD was having little success converting Sylvan. As long as UD had not yet converted Eric Sylvan, and if Gerry Rooth still printed Sylvan's column, UD had not converted *Nordstjernan*.

Swedish-American press opinion bore little relation to Swedish press opinion. The only similarity is the slowly falling support for the American role in Vietnam. The support fell at different times, at different rates, down to different levels. One could best describe the Swedish-American press's support of the war as unclear, unsteady, but slowly falling. Even this general summary does not fit *Svenska Posten*. Its level of support was clear, consistent, and fell like a rock. Its support fell sooner and faster than even *Stockholms-Tidningen*. One can only conclude the emigrant papers were different from the Swedish papers, and often dissimilar from each other.

Support for the Vietnam War fell across the United States from 1965 to 1972. Ever since, researchers have asked why this happened. Put concretely, what led people to decide Vietnam was a "bad war" not worth their support? Recent research has focused on the role of casualties in public opinion. A 1988 poll said 86% of Americans viewed casualties as the most important factor in deciding their support for foreign wars.[29] John Mueller's 1973 *War, Presidents, and Public Opinion* proposes a linear relation between casualties and public support. He concludes, "public approval . . . fell in step with the rise in American killed and wounded, dropping 15 percentage points each time U.S. casualties increased by a factor of ten (going from 100 to 1,000, 1,000 to 10,000, and so on)." Another theory says a tenfold increase in war dead – excluding the wounded – will cause support to fall by 23%.[30] Both of these ratios hold for the

---

[29] Eric V. Larson, *Casualties and Consensus*, Santa Monica, Calif., 1996: 7, 11 note 10.

Vietnam and Korean Wars. It makes sense that casualties should affect opinion. Nobody likes having their sons and husbands die abroad, in long wars, for unclear objectives. Table 26 shows how mainstream American opinion reacted to the rise in war dead.

TABLE 26. *Support for the Vietnam War shown by AIPO polls, compared to U.S. war dead, 1965–1971.*[31]

Date	U.S. Opinion	Total U.S. Dead
May 1965	52%	N/A
August 1965	61%	166
November 1965	64%	924
March 1966	59%	2,415
May 1966	49%	3,191
September 1966	41%	4,976
November 1966	51%	5,798
May 1967	50%	10,341
July 1967	41%	11,939
December 1967	46%	15,695
February 1968	42%	19,107
August 1968	35%	27,280
February 1969	39%	32,234
September 1969	32%	38,581
January 1970	33%	40,112
May 1970	36%	42,213
January 1971	31%	44,109
May 1971	28%	44,980

Source: Mueller, *War, Presidents, and Public Opinion*, pages 55, 143, 271, 275; Larson, *Casualties and Consensus*, page 111.

---

[30] Mueller, *War, Presidents, and Public Opinion*, 62–63; and Eric V. Larson, *Ends and Means in the Democratic Conversation*, Santa Monica, Calif., 1995: 202, and note 280. See also: Mark Lorell, Charles Kelly, Jr., and Deborah Hensler, *Casualties, Public Opinion, and Presidential Policy During the Vietnam War*, Santa Monica, Calif., 1985; John Mueller, Policy and Opinion in the Gulf War, London, 1994; Miroslav Nincic, "Casualties, Military Intervention, and the RMA: Hypotheses from the Lessons of Vietnam," paper presented at the Conference on the Revolution in Military Affairs, Monterey, August 1995.

[31] The May and November 1965 polls asked: "Some people think that we should not have become involved with our military forces in Southeast Asia while others think we should have. What is your opinion?" All other polls, including August 1965, ask: "In view of the developments since we entered the fighting in Vietnam, do you think the U.S. made a mistake in sending troops to fight in Vietnam?"

This table shows a nearly linear inverse relation between war deaths and public support. If one sees the Early View of Vietnam as backing the war, no emigrant paper followed this linear cost-benefit model. *Svenska Posten's* "support" fell far earlier than mainstream opinion, *Nordstjernan's* fell much later, and *Svenska-Amerikanaren's* was irresolute. Table 24 shows the intensity of emigrant press opinion roughly followed the troop strength invested in Vietnam. No paper in table 25, however, had its support fall proportional to how many soldiers died.

One should remember that these three newspapers had different audiences and thus different formats. To serve certain audiences, some papers emphasized their columnis ts. Other papers had active letters-to-the-editor pages, which they felt best served their audiences. Still other papers ran formal editorials. It may be worth considering how each of these different formats addressed the Vietnam issue. Columns are qualitatively different from letters as an opinion medium. Reader letters are more populist by nature. Editorials reflect the views of the newspaper as a social institution. The following table conflates the formal editorials, regular columns, and reader letters in all three papers together.

TABLE 27. *Percentage of Earlier View commentary in Nordstjernan-Svea, Svenska-Amerikanaren Tribunen, and Svenska Posten, by opinion type, 1965–1971.*

Year	Editorials	Columns	Letters
1965	6 of 9 *(66.6%)*	24 of 34 *(70.6%)*	1 of 2 *(50.0%)*
1966	6 of 13 *(46.2%)*	20 of 50 *(40.0%)*	4 of 8 *(50.0%)*
1967	9 of 17 *(52.9%)*	13 of 30 *(43.3%)*	7 of 12 *(58.3%)*
1968	18 of 39 *(46.2%)*	15 of 38 *(39.5%)*	12 of 15 *(80.0%)*
1969	23 of 39 *(59.0%)*	14 of 33 *(42.4%)*	24 of 36 *(66.6%)*
1970	15 of 34 *(44.1%)*	17 of 32 *(53.1%)*	11 of 23 *(47.8%)*
1971	1 of 8 *(12.5%)*	5 of 14 *(35.7%)*	3 of 6 *(50.0%)*
Total	78 of 159 *(49.0%)*	108 of 231 *(46.7%)*	62 of 102 *(60.1%)*

Source: *Svenska Posten, Nordstjernan-Svea,* and *Svenska-Amerikanaren Tribunen,* 1965–1972.

This table warrants several warnings. First, one should note that some percentages come from small samples. Second, these statistics only partly relate to views on Vietnam. There is some opinion "interference" from Swedish Vietnam policy. Third, Swedish-Americans have a traditional relationship with the Republican Party, and a Republican became president in 1969. They may have given Richard Nixon some initial goodwill on Vietnam. Fourth, comment declined exactly when Kjell Öberg wrote his UD study of the Swedish-American press's problems. Lastly, the Swedish-American press's economic problems became severe by the early Seventies. Their comments on Vietnam became more infrequent during this period as well.

Apart from these cautionary notes, this table indirectly suggests why *Svenska Posten*, *Nordstjernan*, and *Svenska-Amerikanaren* were so different. Each paper used an opinion format shaped by the audience they served. *SAT* wanted a national audience, so many of its opinion pieces come from letter-writers across the country. One might expect letter-writers to respond like mainstream opinion as reflected by polls. Table 27 suggests they may not. There is no sign of their support falling relative to casualties: on the contrary. The letters were the most stable opinion format in the Swedish-American press. They remained almost equally divided on Vietnam through the entire survey period. (In 1968, the paper with the most letters forbade letters on Vietnam.) This suggests that editors tried to keep a political balance in their pages. Except for 1968, the letters do seem to present a balanced opinion. It may be that letters-to-the-editor do not reflect public opinion so much as angry public opinion.[32] Only the views of people motivated enough to write to the newspaper appear. On Vietnam there were always plenty of people on both sides of the issue. The letters-editor – called "Urlakaren" in *Svenska-Amerikanaren* – represented each angry side equally. A few letters occasionally protested that "Urlakaren"

---

[32] This also points to different definitions of the term "public opinion." The polling statistics in Table 26 measure the sum of all individuals' opinions with a sampling method. Another definition of public opinion argues only those views in the public debate should count. The letter-writers had submitted their views to the public sphere; the polling data measures opinions largely kept private. (Wijk, *Svarta börsen*, 39–40.)

rejected some of their earlier notes. This suggests there was an editing pattern, but that readers expected editing to be lax.

Nordstjernan was the paper with the most political news coverage. It may not be surprising since that it prints only a few blocks from the Swedish General Consulate and the United Nations. *Nordstjernan* chose to express its opinion largely through formal editorials. Unlike letters or columns, editorials carry the full weight of the newspaper behind it. Editorials speak for the paper as an institution and mouthpiece for Swedish-American interests. The press may well be "the fourth branch of government."[33] It has a certain role in setting the political agenda for debate, presenting ideas that politicians might adopt, and vetting out bad ideas. If the press is an indirect part of government, then editorials are especially so. Unlike other opinion formats, they carry the prestige and gravitas of the entire newspaper. Editorials resist current public opinion trends, but editors think for the longer term. A main function of political editorials is to lead public opinion – not reflect it.

Newspaper editors have to make the same cost-benefit decisions as everyone else when thinking about war dead. They may also have an investor mentality in their role as a government adviser. They also have to think about the future return of a noncommunist South Vietnam. Editorial-writers might think of foreign conflicts as governments do: as investments to redeem. Miroslav Nincic argues the U.S. government did not see Vietnam as a wasted investment until 1969.[34] Other U.S. observers with investment mentalities may have also valued Vietnam in the same way. The Swedish-American editorials appear to lose their ardor for Vietnam after 1969. The slide in editorial support after 1969 is certainly dramatic. It may even be greater than it appears: most papers lapsed into silence toward the end of the war.

---

[33] Phrase coined in Douglass Cater, *The Fourth Branch of Government*, Boston, 1959. (Note that Sweden works under a parliamentary system of governmment and has no clear division between the executive and legislative branches. The press is thus called the *third* branch of government in Sweden.)

[34] Miroslav Nincic and Donna J. Nincic, "Commitment to Military Intervention: The Democratic Government as Economic Investor," *Journal of Peace Research*, vol. 32, no. 4, 1995: 413–426.

The Swedish-American columnists may give a better reflection of American public opinion. In 1965, 70% of the columnists had an Early View of Vietnam, and 61%–64% of the U.S. public backed the war in late 1965. By 1968, 39% of the columns had an Early View, and 37%–39% of Americans supported the war in summer 1968. In 1971, 36% of the emigrant columns had an Early View. In early 1971, 28%–31% of the public supported the war.[35] Unlike the letter-writers, the columnists had few constraints to present a balanced view of the war. (A rare exception was when *SvP*'s Harry Fabbe edited Otto Jacobson's hawkish columns.) *Svenska Posten* had many of Swedish-America's liberal voices, *Nordstjernan* had the pro-war Eric Sylvan and Albin Widén, and *SAT* had guest columnists. Together these different groups reflected U.S. opinion reasonably well.

After dividing the results by opinion formats, it may be worth diving them by subjects. The Swedish-American press found it ever harder to support the war, but this did not always translate into supporting Sweden's positon. Around half the emigrant press's commentary was on Vietnam, and the other half focused on Sweden. The table below shows how *Nordstjernan* commented on each of these two subjects. In Eva Queckfeldt's coding scheme, codes one through seven cover aspects of the Vietnam War. Code eight deals with Swedish Vietnam policy. *Nordstjernan* ran the most news on these issues, and printed more commentary than any other paper. *Nordstjernan* alone ran more opinion pieces than *California Veckoblad, Canada-Svensken, Canada-Tidningen, Covenant Companion, Norden, The Messenger, Svea, The Swedish Press, Texas Posten, Vestkusten,* and *Western News* combined. This makes *Nordstjernan* the most reasonable choice as an example of how an emigrant newspaper looked at Vietnam and Sweden. (*Svenska Posten* focused mostly on Vietnam, while *SAT* commented much less than the other two papers.) Table 28 shows how much *Nordstjernan* discussed Vietnam and Sweden's Vietnam policy. The table counts appearances of codes rather than whole opinion pieces. Many – if not most – items had codes on both Sweden and Vietnam. The table

---

[35] AIPO polling data from Mueller, *War, Presidents, and Public Opinion*, 55, 143, 271, 275.

would count a single editorial with four Earlier View opinions on Vietnam as one Earlier-View Vietnam item. If the same editorial had a Later View opinion on Sweden, I counted it as both an Earlier-View Vietnam item and a Later-View item on Sweden. This is why the number of codes exceeds the number of opinion items printed each year.

TABLE 28. *Nordstjernan's attitude toward the Vietnam War (codes 1–7) and its attitude toward Swedish Vietnam policy (code 8), 1965–1970.*

	Nordstjernan on the Vietnam War			Nordstjernan on Swedish policy		
			Percent			Percent
Year	EARLY	LATER	Earlier	EARLY	LATER	Earlier
1965	13	2	*(86.7%)*	7	–	*(100%)*
1966	15	3	*(83.3%)*	9	1	*(90%)*
1967	10	9	*(52.6%)*	15	–	*(100%)*
1968	11	6	*(64.7%)*	22	7	*(75.9%)*
1969	13	9	*(58.1%)*	28	19	*(59.6%)*
1970	12	5	*(70.6%)*	17	5	*(77.3%)*
Total	74	34	*(68.5%)*	98	32	*(75.4%)*

Source: *Nordstjernan-Svea*, 1965–1970.

As said earlier, it may be specious to separate feelings on the war from feelings on the antiwar movement, or even opinions on Sweden. No such neat divisions exist in life, and issues often connect. Nevertheless, *Nordstjernan's* position on Vietnam appears quite stable over this six-year period. It ran ten to fifteen Early View items every year, while the volume of Later View codes grew slowly. The decline of Later View opinion in 1970 may relate to the Nixon administration's de-escalation of the war. If *Nordstjernan's* position on Vietnam was stable, its view of Sweden was erratic. Early View criticism rose sharply over the years in a pattern that was perhaps predictable. (This sharp rise means Sweden displaced Vietnam as *Nordstjernan's* main topic in 1968.) Later View support of Sweden's position was low for every year except 1969. Rather than supporting Sweden's recognition of North Vietnam, *Nordstjernan* opposed the U.S. pulling its ambassador from Stockholm. *Nordstjernan* began using editorials from *Sverige-Nytt* that year to address the ambassador problem. By 1970, Sweden had a new American ambassador and Later View support of Sweden sank back to usual levels.

Conclusions

This chapter turns to a quantitative content analysis of the Swedish-American press. There are many types of content analysis, but most seem to divide news reports into Positive and Negative stories. This is a problem, because different people may judge articles in different ways. My thesis borrows the method Eva Queckfeldt used in her 1981 thesis *"Vietnam": tre svenska tidningars syn på Vietnamfrågan 1963–1968*. Her method is a proven method with clear guidelines. Instead of labeling news stories as good or bad, she labels opinions as either common in the early Sixties or more typical of the late Sixties. She also has an extensive set of codes, which allow for a certain transparency of standards. Using her method also allows one to compare the emigrant papers to what she found about the Swedish media.

My thesis analyses *Svenska Posten, Nordstjernan*, and *Svenska-Amerikanaren*. It includes editorials, letters to the editor, and columnists' items. This gives a full picture of each newspaper's overall opinion on Vietnam issues. The results show that opinion built rapidly in the mid-Sixties, peaking in 1969. The volume of commentary fell rapidly after that. *Svenska Posten* turned against the war quickly. *SvP* had a Later View of the war as early as 1965. *Nordstjernan* ran the most commentary, holding to an Earlier View through most of the survey period. Its support for the war slipped most from 1964 to 1967, but rising antagonism toward Swedish policy masked some of this development. *Svenska-Amerikanaren's* position on Vietnam remained stable during most of the survey period. The content analysis shows these three newspapers reacted to the Vietnam issue in sharply different ways. None of them resembled the major Swedish dailies that Eva Queckfeldt surveyed. Her newspapers were, after all, news-bearing periodicals. The Swedish-American editors assumed their readers got their world news elsewhere.

Researchers believe public opinion about foreign wars depends largely on the costs borne up to that point. It is unclear whether press opinion reacts the same way. What part of a newspaper would most closely react like public opinion? The editorials, columnists, or letters? Letters to the editor should arguably most closely resemble public opinion – or at least those people angry enough to write their newspaper. Editors realize their editorials are the watchdogs of government, and suggest and discuss policy proposals. Editors for minority groups also realize their editorials define the entire group for the outside world. Editors would write their editorials with an investor's mentality. They know the costs borne thus far, but also see foreign wars as political investments for the future. Columnists may have an advising function on how public opinion should interpret current trends. *Svenska Posten, Nordstjernan,* and *Svenska-Amerikanaren* had different audiences and served them mostly with different opinion formats. I believe the community a newspaper serves influences which opinion format it adopts.

To show this, I combined all the editorials, columns, and letters – across all three papers – into one table. The results were not as clear as I had hoped. I believed the letters would most clearly reflect public opinion, but they did not. They remained equally divided between Earlier and Later Views though most of the survey period. The conclusion is the emigrant papers – *SAT* in particular – worked to keep reader opinion balanced. Another equally plausible conclusion might be that Vietnam was a subject that motivated nearly equal number of readers to write letters to their emigrant paper. Editorial opinion remained stable while a chance remained the U.S. could win the war with more soldiers. When victory proved elusive and the U.S. began withdrawing soldiers, the editorial support fell. Columnist opinion seemed to give a clearer reflection of public opinion than the letters.

The survey of *Nordstjernan,* however, shows that the paper had very unstable and irresolute view of Sweden's Vietnam policy. *Nordstjernan's* commentary about Swedish policy was mostly of the Early View variety. Yet, when the U.S. withdrew its ambassador to Sweden, there was a sharp rise in Later View commentary. It is inconclusive whether swings in later View commentary about

Sweden affected how *Nordstjernan* felt about Vietnam. In the end, I believe it does not matter. Sweden was an integral part of the Swedish-Americans' debate about Vietnam. For them, it would be unnatural to separate Sweden from the rest of the debate, perhaps as unnatural as removing the Republican Party or the Cold War. It does not matter why *Nordstjernan* had an Early View of the war, but only that it did.

This content analysis helps answer how much – and in which political directions – the emigrant press wrote on Vietnam and Sweden's Vietnam policy. So, was UD successful in alterning emigrant opinions? The analysis of the reader letters suggests papers tried to keep letter-opinion evenly balanced. UD thus had little discernable effect on shifting letter opinion either way. *Svenska-Amerikanaren* ran lots of letters, so it was less affected by UD's news-supply policy. Furthermore, *SAT* also did not always consistently get certain UD-supplied news items either.

Table 28 shows *Nordstjernan*'s support for the war fell unevenly from 1965 to 1969. Its share of Early View opinion dropped from 87% down to 59% in those five years. This slide mirrors American public opinion on the war. The numbers are, however, higher than the nation at large – and much higher than in Sweden. *Nordstjernan*'s view of Swedish policy consistently opposed Sweden. The only year when Sweden managed to generate any sympathy was in 1969. Instead of actually backing Sweden's Vietnam policy, this sympathy was really opposing the U.S. policy on Sweden. Table 28 does not show that UD had persuaded *Nordstjernan* or swung its opinion in Sweden's direction. UD's news-supply policy does not appear successful here.

UD may have been more successful in quieting criticism by hanging offers of financial aid before the emigrant papers. Acid criticism of Sweden stopped when Kjell Öberg's committee sought ways to help the Swedish-American press. That may be one reason why commentary dried up in the early Seventies. Also, table 28 shows *Nordstjernan*'s absolute hostility to Sweden's foreign policy softened slightly when UD helped the paper get new printing technology in 1966.

Chapter Seven

Conclusions

The United States and Sweden had strained relations during the Vietnam War. Traditionally good relations soured as the U.S. sent thousands of troops to South Vietnam to support a corrupt and unstable government. Swedish leaders – both in and outside government – criticized the U.S. in occasionally shrill terms. The Swedish government gave North Vietnam diplomatic recognition and foreign aid, and gave U.S. deserters asylum in Sweden. Swedish students raised money for the FNL, the Vietcong's political organization. Perhaps for the first time, the Americans and Swedes clashed openly over foreign policy.

At the time, there were six million citizens of Scandinavian descent living in the United States. That made the Scandinavians the fifth largest ethnic group in America.[1] Most had never known anything but good relations between their homeland and adopted country. Many of them felt uncomfortable with recent developments over Vietnam. Unlike the Germans and Russians – and today Arab-Americans – Swedish-Americans never had to take sides before. They never had to choose between defending their homeland and distancing themselves from it before. If they distanced themselves from Sweden, were they still fully Swedish? Sweden was their totemic symbol of their ethnicity. If they supported Sweden, were they real Americans? As immigrants, they did not want anyone to question their loyalty. Sweden's criticism of

---

[1] White, *Making of a President 1960*, 216, 226.

the United States undermined the Swedish-Americans' sense of their ethnic identity.

This thesis looks into how the Swedish-Americans handled this problem. The approach is to survey Swedish-American opinion as expressed through the Swedish-American newspapers printing in North America. These were the last of the hundreds of papers that targeted Swedish immigrants in the nineteenth century. As the Sixties opened, there were twelve papers left in the United States and three more in Canada. These papers spread geographically across North America. Most were secular publications, but a few had ties to Swedish free churches. They were stylistically similar newspapers, printing news about Sweden and local Swedish-American activities. Many had political editorials about world and Swedish affairs. Most of them leaned to the political right. Anyone who wanted to know Swedish-American opinion could find it here. Anyone who wanted to influence Swedish-American opinion would also have started here.

My broad questions are: How did the Swedish-American press comment on the American military engagement in Vietnam? How did it react to Sweden's criticism of the American war? As I studied these questions, I soon realized the emigrant newspapers were in close contact with UD. They got much of their news either through UD or courtesy of UD. This made me wonder: did the Swedish government influence Swedish-American coverage of Vietnam or Swedish Vietnam policy? If so, how did the Swedish government do it and did it work?

Before looking at Vietnam, this thesis examines the state of Swedish-America as the Sixties opened. The Swedish immigrants that arrived before the Second World War were aging and starting to die off. If the Swedish-language press wanted new readers, they would have to target their audience for younger readers. The Swedish-American press had always defined their ethnic ideology relative to the Republican Party and Lutheranism. Like other young Americans, young Swedish-Americans questioned their parents' values during the Sixties. In the Sixties – a period of change and upheaval – conservative politics and orthodox Lutheranism may have seemed outdated. If ethnicity is an elastic concept, the ethnic press would also have to be elastic. The ethnic leaders – the newspaper editors – had to change their definitions of Swedish ethnicity. This change in ethnicity could influence how these newspapers reported on Vietnam.

The Swedish-American newspapers were often similar in format, presentation, and political color. Chapter Two shows that despite this, similar-looking newspapers often write for different communities. Community-press theory expects a newspaper will approach a divisive issue in a way that reduces internal friction in its community. Different papers with different audiences may approach divisive issues in different ways. The community newspaper works to knit its audience together, build consensus, stress common feelings, play down negative events in the group, and reveal outside threats to the group. Vietnam and the Swedish Vietnam policy were divisive issues the emigrant papers had to address. My thesis focuses on three Swedish-language newspapers with distinctly different communities. *Svenska Posten* served the local Swedish-American community in the Seattle area. Its stable of columnists included liberals and socialists. *Svenska Posten* could run politically unpopular ideas because its columnists were "virtual friends" in the community. *Svenska Posten* stressed this point by printing photos of each writer above their weekly columns. A large regional paper like *Nordstjernan* never did this to identify Eric Sylvan as a virtual friend. *Nordstjernan* targeted a wider regional audience around New York and New England. It ran more political news than most emigrant papers. Its opinions came mostly from editorials and Eric Sylvan's weekly column. *Svenska-Amerikanaren* aspired to reach a national audience across America. Its base, however, was solidly in Chicago and the Midwest. Most of its opinion came in its "Folkets Röst" letters page and some editorials. Chapter Six does a statistical content analysis of these three newspapers. Chapters on emigrant war coverage and comment on Swedish Vietnam policy survey all fifteen Swedish-American papers. Even these chapters often highlight *Svenska Posten*, *Nordstjernan*, and *Svenska-Amerikanaren*'s views.

Chapter Two also examines how the fifteen Swedish-language papers looked at the world around 1960. This was perhaps the last peaceful year in Vietnam. The U.S. increased the number of U.S.

advisers there and expanded their role in counter-insurgency operations the following year. Around 1960, the Swedish-American press had a complex view of Sweden. It supported Sweden, its people and its government, but rarely hesitated to criticize them. If others criticized Sweden, the Swedish-American press vigorously defended Sweden. They might defend Sweden from critical opinions they had voiced themselves. They simply could not let Anglo-America denigrate the main symbol of their ethnicity. The most high-profile U.S. criticism of Sweden came in July 1960. This was when President Eisenhower criticized Swedish society at a Republican luncheon. Eisenhower believed welfare states isolate individuals, creating social problems like suicide and alcoholism. The Swedish government responded by flooding the emigrant press with statistics, memos, and news reports to contradict Eisenhower's comments. Several papers printed these items on their front pages. The editors ran opinion pieces backing the Swedish position, and several readers wrote in to support Sweden. Sweden's government may have felt it had suppressed a potential problem, at least among Swedish-Americans. Spreading news and statistics appeared to be an effective way to handle "unjust criticism" of Sweden.

Chapter Three examines the news sources with which the Swedish-American editors built their newspapers. Some papers cited their sources in bylines, and *Svenska Posten* and *Vestkusten* always cited sources. Four news sources appear regularly in these bylines: ASNE, SIS, FLT, and *Sverige-Nytt*. ASNE was the American-Swedish News Exchange, a semiofficial organ connected to UD. ASNE's Stockholm office collected news from the Swedish dailies, edited and re-wrote it, and mailed it to the New York office. ASNE's New York office sent the emigrant papers a news packet every week. This included the four-page bulletin *Nyheter från Sverige*, special releases, photos and cartoons, short "province notes," and feature stories. In 1966, UD closed ASNE and replaced it with SIS: the Swedish Information Service. SIS filled the same news-supply role as ASNE, but it was strictly a promotional agency. ASNE had an indirect relation to UD, but SIS was strictly under government control.

The Stockholm newspaper *Sverige-Nytt* was another main news source for the Swedish-American press. In 1959, UD arranged for the emigrant papers to get free copies of *Sverige-Nytt* and the rights to its stories. *Sverige-Nytt's* owner resisted this, but he could not easily refuse UD's request. He was also director of the Swedish-International Press Bureau, SIP. SIP was an organ of UD's export and tourist division. His newspaper *Sverige-Nytt* shared office space with SIP – office space that UD owned. *Sverige-Nytt's* news was reliable, but its trade news was pure propaganda for Swedish industry. Its news was arguably just bait to attract foreign media to the promotional material.

The fourth news source in the Swedish-American press was Förenade Landsorttidningar, FLT. FLT provided cultural feature articles and photos, which the emigrant papers got through ASNE-SIS. For years, the emigrant press also got news from Sweden's major wire service, Tidningarnas telegrambyrå, TT. UD paid for this service, but cut it off in 1966. The emigrant papers sometimes also used articles from Swedish dailies. They often reproduced these without permission, but they were rare.

Surveys of *Svenska Posten* and *Vestkusten's* bylines show that both used lots of ASNE-SIS and *Sverige-Nytt* news. By 1969, for example, 46% of *Svenska Posten* news articles came from *Sverige-Nytt*. This was a sharp jump from 27% in 1965. *Svenska Posten* and *Vestkusten* also ran lots of ASNE-SIS's news, but relied heavily on *Sverige-Nytt* to report Vietnam-related news. I define "Vietnam-related news" as including antiwar protests, Swedish government comment or policy decisions, or U.S. responses to Swedish actions. "Vietnam-related" stories directly mention Vietnam or a combatant there. They report events that would not have happened if the U.S. had been at peace. Under this definition, seventy-eight of *Svenska Posten's* eighty-eight Vietnam stories between 1965 and 1970 came directly from *Sverige-Nytt*. Fifty-one of *Vestkusten's* seventy-five Vietnam-related items also came from *Sverige-Nytt* in the same period. It did not print bylines, but a close look at *Nordstjernan's* news reveals the same pattern. It ran 217 Vietnam-related stories between 1965 and 1970, with 159 traceable to *Sverige-Nytt*.

This Swedish news all had a Swedish national perspective. It reported *our* policy decided by *our* leaders. *Our* mistakes were regrettable but understandable, and *our* successes were commendable and idealistic. This perspective painted Sweden's position with more sympathy than having it reported as a foreign government's policy. UD may have hoped this perspective would get Swedish-Americans to identify with Sweden's position. In 1969, however, it frustrated UD the supply of sympathetic news had not stopped hostile editorials in *Texas Posten* over Sweden's Vietnam policy. It ordered a content analysis to find out whether the emigrant papers ran the Swedish news as-is, or if they edited it. UD plainly assumed *Texas Posten* either edited or discarded the "accurate news" it provided. UD may have assumed people would support its policy if only they understood it. Opponents of Swedish policy either did not understand or had gotten inaccurate information. UD's content analysis showed the Swedish-American editors often cut, rewrote, or added onto the news stories they received. This meant UD's influence as a news gatekeeper was weaker than it would have liked.

UD's growing role in information policy may stem from the state's growing role in organizing and protecting the nation's industry. Sweden's industry had become the welfare state's collective possession. Negative publicity abroad might harm the *folkhem's* export markets, hurting Swedish society. A Vietnam-related boycott of Swedish goods might harm Sweden's new ideal society. UD found the *Texas Posten* items especially alarming because they proposed boycotting Swedish goods. Attacking Sweden's main employers was tantamount to attacking Swedish fraternity, equality, and liberty.

Chapters Four and Five move from the front-page news to the editorial page. It is reasonable to presume the news readers get about a topical issue influences the opinions they hold about it. Chapter Four examines how the Swedish-American press commented on the war in Southeast Asia. It is in six broad sections, each focusing on a different major theme or period in the war. During the Kennedy administration, the U.S. sent nearly seventeen-thousand "military advisers" to South Vietnam. None of the Swedish-American newspapers knew much about Vietnam at the time. Comment was thus rare. If communism threatened South Vietnam, it would be reasonable to send foreign aid and perhaps even troops. There were two conditions. First, they did not want another Korean War – a long and brutal land war that the U.S. never really won. Second, they wanted U.S. support to South Vietnam to be strong and effective or not done at all.

In 1964 and 1965, the U.S. openly entered the Vietnam War. The emigrant press backed the White House position during the Tonkin Gulf Crisis and the 1965 intervention. They approved of President Johnson's decisive handling of both cases, but they were also uneasy. Worries over "a new Korea" had returned by late 1965. *Svenska Posten*'s Reinhold Ahleen in particular worried the U.S. had entered a complex civil war with no easy way out. As the antiwar movement grew, some columnists accused its leaders of defeatism or cowardice. *Nordstjernan*'s Eric Sylvan, for example, aggressively attacked its intellectual and religious leaders. This included several columns that branded Martin Luther King a communist pawn. *Svenska Posten*'s Otto B. Jacobson also supported the war and opposed the antiwar movement. Jacobson's editor, however, had already turned against the Vietnam War. In 1966, conflict between the two men over Vietnam forced Jacobson to leave *Svenska Posten*. With Jacobson gone – the lesson perhaps noted by other columnists – *SvP* became Swedish-America's most antiwar newspaper.

An anticlerical current continued in *Svenska Posten*. Instead of blaming the Religious Left for opposing the war, some *Svenska Posten* columnists accused the Catholic Church of starting the war. The Swedish-American press gradually shifted from blaming priests and intellectuals to blaming hippies. The tone of the criticism also changed. Instead of portraying protesters as well-meaning but naive, they painted hippies as unpatriotic slackers. Several Swedish-American writers resisted this simplification, however. A few columnists and letter-writers had served in the military during the First World War. Some had even fought (for the United States) in the European trenches. These veterans could easily sympathize with young people's wish not to fight in Asian jungles.

Some of the most antiwar views appeared in the religious press. *The Covenant Companion* and *The Messenger* were religious papers that targeted Swedish-Americans. Both papers approached Vietnam as a moral issue rather than a political one. They did not support war on religious grounds, but avoided criticizing U.S. policy in Vietnam. They believed negotiations and a nonviolent settlement, followed by political and social reforms, were better ways to help Vietnam. *The Covenant Companion* ran several vivid letters and articles from missionaries based in Vietnam. These are the only "in-country" reports to appear in the Swedish-American press. The *Companion* had become clearly antiwar by the Seventies. Following the My Lai massacre, the *Companion* described America as poisoned by sin. It compared the United States to Isaiah's Israel: "the whole head is sick, and the whole heart faint. From the sole of the foot even to the head, there is no soundness in it, but bruises and sores and bleeding wounds."[2]

Other emigrant papers turned against the war by the Seventies, but none so firmly as the *Companion*. The last few years in Vietnam seemed a pointless nightmare of bombings, massacres, and invasions. The Cambodia invasion pushed *Norden* into the antiwar camp. The emigrant press gave the My Lai massacre wide coverage, mostly focusing on Lt. William Calley's trial. Most newspapers showed little desire to discuss Vietnam any further. The war had become a national obscenity, unfit for printing in a family newspaper. The Swedish-American press lapsed into silence.

Most Swedish-American views on Vietnam did not differ much from mainstream U.S. opinions. There were sometimes Swedish accents, however. Accusing the Catholic Church of starting the Vietnam War, for example, may have its roots in traditional Swedish-American anti-Catholicism. Yet, no emigrant paper ever quoted Prime Minister Olof Palme's speeches in opposing the war. The religious papers – and some secular ones – were far more likely to quote a bible verse instead. Swedish-Americans had no lack of opportunity to read Palme's antiwar opinions during ten years of war. Almost every paper had near-weekly articles on new protests over the war. The emigrant papers often printed Palme's opinions, but few readers or journalists appear to have absorbed them. The

---

[2] Isaiah 1:5–6, quoted in "God Save Our Land," *The Covenant Companion*, 1 May 1971: 32.

emigrants did not absorb these views likely because they no longer saw their Swedish-American papers as news-bearing periodicals. They were social and entertainment media. They may have had some political ideas in them, but that was mostly to advance Swedish-American social and ethnic identity. Few looked to the Swedish-American press as a trustworthy source of political news. Olof Palme's political message on Vietnam went discounted because it appeared in an ethnic social publication.

The Swedish-American press specialized in news about Sweden after all, not Vietnam. It did not compete with the mainstream media over news about Sweden; it had the field almost to itself. In fact, the emigrant press was nearly the only source of detailed news on Sweden's Vietnam policy in North America. Chapter Five shows the Swedish-American press got most of its material on the subject from *Sverige-Nytt*, a paper with ties to UD. Like Chapter Four, Chapter Five also has six broad sections, each focusing on a different theme in Swedish Vietnam politics. These themes may not have been often reported in Sweden, but were the ones that most engaged the emigrants.

The Swedish-American press's first reaction to Swedish criticism of U.S. Vietnam policy was doubt. Many commentators doubted whether the Swedes really knew what the U.S. was doing in Vietnam. If the Swedes did not understand what was going on, then the Swedish media had failed them. The Swedish press was either inept, used biased sources, or was ideologically hostile to America. Those that backed the war thought the Swedish media was either incompetent or filled with communists. Commentators against the war believed Sweden's media used sources that were freer and more neutral.

Sweden's policy of accepting U.S. deserters had become a hot issue by 1968 and 1969. *Nordstjernan* and *Svenska-Amerikanaren* gave "deserter stories" nearly one-third of their Vietnam-related news coverage. Like most of the mainstream media, many emigrant papers opposed Sweden's policy. Perhaps surprisingly, there were also many voices in support as well. Several papers pointed out that Sweden had also accepted deserters from other countries. Others noted that many Swedish-Americans emigrated specifically to avoid the Swedish draft. Some columnists – *Svenska Posten's* Stephen Forslund, for example – had emigrated around the First World War. They could understand why soldiers would want to leave a battlefield like Vietnam.

The emigrants reacted the same way to Sweden's diplomatic recognition of North Vietnam. Many Swedish-American commentators initially saw it as hostile and supporting America's enemy. This view soon faded, replaced with more measured commentary. Several commentators noted that Sweden had been among the first countries to recognize other emerging states as well. This included the People's Republic of China, the Soviet Union, the Algerian Republic, and even the United States. Just because Sweden recognized a state did not mean it agreed with its ideology.

Much of the emigrant press's coverage of the U.S.-Swedish rift focused on personalities. The Foreign Ministers – and particularly Education Minister Olof Palme – often appeared as Swedish policy personified. In February 1968, Olof Palme marched in a demonstration with a North Vietnamese diplomat. The resulting photo appeared on most Swedish-American newspapers. (*Svenska-Amerikanaren* and *California Veckoblad* ran an alternate photo that showed demonstrators holding anti-American placards.)

On a symbolic level, these pictures linked Palme with the enemy in a tangible way. *SAT's* picture also suggested the Swedish government encouraged anti-Americanism. The emigrant papers often reported demonstrators throwing eggs, snowballs, or rocks at U.S. diplomats. This linked the Swedish government to those incidents. Olof Palme recovered some respect among the emigrants when he became Prime Minister. He recovered a little more when he visited the United States in 1970. Yet, the Swedish-American press never trusted him.

In 1970, the Swedish-American press gave Jerome Holland's appointment as ambassador to Sweden wide coverage. The U.S. had left the post vacant since Olof Palme's demonstration, and now the U.S. was filling it. Also, Ambassador Holland was a black man in an era where black ambassadors were rare. His ethnicity drew wide notice when *Svenska Posten's* Reinhold Ahleen wrote that Sweden deserved a white ambassador. Many Swedish-Americans condemned

Ahleen's column as racist, but some wondered if the White House had set a trap for Sweden. If it was, the trap worked. When Ambassador Holland arrived in Stockholm, the American media reported that protesters at the airport and the palace shouted "nigger go home" at him. The Swedish-American press was highly critical, and made this its leading story of early 1970. The story stripped any moral high ground away from Sweden's FNL movement. It also had wide consensus appeal: nearly every paper liked Holland personally. Despite what they thought about Vietnam, all Swedish-Americans opposed racism (at least then) and they wanted their ambassador respected.

Prime Minister Olof Palme returned to the spotlight again in late 1972, during the Christmas Bombings. In a television interview, Palme said the Vietnamese were "being tormented in order to humiliate it." He compared the Christmas Bombings, among other things, to Nazi and Stalinist atrocities. These comments fell with ill grace; Jerome Holland's recent reception in Stockholm was still a recent memory. The emigrant press widely interpreted Palme's words as moralizing. Rather than convincing the Swedish-Americans, Palme's comments sounded antagonistic. I believe this highlighted a change in how Americans – and especially Swedish-Americans – viewed Sweden. Before Vietnam, the emigrants reproached their Swedish cousins for loose morals about sex and alcohol. By the end of the war, the emigrants had come to see the homeland Swedes as self-righteous. Perhaps they were not wrong about Vietnam; yet they were smug about being so right. Swedish-Americans felt little desire to identify with what they saw as mean-spirited criticism.

This qualitative analysis shows the Swedish-Americans did not see Vietnam in the same way as the homeland-Swedes. As a result, they did not sympathize with Sweden's position on the war. Nearly everything they knew on Swedish Vietnam policy came through UD-influenced channels, but that news had little effect on their views. When UD's news on the Swedish reaction to the war clashed with their own understanding of the war – drawn from the mainstream U.S. press – they ignored UD's news. The emigrant press took only the basic facts of Sweden's Vietnam policy from

UD's articles. They interpreted them according to their own values. If UD had hoped to export Swedish values on the war, it mostly did not work. When the emigrants sympathized with Sweden, they usually did so according to their Swedish-American values.

This is an engaging conclusion, a judgment one could support with statistical methods. Chapter Six turns to a quantitative content analysis of the Swedish-American press. There are many types of content analysis, but most seem to divide news reports into Positive and Negative stories. The problem is an American may judge an article one way, but a Vietnamese may judge the same story differently. This form of content analysis often says more about the analyst than the news. I have therefore borrowed the content analysis method Eva Queckfeldt used in her 1981 thesis *"Vietnam": tre svenska tidningars syn på Vietnamfrågan 1963–1968*. Her method has the advantage of clear guidelines. Her codes, in principle, cover nearly every imaginable opinion a newspaper might give. Every opinion gets coded, and the article's viewpoint classified as either one of earlier or later vintage. These labels are also more neutral than positive or negative. Early View editorials usually see Vietnam as a conflict in the Cold War, with the U.S. fighting communism. Later View items see the conflict as a neocolonial conflict, with the U.S. fighting nationalists. Using Eva Queckfeldt's method also allows one to compare the emigrant papers to the Swedish media easily.

Queckfeldt did her content analysis on *Dagens Nyheter*, *Svenska Dagbladet*, and *Stockholms-Tidningen* (and *Aftonbladet* when *ST* closed). My thesis analyzes *Svenska Posten*, *Nordstjernan*, and *Svenska-Amerikanaren*. It includes editorials, letters to the editor, and columnists' items. This gives a full picture of each paper's total presentation of the Vietnam issues. The results show opinion became more intense, with commentary appearing more frequent in the mid-Sixties. Commentary peaked in 1969, the same year when the U.S. had over half a million soldiers in Vietnam. The volume of commentary fell rapidly after that. This fall in commentary came when the U.S. rapidly withdrew its troops after 1969. (The Swedish-American press was also feeling economic strains at the time. The chance of getting Swedish economic help may also have reinforced its silence.) *Svenska Posten* turned against the war quickly.

The Cold War "Early View" had never dominated *SvP*'s opinion items. The Later View dominated its pages as early as 1965. *Nordstjernan* ran the most commentary. It presented an Earlier View though most of the survey period. Its support for the war declined most from 1964 to 1967. Rising hostility toward Sweden's Vietnam policy veiled some of this development. *Svenska-Amerikanaren*'s stand on Vietnam was stable during most of the survey period. One should note that *SAT* banned letters about Vietnam in 1968 and part of 1969. If one discounts this period, one could imagine *SAT*'s opinion gradually moved to a Later View. The content analysis shows these three papers – with different audiences – reacted to the Vietnam issue in sharply different ways. It also shows that none of them resembled the major Swedish dailies.

Researchers believe public opinion on foreign wars depends largely on the costs in American lives borne up to that point. It is unclear whether press opinion reacts the same way. What part of the newspaper would have that retrospective cost-benefit thinking? The editorials, columnists, or letters? I thought printed letters would have most closely resembled public opinion – or at least the readers angry enough to write. Editors realize their editorials have a certain governmental function. Their editorials may even define the entire group for the outside world. They believe current trends should not easily sway them, but instead they should keep an eye on long-term investment goals. Columnists may have an advising role on how public opinion should interpret current events. They arguably approach their subjects as consumer advocates in politics. The three newspapers had different audiences and served them with different opinion formats. I believe the community a newspaper serves will influence which opinion format it adopts.

To show this, I conflated together all the editorials, columns, and letters analyzed in Tables 15 to 22 into one table. Table 27 put the editorials, columns, and letters together, irrespective of which paper ran them. The results were not as clear as I had hoped. I had thought the letters would reflect public opinion most. They did not. They remained equally divided, half with an Earlier and half with a Later View, through most of the survey period. The only fluctuation came in the years when *SAT* banned Vietnam-letters. Some letter-writers had protested *SAT* did not run their letters. Table 27 shows *SAT* worked to keep a balanced opinion. Editorial opinion remained stable while a chance remained the U.S. could win the war with more soldiers. When that proved elusive and the U.S. began pulling its soldiers, the editorial support fell. Columnists also look at Vietnam as a future investment, but they give a better reflection of public opinion than the letters.

The survey of *Nordstjernan*, however, shows tangible "interference" from feelings over Sweden's Vietnam policy. *Nordstjernan* had a strong – if volatile – Early View of Sweden's Vietnam policy. Sweden was the element that made *Nordstjernan*'s statistics so erratic. I believe other Swedish-American papers felt the same way about Sweden. It is a false division to separate opinion on Vietnam and Sweden's Vietnam policy. It does not matter why a newspaper backed the war. It only matters that it did.

●

UD Press Bureau had set up a network of organizations to supply news to the emigrant press. That much is indisputable. What UD's goals were or what it hoped to achieve are harder to fathom. One can only say that UD's news-supply system meant the emigrant papers' news increasingly appeared in Swedish terms. Swedish news services accounted for ever more of their news articles. This Swedish news all had a Swedish perspective. It reported our policies decided by our leaders. If nothing else, UD successfully got this Swedish perspective on Vietnam printed in the emigrant newspapers. Certain words and symbols – the contraction FNL, for example – got into the Swedish-American newspapers. This influence over the words and symbols in the Vietnam debate means UD's news-supply policy was not without success. Through ASNE-SIS and *Sverige-Nytt*, UD also influenced which incidents the emigrant papers would publicize. UD also influenced the agenda of Swedish-American debate as well. It had some sway over what the Swedish-American papers would write about, and the words they would use in their articles. The answer to the question *did the Swedish government influence Swedish-American coverage of Vietnam or Swedish Vietnam policy?* is a qualified Yes.

UD got the Swedish-American press to print its side of the story in its own words. The problem is that UD got its views printed in social and cultural newspapers. These influenced their readers' cultural views, but did not have the political sway of the U.S. dailies or evening TV news. The emigrant papers filled different roles in the mass-communications world than the mainstream media. CBS News and *The New York Times* are primary news outlets: people turn to them for their basic information. For those who want more analysis of this raw data, there are the weekly news magazines. These magazines assume readers have already gotten the raw facts from TV or the daily papers. Even local dailies and afternoon papers fill a complementary role in the news stream. They assume their readers have already heard the top news stories. The emigrant press was almost outside the main news stream. For these papers, the top news stories were not that important. The UD-mediated stories in the emigrant press had little effect on how the Swedish-Americans looked at Vietnam. They got their war news from sources they trusted more.

Also, the UD-mediated news created little sympathy for Swedish foreign policy. Unlike the war news, there were no alternate sources to the emigrant papers. The Swedish-American press had a near monopoly on coverage of Swedish Vietnam policy in America. One might argue the Swedish-American press was indeed a primary news outlet, at least for this particular story. Yet, emigrant readers appear to have taken only the raw facts of Sweden's Vietnam policy from these articles. They interpreted them according to their understanding of the war. Their understanding of the war came largely mediated by the mainstream American press. Table 9 shows Swedish-American editors often changed the Swedish news they received. These changes and additions – editors perhaps saw them as corrections – likely brought the Swedish news into line with how they understood the conflict. This reworking of the UD-mediated news diffused whatever effect the positively-worded items might have had. UD's pro-Swedish news did not produce pro-Swedish editorials in the emigrant press. Thus the answer to the question *did the Swedish government's information policy work?* would largely be No.

All governments have the right to promote their points of view. Governments often spend much time, money, and effort in publicity and media relations. Government may even indirectly exert control through its influence over the national media. In democratic societies, government usually exerts influence through persuasion and agenda-setting. Governments have a right to inform the public at home and abroad of its policies, but are there limits? Did UD violate any unwritten rules? UD was unusually aggressive. It took advantage of the emigrant press's poverty to assure they got non-controversial news. The Swedish-American papers were financially frail and unable to buy their own news articles. UD gave them free news, which it judged the easiest and most legal way to lighten their economic burdens. SIS's Eva Heckscher says UD never meant to turn the emigrant papers into propaganda organs or limit their independence. Still, it may have tacitly expected some measure of gratitude from them. UD did not want to lavish Swedish money on the emigrant papers only to have them acidly criticize Swedish Vietnam policy. UD was not in the practice of subsidizing criticism of its own foreign policy. UD may not have planned to turn them into propaganda organs, but it plainly hoped to make them less troublesome. UD positioned itself as the first gatekeeper in the news flow to the emigrant press.

If UD wanted to help these newspapers, there were better ways to do it. The Swedish-American newspapers were in desperate shape by the early Seventies. Many papers survive now only by the near-heroic efforts of their editors back then to stay open. They pleaded and argued with UD to get more financial help from Sweden, all while fighting a fierce battle for readers against their competitors. My next book will examine in more detail how the emigrant editors kept their papers going during these nadir years.

•

In the first chapter, I planned to examine the Swedish-American press's coverage of the war and Sweden's criticism of it. Sweden's barbed condemnation of America's Vietnam policy put Swedish-Americans in a difficult position. They had double loyalties to both Sweden and America. One was their homeland and the other was their adopted country. They had never seen this double loyalty as a divided loyalty before, much less as disloyal to either one. The Vietnam War put the Swedish-American papers into a difficult position. If a paper backed the war, how did it resolve its love of Sweden with opposing Sweden's Vietnam policy? If a paper opposed the war, how did it reconcile supporting Sweden's Vietnam policy with its U.S. patriotism?

Chapter Two showed the emigrant papers were not always logically consistent. They might criticize Sweden, but resented it when others did the same. The emigrants respected President Eisenhower, and they privately agreed with his 1960 comments. Yet, they rose to defend Sweden when he dared criticize Swedish society. This also went in the other direction during the Vietnam War. For example, *Norden*'s editor was antiwar, and by the end his paper was openly so. While visiting Stockholm, he got into an impassioned argument with a clerk at the department store NK, *Nordiska Kompaniet*. "I tried my best to be patriotic and defend the American involvement in the war," he wrote, "but it was not far from a fistfight. It is not easy to have it both ways."[3]

Immigrants often want it both ways. This often frustrates mainstream society, and perhaps even immigrants themselves. It is the price of having double loyalties. Of course, going into a fistfight to have it both ways is certainly a last choice. Most would rather not have their internal contradictions so easily exposed. Most would rather not fight for such untenable positions. People look for ways to reconcile their positions, often using logical gymnastics. For example, it once shocked my older family members that Swedish actress Ingrid Bergman filed for divorce. They soon argued that she was not a *real* Swede. Perhaps she lost her Swedish values by coming under Italian influences. Few rarely said it, but much of this thinking permeates the emigrant debate on Sweden's Vietnam position. They may have felt most Swedish Social Democrats and FNL-supporters were not true Swedes. Instead they, the emigrants, represented genuine Swedish values.

Table 8 noted *Svenska Posten*'s coverage of Swedish Vietnam coverage was most intense in 1969. It ran twenty-three Vietnam-related stories that year, a year when it ran 447 stories total. The

---

[3] E-mail from Erik Hermans to Edward Burton, 12 February 2003.

other 95% of *Svenska Posten*'s news coverage had little or nothing to do with Vietnam. Most of this was cultural Swedish and Swedish-American news. (Swedish-America's top news story of 1969 could have easily been the filming of Vilhelm Moberg's novel *Utvandrarna* – known in the U.S. as *The Emigrants*.) Other emigrant papers had similarly high ratios of Swedish and emigrant cultural news. In most papers these stories stressed traditional ethnic values. These values included religious faith, honesty, cleanliness, and obedience to the law. For example, *California Veckoblad* ran a Vietnam-editorial on page one of its 7 February 1969 edition. Next to it stood news items with the headlines: "Oregon Youth is Lone Crusader Against Litterbugs," "Law-Abiding Citizens Will Not Be Saddled by Crimes of Few," "Shoplifting Wave Is One of America's Greatest Problems," and a story praising the Boy Scouts. When placed beside news on protests and civil turmoil in Sweden, these items adopt an implied editorial message. They suggest ancestral Swedish values may no longer exist in modern Sweden. News that stresses respect for the law helps build a reader community with its own ethnic identity. Here, the identity is that Swedish-Americans are the real heirs of Swedish values.

That may have been a discouraging thought for many Swedish-Americans. It allowed emigrants to be loyal to Swedishness instead of Sweden itself. That was still not satisfying. Some emigrants wanted to think a Swedish Silent Majority opposed its government's Vietnam policy. *Nordstjernan*'s Eric Sylvan spoke of a "thankfully small number of America-haters" in Sweden. *Nordstjernan*'s Albin Widén wrote, "many Swedes, maybe even most, regret the Swedish mass-media has taken such a one-sided view of the Vietnam conflict."[4] Many emigrants liked this idea of a hostile Swedish media. It helped explain why they so rarely heard from Sweden's Silent Majority. This idea was especially popular when Sweden's criticism of the war escalated. This form of denial remained common, however, throughout the war.

Community-press theory asserts ethnic papers may run news promoting community awareness and ethnic identification. All the

---

[4] Eric Sylvan, "Det Tycks," 28 March 1968: 4; and Albin Widén, "Sverige-Fronten: Anti-amerikansk propaganda," *Nordstjernan-Svea*, 8 February 1973: 2.

news serves some role in meeting that goal. Ideally the news would be positive and would minimize conflict. Vietnam presented a problem. The reports from Sweden were jarring and disruptive, and did little to promote ethnic unity. The immediate reaction was to deny or play down their significance. It may be notable that when *California Veckoblad* could no longer ignore the bad news, it chose to surround the unpleasant Vietnam story with upbeat items. The message was that even if there was friction in the community, the bonds of unity outweighed such problems.

The war clearly was not going well by the late Sixties. This perhaps justified Sweden's criticism of America's decision to enter the war. Only a few Swedish-American commentators argued after 1968 the U.S. was right to enter the war. Few would have repeated the fateful decisions of 1964 and 1965. Yet, the deed was done, and the United States was in Vietnam. The main problem from 1968 onwards was how to leave with dignity, how fast, and how to do it. How the U.S. could uphold its promises to Saigon was another insoluble problem. Continued Swedish criticism during this seemingly endless political nightmare presented another problem for the emigrants. The war had become a long bad dream, and Sweden only criticized the U.S. The emigrants began to see Swedish criticism as mean-spirited. They were more willing than before to see it as smug and moralizing rather than well-meant but wrong.

Swedish-American denials or rebuttals of Sweden's criticism continued. New strains of thought also entered their thinking. Some emigrants tried knitting current events into Swedish and Swedish-emigrant history and culture. They argued Sweden had always sheltered deserters or recognized radical governments. Sweden had a recent custom of accepting some deserters from unpopular wars, but this may be an invented tradition. The emigrants argued Sweden was among the first nations to recognize the revolutionary United States. This meant recognizing North Vietnam was part of a tradition of diplomatic independence. This precedent allowed pride in Swedish traditions while still easing the patriotic conscience. Again, this may be more of a cognitive loophole than a real tradition.

In similar ways, some emigrants recalled how they had fled from conscription in Sweden. The United States did not return them to Sweden, essentially granting them asylum. This allowed some older emigrants reconcile themselves with Sweden's Vietnam policy. It also let them to sympathize with young American draftees who wanted avoid duty in Vietnam.

It was essential for the emigrant press to relate the Vietnam problem into something that could unify the community. The Swedish-American press had developed a talent for this by the late Sixties. The incidents surrounding Jerome Holland in particular could have been a landmine. No Swedish-American paper accepted the claim that the incidents were social criticism. No good would come from opening debate on exposed ethnic groups identifying with immoral governments. It might even split further a Swedish-American community already divided on the war. Most papers instead chose to label the event as a civil rights incident. Civil rights had become a consensus issue in northern cities by 1970. This could only unify the Swedish-American press community. It may be too much to say they consciously planned it that way: such behavior may become instinctive by 1970. They likely identified with Jerome Holland immediately: they felt similarly taunted and abused by the homeland-Swedes. No good would have come from tagging anyone as an Uncle Tom. That might lead to debate whether the emigrant community had its own Swedish Toms.

It may also be that many Swedish-Americans simply did not care to resolve this emotional conflict. Sweden's Vietnam policy dismayed many emigrants. Some emigrants may have distanced themselves from Sweden and Swedish culture. Table 3 shows *Vestkusten* lost nearly half its subscribers in the Sixties. *Nordstjernan* and *Svenska-Amerikanaren* lost nearly a third of their subscribers. This meant several papers had severe economic problems in the late Sixties and early Seventies. Five Swedish-American papers closed between 1966 and 1970. There was clearly a generation shift underway, but some readers may have refused to identify with Sweden. Sweden's Vietnam policy may have led to a renewed desire to integrate into mainstream U.S. society. The result was a wave of unrenewed subscriptions in passive protest over Sweden's foreign policy.[5] From an editorial view, it was thus safer to condemn Sweden's position than to support it.

The late Sixties and Seventies marked the "ethnic revival" period in the United States. This is when the Swedish-American press could have grown rather than contracted. The Swedish-language press did not benefit from the ethnic revival until Vietnam-era tensions were well over. In 1985, for example, *Nordstjernan*'s circulation was down to just 1,100 subscribers. In 2003, its circulation – including a few complimentary copies – is 10,300 subscribers. The paper conservatively estimates that it reaches anywhere up to twenty-five thousand readers. Other papers such as *Vestkusten* have felt similar rejuvenations. *Svenska-Amerikanaren*'s Jane Hendricks thinks the 1976 film *Roots* may have marked the beginning of this change. She credits the film on the African-American experience with prodding Swedish-Americans to reconsider their traditions and language.[6] National Public Radio's weekly syndicated show "A Prairie Home Companion" must have had a similarly positive effect. It stresses down-home midwestern Scandinavian-American culture as warm and neighborly. It makes little distinction among Norwegians, Danes, and Swedes. Its definition of Scandinavian culture is something alive in the U.S. midwest, not northern Europe. The radio show starts with a summary of "News From Lake Wobegone," a humorous sketch of life in the Scandinavian midwest. "News From Lake Wobegone" portrays an ideal society "where all the women are strong, all the men are good-looking, and all the children are above average." Of course, a place where all children are above average does not exist. The news on this radio show recounts fictional events. Listeners eager for real news about Scandinavian-American society have plainly turned back to the Swedish-American press.

---

[5] *Norden*'s editor says he lost subscribers as a direct result of his paper's position on the Vietnam War. It is possible he lost other subscribers indirectly as a result of Sweden's position on the war. (E-mail from Erik Hermans to Edward Burton, 12 February 2003.)

[6] Bengt Hansson, "Drakar för svensk-amerikanar," *Göteborgs-Posten*, 3 November 1996: 31; telephone conversation with Ulf Mårtensson, 10 March 2003; and telephone conversation with Jane Hendricks, 13 November 2000.

Appendix:

Eva Queckfeldt's Earlier and Later View Codes

THEME GROUP 1: *Causes of War*

EARLIER VIEW

1 anf The war in Vietnam is world communist aggression

1d The Domino Theory is correct

1m The war is a mistake by China or by the Communists

1K China is behind the war

1KstN China supports North Vietnam

1KstF China supports the FNL

1SostN The Soviets support North Vietnam

1SostF The Soviets support the FNL

LATER VIEW

1 anf The war in Vietnam is imperialist aggression

1d the Domino Theory is wrong

1m The war is a mistake by the U.S. / has underestimated the enemy / doesn't understand Vietnam, etc.

1inb The war is a civil war

1soc The war's causes are social, economic, political

1befr The war is a national liberation war

1K China is not behind the war

1KstN China does not support North Vietnam

1KstF China does not support the FNL

1SostN The Soviets do not support North Vietnam

1SostF The Soviets do not support the FNL

1r The war is a racist war

THEME GROUP 2: *The FNL*

EARLIER VIEW	LATER VIEW
2k The FNL is a communist group	2k The FNL is a nationalist/non-communist group
2sK China directly controls the FNL	2sK The FNL is independent from China
2hjK China gives the FNL help	2hjK China gives the FNL no / little help
2hjSo The Soviets give the FNL help	2hjSo The Soviets give the FNL no / little help
2sN North Vietnam controls the FNL	2sN The FNL is independent from North Vietnam
2hjN North Vietnam supplies the FNL (via Laos)	2hjN The FNL manages without / with little outside help
2reb The FNL are rebels against the Saigon government	
2agr The FNL is aggressive, breaks cease-fires, attacks first, is attacking force	2agr The FNL is pushed to aggression
2st The FNL has little or no public support	2st Most South Vietnamese support the FNL
2fst The FNL does not represent the South Vietnamese people	2fst The FNL represents the South Vietnamese people
2t The FNL uses terrorism	2t The FNL's terrorism is insignificant, self-defense, etc
2mifr The FNL is militarily unsuccessful	2mifr The FNL is militarily successful
2mifö The FNL suffers losses	
2fr The FNL is politically unsuccessful	2fr The FNL is politically successful
2ben The FNL controls large parts of South Vietnam, but only with terror and at nighttime	2ben The FNL controls large parts of South Vietnam / the entire countryside
2dic FNL soldiers have poor morale and discipline	2dic FNL soldiers have good morale and discipline
2kt An FNL victory will produce a bloodbath, dictatorship, etc.	2kt An FNL victory means popular rule, freedom, justice, etc.
2ök The FNL cannot / will not increase its strength and effectiveness	2ök The FNL will increase its strength and effectiveness
2bpåv Bombing will influence the FNL, force the FNL to negotiate	2bpåv Bombing will not influence the FNL

THEME GROUP 3: *North Vietnam*

EARLIER VIEW

3anf The war represents North Vietnamese aggression

3sK North Vietnam i s controlled / strongly tied to China

3hjK North Vietnam gets help from China

3hjSo North Vietnam gets help from the Soviet Union

3miF North Vietnam supports the FNL militarily / is its base

3inf North Vietnam's regular army infiltrates South Vietnam

3agr North Vietnam is aggressor

3mifr North Vietnam is militarily unsuccessful

3fö North Vietnam suffers losses

3fr North Vietnam is politically unsuccessful / has internal difficulties

3st North Vietnam lacks popular support

3t North Vietnam uses civil and military terror

3kt North Vietnam is a communist dictatorship

3bpåv Bombing will influence North Vietnam, force it to negotiate

3erk Sweden will not recognize North Vietnam

3erk! Do not recognize North Vietnam

3pol North Vietnamese war information is dubious, propaganda

3ök North Vietnam cannot / will not intensify its efforts

LATER VIEW

3sK North Vietnam is independent from China

3hjK North Vietnam gets no / little help from China

3hjSo North Vietnam gets no / little help from Soviet Union

3åSo The war pushes North Vietnam closer to the Soviets

3miF North Vietnam gives no / little help to the FNL

3inf North Vietnam keeps no / few troops in South Vietnam

3agr North Vietnam is not aggressor / forced to attack

3mifr North Vietnam is militarily successful

3fr North Vietnam is politically successful

3st North Vietnam has people's support

3t North Vietnam does not use terror

3kt North Vietnam is voluntarily communist

3bpåv Bombing will not influence North Vietnam

3erk Sweden will recognize North Vietnam

3erk! Recognize North Vietnam!

3pol North Vietnamese war information is accurate

3ök North Vietnam will intensify its efforts

THEME GROUP 4: *South Vietnam*

EARLIER VIEW	LATER VIEW
4dem Democratizing South Vietnam is possible	4dem Democracy is not possible in South Vietnam
4di South Vietnam is a dictatorship	4di South Vietnam is a dictatorship, better than North Vietnam
4stU South Vietnam is an American puppet government	4stU South Vietnam is annoyed at the U.S.
4mkt South Vietnam's ruling generals are ambitious, their government corrupt and brutal	4mkt South Vietnam's ruling generals are ambitious, their government corrupt and brutal
4st South Vietnam's government lacks / is indifferent to the people's support	4st South Vietnam could have had popular support / people want to support Saigon government
4dic South Vietnam's army fights bravely and with good morale	4dic South Vietnam's army is undisciplined and has poor morale
4mifr South Vietnam's army is successful in battle	4mifr South Vietnam's army is unsuccessful in battle
4sv South Vietnam is a weak and unreliable ally	4sv South Vietnam is a weak and unreliable ally
4hjut! South Vietnam should solve its own problems	4hjut! South Vietnam should solve its own problems
4inst Situation is South Vietnam is unstable, many coups, internal decay	4inst Situation is South Vietnam is unstable, many coups, internal decay
4ök South Vietnam cannot / will not intensify its efforts	4ök South Vietnam will intensify its efforts

THEME GROUP 5: *The U.S.*

EARLIER VIEW	LATER VIEW
5anf The U.S. has intervened to stop North Vietnam's / China's aggression	5anf The U.S. has attacked North Vietnam. the war is American aggression
5agr The U.S. was provoked to attack	5agr The U.S. was the first to attack
5dem The U.S. fights (unselfishly) for freedom and democracy in Vietnam	5dem The U.S. does not fight for freedom and democracy in Vietnam
5ek The war is an economic burden for the U.S.	5ek The war is an economic gain for the U.S. The war must continue for economic reasons
5be The war is compromising / a burden for the U.S.	5be The war is compromising / a burden for the U.S.
5mil The military / military apparatus is responsible for the war	5mil Politicians / political prestige is responsible for the war

5m The military has misjudged this situation / works from false premises

5okl The U.S. Vietnam policy is unclear and contradictory

5fo The U.S.'s presence rests on Saigon's formal request. It is legally legitimate

5form Washington's decisions on Vietnam were made in good democratic order

5ompr The U.S. will reconsider its Vietnam policy

5ut The U.S. will not leave Vietnam

5uts The U.S. cannot leave Vietnam. Vietnam will become communist

5ök The U.S. will / is increasing its role in Vietnam

5mifr The U.S. is militarily successful in Vietnam

5hj The U.S. will / does contribute to economic and social programs in Vietnam

5mi The U.S. conducts war through advisers / is advisory / sends military aid

5t The U.S. does not use terror

5st The U.S. has the South Vietnamese people's support

5fr The U.S. is politically successful in Vietnam

5pol American politicians believe in their policy / their information on Vietnam

5kr The nation stands behind the government's Vietnam policy

5ökkr Criticism is decreasing in the U.S.

5kram The U.S. is a society that allows criticism / criticism builds on U.S. sources

5stu There is support for the U.S. policy abroad

5kru The U.S. can / will listen to criticism

5m The politicians have misjudged the situation / work from false premises

5okl The U.S. Vietnam policy is unclear and contradictory

5fo The U.S. presence is legally illegitimate

5form Washington's decisions on Vietnam were not made formally / Congress ignored

5ompr the U.S. will not reconsider its Vietnam policy

5ut The U.S. will leave Vietnam

5uts The U.S. can / will leave Vietnam under certain conditions

5ök The U.S. will de-escalate its role in Vietnam

5mifr The U.S.'s role is a military failure / lacks military success

5mifö The U.S. suffers losses

5hj The U.S.'s assistance programs are insufficient

5mi The U.S. has / will take over the entire war effort itself

5t U.S. troops use terror / commit atrocities

5st The U.S. lacks the South Vietnamese people's support

5fr the U.S. policy in Vietnam is a political failure

5pol American politicians deliberately twist the truth for public opinion / exploit Vietnam

5kr Criticism of the government's Vietnam policy exists in the U.S.

5ökkr Criticism is increasing in the U.S.

5kram News from Vietnam is covered up / facts are silenced or distorted

5stu Criticism of the U.S. policy exists abroad / support is falling

5kru The U.S. does not listen to criticism / criticism meaningless

THEME GROUP 6: *War Events*

EARLIER VIEW	LATER VIEW
6fr World peace threatened because China or Soviet Union may intervene in Vietnam	6fr World peace threatened because China or Soviet Union may intervene in Vietnam
6frSoK Neither the Soviets or China wish war to expand / will not intervene	6utvSoK The Soviets or China may feel forced to intervene / war may expand
6utvU The U.S. will not expand war	6utvU The U.S. may / will expand war
6gr The war is long, cruel, and meaningless. People are exhausted	6gr The war is long, cruel, and meaningless. People are exhausted
6konv Guerrilla wars cannot be won by conventional means	6konv Guerrilla wars cannot be won by conventional means
6g Gas is relatively safe because it is not lethal (also bombing, herbicides, napalm)	6g Gas is dangerous. Using gas violates international law (also bombing, herbicides, napalm)
6bfr U.S. bombing is successful / gives results	6bfr U.S. bombing is not successful / does not produce results
6bök The U.S. will not increase its bombing / starts "bombing pause"	6bök The U.S. will increase number and intensity of its bombing raids / bombing pause ends
6butv Bombing can lead to a peaceful settlement	6butv Bombing can lead to more conflict / intervention of China, etc.
	6bt Bombing raids = terror
	6bfo Bombing is against international law
	6bbe Bombing is a burden to the U.S.
	6bop World opinion is against the bombing
	6bsl! stop the bombing!
6bmil The U.S. bombs only military targets / bombing is limited	6bmil The U.S. bombs indiscriminately
6bdv The U.S. does not bomb schools, hospitals, levees, etc.	6bdv The U.S. does / risks bombing schools, hospitals, levees, etc.
The Geneva Treaty:	*The Geneva Treaty:*
6kG The communists break the treaty	6kG The communists do not break treaty
6NG North Vietnam breaks the treaty	6NG North Vietnam does not break treaty
6FG The FNL breaks the treaty	6FG The FNL does not break the treaty
6SG South Vietnam does not break treaty	6SG South Vietnam breaks the treaty
6UG The U.S. does not break treaty	6UG The U.S. breaks the treaty

6kåf The communists want re-unification

6Nåf North Vietnam wants re-unification

6Fåf The FNL wants re-unification

6Såf South Vietnam wants re-unification

6åfk Re-unification need not mean communism in the whole country

6åfsl Re-unification must be the end of the war

6kåf The communists do not want re-unification

6Såf South Vietnam does not want re-unification

6Uåf The U.S. does not want re-unification

6Fåf The FNL does not want re-unification

6åfk Re-unification means communism in the whole country

6åfsl Re-unification must be the end of the war

THEME GROUP 7: *Peace*

EARLIER VIEW

7sl War will end soon

7mil The war must have a military solution

7k The communists will lose militarily

7K China will lose militarily

7N North Vietnam will lose militarily

7F The FNL will lose militarily

7S South Vietnam will / hopes to win militarily

7U The U.S. will / hopes to win militarily

7konf A conference on Vietnam should be called / a third part can / should mediate the conflict

7ned De-escalation of conflict / cease-fire necessary precondition for negotiations

7nedU The U.S. is willing to cease-fire / Cease-fire shows U.S. willingness to negotiate

LATER VIEW

7sl War will not end soon

7mil The war cannot be won militarily. The war must have a negotiated solution

7k The communists will / hope to win militarily

7K China will / hopes to win militarily

7N North Vietnam will / hopes to win militarily

7F The FNL will / hope to win militarily

7S South Vietnam will lose militarily

7U The U.S. will lose militarily

7knof Conferences are meaningless / a third part cannot do anything

7ned De-escalation of conflict / cease-fire not necessary precondition for negotiations

7nedU North Vietnam is willing to cease-fire / Cease-fire shows North Vietnamese willingness to negotiate

7nedF The FNL is willing to cease-fire / Cease-fire shows FNL willingness to negotiate

7nedUv The U.S. is willing to negotiate under certain conditions

7brned North Vietnam / and the FNL / break cease-fires

7ökned North Vietnam / and the FNL / exploit cease-fires (bomb pauses) to re-enforce

7bfö Bomb pause necessary for negotiations

7bned The U.S. is willing to pause bombing / bomb pause shows U.S. willingness to negotiate

7bnedv The U.S. is willing to pause bombing under certain conditions

7Utr Negotiations with U.S. troops still on the ground possible

7ofr Negotiations impossible / much too early, uncertain, etc.

7Gfö The Geneva Treaty must be the basis for negotiations

7sj The Vietnamese can solve their problems themselves

7sj! The Vietnamese should / will solve their problems themselves

7kfö The communists will not negotiate

7kfö The communists will not negotiate, not under any conditions

7Kfö The Chinese will not negotiate

7nedNv North Vietnam is willing to negotiate under certain conditions

7nedFv The FNL is willing to negotiate under certain conditions

7brned The U.S. / and Saigon / break cease-fires

7ökned The U.S. / and Saigon / exploit cease-fires (bomb pauses) to re-enforce

7bfö Bomb pause not necessary for negotiations

7bned The U.S. is not willing to pause bombing

7bnedv The U.S. is not willing to pause bombing, not even conditionally

7Ntr Negotiations with North Vietnamese troops still on the ground possible

7ofr Negotiations possible / in sight

7Gfö The Geneva Treaty cannot be the basis for negotiations

7sj The Vietnamese can solve their problems themselves

7sj! The Vietnamese should / will solve their problems themselves

7kfö The communists want to negotiate

7kföv The communists want to negotiate, under certain conditions

7Kfö The Chinese want to negotiate

Theme group 8: Sweden-Vietnam

EARLIER VIEW	LATER VIEW

EARLIER VIEW

8ne Sweden risks its neutrality / damages its neutrality by criticizing the U.S.

8krU Swedish criticism is unclear, naive, left-wing

8st Support for the U.S. Vietnam policy exists in Sweden

8stök! Sweden must restrain its criticism of the U.S.

8kr Criticism of the Swedish government's Vietnam policy exists in Sweden

8re The Swedish government / Social Democrats condemn the U.S. Vietnam policy

8ens The Swedish Vietnam criticism is one-sided, aimed only at the U.S.

8op The government has strong public opinion behind it regarding Vietnam

8konf Sweden can mediate the conflict

8demi Rules and interventions at demonstrations are necessary

8demk Demonstrators are fanatics, communists, leftist radicals

8deml Demonstrators are ignorant, naive, deceived / troublemakers

LATER VIEW

8ne Sweden does not risk its neutrality / does not damage its neutrality by criticizing the U.S.

8krU Swedish criticism builds on U.S. material / American critics more insightful than Swedes

8st Criticism of U.S. Vietnam policy exists in Sweden

8stök! Sweden must increase its criticism of the U.S.!

8kr Those who criticize the Swedish policy are Cold Warriors, U.S. sympathizers

8re The Swedish government / Social Democrats do not take a strong enough stand against the U.S. Vietnam policy

8ens The Swedish government has also criticized others, such as the Soviets

8op Certain politicians / circles exploit Vietnam to become popular

8konf Sweden cannot mediate the conflict

8demi New rules on demonstrations needed. Interventions often unnecessary / provocative

8demk Demonstrators against the U.S. Vietnam policy come from all quarters

8deml Demonstrators are knowledgeable and socially aware

Bibliography

Unpublished Sources

Swedish Archives

Riksarkivet (Swedish National Archives, RA), Stockholm
> UD Pressbyrån collection, 1920 års dossierssystem:

> PR4S, boxes I:461–462, files "Svensk-amerikanska pressen"
> NL1, boxes I:318–326, files "Upplysningsverksamhet rörande Sverige-USA"
> U6, box I:605, file "Svenska press- och TV teambesök i utlandet: Vietnam"
> Ä1, box I:174, file "Svensk-amerikaner"
> I1Xv box I:358, file "Upplysningsverksamhet rör Sverige: Vietnam-Vietminh, 1960-"
> I5UaII box I:510, file "Svensk-Amerikanska Nyhetsbyrån, USA-Swedish Information Service"

> Svensk-Amerikanska Nyhetsbyrån collection
> (ASNE Stockholm)

> A:2 box "Svensk-Amerikanska Nyhetsbyråns protokoll"
> A:11 box "Allmän korrespondens"
> A:16–19 boxes "Korrespondens med New York kontoret"
> A:21 box "Korrespondens med Allan Kastrup"
> A:26 box "Korrespondens med UD, amb, och konsulat"
> B:82 box "Operation Västkust 1008"

> Svensk-Internationella Pressbyrån collection (SIP)

> A1:4 box "SIP Protokoll"

Swedish Foreign Ministry Archives (Utrikesdepartementets arkiv, UD)
Stockholm, 1920 års dossierssystem:

PR4S, files "Svensk-amerikanska pressen," UD Pressbyrån
collection
JN1Ua, files "Informationbyrån och upplysningsverksamheten
betr. Sverige-USA"
JN1Xv, files "Informationsbyrån och upplysningsverksamheten
betr. Sverige-Vietnam"
HP1Ua, files "Allmänna ärendena betr. Sverige-USA"
HP1Xv/spec, files "Vietnam: Svenska fredsförmedlingsförsök"
HP1Xv/krigsfångar, files "Vietnam: Krigsfångar"
HP38K, files "Vietnamkriget: Krigsfångefrågan"

Royal Library, Kungliga biblioteket, (KB), Stockholm:
Vilhelm Moberg collection (Moberg)

L:144:1a "Brev till Vilhelm Moberg/Bonniers Förlag"
L:172:1 "Brev till Vilhelm Moberg"

University of Göteborg Library, (GUB), Göteborg:

Reinhold Ahleen collection, (Ahleen)

United States and Canadian archives

National Archives, (NA), Washington D.C.:
Courtesy of Carl-Gustav Scott

United States Information Agency files, Office of Research
(USIA)

Swedish-Canadian Resthome, (SCR) Burnaby:

Swedish Press archives (SP)

Swenson Swedish Immigration Research Center, Augustana College,
    (SSIRC), Rock Island, Illinois:

> American-Swedish News Exchange collection (ASNE New York)

University of British Columbia Library, (UBC), Vancouver:

> Matthew Lindfors collection (Lindfors)
> Olof Seaholm collection (Seaholm)

University of Washington, (UW), Seattle:

> Reinhold Ahleen collection, assession no. 592 (Ahleen)
> Harry Fabbe collection, assession no. 2252 (Fabbe)
> Svenska Posten collection, assession no. 1298-2 (SvP)

Interviews and Correspondence

Arnö, Lars. UD's Press Bureau. UD's press bureau 1949–1952, 1953–1963; press attaché in Ottawa and New York 1963–1971. Telephone conversation, 4 February 2000.

Heckscher, Eva. SIS Informationskontoret 1966–1975, Ambassador to Dhaka 1985–1989 and Bangkok 1992–1997. Telephone conversation, 21 May 2001.

Hendricks, Jane. Editor, *Svenska-Amerikanaren Tribunen* and *California Veckoblad*. Telephone conversation, 13 November 2000.

Hermans, Erik R. Editor, *Norden*. 1963–2003. E-mail, 9 February, 10 February, 12 February 2003.

Holland family. Relatives of Jerome Holland, U.S. Ambassador to Sweden 1970–1972. E-mails from Joseph Holland, 16 and 19 April 2003; and e-mail from Lucy Holland, 17 April 2003.

Mårtensson, Ulf. Publisher, *Nordstjernan*. E-mail, late 1997; telephone conversation, 10 March 2003.

Neumueller, Anders. Editor, *Swedish Press*. Conversation, 13 January 1999; e-mail, 13 June 1999; Telephone conversation, 10 November 2000.

Nilson, Ulf. Reporter, *Expressen*. E-mail, 8 May, 23 September, 30 November, and 6 December 2001.

Stromberg-Brink, Bridget. Editor, *Vestkusten*. E-mail, 15 March 1997.

Trulson, Ruby. Relative of Anton Trulson, editor of *Svea*. Telephone conversation, 14 October 2000; Letter, 10 August 1998.

Wermee, Sture. Editor, *Swedish Press*. 1970–1976, Assistant Editor 1960s. Telephone conversations, 7 June 1999, 13 February 2000.

Öberg, Kjell. UD's press adviser Washington 1955–1961, Ambassador to Beijing 1961–1962, head of College for Swedish Information Abroad 1966–1969, head of Swedish-American Press Investigation 1970–1972. Brief telephone conversation 5 February 2000.

Newspapers
(Found in GUB, KB, SSIRC, and SCR)

California Veckoblad (Los Angeles), 1960–1975
Canada-Svensken (Toronto), 1961–1975
Canada-Tidningen (Winnipeg), 1960–1970
Covenant Companion (Chicago), 1960–1975
The Messenger (Chicago), 1960–1968
Missions-Vännen (Chicago), 1960
Norden (Brooklyn), 1960–1975
Nordstjernan (New York City), 1960–1975
Svea (Worcester), 1960–1966
Svenska-Amerikanaren Tribunen (Chicago), 1960–1975
Svenska Posten (Seattle), 1960–1975
Swedish Press (Vancouver), 1960–1975
Texas Posten (Austin), 1960–1975
Vestkusten (San Francisco), 1960–1975
Western News (Denver) 1960–1975

Official Government Publications

Public Papers of the Presidents: Dwight D. Eisenhower, 1960–1961, Washington: Office of the Federal Register, 1961.

Riksdagens protokoll med bihang. Andra Kammaren. Stockholm: The Swedish Riksdag, 1969, 1970.

Svensk-Amerikanska Pressutredningen. *Utvandrarnas tidningar: Betänkande.* Stockholm: The Swedish Foreign Ministry, 1971.

Swedish Foreign Ministry. *Samverkan mellan organen för svensk upplysningsverksamhet i utlandet: Betänkande angivet av särskilt tillkallad utredning.* Stockholm: The Swedish Foreign Ministry, 1960.

Swedish Foreign Ministry. *Sverige och Vietnamfrågan: Anföranden och uttalanden.* (Ny serie II:19) Stockholm: The Swedish Foreign Ministry, 1968.

Swedish Information Service. *Knowledge of and Attitudes Toward Sweden: Nationwide Studies Among the American Public.* Princeton, New Jersey: Response Analysis Corporation, 1973.

Swedish Information Service. *Princeton Adults' Knowledge of and Attitudes Toward Sweden: A Preliminary Report of the Pilot Study.* Princeton, New Jersey: Response Analysis Corporation, March 1973.

UD Pressbyrån. *Sverige i utländsk press.* Stockholm: Swedish Foreign Ministry Press Bureau: Various years, 1968–1973.

United States. Congress. House. *Congressional Record, 1969.* Ninety-First Congress. First session. Washington D.C.: U.S. Government Printing Office, 1969.

United States Department of Commerce, Bureau of the Census. "Supplementary Report: Country of Origin, Mother Tongue, and Citizenship for the United States: 1970."

The United States Census: 1970. Washington D.C.: U.S. Government Printing Office, 1973.

Unprinted Literature

Ekeblad, Per-Gunnar, and Christer Samuelsson. "Vietnamkonfliktens Behandling i Sveriges Radio-TV Under Perioden 11/2–9/3 1968: Inledning, Syfte och Metod." Unpublished essay. Göteborg University, September 1968.

Person, Karin. "Short History of *Vestkusten*, Swedish-American Newspaper." typewritten manuscript. (undated). Courtesy of Ulf Jonas Björk.

Rydén, Uncas. "Vietnamkriget i svensk press — en kvalitativ analys." AB-uppsats. Historiska institutionen. Göteborg University, VT 1993.

SIFO Research & Consulting AB. Results of SIFO public opinion polls on the Vietnam War, conducted September 1967, March 1968, August 1968. Courtesy of SIFO Research & Consulting AB.

Sjödin, Anders-Petter. "Etnicitet eller assimilation i 'liberala' *Vestkusten*." Unpublished C-uppsats. History department. Uppsala Univerity, 6 October 1980.

Sjöström, Michael. "Sverigebilden i de två svensk-amerikanska tidningarna *Arbetaren* och *Nordstjernan* år 1914." (Adviser: Lars Ljungmark.) B-uppsats. Historiska institutionen. Göteborgs Universitet, HT 1995.

Printed Literature

Allwood, Inga Wilhelmsen, and Knud K. Mogensen, Carl Nosjar, and Martin S. Allwood. *The Norwegian-American Press and Nordiske Tidende*. Mullsjö: Institutet för Samhällsforskning, 1950.

Ander, O. Fritiof. "The Swedish-American Press in the Election of 1892." *Mississippi Valley Historical Review*. vol. 23: 533–554.

Ander, O. Fritiof. "The Swedish-American Press in the Election of 1912." *The Swedish Pioneer Historical Quarterly*. vol. 14. no. 3. 1963: 103–126.

Backlund, J. Oscar. *A Century of the Swedish Press*. Chicago: The Swedish American Newspaper Company, 1952.

Bailey, George. "Television War: Trends in Network Coverage of Vietnam 1965–1970." *Journal of Broadcasting.* vol. 20: 2. Spring 1976: 147–158.

Bailey, George Arthur. *The Vietnam War According to Chet, David, Walter, Harry, Peter, Bob, Howard, and Frank: A Content Analysis of Journalistic Performance By the Network Television Evening News Anchormen 1965–1970.* Ann Arbor, Michigan: University Microfilms, 1973. (Ph.D. thesis)

Baker, Nicholson. *Double Fold: Libraries and the Assault on Paper.* New York: Random House, 2001.

Barton, H. Arnold. "Emigrants' Images of Sweden." *Migrants and the Homeland: Images, Symbols, and Realities.* (ed. Harald Rumblom.) ("Uppsala Multiethnic Papers #44.") Uppsala University, Uppsala, 2000: 97-106.

Barton, H. Arnold. "Svensk-Amerika om femtio år." *Sverigekontakt: En tidning för all världens svenskar.* March 1998: 17–18.

Beattie, Keith. *The Scar that Binds: American Culture and the Vietnam War.* London: New York University Press, 1998.

Beijbom, Ulf A. "The Swedish Press." *The Ethnic Press in the United States: A Historical Analysis and Handbook.* (ed. Sally M. Miller.) London: Greenwood Press, 1987: 379–392.

Björk, Ulf Jonas. "'Folkets Röst,' The Pulse of the Public: Svenska Amerikanska Posten and Reader Letters, 1907–1911." *Swedish-American Historical Quarterly.* vol. 50. no. 2. April 1999:4–17.

Björk, Ulf Jonas. *The Swedish-American Press: Three Newspapers and Their Communities.* Ann Arbor, Mich: University Microfilms International, 1987.

Blanck, Dag. *Becoming Swedish-American: The Construction of an Ethnic Identity in the Augustana Synod, 1860–1917.* ("Studia Historica Upsaliensia 182.") Uppsala: Uppsala University, 1997.

Block, Eva. *Amerikabilden i svensk press 1948–1968.* ("Bibliotheca Historica Lundensis XLIX.") Malmö: CWK Gleerup, 1976.

Board, Joseph P. "Eva Queckfeldt: *"Vietnam": tre svenska tidningars syn på Vietnamfrågan 1963–1968."* [Book review]. *Statsvetenskaplig Tidskrift.* 1982(3).

Braestrup, Peter. *Big Story: How the American Press and Television Reported and Interpreted the Crisis of Tet 1968.* 2 vols. Boulder, Colo: Westview Press, 1978.

Capps, Finis Herbert. *From Isolation to Involvement: The Swedish Immigrant Press in America, 1914–1945.* Chicago: Swedish Pioneer Historical Society, 1966.

Capps, Finis Herbert. "The Views of the Swedish-American Press Toward United States-Japanese Relations, 1914–1945." *Swedish Pioneer Historical Quarterly.* vol. 20. no. 3. 1969: 133–146.

Cater, Douglass. *The Fourth Branch of Government.* Boston: Houghton Mifflin, 1959.

Chrislock, Carl H. *Ethnicity Challenged: The Upper Midwest Norwegian-American Experience in World War I.* Northfield, Minn.: Norwegian-American Historical Association, 1981.

Chrislock, Carl. "The Impact of World War I Nativism on Scandinavian Ethnicity in the Upper Midwest." *Scandinavians in America: Literary Life.* Decorah, Ill.: Smyrna Literary Society, 1985.

Clausen, C. A. "Book Review: *From Isolation to Involvement.*" *The Journal of American History.* vol. 54. no. 2. September 1967: 434–435.

Daun, Åke. *Swedish Mentality.* University Park, Pennsylvania: Pennsylvania State University Press, 1989.

Diamond, Edwin. "Who is the 'Enemy,'?" *Columbia Journalism Review.* Winter 1970–1971: 38–39.

Fishman, Joshua (ed.). *Language Loyalty in the United States: The Maintenance and Perpetuation of Non-English Mother Tongues by American Ethnic and Religious Groups.* The Hague: Mouton & Co., 1966.

Gallup, George H. *The Gallup Poll: Public Opinion 1935–1971.* 3 vols. New York: Random House, 1972.

Gans, Herbert J. *Deciding What's News: A Study of CBS Evening News, NBC Nightly News, Newsweek, and Time.* New York: Vintage Books, 1979.

"Gerry Rooth." *The Swedish-Americans of the Year.* Karlstad: Press Förlag, 1982: 134–152.

Goldwater, Barry. *Konservatismens ansvar.* (trans. of *The Conscience of a Conservative,* 1960) Malmö: Prima-tryck, 1964.

Greene, Victor. "'Becoming American': The Role of Ethnic Leaders — Swedes, Poles, Italians, and Jews," *The Ethnic Frontier: Essays in the History of Group Survival in Chicago and the Midwest.* Grand Rapids, Mich.: William B. Eerdmanns Publishing Co, 1977: 143–175.

Hale, Frederick. "Challenging the Welfare State: The Case of Dwight David Eisenhower." *Swedish-American Historical Quarterly.* vol. LIV. no. 1. January 2003.

Hallin, Daniel C. "The American News Media: A Critical Perspective." *Critical Theory and Public Life.* (ed. John Forester.) London: The MIT Press, 1985: 121–146. Also appears in *We Keep America on Top of the World.*

Hallin, Daniel C. "Images of the Vietnam and Persian Gulf Wars in U.S. Television," *Seeing Through the Media*. (eds. Susan Jeffords and Lauren Rabinovitz). New Brunswick, NJ: Rutgers University Press, 1994.

Hallin, Daniel C. *The Uncensored War: The Media and Vietnam*. New York: Oxford University Press, 1986.

Hallin, Daniel C. *We Keep America on Top of the World: Television Journalism and the Public Sphere*. London: Routledge, 1994.

Hammond, William M. *The Military and the Media, 1962–1968*. ("The U.S. Army in Vietnam.") Washington: U.S. Army Center of Military History, 1988.

Hansen, Marcus Lee. *The Problem of the Third Generation Emigrant*. Rock Island, Ill.: Augustana Library Publications, 1938.

Hedblom, Folke. "Dialect Hunters: In Deepest 'Swedish America' With Microbus and Tape Recorder." *American Swedish '73*. Philadelphia: American-Swedish Historical Foundation, 1973: 63–67.

Helén, Gunnar. *Alltför många jag*. Stockholm: Bonniers, 1991.

"Hell No, We Won't Go." Swedish Television documentary. Channel 2: 24 April 1997.

Herz, Martin F. *The Prestige Press and the Christmas Bombing, 1972: Images and Reality in Vietnam*. Washington, D.C.: Ethics and Policy Center, 1980.

Hindman, Douglas Blanks. "Community Newspapers, Community Structural Pluralism, and Local Conflict with Nonlocal Groups." *Journalism and Mass Communication Quarterly*. vol. 73. no. 3. Autumn 1996: 708–721.

Hunt, Michael J. *Lyndon Johnson's War: America's Cold War Crusade in Vietnam, 1945–1968*. ("A Critical Issue.") New York: Hill and Wang, 1996.

Janowitz, Morris. *The Community Press in an Urban Setting: The Social Elements of Urbanism*. 2nd ed. London: University of Chicago Press, 1967.

Jones, William Parker. *Thor's Hammers: The Swedish and Finnish "Granitklippan" Community of West Concord, New Hampshire*. Master's Thesis. Durham: University of New Hampshire, May 2000.

Karlsson, T. Edward. "Gerhard Rooth: Half a Century as Good-Will Ambassador." *American Swedish '73*. Philadelphia: American-Swedish Historical Foundation, 1973: 21–27.

Kastrup, Allan. *Med Sverige i Amerika: Opinioner, stämningar och upplysningsarbete – en rapport av Allan Kastrup*. Malmö: Corona, 1985.

Kilander, Svenbjörn. *Censur och propaganda: Svensk informationspolitik under 1900-talets första decennier*. ("Studia Historica Upsaliensia 121.") Uppsala: Uppsala University, 1981.

Klein, Barbro. "Folkets Röst: Svensk-amerikanska insändarbrev och folklorens betydelser." *Nord-Nytt*. vol. 52: 85–97.

Knightly, Philip. *The First Casualty: From the Crimea to Vietnam: The War Correspondent as Hero, Propagandist, and Myth Maker.* New York: Harcourt Brace Jovanovich, 1975.

Larson, Eric V. *Casualties and Consensus: The Historical Role of Casualties in Domestic Support for U.S. Military Operations.* (MR-726-RC.) Santa Monica, California: RAND Corporation, 1996. Available at www.rand.org.

Larson, Eric V. *Ends and Means in the Democratic Conversation: Understanding the Role of Casualties in Support for U.S. Military Operations.* Santa Monica, Calif.: RAND Corporation, 1995.

Lefever, Ernest W. *TV and National Defense: An Analysis of CBS News, 1972–1973.* Boston, Virginia: Institute for American Strategy Press, 1974.

Leif-Lundgren, Åke and Linné, Bernt. "Arthur Landfors." *Tiden snöar från trädet.* Luleå: Kantele, 1993: 49–58.

Leifland, Leif. *Frostens År: Om USA:s diplomatiska utfrysning av Sverige.* ("Sverige under kalla kriget"), Stockholm: Nerenius & Santerus Förlag AB, 1997.

Lindahl, Mac. *Svenska-Amerikanska Nyhetsbyrån i New York och Stockholm inför 30-årsjubileet.* Stockholm: Svenska-Amerikanska Nyhetsbyrån, 1951.

Lindmark, Sture. *Swedish America 1914–1932: Studies in Ethnicity with Emphasis on Illinois and Minnesota.* ("Studia Historica Upsaliensia XXXVII.") Uppsala: Uppsala University, 1971.

Link, Ruth. "Ambassador Holland and the Swedes." *The Crisis.* vol. 78. March 1971: 43–48.

Ljungmark, Lars. *Svenskarna i Winnipeg: Porten till prärien 1872–1940.* Emigrantinstitutets vänner: Växjö: 1994.

Logevall, Fredrik. "The Swedish-American Conflict Over Vietnam." *Diplomatic History.* New York: vol. 17. no. 3, 1993: 421–445.

Lorell, Mark, Charles Kelly, Jr., and Deborah Hensler. *Casualties, Public Opinion, and Presidential Policy During the Vietnam War.* Santa Monica, Calif.: RAND Corporation, 1985.

Lundstedt, Bernhard. *Svenska Tidningar och Tidskrifter Utgifna Inom Nord-Amerikas Förenade Stater.* Stockholm: P.A. Norstedt & Söner, 1886.

Marzolf, Marion Tuttle. "The Danish Immigrant Newspaper: Old Friend in a New Land." *From Scandinavia to America: Proceedings from a Conference held at Gl. Høltegaard.* ("Odense University Studies in History and Social Sciences. vol. 103.") Odense: Odense University Press, 1987: 299–319.

Marzolf, Marion Tuttle. *The Danish-Language Press in America.* New York: Arno Press, 1979.

McKay, James, and Frank Lewins. "Ethnicity and the Ethnic Group: A Conceptual Analysis and Reformulation." *Ethnic and Racial Studies.* vol. 1. no. 4. October 1978: 415–417.

"The Media and Vietnam: Comment and Appraisal." *Columbia Journalism Review.* Winter 1970–1971: 26–27.

Mueller, John. *Policy and Opinion in the Gulf War.* London: University of Chicago Press: 1994.

Mueller, John E. *War, Presidents, and Public Opinion.* London: John Wiley & Sons Ltd.: 1973.

Möller, Yngve. *Sverige och Vietnamkriget: Ett unikt kapitel i svensk utrikespolitik.* Stockholm: Tidens Förlag, 1992.

Nilsson, Gunnar. *De sista svenska rösterna: en resa bland emigranterna i Kanada.* Stockholm: Carlsson, 1995.

Nilsson, Torsten. *Åter Vietnam: Memoarer och reportage.* Stockholm: Tidens Förlag, 1981.

Nincic, Miroslav. "Casualties, Military Intervention, and the RMA: Hypotheses from the Lessons of Vietnam." Paper presented at the Conference on the Revolution in Military Affairs, Monterey, August 1995. ("DRAFT and not for quotation.") http://ps.ucdavis.edu/JCISS/cmi.html. (Author has granted permission to quote this article.)

Nincic, Miroslav, and Donna J. Nincic. "Commitment to Military Intervention: The Democratic Government as Economic Investor." *Journal of Peace Research.* vol. 32. no. 4. 1995: 413–426.

Olson, James S., and Randy Roberts. *Where The Domino Fell: America and Vietnam, 1945 to 1990.* New York: St. Martin's Press, 1991.

Opton, Edward M., Jr. "It Never Happened, and Besides, They Deserved It." *Sanctions for Evil.* (eds. Nevitt Sanborn, Craig Comstock, and Associates). San Francisco: Jossey-Bass, 1971.

O'Sullivan, Tim, and John Hartley, and Danny Saunders, Martin Montgomery, and John Fiske. *Key Concepts in Communication and Cultural Studies.* Second ed. London: Routledge, 1994.

Palme, Olof. *USA-kriget i Vietnam.* (Utblick #8). Stockholm: Frihets Förlag, 1968.

Papadopoulos, Kari-Andén. *Kameran i krig: Den fotografiska iscensättningen av Vietnamkriget i svensk press.* Stockholm: Brutus Östlings Bokförlag Symposion, 2000.

Patterson, Oscar III. "An Analysis of Television Coverage of the Vietnam War." *Journal of Broadcasting.* vol. 28:4. Fall 1984: 397–404.

Pettenger, Roger Wesley. *The Peace Movement of the Augustana Lutheran Church as a Catalyst in the Americanization Process.* Ann Arbor, Mich.: University Microfilms International, 1987.

Potter, David M., and Don E. Fehrenbacher. *The Impending Crisis: 1848–1861.* ("The New American Nation Series.") New York: Harper Perennial, 1976.

Queckfeldt, Eva. *"Vietnam": tre svenska tidningars syn på Vietnamfrågan 1963–1968.* ("Bibliotheca Historica Lundensis XLIX") Malmö: CWK Gleerup, 1981.

Redogörelse för Svensk-Amerikanska Nyhetsbyrån: Verksamhet 1/7 1947 – 30/6 1948. Stockholm: Svensk-Amerikanska Nyhetsbyrån, 1948.

Redogörelse för Svensk-Amerikanska Nyhetsbyråns Verksamhet, 1948–1950. Stockholm: Svensk-Amerikanska Nyhetsbyrån, 1950.

Redogörelse för tillkomsten av press och informationorganet i utrikesdepartementet. Stockholm: The Swedish Foreign Ministry, 1939.

Reporting Vietnam: American Journalism 1959–1975. (eds. Milton J. Bates, Lawrence Lichty, Paul J. Miles, Ronald H. Spector, and Marilyn Young). 2 vols. New York: The Library of America, 1998.

Salomon, Kim. *Rebeller i takt med tiden: FNL rörelsen och 60-talet politiska ritualer.* Stockholm: Rabén Prisma, 1996.

Schersten, Albert Ferdinand. *The Relation of the Swedish-American Newspaper to the Assimilation of Swedish Immigrants.* ("Augustana Library Publications no. 15.") Rock Island, Illinois: Augustana Library Publications, 1935.

Schramm, Wilbur, and Merritt Ludwig. "The Weekly Newspaper and Its Readers." *Journalism Quarterly.* vol. 28. no. 2. 1951: 301–314.

Scott, Carl-Gustav. "Swedish Sanctuary of American Deserters During the Vietnam War: A Facet of Social Democratic Domestic Politics." *Scandinavian Journal of History.* vol. 26. no. 2. 2001: 123–142.

Scott, Larry E. "The Swedish-Language Press in Texas." *The Swedish Texans.* San Antonio: University of Texas, 1990: 195–210.

Setterdahl, Lilly. *Swedish-American Newspapers: A Guide to the Microfilms held by Swedish Immigration Research Center.* Rock Island, Ill.: Augustana College Library, 1981.

Skarstedt, Ernst. *Pennfäktare: Svensk-Amerikanska forfattare och tidningsmän.* Stockholm: Åhlen & Åkerlunds Förlag, 1930. (Revised version of *Våra Pennfäktare*, 1897.)

Smith, Anthony. *The Shadow of the Cave: A Study of the Relationship Between the Broadcaster, His Audience and the State.* London: George Allen & Unwin Ltd, 1973

Smith, Timothy L. "Review of Books: *From Isolation To Involvement.*" *The American Historical Review.* vol. 73. no. 2. December 1967: 616–617.

St. Jean, Eva. "From Defiance to Defence: Swedish-Canadian Ethnic Awareness During the Two World Wars." *American Journal of Scandinavian Studies.* (forthcoming.)

St. Jean, Eva. "The Myth of the Big Swede Logger: An *Arbetskarl* in the Vancouver Island Forests 1920–1948." Unpublished M.A. thesis. University of Victoria, 1999.

The Statistical History of the United States: From Colonial Times to the Present. New York: Basic Books, 1972.

Stephenson, George M. "The Attitude of the Swedish-Americans Toward the World War." *Mississippi Valley Historical Association Proceedings.* vol. 10. 1918–1921: 70–94.

Swanson, Alan. *Literature and the Immigrant Community: The Case of Arthur Landfors.* Carbondale, Southern Illinois University Press, 1990.

Söderström, Alfred. *Blixtar på tidnings-horizonten.* Warroad, Minn. (no publisher given): 1910.

Tallgren, Henrik. *Svensk-amerikaner i Kalifornien: En studie av lågaktiv etnicitet.* Göteborg: Socialantropologiska institutionen, Göteborgs universitet, 2000.

Thorén, Stig. "Vietnamkonflikten i telegramens belysning." *Studier i förmedlingen av utrikestelegram.* Stockholm: Beredskapsnämnden för psykologiskt försvar, 1966: 64–103.

Tuchman, Gaye. *Making News.* London: Collier Macmillan Publishers, 1978.

Tuchman, Gaye. "Objectivity as a Strategic Ritual: An Examination of Newsmen's Notions of Objectivity." *American Journal of Sociology.* vol. 77. no. 4. January 1972.

Turner, Kathleen J. *Lyndon Johnson's Dual War: Vietnam and the Press.* Chicago: University of Chicago Press, 1985.

"U.S. Envoy In Sweden Told, 'Nigger, Go Home.'" *Jet.* vol. 38. 30 April 1970: 4–5.

Utlandssvenskarnas Förening and Riksföreningen för Svenskhet Bevarande i Utlandet. *Svenskar i utlandet: Biografisk uppslagsbok.* Stockholm: P.A. Norstedt och Söners Förlag, 1969.

Weibull, Jörgen. "Censur och opinionsutveckling," *Norden under 2. verdenskrig,* Copenhagen: Nordisk Ministerråd/Gyldendal: 136–172.

Westerståhl, Jörgen. *Vietnam i Sveriges Radio: En studie av opartiskhet och saklighet i nyhetsförmedlingen utförd på uppdrag av Radionämnden.* Göteborg University, Statsvetenskapliga institutionen, August 1968.

White, Theodore. *The Making of a President, 1960.* London: W.W. Norton, 1963.

Wijk, Johnny. *Svarta börsen – samhällslojalitet i kris: livsmedels ransoneringen och den illegala handeln i Sverige 1940–1949*. Stockholm: Almqvist & Wiksell International, 1992.

Williams, Anna. "Providing an Ethnic Identity: Journalist in Swedish-America." *Swedes in America: Intercultural and Interethnic Perspectives on Contemporary Research.* ("A Report on the Symposium Swedes in America: New Perspectives.") (Ed. Ulf Beijbom) "The Swedish Emigrant Institute Series #6." Växjö: The Emigrant Institute, 1993.

Wilson, Marshall. "Fabbe: Northwest Swedes' Editor." *Swedish Pioneer Historical Quarterly.* vol. 26. 1975: 185–192.

Wittke, Carl. *The German-Language Press in America.* Frankfort: University of Kentucky Press, 1957.

Wyatt, Clarence R. *Paper Soldiers: The American Press and the Vietnam War.* New York: W.W. Norton & Company, 1993.

Östergren, Bertil. *Vem var Olof Palme?* Stockholm: Timbro, 1984.

DISSERTATIONS FROM THE DEPARTMENT OF HISTORY
GÖTEBORG UNIVERSITY

ISSN 1100–6781

1. Ingemar Karlsson, *Historien som biologiskt öde. Om perspektivförkjutningar inom mellankrigstidens tyska historieskrivning* (1989).

2. Helen Lööw, *Hakkorset och Wasakärvan. En studie av nationalsocialismen i Sverige 1924–1950* (1990).

3. Martin Åberg, *En fråga om klass? Borgarklass och industriellt företagande i Göteborg 1850–1914* (1991).

4. Anna Götlind, *Technology and Religion in Medieval Sweden* (1993).

5. Henrik Glimstedt, *Mellan teknik och samhälle. Stat, marknad och produktion i svensk bilindustri 1930–1960* (1993).

6. Lennart Andersson Palm, *Människor och skördar. Studier kring agrarhistoriska metodproblem 1540–1770* (1993).

7. Erik Husberg, *Honung, vax och mjöd. Biskötseln i Sverige under medeltid och 1500–tal* (1994).

8. Göran Malmstedt, *Helgdagsreduktionen. Övergången från ett medeltida till ett modernt år i Sverige 1500–1800* (1994).

9. Christer Thörnqvist, *Arbetarna lämnar fabriken. Strejkrörelser i Sverige under efterkrigstiden, deras bakgrund, förlopp och följder* (1994).

10. Britt Liljewall, *Bondevardag och samhällsförändring. Studier i och kring västsvenska bondedagböcker från 1800–talet* (1995).

11. Margaretha Mellberg, *Pedagogen och det skrivna ordet. Skrivkonst och folkskollärare i Sverige 1870–1920* (1996).

12. Ingrid Lomfors, *Förlorad barndom, återvunnet liv. De judiska flyktingbarnen från Nazityskland* (1996).

13. Eva Jakobsson, *Industrialisering av älvar. Studier kring svensk vattenkraftsutbyggnad 1900–1918* (1996).

14. Sven–Olof Josefsson, *Året var 1968. Universitetskris och studentrevolt i Stockholm och Lund* (1996).

15. Bertil Rimborg, *Magnus Durell och Danmark. Studier i information* (1997).

16. Jan Christensen, *Bönder och herrar. Bondeståndet i 1840–talets liberala representationsdebatt. Exemplen Gustaf Hierta och J. P. Theorell* (1997).

17. Anita Pärsson, *Dövas utbildning i Sverige 1889–1971. En skola för ett språk och ett praktiskt yrke* (1997).

18. Reine Rydén, *"Att åka snålskjuts är icke hederligt". De svenska jordbrukarnas organisationsprocess 1880–1947* (1998).

19. K. G. Hammarlund, *Barnet och barnomsorgen. Bilden av barnet i ett socialpolitiskt projekt* (1998).

20. Carl Holmberg, *Längtan till landet. Civilisationskritik och framtidsvisioner i 1970-talets regionalpolitiska debatt* (1998).

21. Henrik Janson, *Templum Nobilissimum. Uppsalatemplet, Adam av Bremen och konfliktlinjerna i Europa kring år 1075* (1998).

22. Henrik Olsson, *Öst och Väst eller Nord och Syd? Regionala politiska skillnader inom den svenska bondegruppen under 1800-talet* (1998).

23. Lizelotte Lundgren Rydén, *Ett svenskt dilemma. Socialdemokraterna, centern och EG-frågan 1957–1994* (2000).

24. Lars Hermanson, *Släkt, vänner och makt. En studie av elitens politiska kultur i 1100-talets Danmark* (2000).

25. Karl Magnusson, *Justifying Oppression. Perceptions of Race in South Africa between 1910 and 1961* (2000).

26. Maria Eugenia Chaves, *Honor y libertad. Discursos y recursos en las estrategias de libertad de las eslavas en Guayaquil a fines del periodico colonial* (2001).

27. Anders Simonsen, *Bland hederligt folk. Organiserat sällskapsliv och borgerlig formering i Göteborg 1755–1820* (2001).

28. Kenneth Nyberg, *Bilder av Mittens rike. Kontinuitet och förändring i svenska resenärers Kinaskildringar 1749–1912* (2001).

29. Audur Magnúsdóttir, *Frillor och fruar. Politik och samlevnad på Island 1120–1400* (2001).

30. Tommy Isidorsson, *Striden om tiden. Arbetstidens utveckling i Sverige under 100 år i ett internationellt perspektiv* (2001).

31. Renzo Ramírez Bacca, *History of Labor on a Coffee Plantation. La Aurora Plantation, Tolima-Colombia, 1882–1982* (2002).

32. Laila Nielsen, *Unfree to Develop. A Comparative Study of Kuria and Ukerewe under Colonial Rule, Tanzania 1850–1961* (2002).

33. Lars Nyström, *Potatisriket. Stora Bjurum 1857–1917. Jorden, makten, samhället* (2003)

34. Edward Burton, *The Swedish-American Press and the Vietnam War* (2003)